With Malice toward Some

The Littlefield History of the Civil War Era

Gary W. Gallagher and T. Michael Parrish, editors

Supported by the Littlefield Fund for Southern History,
University of Texas Libraries

With Malice toward Some

Treason and Loyalty in the Civil War Era

WILLIAM A. BLAIR

The University of North Carolina Press // Chapel Hill

© 2014 The University of North Carolina Press
All rights reserved
Set in Miller by codeMantra
Manufactured in the United States of America

Library of Congress Cataloging-in-Publication Data
Blair, William Alan.
With malice toward some : treason and loyalty in the Civil War era / William A. Blair.
pages cm. — (The Littlefield history of the Civil War era)
Includes bibliographical references and index.
ISBN 978-1-4696-1405-2 (hardback) — ISBN 978-1-4696-1406-9 (ebook)
1. United States—History—Civil War, 1861–1865—Collaborationists. 2. Traitors—
United States—History—19th century. 3. Treason—United States—History—
19th century. I. Title.
E458.8.B83 2014
973.7—dc23
2013046758

18 17 16 15 14   5 4 3 2 1

To George Richards,
who encouraged us to dream big dreams

CONTENTS

With Malice toward Some

INTRODUCTION

Roughly twenty years ago, a graduate seminar planted the seed for this book. The professor raised the intriguing notion that perhaps the history of the U.S. South would have turned out more favorably for African Americans had Union authorities lined planters against a wall and executed them. The statement contained just enough seriousness to make it provocative. Students chuckled at the outlandish thought. Such a thing could not happen, could it? But the idea of a different outcome to the war intrigued. Additional reading yielded ample examples of those who sought revenge, not only northerners railing against Confederates but also Republicans condemning Democrats who opposed the Lincoln administration. Further investigation found letters from citizens housed in the National Archives that asked authorities to hang Confederate leaders higher than biblical proportions so that Jefferson Davis could replace Haman as the new standard for the height of a symbolic noose. But in the real world, no one beyond the Lincoln conspirators and the commandant of Andersonville faced execution, although plenty of former Confederates were indicted for treason. How can one reconcile what appeared to be a heartfelt hatred of the rebels, and expressions of vengeance, with the demonstrable record of leniency?

Finding the answer prompted a journey into understanding how Civil War era northerners conceived of, and acted upon, treason. The first revelation came in the extent to which ideas about treason proliferated as a primary means of constructing policy during the conflict—especially in guiding the military in defining the contours of loyalty on the northern and Confederate home fronts. Treason pervaded public discourse. It represents a challenge for a researcher to find a northern newspaper or periodical during any day of the war in which the words "traitor" and "treason" *do not* appear as a characterization of the rebels, of political opponents, or of the people suspected of holding divided loyalties in the United States. Popular conceptions of treason—or opinions formed outside of civil courts but in tracts, legislative halls, and executive chambers, and through actions in the streets—justified confiscation of rebel property, including slaves, ships, and other contraband; allowed soldiers to arrest women who taunted them; enabled a Union general in New Orleans to hang a man for tearing down a U.S. flag; caused thousands of arrests by the military in the loyal states for something called "treasonable behavior"; encouraged as patriotic acts informing on neighbors with little or no evidence; enabled soldiers to prevent people from voting; allowed authorities to suppress newspapers and arrest editors who criticized the Lincoln administration; allowed them also to arrest political figures and judges; and motivated soldiers in their efforts to remove a clergyman in Virginia in the midst of an Episcopalian worship service because he refused to administer the prayer for the president. Numerous examples indicate an excessive use of force against so-called treasonous behavior, yet supporters of the administration shrugged such things off as necessary actions to save the nation and as the just deserts for traitorous behavior, imperfectly defined.

This realization raised another contradiction to resolve. The popular interpretation of treason, one that most served the interests of the United States during the war, often failed to meet the test for the highest crime against the nation-state, at least in peacetime. Treason is the only crime specified in the Constitution, put there deliberately to make it hard to prosecute. As chapter 1 discusses, it had been a political and personal crime under the British. Declare that you wished for the demise of the king, and you could swing from the gallows or suffer a death by torture. The framers tried to eliminate this British interpretation known as "constructive" treason, which allowed the king to punish people who had committed no actual crime beyond expressing disloyalty. Treason in the British system even allowed members of a traitor's family to be executed or prevented from inheriting the property of the convicted. Corruption of blood or forfeiture, it was called. In the United States, one has to earn a treason conviction, first by levying actual war against the nation or aiding its enemies and, second, by having two witnesses, not one, swear you had done so. That mandate makes for a careful guarding of liberty, consistent with a desire to protect freedom of speech. This check on abuse of power, however, did not stop people either in the antebellum era or especially during the war from doing their level best to stifle speech that was determined to be offensive to the health of the national state. Yet during the Civil War, as detailed in chapter 2, thousands of northerners supported that the *expression* of treason, on the basis of popular conceptions of this crime rather than legal decisions, informed a range of policies against the suspected traitors at home.[1]

As troubling as this sounds, northerners did not check their respect for legal traditions at the door when it came time either to kill the enemy or to imprison each other. In fact, the contrary case can be made. As much as administration supporters seemed to stretch the Constitution, Civil War Americans felt bound to explain their positions in legal terms. Law and the Constitution provided the common vernacular for people on all sides of this civil conflict. Actions had to have, as one historian has noted, constitutional plausibility. Others have argued that the times called for extraordinary measures, which the Constitution permitted through its charge for the preservation of republican self-government.[2]

What is missing from the literature of the war is the extent to which the courts, Congress, and the executive branch employed transnational currents of thought in order to create this plausibility. The Constitution assigns the president the power to defend the country from invasion or insurrection, but it does not say how. Are there limits to this power? What kinds of punishment can be visited upon an enemy or an insurrectionist according to the rules of war? Chapter 3 reveals that legislators, politicians, judges, and even public intellectuals borrowed from international law and the practices of warfare in the Atlantic world to determine how the country should treat the rebel traitors—how they could act as if the rebellion were a public war between foreign nations without losing the ability to prosecute Confederates as traitorous citizens. Particularly influential were two works, an eighteenth-century compilation called *The Law of Nations* by Emmerich de Vattel and an antebellum-era tome titled *Elements of International Law* by Henry Wheaton.[3] Although a wing of constitutional history suggests that the fundamental law of the land was adequate to handle the crisis, this is true only if we add international law and customary practices of warfare in the Western world to supplement the Constitution. These precedents fortified the logic for emancipation, among other policies. The transnational ideas embodied in the laws of war and the laws of nations resolved the seeming contradiction of considering Confederates as enemies in a public war, yet remaining as citizens subject to prosecution as traitors. These sources, some of them unwritten, were used by Congress, courts, and the code of war by Francis Lieber that emerged in 1863.[4]

But this book does not focus on constitutional theory. It is far more concerned with practice, or the social and political consequences of ideology. Those who wish to learn about legal cases, lawyers, and judges will certainly be disappointed. Nowhere in these pages appears a discussion of original intent or of judicial review. In fact, much of the attention must be elsewhere than civil courts because the restrictive nature of treason law chased authorities toward using executive power to combat disloyalty. Plus, Lincoln and many of his advisers were not concerned with splitting constitutional hairs. They were interested in finding the practical tools to win the war, while ensuring that they maintained a toe in the water of constitutional plausibility.[5] The purpose of this project was to learn how authorities and the public deployed their notion of treason—that is, the practical application of these ideas on people. The goal was to show the intersection of high policy with low practice, not to justify the actions or ideology but to try to put a face onto the prosecution of disloyalty. Consequently, I tried as much as possible to see how decisions in Washington informed what happened in communities, and vice versa. The understanding of treason, what it allowed Civil War people to do and not to do, came about not through Lincoln alone but through a collaboration among the many who supported the administration's prosecution of the war, including editors, public intellectuals, politicians, citizens passing resolutions in public meetings, and crowds destroying newspaper offices.[6]

If any entity provides a consistent thread weaving its way throughout this story, it is the military, as a partner in shaping policies for civilians under its charge on both sides of the conflict. Scholars of emancipation during the war have shown the military's impact on pushing forward an antislavery agenda. Through the orders of John C. Frémont and David Hunter that were countermanded by the president and the creation of the contraband concept by Benjamin Butler that overturned the Fugitive Slave Laws—even the geographic location of troops in encouraging flight by the enslaved—historians have argued for the army's role in keeping emancipation in the forefront of national discussion.[7] Yet they have been slow to recognize the same dynamic in the Union army's enforcement of loyalty.

Washington bureaucrats often had to react to the stands taken by generals, soldiers, or provost marshals on the ground. Soldiers stationed in all corners of the Union, even the loyal sections, had to deal with guerrillas, spies, recalcitrant women, citizens taking loyalty oaths, election officials, and more, and do so without a script, especially early in the war. They encountered conditions peculiar to situations in communities without the time, or sometimes inclination, to consult with Washington. In Missouri in 1861, General Henry Wager Halleck sorted through difficult situations involving guerrilla fighting with citizens who had burned bridges; some were hauled before military commissions where many were convicted on treason charges. No rulebook counseled how to handle these kinds of cases, and it took time before a code of conduct appeared. Similarly, as we will see in chapters 2 and 5, Lincoln stepped in to overturn military interference with ministers and churches. Historians typically cast the most famous military arrest, that of Clement L. Vallandigham, as one that the president probably did not prefer but accepted because he did not want to weaken the military's ability to regulate traitorous speech. In other words, the overarching narrative of the war has not recognized what stares it in the face: the military's contribution to defining traitorous behavior, sometimes independent of superiors.

Lincoln did not concede his executive power to subordinates; the lack of effective administrative control testified to the strains of supervising problems over a vast territory without the necessary administrative infrastructure or policy precedents. The executive branch supervised the military, and Lincoln remained a strong commander in chief.[8] He certainly stepped in and overturned actions by subordinates that he considered imprudent. He also took the lead. The president, with eventual support from the Congress, suspended habeas corpus, which treated loyal states with functioning civil courts as under military jurisdiction and allowed for numerous arrests from the concern that traitorous speech could interfere with raising troops or encourage desertion. Lincoln's power and prominence cannot be denied in the story of civil liberties. The argument here, though, is that the military must be inserted into this story—not just as an enforcer of stated policies but also as a collaborator and, perhaps even more often, as the instigator. If, as Mark E. Neely Jr. has argued, the constitutional history of the Civil War must be sought less in the courts than in political tracts and newspapers, then military officers should receive just due among the contributors to the constitutional history of the United States.[9]

Over the course of the war the enforcement of loyalty in the North increasingly fell to provost marshals. Chapter 4 shows a complicated system, which modifies the picture of a centralized force in the scholarship of the war. By midway in the war, three different kinds of provost marshals might patrol a community, all with slightly different responsibilities and chains of command. The army had its own provosts who focused primarily on soldiers; military departments assigned to monitor a certain territory had their own authorities; and then came the administrative arm represented in most scholarship of the war, the provosts who supervised and enforced conscription throughout the North. This last, "centralized" bureaucracy rested upon a base of localism—of "special" provosts who had arisen at the local level early in the war to help monitor loyalty, as well as of police and other agents. While it is true that conscription was part of "nationalizing tendencies," the enforcement arm for conscription at the federal level depended on state patronage and local people.[10] These provost marshals, especially in more isolated areas, rarely had enough people working for them to handle resistance. They functioned best in Republican communities that supported the war. They struggled in areas dominated by peace or antiadministration Democrats, such as the upper tier of Pennsylvania known as the lumber region. At the ground level, this centralized force could appear fragmented and subject to local pressures. Even in urban areas, staying out of the draft, as historian Tyler Anbinder has demonstrated, was achievable. "By either failing to report or obtaining an exemption," he has noted, "eight out of ten draftees in the urban areas sampled managed to avoid army service."[11]

Once it went into Confederate territory, or contested areas of the Union like Missouri that contained southern sympathizers, the U.S. military's experience with civilians underscored the ways in which women were treated seriously as potential enemies of the state. Chapter 5 reveals how the war conflated the domestic world with the political one. In many respects, loyalty became a struggle over the security of households. Union military officials and provost marshals in occupied areas began to use access to livelihood to coerce faithfulness, by trading provisions and the ability to practice their professions for oaths of loyalty. The military realized that this ritual, far from guaranteeing fidelity to the nation, often represented nothing more than lip loyalty rather than sentiments of the heart. Goods were seized, as well as slaves, on the basis of their owners committing treason that was never tried in a court. The Second Confiscation Act, designed to punish traitors, did give some legal standing to the military in taking property. General William T. Sherman, in fact, awarded to objects the power of a capital crime against the state when he said, "All cotton is tainted with treason, and no title in it will be respected."[12]

The next two chapters return to the North to encounter the military meddling in the sacred public ritual of a democracy, the ballot box. As with so much of the executive actions against treason, this occurred most often in the border states. Soldiers tipped the results in at least one congressional race in Maryland. And in Delaware, the policy of stationing troops at polling precincts, where a voter's intention could easily be discerned because there was no secret ballot, caused Democrats to boycott an election, sending an antislavery Republican to Congress. The 1864 presidential election took place in the shadow of these actions, which Democrats used to illustrate their lament about the administration's abrogation of the Constitution as the best strategy to put forth in the campaign. In the Congress, border state representatives pushed for legislation to prohibit the troops from being within a mile from precincts on election days. They eventually won, but not until Republicans delayed the bill until 1865, or after it had any practical impact on the war. Unaccountably, this activity by the military at polling precincts—appearing in certain state studies and especially earlier works by revisionist historians—has fallen out of the general literature of the war and does not appear in recent biographies of Lincoln.[13]

The army was also used in ways that were not quite so coercive but that stand out as unusual in comparison with today. In the Civil War, it engaged in more partisan activities than is fashionable in the twenty-first century. Political positions were encouraged, as long as they supported the Republican administration. Military theorists in our time debate the role of officers in engaging in politics. The expectation is that officers will not openly campaign for candidates. Nor is it expected that officers would pressure subordinates to vote for a particular public official.[14] Nor would it be condoned—even if absentee ballots make it unnecessary now—to solicit officers to furlough soldiers to go home to vote for a particular party. Yet this happened in the Civil War. Lincoln encouraged general officers to leave the ranks so they could speak on the political stump in key districts. He also let army leaders send soldiers home to vote if they could not do so via absentee ballot if it appeared they could help the Republican cause back home. In the army, commanders banned so-called treasonable material from camps, which often meant Democratic tracts and newspapers.[15] Of course, Democrats had less power to do this. The administration was not bashful about using its control over the army to help political ends. Nor should it have been: politics was played differently in the nineteenth century. Democrats certainly would have done the same.

The final two chapters deal with why the traitors did not hang and how Republicans still tried to use charges of disloyalty in the postwar world to reconfigure political power both in the former Confederacy and in the North. Despite the expressed desires to hang some of the leading rebels, such as Jefferson Davis, and the indictments of nearly forty ex-Confederates, including Lee, in civil court for treason, none of these men hanged for the crime. The military played a role in the movement toward clemency in the form of the paroles given to Confederate soldiers in exchange for their promise of loyalty. Although this seemed to close the book on prosecuting the rebels in arms, it did not. Popular legal opinions, including the writings of Columbia law professor Francis Lieber, suggested that the lenient terms of surrender did not preclude rebels from being prosecuted as traitors. The paroles, in this view, had died with the war in a way similar to the prisoner exchange system. Plenty of discourse suggested that paroled soldiers could, and should, be tried. But the political will did not exist to sustain the effort. Or perhaps it is more accurate to say that other political goals took precedent. Reunion was the primary goal of the war, and it did not pay to create martyrs who might inflame the people expected to embrace renewed dominion by the federal government.[16] It especially did not pay to lose court cases that might prove secession possible, which legal advisers considered a real possibility. As the battles intensified between President Andrew Johnson and Congress over the goals of Reconstruction, concern over the fate of rebels indicted for treason faded.

But two groups of people lent their voices to the movement of reconciliation with traitors. One was a wing of abolitionists typified by Horace Greeley and Gerrit Smith, both of whom argued for clemency for the rebels. Their support for reconciliation rested, it seems, on their broad interests in societal reform that included repugnance for capital punishment and a belief that hangings reformed no one. African Americans, meanwhile, also found themselves rejecting vengeance on slavemongers because it did not serve their political efforts for equality. They banked their hopes on reminding white politicians that black people had been loyal to the Union and that restoring the slaveocracy to power without enabling black men to vote gave power back to traitors who could undermine the victory. Reconciliation-minded abolitionists and African Americans consequently found themselves in agreement concerning mercy for traitors, although for different reasons.

But the lack of civil action does not mean that the rebels escaped punishment legislatively or politically. One of the underappreciated issues in Reconstruction has been the extent to which Republicans debated and experimented with various means to restrict the suffrage and the national influence of traitors, with mechanisms for this finding their way into the Fourteenth Amendment. Black people were considered as the loyal constituency in the South and a possible balance against the restored power of rebels in politics. Yet early in Reconstruction it was clear that voting rights for African Americans in the Confederacy raised mixed feelings among many white people in the North, where most black people did not have the right to vote. Because of federalism, or the recognized right of states to determine who could vote, advancing the cause of black rights required a dual fight at national and state levels. Northern blacks in the Equal Rights Leagues developed multiple approaches, realizing that they had to push for changes to constitutions in states like Pennsylvania, which reserved suffrage for white freemen. One avenue to explore more precisely for Reconstruction is the extensive restructuring of state constitutions in the North, almost all of which had to conform to the new standards of freedom established in the national Reconstruction Amendments. The former Confederacy was not the only place rewriting its state constitutions; states in the North also had to revise their fundamental laws.

Chapter 9 demonstrates how, especially in the border states, various means were employed to prevent former Confederates from voting. Loyalty oaths in Missouri and West Virginia were particularly effective in keeping Republicans in power by preventing those who had served the Confederacy from exercising the franchise. Other techniques that became popular included new voter registration laws, ostensibly designed to protect against voter fraud but also giving judges of elections sitting at precincts broad powers to deny a person suspected of disloyalty in the war access to the ballot box. But there were additional attempts to keep disloyal people from exercising the franchise. Republicans in perhaps seven northern states took advantage of a federal law passed near the end of the war that stripped deserters from the Union army of their rights as citizens. It was commonly believed that most deserters were Democrats, so these efforts were partisan. At the same time, northerners were trying to overcome the problem of the three-fifths clause in the Constitution, which became moot with the freedom of African Americans. The irony: black people now counted as full persons for apportionment, giving white men more representation in Congress and the Electoral College without having to represent the interests of a sizable portion of their electorate. Sections 2 and 3 of the Fourteenth Amendment were intended to rectify this by reducing congressional seats in the South if leaders did not recognize black suffrage and by banning former Confederates from public office. These two provisions angered the white South the most, not the most famous first section that declared citizenship and protection under the law for everyone born in the United States.

Various conclusions stand out as a result of this exploration into the uses and abuses of treason. The military served as a significant intruder into the liberty and property of civilians on both sides of the Mason-Dixon Line, at times justifiably and at times before Washington could endorse the decisions. Arrests based on speech were made on the basis of treason expressed or implied, and women were considered serious enemies capable of undermining the Union war effort. But it is also true that the punishment of traitors took place outside of the judiciary and often without the oversight of the executive branch. People who spoke out against the administration could find themselves visited by soldiers at night, chased by a crowd intent on violence, expelled from a job, ostracized socially, or taken to jail by local police. Establishing the boundaries of free speech and loyalty in the Civil War era was a collaboration of more people than Lincoln, involving more than the domestic laws of the United States. Although it is true that the view from Washington was one of targeted, rather than arbitrary, application of power, the experience on the ground often conveyed the impression that such actions were capricious and designed to stifle political speech, even when they were not sanctioned by the administration.[17]

Although federal activity fell most on the border and insurrectionary states, there were enough arrests in the upper North that involved political candidates and community leaders to infuse a partisan Democratic critique with substance. Historians have dismissed the Democratic characterization of Lincoln as a dictator, as well they should. It is, in fact, a ridiculous charge, given the extent to which the press and other institutions and activities continued, such as the 1864 election for president.[18] But the reverse is also wrong—to think that the opposition's complaints about arrests were secondary to its racism. They were of a piece. Besides the obvious racial attack against the Republicans, there was much to criticize concerning abuses of liberties. Also, the Democratic opposition to Lincoln retained political awareness. By the time Democrats arrived at the 1864 presidential election, the people who crafted the platform realized that complaints against emancipation could not win nationally. The logic might work locally or in state campaigns—and racist images certainly proliferated. But by 1864 the anti-emancipation stance took a back seat as an *official* party position for a presidential campaign. However, the criticism about the unconstitutional use of power did not. In 1864, it provided arguably the best critique for why Lincoln had to go and why someone with more respect for the Constitution had to enter. Although it is true that Democrats failed to lay out a specific plan for how they intended to protect the Constitution as it was, their position suggested finding a leader who did not allow the military to arrest them for criticizing the government or stationing soldiers at precincts to influence voting.[19]

Also running throughout this story is a subtheme about the problems of centralized administrative control and the endurance of limited government and state rights as a mentality even among northerners. The centralized government was not a figment; the national apparatus grew during the war in the form of a national currency, conscription, and various other means. But it also was far from complete. It had to use local people and depended on state support. Centralization did not enjoy a nonpartisan commitment. Government grew because authorities tried to find pragmatic ways of defeating traitors in their unprecedented insurrection, which necessitated creating institutions such as conscription and the Provost Marshal General's Bureau. But these innovations were not appreciated by many in the United States, or even by the people who put them into place. If we use Lincoln's election in 1864 as a barometer, at least 45 percent of the North did not believe in the direction the country traveled. When we add the former Confederacy to this mix, it provides additional weight to the endurance of state sovereignty. This concerned Richard Henry Dana, a prominent attorney and one of the government's attorneys in the potential trial for Jefferson Davis. He feared trying people for treason in areas in which the crimes were committed because he could not be sure the government would win a conviction. The possibility of facing a jury with the wrong set of beliefs presented too much of a risk.

Finally, what do we make of Lincoln and the Republicans who used the military, and whatever other powers at their disposal, almost like an extension of a political machine to move their policies forward? Does this book fall within an orientation that one historian of Civil War scholarship defines as "neo-revisionism"? Historians today have discarded the triumphalist narrative of the Civil War as a progressive story of freedom and nation-building; many focus on the horrors, atrocities, and tragedy of using war to settle political differences. This position echoes the revisionist writers of the early to mid-twentieth century, especially beginning in the 1930s, who assumed a more critical view of the nation and saw the war as needless and even synonymous with organized murder. Various books in the past decade have analyzed the less appealing aspects of the conflict, especially guerrilla warfare.[20]

This work only partially fits the description. Yes, it will not feature a triumphalist narrative. The Civil War was a harder war than the public today usually acknowledges, one in which leaders had to reach for unusual, even legally malleable, measures. Lincoln and his advisers faced an incredible array of problems on the home front ranging from guerrilla actions in the border states to divining what it meant when a rebel woman goaded her son into throwing stones at Union soldiers. Sometimes, Union officials went too far. In the following pages, there will be examples of horrible behavior by the Union military, such as its vandalism in Alabama that resulted in the destruction of homes, private papers, Bibles, and the sexual molestation of two enslaved women. Also, it seemed unnecessary for soldiers to pistol-whip a Maryland judge as they removed him from the bench to take him to prison. Nor was it clear that soldiers needed to interfere in voting in Maryland during the 1863 congressional races, stationing themselves at the polls to prohibit the "disloyal" from voting. On one level, the measures employed by the Union deserve questioning and, at times, condemnation.

But the greater context must factor into any critique of the administration, rendering the excessive measures as at least partially understandable. Administrative controls were poor and pieced together to handle situations as they emerged. Real dangers existed in guerrilla activity in the border states, which also contained rebel sympathizers. Overzealous citizens took matters into their own hands to persecute real and imaginary traitors in communities, as did army officers. The unprecedented nature of threat and the willingness on the part of Lincoln to retract the claws of excessive force when things went too far must be acknowledged. The ultimate goal was to win the war, not to suppress liberties. Additionally, there were achievements worth recognizing. The war resolved whether slavery remained as a sanctioned institution in the United States. It also resolved whether the United States survived intact. Yet war and coercion were the blunt, tragic instruments necessary to accomplish these ends.

Consequently, the ingredients featured in most of the discussion throughout this study come down to the following. Popular understanding of treason, not legal definitions in civil courts, guided actions by Union functionaries, both high and low, throughout the Union and Confederacy. A "centralized" Union existed in a partisan way and functioned most efficiently where it found welcome from local people—in collaborations involving such novelties as special provost marshals and privately formed militia groups. The situation prompted supporters of the war to equate patriotism with spying on neighbors and with turning them in to authorities, no matter how slim the evidence. Often the residents in a region moved more swiftly than federal agents. Questionable policies resulted as Lincoln pushed the law to its extremes; however, when the country teetered on the edge of the constitutional precipice, he pulled it back from the edge. But he also allowed the government to do things that should give one pause. One scholar has characterized the assaults on liberty as lying between state repression of suffrage and spontaneous intimidation of friends and neighbors.[21] But focusing only on Lincoln misses the fuller picture of dealing with alleged disloyalty, including the attempts after his death to control white suffrage by disfranchising former Confederates and Union deserters during Reconstruction. To watch this unfold requires embarking on the journey laid out in the pages ahead.

1

TREASON BEFORE THE

CIVIL WAR

As John Brown faced the hangman on a December morning in 1859, it likely provided little solace to know that he was setting a legal milestone. By the time authorities eased John Brown's body from the noose, he had become the first person to be executed for treason since the ratification of the Constitution. Whenever mentioning the history set at that execution, honesty demands the confession of two technicalities. First, Brown hanged not only for treason but also for two other charges: inciting insurrection among slaves and murder. Both were capital crimes, with either one enough to make him just as dead as if treason had not been thrown into the bargain. The second technicality, though, is more interesting. Although he had attacked a federal installation—the armory at Harpers Ferry—Brown's treason was committed not against the United States but against the Commonwealth of Virginia. His trial took place in a state court, with the governor of Virginia orchestrating the event. Having the state of Virginia handle the trial of John Brown suited the political needs of the moment and, because of the peculiarities of its own treason statute, virtually guaranteed a conviction.

The sectional crisis revived the use of treason cases as the country inexorably rolled toward a bloody resolution of its ills. During the 1850s, proslavery forces—along with people who opposed abolition or simply endorsed upholding laws to protect slavery—resorted to treason charges in at least three impassioned political circumstances with the intention of quashing antislavery activity. Two of these occasions, ironically, featured members of the John Brown family. Each one became a cause célèbre for the abolitionists and Free-Soilers. None of these cases served as a model for the kind of justice envisioned by the framers of the Constitution. They originated and assumed their direction from political motivations, with the intent to curtail the Free-Soil movement through the overwhelming might of the government. This application of treason included attempts to criminalize even spoken or written words. Antiabolitionists merely followed the habits of American politics that had emerged since the writing of the Constitution in 1787. And they did this, in their own minds, for patriotic reasons: they believed they were protecting the country from potential disunion caused by the extralegal agitation of an unwelcome faction known as abolitionists. The mentality among northern Republicans would be very similar during the Civil War as they saw a wide range of behavior as involving disloyalty and a threat to the national state.

The Christiana Riot of 1851 provided a federal stage to reinforce the government's commitment to the new Fugitive Slave Law that had emerged from the Compromise of 1850. With the encouragement of the Fillmore administration, the government prosecuted the suspects not on the basis of violating the fugitive law, which obviously had been committed, but for treason against the United States. In middecade, proslavery forces in Kansas charged or held a half dozen or more antislavery men on high treason. One of them was John Brown Jr., the son of the famous insurrectionist, but he was nowhere near as well known as the others indicted, including the first territorial governor, the antislavery governor of the contested government at Topeka, a prominent editor of an antislavery newspaper in Lawrence, and a former Indiana congressmen who would become one of the first U.S. senators from the state. Proslavery leaders failed in these two attempts to convict for treason but succeeded with the trial of John Brown. None of the cases derailed the Free-Soil movement that found a home in the emerging Republican Party. To the contrary, proponents of Free-Soil used such occasions to rail even more loudly against a slaveholding aristocracy that, they claimed, conspired with northern men to control the institutions of power in order to force slavery into becoming a national institution.

The trials from the early republic through the eve of the Civil War suggest a pattern. Since the 1790s, federal court rulings have narrowed the definition of treason to make it difficult to prosecute, yet this had not discouraged people from trying to use the charge broadly. There had been a tension between the application of treason by the polity and the definition of the crime in case law, or between the public's conceptualization of the crime and that of the judiciary. No matter how narrow the court's rulings, this had not stopped politicians or the public from trying to push the boundaries of treason's definition to serve political needs, including in the hands of George Washington and Thomas Jefferson.[1] Sometimes, this may be justifiable, such as when Washington thought he was saving the republic by trying the leaders of the Whiskey Rebellion. It becomes dubious, to say the least, to see this tactic in the hands of dough-faced, Democratic politicians and proslavery forces in the 1850s: the very people who proclaimed to honor state rights and limited construction of the Constitution, yet who did not hesitate to muster the fullest power of the national state to protect local sovereignty over slavery.

Origins of Treason

Treason is the only crime defined by the U.S. Constitution, and it was limited by both definition and a special test for evidence to increase the difficulty of deploying it for partisan purposes. Article III, section 3, of the Constitution establishes treason as levying war against the United States "or adhering to their enemies, giving them aid and comfort." It takes the testimony of two persons witnessing the same "overt act," or a confession in open court, to win a conviction. Congress can establish the penalty for treason, such as imprisonment instead of death, but cannot extend the effects beyond the lifetime of the person. Conspiring to overthrow the government is not enough to qualify; nor is wishing for or plotting for the death of leaders, unless these intentions became part of an actual campaign to wage war against the United States or to aid its enemies. Except for a brief moment in the Federalist period, sedition and conspiracy did not exist as a crime at the national level before the Civil War.[2]

By specifying what it took to commit this capital offense, the framers hoped to avoid arbitrary acts that had occurred in England, especially under the Tudors. But the Committee on Detail could not cut itself loose from precedents: English law remained in the blood of the new country. The committee borrowed language directly from Edward III that had existed since the 1300s and considered it a crime to levy war and to aid enemies of state. On the other hand, the framers avoided some of the more abusive elements. The English statute also made it a capital crime to "compass" (bring about) or imagine the death of the monarch. Judges over the years expanded this by construction, or interpretation, to include spoken or written words critical of the government. This became known as constructive treason.[3] Additionally, one could not threaten the continuity of the king's family in any way or murder a lord, master, clergyman, or other person to whom one owed fidelity in the hierarchy of feudal relations. The framers of the U.S. Constitution purposely omitted these matters from the treason clause. By locating this clause under Article III, or the powers pertaining to the judiciary, the framers denied to the Congress the power to change the parameters of treason through legislation. Finally, unlike in England, where the traitor might have his lands seized and his heirs held responsible, no penalty could affect anyone other than the person convicted. (This factor will have repercussions for confiscation of property during the Civil War.)[4] As one historian has noted, "The framers' omission of this definition of treason was intended to restrict the concept of 'constructive treason'—in other words, speaking or acting to encourage treason—that in England had been exploited to suppress dissent and political opposition."[5] The result has been the prosecution of fewer than forty treason cases over the course of U.S. history, with John Brown remaining the main figure executed for the crime since the birth of the Constitution in 1787.

Despite the relatively clear language, the treason clause in the Constitution resolved neither how it would be interpreted nor applied. Constructive treason had not been banished from popular attitudes or, for that matter, from the government. As one historian has argued, the meaning of levying war was not quite so clear at the time. Some of the first cases to emerge after the adoption of the Constitution featured citizens resisting particular legislation, usually involving taxes. The distinctions between riot and treason remained muddy. Historian Thomas P. Slaughter has concluded: "The realities of the treason clause would be worked out on the battlefield and in the courts, in those moments of intense political turmoil that the Founders most feared."[6]

George Washington faced the first practical tests of the treason clause, with the Federalist era favoring protection of the national state over the rights of individuals. In 1794 four western counties of Pennsylvania broke into open rebellion over federal excise taxes on whiskey. The protesters terrorized revenue collectors, robbed mails, and disrupted courts. One tax collector's home was burned down, which also destroyed the official records for administering the levy. At one point, the rebels massed 5,000 men outside of Pittsburgh at first apparently to attack a federal installation but then changed their mind and marched through the town in a show of force. To restore order, President Washington raised nearly 13,000 militiamen from four states. The opposition melted by the time the troops crossed the Allegheny Mountains. The administration pushed forward with prosecutions for treason. Out of the two dozen indicted, two men were convicted, Philip Vigol and John Mitchell. Their convictions and death sentences became the first cases of treason to be upheld after ratification of the Constitution. Once the point had been made, the president pardoned the defendants, ostensibly using clemency to allow passions to cool or to deny further reason for uprisings.[7]

These first treason cases flirted with restoring the interpretation of constructive treason from England that had blurred the boundaries of riot, resistance, and rebellion. The charges against the defendants, Vigol and Mitchell, dealt with actions involving an armed confrontation of a mob at Couche's Fort and the subsequent burning of a home belonging to the tax collector, John Neville. The mob challenged the collection of the excise tax placed on whiskey. During the trial in the Circuit Court of Pennsylvania, the defense logically argued that treason did not apply in this case, both because of the nature of the act and because of the test of evidence required by the Constitution. "Constructive, or interpretative treasons, must be the dread and scourge of any nation that allows them," they contended, adding that under the district attorney's construction "a mob may easily be converted into a conspiracy; and a riot aggravated into High Treason."[8] They pointed out that Congress already had a perfectly good law on the books to handle such acts described in the indictment—obstruction of an officer in the performance of his duty, which was a misdemeanor. Even if the defendant had conspired to levy war, it was not the same thing as doing so. Plus, they concluded, the state of the evidence dictated an acquittal. It was clear even to the judge that only one witness had established Mitchell at the scene of the burning of Neville's home. Another thought he saw the defendant with the mob. As Slaughter explains, "The prosecution sought to define the overt act constructively to include both events—the meeting at which Mitchell, among many others, was heard to express opinions of a 'treasonous' design and the burning of excise inspector Neville's house—as part of one overt act that also included a subsequent gathering at a later date."[9]

In 1799 Fries Rebellion in Philadelphia presented another instance when the court seemed to be heading toward an expanded interpretation of treason. Citizens protested a tax that fell on dwellings. They caused trouble for the assessors who entered communities to establish value according to the number of windows. Farmers threatened violence and, in one instance, a woman poured scalding water from a story above onto an assessor, which gave rise to the colorful nickname of the "hot water war." A federal marshal began gathering those who resisted paying the tax and imprisoned them; they then went to the town of Bethlehem. Community members were furious. Men organized an attempt to release the prisoners, mustering about a hundred to march on the jail, causing the marshal to release the prisoners. The intention of these liberators scarcely seemed to involve the overthrow of the government; they protested one law and the assessors who came into their neighborhoods. Yet Fries and two others were convicted of treason and sentenced to hang. After deliberation with his cabinet, President John Adams decided that the case had gone too far in employing constructive treason. He acknowledged that the attack on the marshals had been dangerous, with serious implications for law and order; however, he considered that the crime better fit the definition of riot rather than treason. Despite the opinions of his cabinet, which wanted him to support the executions, Adams pardoned the men.[10]

From the turn of the nineteenth century to the Civil War, however, the federal judiciary followed a course that narrowed the definition of treason. The turning point came with the trial that involved the still unclear designs of the vice president of the United States against his own government. In 1804, Aaron Burr killed his rival Alexander Hamilton in a duel. He never was tried for the offense, but it cost him his political career. He sought other opportunities in the western areas of the emerging nation. Some believe he wanted to drive the Spanish from Mexico, paving the way for expansionism. In this case, he would have been serving the interests of the United States. Others suggest that he intended to dismember the Union by severing western territories from the United States and forming a new country with him as the leader—a potentially treasonous act. After first ignoring the situation, President Jefferson actively pursued the prosecution. Had the president succeeded, he would have nudged treason law in the United States closer to the practices of England that he was on record as hating.[11]

Burr evolved his scheme over a couple of years. In 1805 he traveled down the Ohio and Mississippi Rivers to New Orleans. A good reception by the people there encouraged him. He linked up with Harman Blennerhassett, an immigrant Irish lawyer who offered Burr a staging point for his campaign from an island in the Ohio River in western Virginia. But General James Wilkinson, who served as governor of the Louisiana Territory, shifted from an ally to an informant, sending the president a copy of a ciphered letter allegedly from Burr. A presidential proclamation declaring a conspiracy virtually caused the project to shut down and scattered whatever forces had assembled. Burr himself had left Blennerhassett's island and was not present when federal authorities came for him. Meanwhile, Wilkinson began rounding up suspects in his region. Burr eventually was arrested in 1807 in Mississippi Territory, but it was not his case that served as the turning point in treason history.[12]

The important actions involved two of Burr's alleged conspirators, Samuel Swartwout and Eric Bollman. Burr had engaged them as messengers to Wilkinson. Chief Justice Marshall composed the opinion. A

Federalist, Marshall knew the stakes of this event—that there was an attempt to expand executive powers and to politicize the use of treason. He urged for calm, rational decisions, adding, "As there is no crime which can more excite and agitate the passions of men than treason, no charge demands more from the tribunal before which it is made a deliberate and temperate inquiry."[13] In the end, he judged that there was neither the overt act nor the standard of evidence to meet the test for treason. In *Ex parte Bollman* and *Ex parte Swartwout*, Marshall ruled that in order to have an overt act, there must be an assemblage of men who were to use force to achieve a treasonous end. It was not enough to conspire to overthrow the government: that act would constitute a high misdemeanor. Violent force must be applied, even if it consisted of strength insufficient to achieve its goal.

In other segments of his opinion, Marshall created an interpretation that left an impact on the Civil War generation. The issue arose as he sorted through what constituted an act of levying war and whether someone who was not present during an assembly under arms could be convicted of treason. In *Bollman* and *Swartwout* he wanted to make it possible to hold accountable the people who had spawned and directed the treasonous acts. Marshall embraced a theory of English law that stated that in treason there was no such thing as an accessory to this crime—that, in fact, all the men involved were principals even if a person did not appear in arms against the country. Once the necessary ingredient was proved—the act of waging war—then all were guilty, no matter how minute their connection.[14] This judgment had a bearing on the prosecution of Confederates after the war, creating a problem for northerners who entertained ideas of vengeance against the defeated rebels. If Jefferson Davis hanged for his crimes, should not every officer and soldier who fought against the United States? Where did one draw the line against prosecutions for treason?

Burr eventually escaped the hangman's noose as treason became a more difficult charge to prove, but the case left another legacy for the post–Civil War discussion of treason. Legal advisers within the Johnson administration pondered over where to hold a trial for Jefferson Davis, should a civil action move forward. The consensus became that Richmond should serve as the site, because it was the city where he lived and worked as president of the Confederacy. This presented a real challenge for the success of any trial, which needed only one person to rule "not guilty" in order to hang the jury.

There is little doubt that Jefferson deployed all the powers of the executive in an attempt to wage political warfare of his own.[15] Some in his own party thought so, and the trial reinforced the breach growing between the president and fellow Virginian, John Randolph. After he learned of the messages to Wilkinson, the president had given a special address to Congress in which he condemned Burr as a traitor before a trial. He supervised all aspects of the prosecution, issued blank pardons, and allowed a collection of false affidavits. Here was one of the most storied founders—a man renowned for his concerns about the powers of a central government—using treason as a political weapon. But Jefferson was not alone. As the country advanced toward civil war, the government's leaders resurrected an interest in treason as a means of stifling a political opposition.

Christiana and Kansas

Right after the Mexican War, the possibility of disunion faced the country. The United States had acquired the remainder of most of its continental territory. But this prime real estate was purchased with bitter consequences. As the Mexican War raged in 1846, a proposition offered by Pennsylvania congressman David Wilmot said that the president could have his money to continue the war with Mexico but only with the proviso that slavery would not be allowed in any future states in the territories. Delegates from some southern states met at Nashville to talk about disunion but held off until they could see how the situation played itself out. The crisis was averted with a compromise that seemingly favored the free states except for one important element—a renewed commitment on the part of the United States to enforce the capture and return of fugitive slaves. Slave owners had become increasingly irritated by the loss of their human property without receiving justice in northern state courts. In the 1850s, the government featured three successive Democratic administrations determined to use whatever means possible to hold the Union together, even if it meant using the charge of treason to head off the antislavery movement and, in their minds, prevent disunion. One historian of the Supreme Court has observed about this period that "politics at times seemed to conceal the law within its shadow."[16]

One such instance came relatively soon after the compromise with the so-called Christiana Riot in Lancaster, Pennsylvania. In late 1849, four male slaves of Edward Gorsuch, a Maryland slaveholder, fled from Baltimore County to Pennsylvania. Gorsuch wanted them back. He filed the proper paperwork and in 1851, accompanied by Deputy Marshal Henry H. Kline, went to Christiana where he cornered the fugitives in the home of William Parker, a former slave who had won freedom through flight.

This part of Pennsylvania contained residents with mixed emotions about slave captures, with some supporting the activity but others who resented the wrongful kidnappings of African Americans. One confrontation before the passage of the Fugitive Slave Law at Lancaster had left two kidnappers mortally wounded. So Gorsuch should have expected trouble. But he wandered into a passionate situation without due caution. A first assault inside the house failed. As the men regrouped, African American and white neighbors from the region came to the rescue, some of them answering an alarm or horn sounded from the Parker house. Thus began the "Christiana Riot." Then, as Gorsuch and one of his former slaves argued with each other, the slave owner was clubbed from behind. As he rose, he was felled by shots and then beaten where he lay. The fugitives, including the men who had pulled the triggers, escaped beyond reach of the law, as they were shuttled through to Canada by abolitionists.[17]

This was heady stuff, to say the least. African Americans had banded together with a few white allies to resist a federally sanctioned posse. In the aftermath of the riot, the government rounded up more than thirty African Americans implicated in the crime, along with five white men. One of those, Castner Hanway, was a white miller living next door to Parker who heard the alarm and went to the scene of the crime to find out what was happening. He had watched as the events unfolded and had refused to help the marshal when asked. As a Quaker, he was against such involvement. According to testimony, he also affirmed the right of the African Americans to resist, as did one of the other white defendants who said he would not help the posse.[18]

Southerners greeted the murder and breach of the Fugitive Slave Law with outrage and the conviction that northerners had better show that they intended to uphold the laws of the land or else the Union meant nothing. In an open letter, Governor E. Louis Lowe of Maryland pressed Democratic president Millard Fillmore to prosecute the prisoners not on murder or a violation of the Fugitive Slave Law but on treason. He believed the importance of the controversy, and the inflammatory condition of the country, demanded a powerful statement. Lowe continued that if prosecution for treason did not take place, or if passion should dictate the outcome of the verdict, he feared the Union would split apart.

The case became one of the important political trials of the nineteenth century, with Fillmore ensuring it achieved this status. After consultation with his cabinet, he held a meeting with U.S. Attorney John Ashmead, Secretary of State Daniel Webster, and Attorney General John J. Crittenden and decided to move ahead with a treason trial. Fillmore was hoping to gain political capital in the South and to prove that the Fugitive Slave Law could not be violated. Legal historian Paul Finkelman makes the point that winning for the government was not really necessary—that simply the gesture of seeking a treason verdict was enough to earn high marks for enforcing the law. With little to lose, Finkelman argues, the government could lct the trial take on a partisan appearance even in the composition of the prosecution.[19]

The problem for the government's prosecutors was that they had the wrong defendant for winning a conviction. The men who had pulled the trigger had fled from the area. This show trial featured Castner Hanway, a white miller whose connection to a conspiracy was difficult to prove. The prosecution contended that he had taken part in a planned effort to overthrow the laws regarding slavery and had served as a leader for the conflict, yet there was no preconceived action intended to culminate in an attack on the United States. Hanway had ridden over on his horse on an impulse when learning of the commotion next door. The prosecution tried to implicate him by suggesting that he distributed pamphlets and other written material that encouraged resistance to the act. Even this tactic, however, incorporated the lamentable concept of constructive treason. There also was the problem of having no witnesses—much less the two required—to Hanway's alleged intentions. There had been no overt act of war making on his part. As one scholar has noted, "The only capital crime the federal prosecutors had in their arsenal to help establish their commitment to the Fugitive Slave Law was treason. The only white men they had to sacrifice had carried no guns in 'levying war' against the government." The trial had been exactly what the founders had hoped to avoid—one based far more on politics than on legal principles.[20]

When it came time to charge the jury, Supreme Court Associate Justice Robert C. Grier, who was assigned to the circuit, recognized that he had to deal with issues beyond simply the interpretation of treason and for an audience beyond the courtroom. Knowing full well that treason was inapplicable, he tried to allay the fears of Marylanders, their fellow southerners, and conservative northerners that Pennsylvania contained unconstitutional rebels who discarded the law of the land when it suited them. He was embarrassed to admit that Pennsylvania had contained "the only trials and convictions on record for armed and treasonable resistance to the laws of the United States since the adoption of the Constitution." He hurriedly reassured the courtroom and the readers who consumed the news reports that these first cases had occurred roughly a half century ago. According to Grier, most of the state looked with "abhorrence upon this disgraceful tragedy," except for "a few individuals of perverted intellect, some small districts or neighborhoods whose moral atmosphere has been tainted and poisoned, by male and female vagrant lecturers and conventions." He referred, of course, to abolitionists who appeared to conservatives and moderates in the United States to be extremists agitating for extralegal measures that would create an unwelcome social revolution.[21]

Grier defended what was not even before the court by declaring that the Fugitive Slave Law was constitutional. This underscored his desire to reassure the country that the court took these matters seriously. He criticized the clergymen in the North who preached otherwise and who said that their congregants should not obey the law. The justice said he respected their opinions when confined to theology but "cannot receive their decisions as binding precedents on questions arising under the Constitution." In the comments, Grier dealt with the notion of a "higher law" that permeated abolition rhetoric. Typified by William Henry Seward, senator from New York, the logic stressed that parts of the law were immoral and that God provided greater guidance than the Constitution concerning slavery. The law may not be perfect, but the judge believed that no one could have made a better compromise for this particular moment. He ended this part of his commentary with: "Let us suffice, for the present to say to you . . . that this law is constitutional; that the question of its constitutionality is to be settled by the courts, and not by conventions either of laymen or ecclesiastics; that we are as much bound to support this law as any other; and that public armed opposition to the execution of this law is as much treason as it would be against any other act of Congress to be found in the statute book." His frustration showed when he proclaimed the participants in the Christiana affair guilty, but of the wrong crime. He believed that the evidence "has clearly shown that the participants in this transaction are guilty of riot and murder at least—whether the crime amounts to treason or not will be presently considered."[22]

Despite the judge's diatribe against a criminal act that outraged him, he could not counsel the jury to render a verdict of guilty. Grier felt bound to follow the law. He asked the jurors to consider the intent of Hanway, or whether the defendant had come to aid or encourage the rioters. If that were the case, then he was guilty of any act committed by any individual in the riot, including a treasonous one. There was no evidence that Hanway had done so, and none existed to support the government's contention that he belonged to an abolition group. Hanway stood by as the events unfolded, just as a man might watch a madman attack father or friend and refuse to help. "We may wonder at his philosophic indifference," the judge said, "though we cannot admire the man."[23] The judge reminded the courtroom of the findings in the cases of *Bollman* and *Swartwout*, as well as *Fries*, to reinforce that there must be a specific overt act involving an assemblage of persons intending to conduct an insurrection or oppose the execution of a statute of the United States by force in order to compel its repeal. Debtors may gather to resist the sheriff from seizing their property, and they may even kill the authorities who do so, yet they cannot be considered traitors because they did not conduct an insurrection of a public nature. Similarly, fugitive slaves may resist their capture and murder or rob the authorities, making them liable for punishment of a felony, but not treason. "But when the object of an insurrection is of a local or private nature, not having a direct tendency to destroy all property and all government, by numbers and armed force, it will not amount to treason."[24]

The jury took less than fifteen minutes to decide on an acquittal. This did not necessarily absolve the defendants from prosecution on other charges, including riot or accessory to murder. The grand jury sitting in Lancaster considered raising such a possibility. The problem remained, however, that the people who were truly guilty of the crime were beyond reach of the law. In the end, no one was convicted for the death of Gorsuch and none of the formerly enslaved was returned.[25]

■ Kansas of the 1850s and early 1860s certainly qualifies as one of the ugliest episodes in U.S. history. It earned this infamy not only for the brutality that took place but also for the lack of justice. Within the span of a decade, a number of people died from bushwhackers, marauding Border Ruffians, posses persecuting in the name of law and order, and vigilantes who used firearms, swords, bowie knives, hatchets, and lynch rope. This violence comes as no surprise to historians who have long considered the territory as containing the first examples of civil war. The attempts by the proslavery Lecompton territorial government to eliminate the opposition through the trampling of civil liberties, and the federal government's role in the pattern of injustice, provided part of the motivation behind John Brown's grisly executions of five proslavery residents. The federal government's position on treason provided more fuel to a growing fire and highlighted how constructive forms of this capital offense remained important and symbolic.[26]

Early in 1856, Democratic president Franklin Pierce issued a statement that branded the antislavery efforts as revolution and defined opposition to the proslavery territorial government as an act of treason. The federal posture encouraged the chief justice of the territorial Supreme Court, who in May presided over a grand jury that voted on a number of indictments for treason. Targeted were key leaders of the antislavery shadow government that had formed early in the year. Once U.S. marshals had tried to exercise their writs, a county sheriff took over and called for the destruction of certain buildings as public nuisances. In the process, the Free-State Hotel sustained considerable damage and at least one home was burned. Newspaper offices were ransacked and presses destroyed. This occurred after an autumn of murders in which killers of a handful of antislavery men went free, and more deaths were promised daily in the public press. For Free-Soil settlers, the president, cabinet, Congress, and courts, in the words of one chronicler of events, appeared "as the accomplices of murder, arson, and pillage, and as the champions of pettier tyrants who would hesitate at no crime." Facing a local government that shut down free speech and branded the Free-Soil government as against the law, and seemingly shut out of a sympathetic hearing from the chief executive, John Brown "now took the field."[27]

Brown and his Free-Soil compatriots found Pierce's analysis of treason anathema because they understood that the Lecompton government existed through fraud and coercion. Missouri slave owners cared a great deal about Kansas because their slave state had stuck out like a thumb above all other slave states as it jutted into the freedom side of the 36°30 line established by the Missouri Compromise. Should Kansas and Nebraska organize on the basis of antislavery, Missourians believed it would increase the pressure on maintaining their institution of slavery. They flooded the territory with Border Ruffians, men who descended upon the region just before an election for representative to Congress in late 1854. Armed men took over the polls and prevented Free-Soilers from participating. A later congressional investigation concluded that 1,700 votes were fraudulent. What worked well once was worth another try. At the election for the territorial legislature of March 30, 1855, more than 6,000 votes were cast when the census had determined that only 2,905 citizens were eligible to vote. Not surprisingly, the proslavery vote totaled 5,427.[28] Yet this became the government that Pierce recognized.

Foreshadowing sensitivity to speech in the Civil War, the proslavery government adopted legislation that made spoken or printed language against slavery a crime deserving hard labor. In fact, the code for the protection of slave property described three offenses that required the death penalty: raising an insurrection of slaves or free blacks; aiding in such an insurrection; or speaking, writing, or printing material designed to encourage such an act. The code contained stiff prison sentences for what one might expect, such as defendants found guilty of helping slaves run away, procuring slaves for the purposes of giving them freedom, or obstructing the capture of fugitives. Toward the end of the code, sections eleven through thirteen impinged even further on the liberty of Free-Soilers. People faced the possibility of hard labor if they spoke out against slavery, wrote these sentiments down, or circulated the statements in written form. More to the point, no one could hold elective office, or sit on a jury, if the person did not endorse the right to own slaves in the territory.[29] The message was clear: accept slavery, keep quiet about it, help authorities enforce it, or face prison and possibly hanging. Language, whether spoken or written, was considered to be a threat instead of a protected right.

Antislavery settlers responded by establishing their own government, which became viewed by the federal government as an extralegal one. Antislavery proponents had established the Free-Soil Party as early as August 1855. At public meetings, the leadership passed resolutions that vowed resistance to paying taxes or obeying the edicts of the proslavery legislature and courts. They boycotted the territorial election and, by mid-January 1856, had established a rival government at Topeka, which elected Dr. Charles Robinson to serve as governor. Among the people chosen as legislators was Representative John Brown Jr., a son of the old revolutionary. Faced with this movement, the ruling opposition described itself as the law and order party fighting against a faction that agitated for illegal social revolution.

In response, Pierce used a special address to Congress to excoriate the Free-Soil movement. It was an unusual gesture, whose timing raised commentary, especially among the people in the chambers who had begun referring to themselves as Republicans. Pierce had avoided the Kansas issue in the annual message of a few weeks earlier in December. Coming as it did on January 24, 1856, the special message sent a strong message to the antislavery people in Kansas to support the "legitimate" government or face potentially fatal repercussions. In this address, the president claimed that the proslavery government was a lawful entity whose legislation must be obeyed. He admitted that there had been fraud in the elections, but asserted that the first territorial governor had screened the ballots and authenticated the ones used to establish the legislature.[30] Pierce could not resist taking shots at the abolition movement, which he characterized as "pernicious agitation" that "disturbed the repose of our country" in the attempt "to propagate their social theories by the perversion and abuse of the powers of Congress." In Kansas, abolitionists had set up an illegal government. Pierce wrote, "In fact, what has been done is of revolutionary character. It is avowedly so in motive and in aim as respects the local law of the Territory. It will become treasonable insurrection if it reach the length of organized resistance by force to the fundamental, or any other federal law, and to the authority of the general government." Treason, the president promised, faced the full weight of the government.[31]

Congressional and newspaper reactions fell along partisan lines. It was an election year with the presidency on the table and the Republican Party, which had emerged in the North, facing its first national campaign. Both sides looked for issues to define themselves and mobilize their constituency; in the process, they escalated tensions in the territory through their partisan battles. Supporters of slavery and popular sovereignty tried to marginalize the abolition efforts. They virtually ignored the memorials and petitions that came into the congress from the Free-Soil settlers who requested protection of the government. Picking up from the theme of the president and the Kansas allies, they cast the recognized government in the territory as the law and order party. Senator Isaac Toucey of Connecticut in particular defended the president. Even if fraud had occurred in the elections, he said, there had been no official challenge to Governor Reeder's qualification of the vote. "There is but one government in the Territory of Kansas—a government organized in pursuance of an act of Congress. There is a legislative department to prescribe the laws; there is a judicial department to adjudicate them; there is an executive department, with ministerial officers at its command, to execute those laws. There is no other government in Kansas."[32]

Kansas lies a thousand miles from Washington, but the capital may as well have been next door. This was a moment in antebellum history when the local and the national merged. As a territory, Kansas was administered directly by Congress. The Senate committee for the territories consisted primarily of conservative men who favored popular sovereignty. Stephen Douglas led the group of all Democrats and one Republican, Jacob Collamer of Vermont. Plus, the officials in the territories owed their positions to the Democratic administration, especially the governor who validated elections and the judges who administered the daily practice of the law. Officials in Washington were occupied by far more than what was happening in Kansas and let their own political needs set an agenda for the territories. With an established pattern of violence engaged in by local authorities—and without justice for the victims—the policies adopted by the federal government set the boundaries in which injustice operated and added an additional impact to those experiencing these effects within the turbulent atmosphere of Kansas.

John Brown understood this as well as anyone. He had been in the territory since the prior year and witnessed examples of prejudice among legal authorities against the Free-Soil settlers. At least four antislavery men had been killed in 1855, leading to a siege of Lawrence by 2,000 or more Border Ruffians and militia. Free-Soil settlers had dug in and armed themselves. One of their number, a man named Barber from Ohio, was gunned down as he traveled unarmed in the countryside with two companions. His body was retrieved and brought to town. It made an impression on Brown as he watched the arrival of the victim's wife and friends who gathered around the body. He called the scene "heart-rending, and calculated to exasperate the men exceedingly, and one of the sure results of civil war." Tensions cooled somewhat through a truce arranged by Wilson Shannon, the territorial governor. Yet all knew that more violence percolated beneath the seeming calm and that the federal government's position on these matters meant a great deal. In February 1856, Brown wrote his family: "We are very anxious to know what Congress is doing," he said. "We hear that Frank Pierce means to crush the men of Kansas. I do not know how well he may succeed; but I think he may have his hands full before it is all over." To Brown and others of his camp, the Pierce administration was an extension of the enemy who patrolled beyond the Wakarusa River.[33]

Brown was by no means alone in this opinion. Sara Robinson, the wife of the Free-Soil governor, typified the Free-Soil mentality. She considered the national government as infiltrated by slave-owning southerners who easily coaxed weak-willed men like Pierce into doing their bidding. She believed that the real head of government was Jefferson Davis, who served as secretary of war. She experienced a moment just before the sack of Lawrence that resonated with John Brown's conflation of the enemy with Franklin Pierce. She attended to a woman who, with her husband, had been driven from their home "by these villains, under the cover of law." In a little while, the husband came into the building. He cradled his rifle as he sat and wiped his brow, vowing that he would not run from the enemy again. Robinson asked him what he would do, and he responded with, "I will protect myself." When she pressed him if he would resist the U.S. soldiers, he said, "Yes, I will fight anybody. If I live under a government that does not protect me, then I will protect myself, Frank Pierce or no Frank Pierce."[34]

In early May, the territorial court called for the indictments of eight men for treason. Targeted were important leaders of the opposition: the first territorial governor, Reeder; the current Free State governor, Charles

Robinson; newspaper editor, George W. Smith; former Indiana congressman, future U.S. senator, and ruthless military chieftain James Lane; and others instrumental in the resistance to the Lecompton government. Led by the U.S. district attorney, the grand jury complied with the requests and handed down the true bills necessary for the arrests. After initial difficulties, the U.S. marshal organized a posse and rounded up as many of these men as he could on May 20 in Lawrence. A few of the key individuals escaped: Lane was out of the state, Robinson fled, and Reeder proclaimed immunity because he was a representative to Congress with the Free-Soil Party.

Consequently, the charge of treason proved instrumental in igniting one of the most infamous episodes in the history of Kansas and the sectional crisis. At this point in the story, Sheriff Samuel Jones rode into the picture. He was a notorious county official who had collided with Free-Soil settlers repeatedly and had been wounded in an assassination attempt about a month earlier. He directed the men to destroy the Free-State Hotel and two newspapers as nuisances. The hotel served as the main meeting place for the settlers to discuss political affairs, and it was constructed like a fortress with thick stone walls that jutted over the roof. Thus followed what the Free-Soil faction, and subsequent historians, have called the Sack of Lawrence. On May 21, the hotel was destroyed, as were the printing presses of the *Herald of Freedom* and *Kansas Free State*. Against orders to respect private property, someone in the crowd burned the home of Robinson. Although a notorious act, the destruction and pillaging was not as great as the antislavery people alleged. No Free-Soil residents were killed, and the violence had fallen on targets that aided the resistance to the Lecompton government.[35] For a while, the prisoners held for treason remained in limbo because of the political struggle in Washington and the violence that erupted with vigor notorious even for Kansas.[36]

After the raid on Lawrence, John Brown cemented his notoriety with the nighttime activity that resulted in the grisly executions of five proslavery settlers, and the next month, two of Brown's sons were arrested by local authorities. One of them, John Brown Jr., had become temporarily addled under the tension and from beatings he suffered at the hands of rival Missourians. His captives did not help his sanity by tightly binding Brown in ropes for more than twenty-four hours as they marched him to prison. When they arrived at Lecompton, one son was released but John Jr. was held for treason as a member of the Free-Soil legislature.[37] Robinson was also captured and added to the pool. Eventually, the "state prisoners"—as Republicans referred to them—sat in Lecompton with some of the more prestigious men living in tents. Freedom came for the prisoners in early September. Pressure had come from Washington to make this issue go away. In early August, Senator Henry Wilson of Massachusetts submitted a resolution that the committee on the judiciary authorize the president to direct the attorney of the territory of Kansas to enter a *nolle prosequi* on the indictments.[38] Lecompte convened a hearing on September 9, but the disorder in the territory was such that key witnesses and attorneys could not make it to court. The judge finally issued a continuance but allowed the release of the prisoners on bail. John White Geary's arrival on the same day as the new Democratic territorial governor signaled a change in administration that contributed to ending future prosecutions. He immediately disbanded the militia dominated by Border Ruffians and tried to restore justice to the region, and even conducted a feud with Lecompte, urging Pierce to remove the judge. Although he ultimately could not secure the peace—or win the support of the next administration under Democratic president James Buchanan—the government eventually entered the plea of *nolle prosequi* that indicated the prosecution would proceed no further.

Harpers Ferry and Hanging

Twice then in the 1850s, the charge of treason was raised without achieving the goal of blunting the antislavery cause, but the third time resulted in a successful prosecution. John Brown attacked Harpers Ferry with twenty-one followers on October 16, 1859. They had targeted the small town at the confluence of the Shenandoah and Potomac Rivers because it was the home of one of two federal armories in the country. The town had weapons and was, unlike the other armory at Springfield, Massachusetts, in a slave state. Brown hoped to entice African Americans to fight for their liberty. Even though this was not an area of large slaveholding, it was a region offering slaves rugged terrain that potentially aided their flight. Here might be found fugitives ready to join Brown's cause or help enlist other African Americans. In winning them to his side, he would weaken the institution of slavery—at least, so he reasoned.[39] The entire affair lasted for fewer than forty hours. Seven of his men were killed. Brown and four others were captured and held for trial. He was guilty of many things: accessory to murder, insurrection, and inciting a slave rebellion, to name a few. But it was treason that became a key point and counterpoint by the prosecution and defense, especially whether he could be tried in a state court for a crime committed on federal property.

John Brown's road to the hangman's noose began in Philadelphia with the crafting of the Constitution. Considerable debate occurred over whether the power to prosecute treason belonged solely to the federal government. What at first seemed sensible, self-evident, and clear—the need to have treason tried only by the United States—grew murky, debatable, and complicated as the committee's discussion unfolded. During a meeting on August 20, Pennsylvania delegate James Wilson stubbornly maintained that treason could be committed only against the United States. He and fellow Pennsylvanian Gouverneur Morris favored language that clearly specified this sovereignty in the Constitution. James Madison leaned to this position, but seemingly because he believed the clause, as phrased, left concurrent jurisdictions, which might allow for double punishment. On the other side, men claimed there was a need to maintain sovereignties particular to both areas.[40] Eventually, all sides capitulated and let the ambiguity stand.

The abstract arguments of the framers faced a test run long before John Brown's raid. In 1842, violence erupted in Rhode Island as Thomas Wilson Dorr led more than 200 men on an assault against the arsenal at Providence. Dorr and his followers contested the restricted rights of an anachronistic regime that was holding on to limited suffrage based on the original 1663 charter for the colony. Dorr wanted to expand suffrage and create a new constitution. In 1841, two constitutions were laid before the state: a Freeman's Constitution that restricted suffrage to property owning or taxable eligibility and a People's Constitution that was far more liberal. Dorr won the people's support as governor. But the established governor declared martial law and began arresting the leaders of the Dorr opposition. On May 17, Dorr stormed the arsenal with his followers. They fired on the place without result. With daylight, his men had melted away. The sitting government declared martial law and began arresting anyone suspected of participating in the conspiracy. Dorr had fled the state, but after a new constitution was adopted by voters in 1843, he returned and was arrested for high treason.[41] The case went before the Rhode Island Supreme Court in March 1844. The court found him guilty and sentenced Dorr to solitary confinement for life. Eventually, his civil and political rights were restored, although he was broken by the events and died fairly soon afterward.

Jurisdiction of the John Brown trial became an issue in 1859. By October 19, two commitments had been lodged, one by Virginia and the other by the United States. Publicly, it was assumed that Virginia should handle the murder cases. Treason against the United States could be tried subsequently by the federal judiciary if needed.[42] In truth, the federal government did not put up much of a fight for jurisdiction, but few scholars have mentioned that the odds favored a conviction at the state level because of the nature of Virginia's law concerning treason. The statute's first section replicated much of the wording from the U.S. Constitution, but the next three provided for a much more expansive interpretation that seemed tailor-made for the Harpers Ferry insurrection. They provided punishment for free persons who failed to divulge knowledge of plots, who attempted to establish a government or instigate others to do so through writing or speech, and who conspired with a slave or a free person to induce a slave insurrection, whether or not it was carried out. The wording did not require the accused to be a citizen of the state of Virginia. As we will shortly see, the prosecution leaned heavily on the sections of the statute that prohibited establishing any government within its boundaries other than the existing one.[43]

The trial in the Circuit Court of Virginia consumed five days, with the defense trying to discredit the case for treason, first by arguing that the state had no jurisdiction in the matter and then that the incident itself did not meet the test for waging war against the government.[44] The incident had occurred, various attorneys for Brown claimed, on federal property. In closing arguments, the defense pushed the matter further, proclaiming that treason was inappropriate because Brown was neither a citizen nor a resident of Virginia; thus he owed the commonwealth no particular allegiance. "Rebellion," explained defense attorney Henry Griswold, "means the throwing off allegiance to some constituted authority. But we maintain that this prisoner was not bound by any allegiance to this State, and could not, therefore, be guilty of rebellion against it."[45] He went on to challenge that Brown had waged war. His men had only hoped to repeal "obnoxious laws" but never intended to overthrow the state government.[46]

When the prosecution had its turn, Andrew Hunter, an attorney from Virginia, built his case on the premise that Brown had intended to supplant the government of Virginia with his own republic. Before the trial opened, authorities had found in the group's headquarters at the Kennedy farm in Maryland a cache of papers that revealed components of Brown's planning and his support by important manufacturers, philanthropists, and clergymen from the Northeast. Among the documents was a constitution for a provisional government. The constitution had been adopted by Brown and his followers during a convention that they held in Chatham, Canada, during May 1858. Hunter introduced as evidence the first two clauses of the preamble, along with Articles 7, 45, and 48. The preamble referred to slavery as "the most barbarous, unprovoked, and unjustifiable war of one portion of its citizens against another portion," and promised to establish a government that protected the oppressed who had been denied the rights of citizens by the Dred Scott decision. The other articles set up a commander in chief, allowed for the arrest without a warrant of armed persons who did not belong to the organization, and prescribed oaths to obey this constitution by civil or military officers.[47] These facts arguably met the test for treason against the state of Virginia.

As to the question of jurisdiction, the prosecution repeatedly affirmed that the state had the right to try criminal offenses that occurred at Harpers Ferry. Felonies occurring at the federal armory, the attorneys argued, had been handled by state courts, not federal. There was no such thing as exclusive jurisdiction by the United States over this region, and, Hunter maintained, the state had never ceded its authority with the sale of property. Besides, the attorney argued, the concept of state treason did not "require that the offender should be a citizen according to our system of government." The state code defined citizens as "white persons born in any other state of the Union who may become residents." Hunter believed that when Brown planted his foot on the commonwealth's soil, he did so to "reside and hold a place permanently." He conceded that the actual living quarters for the group had been a few miles away in Maryland, but this was not meant to be a residence, merely a launching point "for the nefarious purpose of rallying forces into this Commonwealth, and establishing himself at Harper's Ferry as a starting point for a new Government." He had to deal with Article 46 of Brown's constitution, whose title conveyed the meaning of the section: "These Articles Not for the Overthrow of Gov'm't." Although the document stated that the group would adopt the flag of the Union, Hunter would have none of it. He advised the jury that it needed to consider the document as a whole and what it advocated: "The property of slaveholders was to be confiscated all over the South, and any man found in arms was to be shot down."[48]

The jury of twelve men from a slave state easily accepted Hunter's reasoning. Within forty-five minutes, the jurors returned the verdict of guilty. On November 2, Brown faced the judge for sentencing and added a statement that electrified northern abolitionists. First, the defense made a final appeal to throw out the treason charge by claiming it could not be committed against a state. The judge refused, adding that most states had passed laws against treason. The clerk then asked Brown if he had anything to say. Even though there had been evidence to the contrary, the convicted traitor maintained that he never intended an uprising but sought only to free the slaves. He said he had done something similar the prior winter in Missouri, when he took slaves "without the snapping of a gun on either side" and transported them out of the United States to Canada. "I designed to have done the same thing again on a larger scale," he said, adding, "That was all I intended to do. I never did intend murder or treason, or the destruction of property, or to excite or incite the slaves to rebellion, or to make insurrection." Then he said that had he taken these actions on behalf of the rich, powerful, intelligent, "the so-called great," or any of their friends and acquaintances, "it would have been all right, and every man in this Court would have deemed it an act worthy of reward rather than punishment." Finally, he pointed to the Bible and used its presence to affirm the abolition notion of a higher law. He claimed to follow the New Testament, with its emphasis on remembering those in bonds. "I believe that to have interfered as I have done, as I have always freely admitted I have done in behalf of His despised poor, is no wrong, but right."[49]

While stirring to abolitionists, the statement by Brown and the claims of his defense counsel were not convincing to a majority of Americans. The jurors were not alone in their opinion that Brown had committed treason. Most people took it at face value that he and his men had waged their own kind of war against the United States, with only hard-line abolitionists—especially from New England and Free-Soilers in Kansas—offering a contrary view. The bulk of the Republican Party was doing its best to distance itself from the Harpers Ferry raid, and most of its leadership denounced the actions of Brown and his men. They could not afford to do otherwise and hope to vie for the presidency in 1860. Senator William Henry Seward, a leading antislavery voice in Congress, came out against the attempted insurrection. Abraham Lincoln expressed the party line when he told a group in the Kansas Territory, "Old John Brown has just been executed for treason against a state. We cannot object, even though he agreed with us in thinking slavery wrong. That cannot excuse violence, bloodshed, and treason." Lincoln made no attempt even to argue about the jurisdiction of the case. Later, in his inimitable fashion, he turned the position back on his audience, adding, "So, if constitutionally we elect a President, and therefore you undertake to destroy the Union, it will be our duty to deal with you as old John Brown has been dealt with. We shall try to do our duty."[50]

In the context of debating jurisdiction of the case, it was not unusual to see allusions to the Castner Hanway trial of eight years earlier in order to make a political point about the weakness of the Democratic administration. The *National Era* in Washington, D.C., introduced this idea just a couple of days into the Harpers Ferry trial. It remarked with considerable irony how in the former case the federal government labored strenuously to establish treason where it had not occurred. There had been no attempt to overturn the government, seize arsenals, or establish a provisional government by Hanway. Yet strong effort was made to convict the offenders of treason. "In the present case, where the offenders avow a treasonable purpose, and wage actual war upon the Federal Government, the affair is unceremoniously turned over to State authorities, as a mere riot attended with murder!" According to this report, the Buchanan government caved in to the wishes of Governor Wise, providing further evidence, according to this writer, that the federal government was under the control of the Slave Power.[51]

What no one was saying was that a shift in jurisdiction may not have changed the outcome. Most people considered Brown guilty as charged, except for abolitionists. And no one presented an alternative for what would happen if the federal government had assumed authority over the case. So John Brown hanged for treason against Virginia, as well as inciting slaves to insurrection and murdering five people. And a president did not have to intervene.

The court's position in these antebellum cases mattered for Civil War–era public officials, if only in instructing them to find other ways than civil courts to punish treason. The sectional crisis had reawakened interest in treason to avert antislavery and disunion. It had revealed that treason was a subject very much on the minds of antebellum Americans, alive in public discourse and in legal proceedings. A grand jury empanelled in Pennsylvania felt compelled to comment on the crime because Brown had met with conspirators in the state. In a presentment dated February 24, 1860, the jurors pressed for a thorough investigation and offered their services in the courts of justice "to enforce the law against all treasonable and tumultuary combinations or transactions by ill advised persons, *to prevent* or *obstruct* the regular and peaceable execution of all laws of the United. States."[52] The past had shown that either state or federal authorities might resort to treason, but that the judiciary, for the most part, adhered to precedent. The Civil War hit well-established legal joints of the nation, prompting an expected reflex. And it would do so under different circumstances, when the exigencies of war limited the intervention of the judiciary and enhanced the power of the executive.

2

TREASON EXPRESSED
OR IMPLIED

As the war came, the United States confronted the reality of a vastly deficient system for protecting what we now call national security. In fact, to call it a "system" gives it a stature that did not exist. Other than customs collectors, whose focus remained on trade along the borders of the country, no agency monitored internal affairs. There was no Federal Bureau of Investigation or Department of Homeland Security—not even a Department of Justice. At the same time that the North dealt with the problems of mobilizing massive amounts of troops—more than ever in the country's history—officials had to worry about how to construct a network to catch traitors. Northern leaders who conducted this mission identified a variety of problems: travelers coming in and out of the nation who might be spies, Confederate sympathizers in sensitive public positions, northern business people who communicated with the South, carriers of trade and commerce from the high seas that might help the enemy. Virtually any kind of goods or information that could provide the South with human, material, and intellectual resources became a threat to a government fighting to hold itself together.

Unionists had no vocabulary beyond the word "treason" to describe and respond to the enormity of what was happening. The laws of the nation did not recognize the crime of "plotting" or "designing" war against the nation. Treason served as the reflex response against the men and women who took up arms against the United States or who, in actions much less worthy of a capital offense, cheered for Jefferson Davis or carelessly toasted in public to the health of the new Confederacy. Groping in the dark, the northern public and authorities often resorted to excessive means, especially when it came to examining the behavior of neighbors. Yet treason as a means for containing disloyalty was not useful in a rebellion. The procedure demanded individual cases—court trials for each offense—rather than collective action. Also, anyone who had paid attention during the antebellum period would have realized that treason served the cause of conservatism, and even then it had failed to stop the march of antislavery before the Civil War. Needed was a weapon that was more radical and more flexible to punish the traitors.

Two issues flowed from the problem of how to handle treason. The first was deciding what actions were dangerous. This was not as simple as it sounds. Some things were obvious, such as spying, betraying information to the enemy, running guns, committing sabotage, or leaving home to join the Confederate army. But others were not so obvious. Could speech apply? What about criticism of Lincoln and the Republicans, or failing to pray for the president in church services? That kind of talk, seemingly harmless, might lift the morale of secessionists, which could be construed as furnishing aid and comfort to the enemy. What about selling butter to one of the states in rebellion? Was this lowly transaction worthy of a capital crime for which the seller could hang? And how about men and women who lived in the United States while their sons and brothers fought for the Confederacy? Did they need special monitoring? Routine activities considered personal in peacetime became potentially dangerous in a civil war.

The second issue concerned how to police infractions that posed a threat to the nation. Who should make an arrest and at what level: local, state, or federal? Might all become involved? Could the civil courts handle the myriad cases likely to arise, with many based on suspicion, poor evidence, and insufficient intelligence? What entity should oversee national security at a time when no mechanism or manpower existed for this purpose? To answer these questions, the country patched together what it needed. Gearing up for war demanded paying attention to priorities everywhere at once, including raising soldiers, expanding the bureaucracy, and appropriating the money to fund the war. Secession jolted the United States into piecing together an enforcement system against treason that rested with municipal authorities, State Department detectives, state militia, and eventually an increasing presence by the federal military.

Instrumental in tackling this problem was a popular conception embraced by civilians and public officials of "expressed or implied" treason that had its roots in the constructive treason practiced by the British and that hardly reflected a narrow interpretation of the Constitution. Ambrose Burnside employed this phrase as the basis for his famous arrest of Copperhead Clement L. Vallandigham. Others used adaptations of the concept, such as Major General Henry Wager Halleck referring in 1863 to "military treason." Still others simply used the term "treasonous behavior."

And one woman was tried by a military tribunal for treason under the laws of war, which arguably did not exist as a charge. The purpose behind these various terms was the same: to sanction measures against suspicious individuals without following the letter of the law. Even the wrong kind of speech came under this umbrella. Political arrests bolstered by this rationale allowed for detentions without hearings in civil courts as Union officials tried to defend the country against possible enemies of the state. Although called political arrests, they were not at first partisan in nature. Even Democrats could support them until differences between the parties widened after the Union's failed campaign on the Virginia Peninsula in 1862.[1]

Despite the urgency of the situation, and the tensions that existed in neighborhoods over suspected traitors, it is remarkable that greater disturbances did not happen. Most of the people backing the administration welcomed the imprisonment of the people who called for the demise of the government. In the beginning of the conflict, even Democrats who opposed Lincoln saw secession as a threat that required a strong response. Although there were dissenters, most public commentary in the beginning of the war did not question the doctrine of implied treason. Arrests on flimsy evidence were looked upon as excusable; they were not only a necessary evil to combat disloyalty during an insurrection, but also constitutionally plausible because of the executive branch's charge to guard against insurrection or invasion.[2]

Formulating a Policy

In late December 1861, Attorney General Edward Bates clarified the nature of arrests made against civilians by the federal government. When civil authorities in Kentucky challenged the imprisonment of citizens by the military through Major General Don Carlos Buell, Bates was asked to provide an opinion on the legality of the actions. He identified two kinds of detentions, judicial and political. Judicial arrests were the more familiar kind of punishment, handled by the civil system and following the ritual of charges, tests of evidence, representation by an attorney, and trials by jury. These, of course, were supervised by the judiciary, particularly the federal circuit and district courts, but also at the local and state levels. Political arrests were different. According to Bates, these were overseen by the military to secure a prisoner and "hold him to somewhat broad, and as yet undefined, discretion of the President, as political chief of the nation." It was the "political power" of the president that allowed these actions. Consequently, judicial officers of the United States had no authority over these prisoners. In a few neat paragraphs, Bates had identified the tool that the Union employed to combat treasonous behavior through arrests by the executive department. The resulting detainees were prisoners of state—civilians held by the military at the discretion of the chief executive.[3]

The extent of political arrests has been known, but until recently most scholarship has overlooked the fact that implied treason—what legal theorists term "constructive treason," which had been used by the English crown—became the justification for many of the arrests of these kinds of prisoners. Before the past few years, James G. Randall's *Constitutional Problems under Lincoln* remained the principal voice on the subject. Randall did not notice that constructive treason had not perished but was alive and well as a triggering mechanism for arrests, if not for prosecuting a capital crime in civil courts. Consequently, Randall portrayed a government that remained true to the fundamental nature of the legal code. The point is more debatable than Randall acknowledged, even though the case can be made that the Constitution allowed the use of broader powers by a chief executive facing an insurrection. Jonathan W. White's recent research has clearly shown the connections of the American Civil War with the British formulation of treason. Excessive arrests were readily employed, and freedom of speech had a much different meaning when facing the possible dissolution of the Union. A recent study Mark E. Neely Jr. argues that interpretation of constitutionality remained a battle often waged within partisan politics. Even in the antebellum period, the parties tended to exploit provisions that served their positions. For Randall's position to work, it requires ignoring the Democratic critique.[4]

Authorities normally could not touch a person for uttering words that encouraged war with the United States, yet spoken or printed opposition to the government—what we call political speech—landed hundreds of people in prison during the Civil War. The officials who executed the acts, and the newspapers that endorsed them, declared that the arrested had committed treasonable behavior or treasonable language, without seeking confirmation through civil proceedings. In the first months of war, it was natural for Democrats or Republicans to condemn activities that contained less than unconditional support of the Union as constituting potential aid to the enemy. Lincoln, for instance, in his July 4, 1861, address to the Congress, referred to armed neutrality in the border states—meaning blocking the advance of Union soldiers through the region—as "treason in effect."[5] This represented an elastic way of considering a narrowly defined concept.

The concept manifested itself in a variety of phrasings. Most people referred generally to "treasonable behavior" to describe a range of activities from something as vile as supplying weapons to Confederates to something as mundane as the person who praised Jefferson Davis. It also encompassed noncombatants who showed disrespect to occupying military personnel, or women who wore dresses bedecked with the Confederate flag or other secession emblems. Some used the phrase "treason expressed or implied" or treason "actual and implied" to describe behaviors that were prohibited.[6] "Latent" treason was employed to denote the disguised, hidden traitor. In 1862, the *New York Herald* invoked this terminology to describe the members of secret societies, such as the Knights of the Golden Circle. In occupied zones, military officers used the term "latent treason" to include the Confederate sympathizers who festered and required careful vigilance. Leaders of occupation forces recognized that although the army held secessionists under control, their charges had not given their hearts to the Union and might use any means—sabotage, spying, preaching, and writing—to keep the rebellion alive. In this case, even sullenness or silence could be construed as treasonous. In 1863, Major General Henry Wager Halleck introduced the notion of "military treason," when clarifying for Major General Rosecrans the policies that the military could pursue against noncombatants in Tennessee. In this case, Halleck meant noncombatants who displayed armed resistance against the occupation force.[7]

Popular thinkers offered similar ideas about how to meet the challenges of the rebellion, even if they did not use the phrase "implied or latent treason." One of the most influential arguments came from Horace Binney, a retired lawyer from Pennsylvania well known in the legal community, who defended the president's power to employ martial law. He produced three versions of a famous pamphlet entitled *The Privilege of the Writ of Habeas Corpus under the Constitution*. Binney wrote this tract because of the criticism that Lincoln received for invoking martial law and suspending the writ of habeas corpus in handling unrest in Maryland early in the war. Opponents had said that only the Congress had the right to waive the writ, but Binney disagreed. He said no one had to declare such a thing; the Constitution authorized the suspension in the specific case of invasion and rebellion. In such circumstances, it naturally became connected with the president's duty to defend the country from insurrection. So the waiving of habeas corpus did not have to be declared by anyone. Binney's work circulated widely as one of the earliest arguments that outlined how to handle a rebellion.[8]

Although he did not provide a specific term for it, Binney's pamphlet captured the ideas floating among northerners that mirrored the concept of implicit treason. He saw the courts as lacking sufficient enforcement powers during a rebellion. In a rebellion, Binney wrote, the courts could be obstructed. "In some instances they are closed, and their officers are put to flight." This accurately described most of the federal acts in the Confederacy and perhaps parts of the border states. "In some," he continued, "their judges and officers are parties to the rebellion, and take arms against their government. In other instances, the people, the jurors, the officers of courts, are divided in their opinions, attachments, families, affinities. Calmness, impartiality, and composure of mind, as well as unity of purpose, have departed." Like most northerners, he saw the impracticality of arresting and trying even the people considered as guilty. And traitors did not play fairly. Rebels resorted to lying, spying, and disguising their intentions. He captured perfectly the sentiments of many when he wrote:

A part of this disguise may sometimes be detected, and not often the whole. An intercepted letter, an overheard conversation, a known proclivity, an unusual activity in unusual transactions, in munitions, or provisions, or clothing,—a suspicious fragment and no more, without the present clue to detection, may appear—not enough for the scales of justice, but abundantly sufficient for the precautions of the guardian upon his watch. Such are the universal accompaniments of rebellion, and constitute a danger frequently worse than open arms. To confront it at once, in the ordinary course of justice, is to insure its escape, and to add to the danger. Yet the traitor in disguise may achieve his work of treason if he is permitted to go on; and if he is just passing from treason in purpose to treason in act, his arrest and imprisonment for a season may save both him and the country.[9]

The logic behind Binney's treatise concerning the need to arrest people before treason in purpose became treason in action served as one of the arguments employed by Lincoln to defend the arrest and banishment of Vallandigham in 1863. This does not mean that Binney influenced the president, who more than likely arrived at his own conclusions. However, such thoughts were common and not created by Lincoln alone.[10]

Similarly, the arrests that have captured attention among historians and buffs for breaches of civil liberties, such as the imprisonment of the police board and legislators in Maryland, were among many instances taking place in communities throughout the Union. In other words, there was little unusual about them. The arrests were not always on the same scale in terms of numbers or political officials involved outside high-profile areas such as Maryland. Nor were they carried out as intensely elsewhere. But they occurred with some regularity nonetheless. Small wonder that one northerner commented in his diary in the summer of 1862 that "treason now is broader than ever. Silence is treason, the purchase of specie is treason, and what is not treason now? I can't say, except villainy, robbery and abolitionism, and 'the end of all these is death.'"[11]

The truth is that a seemingly draconian approach appeared defensible and necessary at the time. In 1861 traitors did seem to be a menace, especially in government departments where long-term bureaucrats had served at the pleasure of the Democratic administrations of the 1850s and retained their posts when the southern states seceded. There was no telling what mischief they could make.

Before the war came, the country had witnessed the damage that "traitors" could render in public office. Controversy had plagued Buchanan's administration, which featured a cabinet containing secession sympathizers. In December 1860, before his state seceded, Secretary of War John Floyd resigned and returned to Virginia. Word circulated that as one of his last acts he ordered the transfer of artillery pieces from Pittsburgh to the Deep South. Although the order was countermanded, it appalled northerners that a secretary of war had tried to divert weapons to people who could make war on the United States. In fact, a lawyer in New York, F. C. Treadwell, filed an affidavit with Supreme Court Chief Justice Roger B. Taney charging Floyd, Howell Cobb, Robert Toombs, Alfred Iverson, Jefferson Davis, and Joseph Lane of Oregon with treason. Taney apparently held the note for three days before ordering the clerk to return it to Treadwell.[12] Although the legal terms of treason were not met in this case, Taney had not alleviated the concern. Who else might be tempted to do something similar, especially with so many southern men put into their positions by a dough-faced president like Buchanan, who seemed to detractors to be more interested in placating the South than saving the Union?

To address the problem of national security, Lincoln turned to Secretary of State William Henry Seward, who supervised the arrests of prisoners of state. For the first ten months of the conflict, or until February 1862, the State Department took the lead on this assignment and established patterns that continued for much of the war. Seward was a more competent administrator than Secretary of War Simon Cameron and was more zealous about preventing treason than Attorney General Bates, who controlled the U.S. District Attorneys who were making arrests in the early going. Bates, however, viewed his authority as restricted to judicial, not political, arrests. He would not actively pursue this policy. Neither man presented the right choice for the job of hunting down traitors. It was also the case that the individual overseeing the formation of an internal security system dealt with a great deal of foreign or nondomestic concerns. Seward was as sensitive about key ports and the Canadian border as he was about anything happening within the interior of the country.[13]

One of the first tasks confronting the Union was to stop the flow of supplies and information to the Confederacy. The United States appeared to be leaking like a sieve. Foreigners hoped to capitalize on new business opportunities in supplying the Confederacy. Diplomats appeared to use their immunity to pass vital information to the enemy. Smugglers tried to bring medical supplies from Canada through the Old Northwest and into the South. Spies gathered information on troop strengths. Loyal newspapers unwittingly turned over valuable information to the enemy through their patriotic reports on the army. Correspondence between families or acquaintances caught on opposite sides had the potential to contain valuable details about how communities organized for the conflict. Under the circumstances, it is not surprising that the communications from the State Department reveal great attention paid to the port cities of Boston, New York, and Baltimore. These sites demanded attention, not only to cut off contraband but also to restrict unwelcome or suspicious foreigners.

In addition to the port cities, Seward tried to shore up intelligence along the Canadian border. On the day that the Confederates opened fire on Fort Sumter, he ordered a special agent there to clarify the U.S. position on the conflict, as well as report "to this Department such facts of interest as may come to your knowledge."[14] To patrol the border and watch for treasonous activity in general, Seward enlisted agents to work under cover for fifty dollars per month. One such man received the following charge: "You will be particularly on the watch for such persons who may pass into or from Canada on their way to or from Europe. In case any well founded suspicion should be entertained against any such person, you will arrest him, secure his papers and give immediate notice by telegraph to this Department."[15] Agents enjoyed broad powers to make arrests and to confiscate property that appeared to benefit the enemy. Their interpretation of events was what mattered, rather than legal evidence. Such leeway to act was believed to be necessary. As the war continued, more and more insurgent activity was planned by the Confederates to be launched from the Canadian border.

Because the Union hoped to seal off war materiel from the Confederacy, merchants and businessmen came under close scrutiny. Seward on occasion ordered police to watch a house in order to arrest members of a firm if there was evidence of disloyalty.[16] The concern was obvious: even a loyal man could cause harm by conducting business with the wrong people. When the merchants or citizens were disloyal, the potential consequences were even worse. Stephen A. Hurlbut, a brigadier general in Quincy, Illinois, urged discretion by his men so they would "not confound the innocent with the guilty." He did order his men, though, to fire upon citizens who tried to sabotage the railroad and asked them to capture those who "furnished horses, provisions or money or any article to assist" men who attempted to raise troops for the Confederates. These prisoners would be charged with treason and sent to brigade headquarters for further action.[17]

However, not every case of exchange with the enemy was this serious. What constituted dangerous goods remained in the eye of the beholder. In June 1861 a commission merchant named John A. Skiff of Cincinnati was taken before a U.S. commissioner in the city to answer a charge of treason for shipping contraband goods to the seceded states. What was the reason that he faced possible conviction for a capital crime? He had packed butter in ale barrels that were sent to Louisville, Kentucky, for reshipping to the Deep South. The government does not appear to have pursued the case, and the merchant escaped potential hanging for peddling butter to the Confederacy.[18]

The records of the State Department and reports in the postwar *Official Records* of the Union reveal the pattern that emerged with these political arrests. It was typical for proceedings to begin with the confiscation of private mail. Authorities in 1861 were obsessed with strangling communications with the South. The mail aided treason by reporting troop movements or allowing business transactions that might give the rebels military supplies or funds. In May 1861 the U.S. District Attorney for the Southern District of New York had the marshal seize from the telegraph office all correspondence to the South for "a year and upward." By his estimation, this involved from 200,000 to 300,000 dispatches.[19] In other cases, mail was seized because it was addressed to someone in the Confederacy or contained inflammatory sentiments, such as hostility to Lincoln. Sometimes mail was intercepted after an unnamed person notified officials that a neighbor was conducting suspicious business.

In the summer of 1861, Lincoln moved to shut down communication with the Confederacy. By a proclamation of August 16, he cut off commerce and turned over enforcement to Postmaster General Montgomery Blair. Letters were allowed to be seized and forwarded to the Post Office

Department. Popular opinion supported the actions. By the fall of 1861, the *New York Times* noticed that arrests were on the rise for this activity. "Transmitting letters [to] the Confederacy is treason," the writer firmly stated, "as much as is transmitting munitions of war."[20] These were attitudes that had arisen fairly quickly after the war began. In May 1861, a Philadelphia newspaper worried about "the codfish aristocracy" that "closely sympathize with the cotton oligarchs." It added: "Every day letters leave our Post Office directed to leading traitors in Montgomery, Charleston and Richmond." Every night these men, the report alleged, held secret meetings. "It may be that this treason will not do us any harm. But to make matters perfectly sure it should be detected and punished."[21]

When community members reported treasonable behavior, such accusations were enough to spark action. Whisked to one of the forts near Boston, New York, or Baltimore, the offenders invariably pleaded that there must be a misunderstanding, for they were indeed loyal. Seward often refused leniency during the first appeals, letting the person sit a little while in prison, although it is not necessarily the case that he intentionally let the person squirm. Bureaucratic inefficiencies account for much of the blame. In many instances, he had little knowledge of the cases and needed to find out more before making a decision. Petitioners wrote the secretary directly, and he had to request more information from subordinates. Ultimately, most offenders were let go, sometimes after another round of petitions, but only after taking the oath of allegiance and promising not to have transactions with people conducting insurrection.[22] In one case, Seward added another condition. With a group of ten men held in prison, he released all but one—until the man agreed not to pay a fee to the attorney who pleaded his cause with the government. Everything possible was done to protect the government from legal procedures that could challenge authority.[23]

In these situations, being from humble ranks of society could have its advantages by speeding release from custody. A clear example of this came in Maryland in September 1861. Major General John A. Dix, commanding the department, reported the capture of twenty-four men who tried to make their way to the Confederate army. Dix noted that a thorough investigation by police determined that twelve of the men ought to be released after taking the oath of allegiance. The reason spoke volumes about how the government viewed common people in the battle for stamping out disloyalty. "They are all laborers or mechanics," Dix said, adding, "and of no social importance." This was a harsh commentary. Dix thought that their initial purpose for entering Maryland had been to find work. Even if they had decided to press on to Virginia, and Confederate service, Dix thought they had been punished enough by arrest and imprisonment. To the government, they represented a very limited threat.[24]

Prominent people, especially public officials, *were* of social importance and *their* detention could make an impact even if they could not be successfully prosecuted for treason. Evidence of disloyalty in high offices, in fact, fed the popular appetite for excessive arrests as time and again people expressed the wish that prominent traitors could suffer some discomfort for the example it would make. George Templeton Strong, who became influential in the U.S. Sanitary Commission, was typical when he wrote in August 1861: "The first duty of the government at this time is to hang some highly respectable, gentlemanlike, wealthy, and well-connected person, after due trial and condemnation, for treason." Claiming that many cases existed for this purpose, he added: "One such proceeding would do more to consolidate the nation and invigorate its life than all this Cabinet has done since the Fourth of March."[25]

This was something that Attorney General Bates understood as well, although he also anticipated repercussions better than Strong. Using treason to make an example—and to make the opposition more careful—did have its merits and led to the occasional appearance of treason cases in civil courts. Bates, though, cautioned his U.S. Attorneys from advancing cases to trial too readily, because treason was hard to prove. Once again, a lower social status proved to be an asset if one were to avoid prosecution. He advised a U.S. Attorney in St. Louis about the desirability of wasting energy on small fish: "I would use indictments *for treason* sparingly— especially against *small men*. There are some magnates however, who are not now in the State & may never be there again, against whom a pending indictment for treason might be made useful in the future." This struck him as having a potential reward even beyond the conflict: "When the war is mainly over, it may be a good thing to have that hold upon them, wherever they may then be."[26] He could be more pointed still. With its powerful core of Confederate sympathizers, Baltimore presented a number of problems to federal control. Bates appreciated using a strong hand there. He counseled General Nathaniel P. Banks, "Among the malcontents in Baltimore there are some men of position and influence, who are now so far perverted and so deeply committed that it is a waste of reason to argue with them. To keep them quiet we must make them conscious that they stand in the presence of coercive power."[27]

Bates was not the only public official to come to the conclusion that displays of force against community leaders of suspicious intentions could reap benefits. Superintendent John A. Kennedy of the New York City Police saw the merits of using arrests without hearings to make newspaper editors more cautious about what they wrote. Kennedy mentioned to Seward in 1861 that the best way to hurt uncooperative newspapers was not to seize the printing offices or restrict circulation by denying mailing privileges. Better, he believed, to arrest the editors and publishers without worrying about advancing them to trial. Such a ploy "would lead to a modification" of the newspaper's tone. Historians have judged this policy as causing some of the more venomous critics to withdraw their fangs.[28]

One significant case of targeting elites occurred in Philadelphia, where authorities arrested Pierce Butler in August 1861 and almost had the tactic backfire. The Quaker City contained a serious group that opposed the Lincoln administration and also expressed sympathies with southern secession. Butler was the grandson of a prominent South Carolinian who had been a hero in the Revolutionary War and one of the architects of the fugitive slave provision of the Constitution. Born in Philadelphia, the younger Butler inherited two of the grandfather's plantations but, just before the war, had to sell off slaves to save the family's fortunes. Nevertheless, he retained holdings in the South, which complicated his life during the war. It was the mail that gave authorities the excuse to apprehend Butler. He had sent letters to the South, claiming he wrote only about personal business. Unionists were unconvinced and believed he had expressed strong opinions in favor of the Confederacy. Butler was arrested by federal marshals, charged with something resembling treason (the actual charges were murky), and sent to prison at Fort Lafayette, New York.[29]

Local supporters of the administration heartily applauded. A core of them who would become prominent in the Union League, a patriotic club that formed later in the war, routinely gathered at the newspaper office of Morton McMichael, editor of the *North American and United States Gazette*. One of them, George Boker, was a minor literary figure who would become a secretary of the local league. As they discussed the Butler affair and other aspects of the war, they thought it appropriate to "bring social opinion to bear upon those who expressed sentiments hostile to the government and the war." Sidney George Fisher, the diarist who recorded the meeting, thought this went a bit far because it encouraged mob action. And the public needed very little encouragement for violence.

While he decried such actions, Fisher had no trouble with the principle of arresting people who *might* cause trouble, and he was unhappy with the decision to release Butler after about a month in prison. "It is true that no overt acts of treason were committed by Butler," Fisher admitted, adding, "nor was he committed for punishment or trial, but as a precaution & because his general conversation was seditious & tended to strengthen the influence of the rebellion in this part of the country." It disheartened Fisher that Butler refused to take the oath of allegiance. He was released upon signing a pledge that he would do nothing to help the South. He had resisted the oath, claiming it would have endangered his southern property by identifying him as an alien enemy to the Confederacy. Still, Fisher considered him "morally as much of a traitor as any man in the Confederate army. His arrest had a very good effect here and his release will have a bad effect."[30] Neither a radical nor a hothead, Fisher favored the Republicans and saw the silencing of Butler as beneficial to the Union cause. He did not consider the arrest a breach of civil liberties. He expressed a desire for preventative arrests a couple of years in advance of Lincoln, who would profess a similar concept in response to criticism over the arrest of Clement L. Vallandigham.

Targeting men of means had its benefits for curbing unwanted behavior, but it also contained dangers: they were well connected, were used to pulling the strings of power, and had the financial ability to fight back. Fisher hoped that Butler would banish himself from the Union, but he did not. Instead, Butler decided to fight for retribution. Simon Cameron had initiated the actions against Butler while serving as the first secretary of war under Lincoln. The following spring, Butler sued the former secretary in the Pennsylvania Supreme Court for trespass, assault and battery, and false imprisonment. The government had no policy to help in the defense of the people who acted on behalf of the president. Early in the war, most district attorneys and federal marshals were left to fend for themselves without government support.

This incident contained enormous consequences. If Butler succeeded in his suit, the government was vulnerable to actions from thousands of individuals. Merely handling the caseload, no matter how many actions may be frivolous, could prove insurmountable. But the suit also opened a Pandora's box: if successful, state courts could detain federal officials, diverting them from handling the business of the nation. Indirectly, such suits struck at the right of the president to order political arrests, thus eroding executive authority. Small wonder that Bates told a subordinate that the president "was wanting the case to be defended." The attorney general considered this a "matter which deeply concerns the public welfare, as well as the safety of the individual officers of the Government."[31] For some reason, the case never made it to trial; Butler apparently dropped his suit.

This and similar actions that occurred against other public servants—including district attorneys, marshals, and a governor—led to provisions in the Habeas Corpus Act of March 3, 1863, to protect soldiers and government employees who executed orders of the president. The main thrust of the sections concerning federal employees was to transfer such cases from state to federal courts. Local and state courts were viewed suspiciously because they might contain judges who sympathized too much with, or felt beholden to, the prominent men in their communities. In these circumstances, federal courts presumably would be friendlier to the government's position.[32]

Should we conclude that the government wanted to target only influential citizens and public officials? Not completely. The government was not efficient enough to pull off a campaign of such precision, even if it had wanted to. And in many cases men were arrested by community authorities acting without direction from higher officials. Common people and social elites were subject to similar kinds of treatment. What mattered most were particular kinds of behavior as an indicator of treason: communications with the Confederacy, expressions of support for the southern secessionists, failure to take the oath of loyalty, lack of enthusiasm for displaying the U.S. flag, to name a few. But prominent people elicited the most coverage from the press and provided the most compelling examples of what awaited persons who drew attention to themselves for questionable patriotism. While ministers, newspaper personnel, and key community leaders were not the only ones arrested, they were among the first to gain scrutiny from arresting agents. These were the people feared for their ability to mobilize citizens against the government. This is also why playing the numbers game alone as an analysis of egregious arrests does not tell the whole story. Some arrests mattered more than others and left a greater impact within communities.

The unintended consequence of having elites as vulnerable, if not more so, than the middling and working classes for arrests was that it virtually guaranteed that public outcry or resistance came through traditional institutional channels, such as political parties and the courts. Community leaders such as merchants, businessmen, political figures, editors, and preachers rarely espouse revolutionary, extralegal measures as solutions to problems. Although secret societies such as the Knights of the Golden Circle existed, they never gained enough adherents to make an impact outside of institutional forums. And when the Irish dockworkers and other working-class immigrants took over the New York City draft riots, as historian Iver Bernstein has shown, many of the German and other Democratic leaders dropped out. The people with a greater stake in property also have the most to lose.[33]

The concern over traitors extended to people within the government itself. Unionists feared that the enemy thrived in places such as the Treasury Department and various bureaus of the War Department, where those so inclined could easily raise numerous obstacles to the northern war effort. In fact, it was a commonplace to see headlines screaming about the traitors and spies who infested Washington.[34] Actually, a good number of southern sympathizers probably did work in government as war broke out. Despite the long sectional crisis, war had erupted quickly enough that many persons who hailed from states that joined the Confederacy suddenly found themselves in a strange position—supportive of the rebels, and maybe even with family in the Confederacy, while receiving a paycheck from the Union.

The Lincoln administration tried to protect against traitors by using oaths of loyalty. All government workers were required to repeat the oaths whenever they received an appointment. But these first oaths, in which the swearer simply promised to obey the Constitution, seemed too weak. In August, the U.S. Congress instituted new loyalty oaths, keeping the provision to obey the Constitution but adding that the individual pledged allegiance to the Union, "any ordinance, resolution or law of any State Convention or Legislature to the contrary notwithstanding." This rejected the belief in state sovereignty and forced individuals to pledge themselves to the national government.[35]

The new oath meshed with a congressional effort to purge government departments of potential traitors that contained parallels with the 1950s efforts to identify and punish so-called card-carrying communists. In mid-July, John F. Potter, like Joseph McCarthy a Republican from Wisconsin, successfully petitioned his colleagues to form a committee to investigate the loyalty of government employees. The resolution establishing the select committee started out by targeting people who had refused to take the oath of loyalty since Lincoln's inauguration of March 4. It quickly exceeded its original charge and began collecting allegations on anyone in public service. From July to October, the committee assembled 550 charges, interviewed 450 persons, and determined 320 of them as disloyal. It met in secret. In order to encourage people to come forward, the committee kept the accusations anonymous. There was no attempt to interrogate the accused or give them a chance to defend themselves. Potter justified this by claiming that the committee was one of inquiry, not adjudication. He maintained that the congressmen in all cases tried to be fair and scrupulous, adding that questionable cases were turned back to the department heads so they could establish the loyalty of the employee.[36]

It is difficult to know how many of these cases were valid. The committee's own report admitted that errors could have been made but dismissed the harm to individuals by reminding people of the dangers faced by the republic. The committee noted that the worst that happened was that these men lost their jobs, as if that was no cause for concern and no great punishment. Occasional criticism came from the press and even from within the government. Benjamin B. French, the commissioner of public buildings, had doubts privately about accusations made against some employees in the White House, but he wondered if the president might not diminish the public clamor on this issue by dismissing some of the accused, whether guilty or not.[37] Each of the department heads, especially Salmon P. Chase and Montgomery Blair, made his own investigations and retained some of the people accused by the Potter Committee.

The remarkable thing about this purge was that it elicited such little public outcry. Most of the accused stepped down quietly or, even if they lingered, eventually lost their positions without any furor. This outcome seemed wholly appropriate at the time and was justified on the basis of treason, even though no overt act had been committed. Not everyone agreed with the situation. Representative Clement Vallandigham of Ohio, who still held his seat in Congress, put up a little fuss when Potter first raised his resolution, but then quickly backed away from the issue. For the most part, northerners seemed to accept the work of the committee as necessary or unable to be challenged politically. In fact, when it learned that the secretary of the interior disagreed with many of the accusations concerning people in his department, the *New York Times* commented: "The sympathies of the country will be with the Committee, for the people know that the Government has been harassed and nearly ruined by spies in Washington."[38]

During the oversight of arrests by the State Department, the actual numbers were not high, considering the proportion of the population. Part of the reason lies in the limited bureaucratic machinery that had no ability to coordinate a systematic, widespread effort against civil liberties. Mark Neely's study indicated that the total arrests made under Seward's tenure, which lasted until February 1862, amounted to fewer than 900.[39] But this certainly is understated because it represented federal arrests and did not take into account activity by state or local authorities, many of which resolved cases without reporting on the federal level. Unknown, too, was the extent of mail and personal property, such as cash, that was confiscated from suspects and never returned. But the arrests by the State Department accomplished several things. They curtailed the correspondence between North and South and established the pattern followed by authorities: arrest first and sort out the particulars later. They used the threat of treasonable acts as the rationale for doing this. And clemency came fairly easily for those who swore an oath of loyalty.

It should be noted that the judiciary was also active in regard to treason. Indictments during the war easily numbered in the thousands. But while the indictments were many, the trials were few. They happened periodically, and when they did, it was notable that the federal courts remained levelheaded in the handling of these cases. One of the first dealt with Charles A. Greiner, arrested and charged with treason for aiding in the seizure of Fort Pulaski in Savannah, Georgia. On January 2, 1861, Greiner served as part of an artillery company acting according to orders of the governor of the state of Georgia, which had yet to secede. Greiner originally hailed from Philadelphia and had apparently sent his family to a boardinghouse in the city at an unfortunate time. When he went to visit them, he was arrested, charged with treason, and brought before Judge John Cadwalader of the Eastern District of Pennsylvania. In early May the trial convened before a packed courtroom, as the curious came to see the tall man of roughly forty-five, with supposed military bearing, dressed neatly with a heavy mustache, which, like his hair, was sprinkled with gray. These descriptive details in newspaper accounts attested to the interest that the case drew beyond its importance.[40] Cadwalader set Greiner free, and appropriately so. The trial for such an offense needed to be held where the crime was committed, which meant Georgia. He placed Greiner under recognizance of $10,000 to keep the peace and obey the Constitution.[41]

A few additional treason cases made their way into the federal court system but with unsatisfactory results for people hoping to punish traitors. In 1862 the case of James W. Chenoweth briefly made headlines. A grand jury in Ohio had indicted him for treason for providing weapons to the Confederacy in 1861. In May 1862 the U.S. Circuit Court for the Southern District of Ohio heard a motion to quash the indictment, claiming that treason did not apply because there was no war technically but a rebellion. The defense argued that the English statute on which the federal practice was based called for a war with the subjects of a foreign power. Justice Noah Swayne, recently appointed to the court, quashed the indictment and wrote: "We sit here to administer the law, not to make it. With the excitement of the hour, we, as Judges, have nothing to do. They cannot change the law nor affect our duty. Causeless and wicked as is this rebellion, and fearful as has been its cost already in blood and treasure, it is not the less our duty to hold the scales of justice, in all cases, with a firm and steady hand." The *New York Times* would not criticize the ruling but hoped that men who traded with the enemy would not go unpunished.[42] Two other cases made it to the hearing stage. In late 1862, newspapers touted the case of Andrew J. Houston as the first treason trial of the war. He had participated in a raid by Confederate guerrillas on the town of Newburgh, Indiana, in July 1862. His case remained active for a little while, until he was finally found not guilty in 1863. In Kentucky, meanwhile, a man named Thomas C. Schachlett apparently served in the Confederate army, returned to his native county, and killed a postmaster. He was tried before U.S. Judge Ballard and found guilty of treason.[43]

Much more common was the tendency for the federal courts to leave the indicted prisoners in legal limbo, sometimes for the entire war. This happened with one of the most famous controversies concerning habeas corpus. In 1861 the Lincoln administration ignored Chief Justice Taney's order to produce the body of John Merryman. Eventually, he and numerous other Maryland rioters were turned over to civil authorities. Merryman was officially indicted on July 10, 1861, and ordered to appear in the District Court of Maryland, where he posted $20,000 bail. It took until April 1867 for the charges against him to be dropped.[44] Similarly, William Perry and thirty-five of his colleagues who fitted a schooner called the *Petrel* with weapons to wage war were captured and indicted for high treason in the U.S. Circuit Court for the Eastern District of Pennsylvania. They had been arrested July 28, 1861, and never faced trial. The government walked away from the case in April 1865 by entering *nolle prosequi*, or a refusal to proceed any further.[45]

This should not leave the impression, however, that the civil courts had no engagement with cases of disloyalty. A study of the federal courts of southern Illinois found hundreds of cases adjudicated. But the legal community, and the Congress, realized fairly quickly that treason charges could not handle such matters as suspicious behavior and plotting against the government. The Congress responded by passing the Conspiracies Acts in 1861 and 1862. And confiscation of contraband goods became another method for punishing traitors.[46] However, from the perspective of the U.S. government, the civil courts provided poor remedy for stamping out treason. Attorney General Bates discouraged such prosecutions. Better to try a person for vulgar felonies and misdemeanors, he warned, "than for romantic and genteel treason. The penitentiaries will be far more effective than the gallows."[47]

The War Department Takes Over

The transfer of authority over political arrests took place in fairly routine fashion during February 1862. Edwin Stanton had replaced Simon Cameron as secretary of war. The initial anxiety over traitors in the country and in government offices had calmed. The military situation seemed to have brightened, and many northerners hoped for an end to the conflict in the coming season of campaigning. Yet success also created problems. Capturing territory meant more rebels had to be supervised and watched for latent treason. The State Department had neither the staff nor the administrative mission to continue to monitor treason as the war expanded geographically and soldiers penetrated deeper into the states conducting the insurrection. The army, and its agents in the form of provost marshals installed in communities, became the principal police force against treasonous behavior. Although the supervising agency had changed from the State Department to the War Department, the pattern of arrests did not: they would still be employed vigorously as a precaution against disloyalty, with most cases failing to go to a trial, and most of the accused released if they would swear to behave as good citizens and not support the insurrection.

Stanton ensured that the transition to the War Department enjoyed the forms of legality by appointing a special commission to visit the prisons and determine which inmates should be retained and which let go. Composed of Major General John A. Dix and Judge Edwards Pierrepont of New York, both respected moderate Democrats and men who represented the military and civil arms of the republic, the commission sifted through roughly a couple of hundred cases at prisons in the Washington-Baltimore region, New York, and Boston. A general amnesty for most of the prisoners, and the careful scrutiny of the cases by known Democrats, sent a signal that the administration, contrary to the increasing accusations of the opposition press, had not abandoned the Constitution and civil law.[48]

Stanton's explanation for the transition revealed how the administration explained political arrests, sending a clear message that authorities from the president on down considered it appropriate to quash treason before it could flourish. Although the secretary of war signed the document that appeared in newspapers, he was acting on an order of the president and clearly had Lincoln's approval. The Confederates had committed treason by forming an army against the United States, every department of the government "was paralyzed by treason," the capital was beleaguered, military posts and federal installations were betrayed, and the Congress and the courts were powerless to meet this emergency. In such a situation, the president merely deployed the extraordinary powers granted to him by the Constitution to battle insurrection. He prevented the use of the Post Office for treasonable correspondence, suspended habeas corpus in various places, used the military and other agents to arrest people about to engage in "treasonable practices," and detained them in military custody. But, the message alleged, the government was stronger and more stable now. "The insurrection is believed to have culminated and to be declining." The public exhibited fewer apprehensions and "treasonable practices have diminished with the passions which prompted the heedless persons to adopt them."[49]

The transfer of power to the War Department passed without undue clamor against the specter of military repression. Supporters of the administration typically cast the arrests as no longer needed because the end of the rebellion appeared to be in sight. The *Springfield Weekly Republican*, for instance, closed its discourse on the changing times of February 1862 by proclaiming, "The necessity for such arrests is now at an end, except along the line where civil war prevails and 'due course of law' is out of the question."[50] It was a fine statement. But the necessity for political arrests would not go away: the military continued to apply implied treason on thousands of more civilian prisoners.

The military was certainly not new to combating treason through arrests under martial law. Soldiers had done so from virtually the opening of the conflict. Operating in sensitive areas such as the border states, military personnel were on the front line of contact with citizens who were deciding on their loyalties to Union or Confederacy. The army experienced a fast learning curve concerning civil-military relations that began early in the war, especially in horribly divided and violent Missouri. Historians have often concentrated on Maryland for assaults on civil liberties in the border region and considered Missouri as the extreme of the story with some of the worst guerrilla fighting and intercommunity strife of the war. Yet Missouri provided a laboratory for experimenting with how to deal with civilian enemies. More to the point, it was the experience in the western border region that taught quick lessons to military commanders about the problems of combating treason through courts. Missouri suffered from a severe case of legal and institutional disorder. Confederates and Unionists both claimed it, and for a while it lacked a state government. In place of a legislature, a convention that had been called and elected in order to decide on the question of secession administered state affairs. Marauders roamed much of the western border states but were especially active in Missouri. They shot and killed straggling soldiers and harassed the operations of the North Missouri Railroad by burning bridges, destroying track, and firing upon trains. The state presented a supreme challenge against maintaining law and order, and it became very clear, very early on, that the solution would have to come outside of traditional legal channels.[51]

One of the tools that the army employed was the military commission. These special bodies had begun during the Mexican War and were to be used when regularly established courts could not handle the transgressions. Even though they operated outside of civil law, they were tightly administered. Only the general in chief of the army or the commander of a military department could establish these courts, which were to have a minimum of three members and often had many more. Major General Henry Wager Halleck took pains to outline for subordinates the rationale and scope of these bodies as he assumed command of the Department of Missouri. His orders set the pattern for other departments. The commissions were to follow the procedures for courts-martial. The sixth section of his orders dealt specifically with treason, which Halleck identified as an offense defined by the Constitution that must be tried by civil authorities. He did, however, leave the door open for prosecution, adding, "But certain acts of a treasonable character, such as conveying information to the enemy, acting as spies, &c., are military offenses, triable by military tribunals, and punishable by military authority." Over the course of the war, the army conducted a little more than 4,000 military commissions. Neely's study of civil liberties found that 1,940 of these trials occurred in Missouri or, as he put it, "a staggering 46.2 percent."[52]

But the military seems to have followed Halleck's guidelines—at least when it came to formal proceedings. A database compiled by two researchers that indexes cases from the 80,000-plus records of courts-martial housed in the National Archives identified only 106 cases in which military commissions tried men and women for treason, with 87 of these hearings involving civilians (see appendix A). The *Official Records* of the Union and Confederate armies contained another 8 cases in Missouri in the first year of war that were not accounted for in the index. Missouri claimed 42 of the total cases, or more than a third and about 45 percent of the hearings involving civilians—figures roughly proportional to Neely's findings for military commissions in general.[53] These were not frivolous cases but dealt with violent resistance to the government, with the accused taking up arms against the United States or aiding in the destruction of railroad bridges and track. In effect, these may have been some of the most viable cases to prosecute during the entire war. With rare exception, the commissions in Missouri found the defendants guilty of the charges.[54] But it is clear that the U.S. Army did not promote treason trials to handle either the rebels or the enemy within.

Even when widening the search to include the more ambiguous charge of disloyalty, the database yielded limited results numerically. Sixty-five soldiers and civilians faced this particular charge in courts-martial, although usually in combination with other offenses (see appendix B). But what is striking is the extent to which language was taken as a serious threat to the nation-state. Fifty-one of the sixty-five files dealt with disloyal utterances, or a surprising 78 percent. It is not a stretch to say that speech, whether written or spoken, was central to determining disloyalty in the minds of Unionists in the Civil War. The kind of speech ranged widely and defies easy categorization. Language was prosecuted if the defendant tried to discourage enlistments or encourage desertion. It was also taken seriously if a person declared he had served with the guerrillas or the Confederate army. For instance, George J. Johnston of Missouri was found guilty of violating his oath of allegiance before a military commission that presided in March 1865. He said he was a Quantrill man—referring to the guerrilla leader William Clarke Quantrill—and openly praised Jefferson Davis. For this, the commission awarded him six months at hard labor.[55] Less serious charges, however, easily could be found. In Kentucky, Richard Rutter was fined $100 in March 1863 for proclaiming he was still a secessionist. Yet not every sectional epithet resulted in punishment. John Dearth of Tennessee escaped a conviction for saying that the South would whip the North, and James Wilkinson of Kentucky was let go despite taking the more vindictive position that all Union men should be killed.[56]

But the military's influence was felt beyond formal proceedings. Far more common was its involvement in the enforcement of community-level standards for treasonous behavior. In a search of a newspaper database across the four years of war, the hunt uncovers hundreds of incidents in which people faced arrest or investigation by the military for a variety of crimes. A random sampling of just under 400 arrests that appeared in selected newspapers from 1861 to 1865 allowed for a closer view of the process (see appendix C).[57] Out of the charges that could be discerned in these reports, disloyalty led the way, with 117 persons accused.[58] Treason was not far behind, although an unambiguous, specific allegation of treason occurred only 39 times. The more ambiguous "treasonable activities" accounted for another 17 charges. Treasonable language—again not defined—drew military attention to another 29 civilians, bringing the total instances spread across these three categories to 85. One could make the case, however, that treason was at least an unstated part of some of the other charges. For instance, citizens were arrested for "aiding the enemy," encompassing everything from printing money for the Confederacy to revealing troop positions. These acts could qualify as one of the litmus tests for treason under the Constitution. It should be noted, nonetheless, how little even in a sampling geared to finding treason and disloyalty that these charges appeared. The two charges accounted for exactly half of the total arrests charted in this sampling. That means another 202 of the accusations did not. The tendency of officials was to arrest on the basis of a presumed treasonable act, yet to discriminate when it came time to move a case forward.

It is also clear that public speech was viewed as dangerous, whether in newspapers, in the pulpit, or in someone's yard. As in the military commissions, most involved similar matters of speech: professions of support for the Confederacy, prayers for the South, newspaper columns sympathetic to secession, or failures to declare an oath of allegiance to the United States.[59] Four citizens of Maryland were arrested in 1863 for cheering for Jefferson Davis.[60] Military officers were often adamant in their instructions to noncombatants in their charge to withhold criticism of the Union. In April 1862, orders issued in the Union-occupied areas of North Carolina warned that anyone who uttered "one word against the government of these United States, will be at once arrested and closely confined. It must be distinctly understood that this department is under martial law, and treason, expressed or implied, will meet with speedy punishment."[61] Similarly, General Orders No. 1 for the military department of Utah in 1862 urged all commanders to promptly arrest "all persons who from this date shall be guilty of uttering treasonable sentiments against the Government." It added: "Traitors shall not utter treasonable sentiments in this district with impunity, but must seek a more genial soil, or receive the punishment they so richly merit."[62] Freedom of speech was not so free, after all, as a civil war exacerbated the public's fear of the power of words.

The Press and the Clergy

In February 1863 an estimated seventy-five soldiers convalescing in a hospital in Keokuk, Iowa, mustered enough energy to rise from their sickbeds so they could wreak havoc on an allegedly disloyal newspaper office. About three o'clock in the afternoon the soldiers marched to the office of the *Daily Constitution*, led by three or four persons wielding sledgehammers. Their comrades spread out along the street to guard them. The men with hammers demolished a printing press on the first floor. The crowd then went to the second floor, cleaned out the type and destroyed another press. On the third floor, it encountered yet another press and threw it out the window in an obvious fit of pique. One imagines cheers or unrepeatable oaths greeting the fall of one of the tools of a free press in a democracy. Armed soldiers arrived at the scene to curb the destruction. The convalescents were not immediately intimidated. The destroyers resisted until the arriving military trained their weapons, although there was a moment when revolvers flashed from pockets of the vandals who threatened that if the soldiers fired so much as a shot, "they, along with their commander, were dead men." Eventually, the convalescing soldiers formed into line and marched off, but not before they had dragged the presses to the river.[63]

It is not known what triggered these men to shake off their various ailments to attack a mechanism essential to a free society, but it was not uncommon to have such runs on presses or to have the government arrest editors whose columns appeared to aid the rebellion. Prominent people could be a problem, especially if they could mobilize public opinion and dissuade men from volunteering. One study of Pennsylvania notes that, since the first months of the war, "Republican crowds had acted as informal enforcers of loyalty in urban communities." Popular crowd actions against papers occurred in Philadelphia, but they also appeared in the lumber region, Kittanning, Carlisle, and Huntingdon. Soldiers vandalized the press of the *Monroe Democrat* in Stroudsburg. One study has suggested that throughout the Union 111 newspapers were damaged by angry citizens. More often, however, editors who published unpopular opinions faced suppression of their papers, the loss of mailing privileges, or imprisonment. For the most part, the jail time was brief, mirroring the usual practice in political arrests to gain a public pledge of loyalty and sometimes a statement of contrition. Often, the reason for such assaults, and suppression of newspapers by the government, was rather flimsy and represented an attack on political speech.[64]

The public's hand in establishing the boundaries of loyalty revealed itself in such events, as it would in the harassment of unpatriotic preachers. Editors and ministers enjoyed no special protection during the war. Part of the reason lies in the nineteenth-century sensibilities over free expression that were very different from today. Struggles over free speech and worship in the Civil War era occurred primarily outside of the upper courts, which did not become more involved in these affairs until closer to World War I. Historians recently have made the case that the constitutional history of the United States may be found less in the courts than in newspapers, political tracts, and legislative halls. We might add to the list the military and crowd behavior.[65] A study of free speech by Michael Kent Curtis similarly has argued that a popular tradition emerged before the war among antislavery activists, editors, ministers, and politicians who rejected the claim, very much in vogue at the time, that speech deemed dangerous could be suppressed. From the Alien and Sedition Acts of 1798 through the Civil War, scholars, judges, politicians, legislators, and others considered that speech that *could* produce harmful results was not protected. Curtis notes that federalism complicated the story, giving the impression that the Constitution prohibited the central government from regulating free speech but allowed the states this power. Hence, the state of North Carolina convicted a minister in the 1850s for selling copies of a book by Hinton Rowan Helper that critiqued slavery as damaging the liberties and economic advancement of white people in general. The government in a slave state viewed criticism of the institution as dangerous for promoting possible slave unrest. "In the Northern states," on the other hand, "serious legal incursions on abolitionist speech, press, or petition were checked, not by courts, but by citizens urging a broadly protective understanding of free speech."[66]

For antebellum Americans, state and local communities determined what constituted dangerous speech. They implicitly understood the possibility of taking action based on their own understanding of rights and the dangers of certain kinds of expression. The terms free speech, freedom of the press, and freedom of religion or worship certainly occurred in the nineteenth century. Democrats known as Copperheads during the Civil War railed against the Lincoln administration for ignoring this constitutional right. Some editors and ministers also appeared before civil courts. An Ohio newspaperman was indicted on four counts of treason in the U.S. Circuit Court for the Southern District of Ohio because of his editorials. He was never convicted. But more often it was either local pressure or the military that stepped into the picture. In general, this was a battle fought more often than not outside of the high legal chambers.[67] And the public's right to take matters into its own hands became a matter of comment. *Frank Leslie's Illustrated Newspaper*, in an item titled "Printed Treason," suggested that the country was waking up to the reality of war and rejected treating mutineers, rebels, spies, and others leniently. The country insisted "that printed treason, as well as spoken and acted treason, shall be amenable, if not to legal at least to popular restraint."[68]

At least three things changed during the Civil War; otherwise one could argue for an incredible amount of continuity from the antebellum period concerning the public's consideration of free speech and worship. First, the targets shifted. Whether going after editors or ministers, the antebellum era featured abolition as a principal instigator for crowd reaction. One of the more famous instances came in Alton, Illinois, in 1837 when a crowd murdered abolitionist editor Elijah Lovejoy as he tried to defend his press. Also, public discourse featured the term "political preacher" most often as a synonym for antislavery sermons.[69] But when the war came, the focus turned in the direction of the citizens who criticized the administration or who did not show enough support. Abolitionists were still vilified in the beginning of the war as traitors whose agitation caused disunion. However, they underwent less suppression for their printed views than Democrats and southern sympathizers. Especially if the clergy failed to say a prayer to the president, or if editors told readers not to enlist in the Union army, they faced not only condemnation in public commentary but also possible arrest. The second change came in the use of the military to enforce and to shape the contours of disloyalty. We ought to think of the military as more than simply an enforcer. It was an active agent of social, moral, and legal influence during the war. Officers making decisions on the ground left their imprint on popular constitutional ideals and sometimes forced civilian leaders to construct new policy.

Finally, a civil war added a new dimension, making northerners rethink the definition of loyalty and disloyalty and the need for the government to employ whatever means possible to battle implicit treason. Columbia University law professor Francis Lieber expressed to the attorney general in 1862 his concerns over the mischief that the press could cause. He was not sure what should be done, but Lieber added, "The simple peace answer based on the principle of the liberty of the press will not do in urgent times of war." Similarly, the *New York Times* noted the necessary limits to liberties. "Speech is free—but no man can exercise that freedom in persuading soldiers to desert—or in bargaining for murder, theft or any other crime."[70]

The government's suppression of newspapers and arrests of editors earned very little disapproval from the fourth estate as a unified force. Today, assaults on press freedom generally encourage the media to close ranks and file protest. But in the Civil War, most arrests of editors passed either without comment or, more likely, with cheers from rival organs. According to one study, the partisan nature of the press made journalists "serious enemies of freedom of the press in wartime." The same scholar noted not a single Republican newspaper from the Civil War period consistently defended freedom of the press; all endorsed suppression of the opposition.[71]

The most famous case of suppression involved the *Chicago Times*. Wilbur Storey, editor of the *Chicago Times*, excoriated the arrest of Clement L. Vallandigham in May 1863. He referred to it as "the funeral of civil liberty." Subsequent columns continued the attack. Burnside ordered the *Times* to cease publishing. Storey refused. Soldiers broke into the building during the night and destroyed all the issues of the newspaper. Illinois's Senator Trumbull and Congressman Isaac Arnold begged Lincoln to overturn the order. So did Supreme Court Justice David Davis. Lincoln did cause the order to be revoked.[72] But even though some Republicans blanched at the order, the sentiment was hardly unanimous. Lincoln's action disappointed members of the Union Leagues of Chicago who met to pass resolutions that called the vacillation "an exhibition of weakness." Its resolutions declared, "We have no more sympathy with Traitors at home, than we have with Traitors abroad." They urged the president to suppress disloyal newspapers and "summarily try, banish and send without the military lines of our Armies, blatant spouters of Treason."[73]

Yet there was no coordinated campaign to stifle the opposing press. Most antiadministration papers faced no suppression, and editors left too big of a paper trail of stinging columns to support any contention of wide-scale assaults on such speech. Newspapers felt this pressure primarily in the border states, although editors were arrested and newspapers shut down in New York, Ohio, Pennsylvania, and Indiana. Historian Richard Carwardine argues that Lincoln approached this subject with ambivalence, convinced about the problems that editors could cause in shaping public opinion, supportive of shutting down the worst cases, but aware of the legal limits. In fact, this echoes the assessment by James G. Randall that the war and "demands of military men tended to pull the Government in the direction of arbitrary measures, while that deeper sense of regard for law was at the same time operating as a powerful restraining force."[74]

Ministers faced similar scrutiny. Although Americans believed in the separation of church and state, they also considered preachers molders of opinion and potentially dangerous. This was especially so because many denominations had their own newspapers circulating among the faithful. Recent studies have begun to reclaim the extent to which ministers, typically shown as generating nationalistic sentiment, spoke against the administration and faced arrests. Ministers, according to historian Timothy

L. Wesley, faced arrest repeatedly in New York, Pennsylvania, and Ohio. Sometimes, they attracted attention because they edited denominational newspapers that printed caustic commentary. More often, they stood out for their sermons that criticized the government, such as arguing against emancipation. But they also could earn rebuke from soldiers for silence, such as failing to pray for the president, not encouraging support for the prosecution of the war, or failing to take oaths of loyalty. In fact, Wesley argues that the Civil War posed the first true test of ministerial authority in U.S. history.[75]

The religious story of loyalty underscores once again the importance of shifting the focus to nongovernmental actions in combating treason. The military did not always need to be on the front lines of monitoring pastors. Church organizations policed their own. From 1860 to 1865, formal complaints were lodged against 121 ministers at annual conference meetings by twelve conferences in Illinois, Indiana, and Ohio. Bryon C. Andreasen adds that this does not include action taken against local ministers that never made it to this level. Thirty ministers were expelled, and the number of challenges to the ministerial fitness of individuals increased. Andreasen also found that the largest numbers of expulsions coincided with years featuring congressional and presidential elections, suggesting a political dimension to the actions. He concluded that "political tests became the measure of religious faith."[76] Similarly, a reverend in a Methodist Episcopal church in Illinois was tried before a fifteen-member district body. He had criticized the church for conducting political preaching and suggested that Democratic members might form a more conservative body. He was expelled.[77]

Under the circumstances, conference meetings could be quite lively as clergy assembled with different opinions about political affairs. Loyalty declarations and resolutions were often featured in these gatherings. For the most part, they declared their support for the government in its prosecution of the war. A Methodist Episcopal Conference in New York in 1863 featured resolutions that expressed unconditional loyalty to the United States. It added that "those who oppose every warlike measure under the pretext of discriminating between the administration and the government, are guilty of covert treason." The resolution that denounced slavery as treason "created a scene of almost wild enthusiasm. The clergy rose *en masse* and marked their approval of them by cheers, clapping of hands, stamping their feet on the ground and other modes of applause to which a council of reverends might be supposed a stranger." Two of the members stirred up the crowd by expressing dissenting views. They supported the resolutions for Union but did not approve of the stand against slavery. Loud cries came for the men to explain themselves. One finally did go before the assembly and professed his loyalty but also his opinion that emancipation was unconstitutional. He was hissed and told to sit down. He added that he would support the government "in every just constitutional measure to carry on the war, but he would never give up his right to free speech."[78]

Less formal action greeted ministers whose views ran contrary to congregants. They faced ostracism, firing, and even the threat of violence. Or they could be ignored. A guest minister at a church in central Pennsylvania misgauged the mood of his audience. He launched into a discussion about the equality of African Americans, which caused a large portion of the congregation to bolt. In 1864, in another Pennsylvania congregation, Democrats came into a church and interrupted the preacher during a sermon, asking him "whether he was a Democrat or an Abolitionist, saying that if he was the former he might continue to preach, but if the latter they would hang him." He escaped through a window.[79] Orders from church leaders to ministers did not always work. A bishop of the Episcopal Church in Maryland tried to cooperate with the government's request to observe fast days and thanksgiving. A letter to his clergy encouraged the observance and sent along prayers. But congregants under his charge protested. The prayers were rebuffed. Similarly, some ministers in Baltimore churches faced congregations that refused to say the prayer to the president even when requested by the pastor, causing some of the clergy to leave their charges.[80]

The government played its part in controlling speech and freedom of worship through the actions of military officers and state regulations that increasingly required people practicing various professions to swear oaths of loyalty. Missouri eventually included ministers, requiring them to take ironclad oaths of past loyalty before they could preach. Similar oaths existed in other states.[81] Provost marshals sometimes stepped in to arrest ministers and shut down congregations. In St. Louis, as discussed in chapter 5, discord over a Presbyterian minister's Confederate sympathies caused his imprisonment by a provost marshal. Washington interceded, and Lincoln issued a famous letter to the military commander in the region that "the U.S. government must not, as by this order, undertake to run the churches. When an individual, in a church or out of it, becomes dangerous to the public interest, he must be checked; but let the churches, as such take care of themselves." This position recognized the government's right to detain and punish ministers but called for caution.[82] Similarly, in the spring of 1864, Major General William Starke Rosecrans issued Special Orders No. 61 requiring members of religious meetings to take oaths of allegiance. The general also instructed provost marshals to attend such sessions to ensure loyal commentary occurred. Lincoln responded with a gentle letter that he called "more social than official," but he left the clear impression that he did not like the policy. "I somewhat dread the effect of your Special Order, No 61 dated March 7, 1864," he wrote, adding, "I have found that men who have not even been suspected of disloyalty, are very averse to taking an oath of any sort as a condition, to exercising an ordinary right of citizenship. The point will probably be made, that while men may without an oath, assemble in a noisy political meeting, they must take the oath, to assemble in a religious meeting." He ended by congratulating Rosecrans for acting better in Missouri than he had dared to hope.[83]

Overall, the handling of treason in the Union contained common ingredients, whether involving interdiction of mails, capturing spies, suppressing newspapers, enforcing loyalty in the churches, or making political arrests in general. First and foremost was the tendency to use a popular conceptualization of treason that had questionable constitutionality but that did not bother the people who employed it. The rationale to fight treason expressed or implied through military arrests and oversight by the executive branch, rather than civil courts, enjoyed wide currency among those most committed to the administration's goals for fighting the war. At times, attitudes among residents in communities—and their actions taken without waiting for federal direction—pushed the national government to act rather than the other way around. Increasingly, conflict between military authorities and civilians assumed a character defined by the peculiar traits and difficulties within different parts of the Union. The national government exerted its influence, to be sure; suspending habeas corpus and empowering provost marshals to arrest people for discouraging enlistments sparked increased arrests, especially after the failure to take Richmond in the summer of 1862. But the campaigns against disloyalty featured a dialectic of civilians and soldiers engaged with community action, out of which came new syntheses for policies.

Thus, the characterization of the administration as using hard but targeted measures, as well as the more critical assessment by historians of what happened, may both be right. From the high ground, the picture looked more restrained. The closer one gets to the ground level, however, the messier matters appeared. But before exploring this perspective in the loyal states and the occupied Confederacy, it will help to consider once more the view from above.

3

A THREE-BRANCH WAR,

WITH AN

ATLANTIC-WORLD FLAVOR

Given how much the country applied the logic of implied treason, it is tempting to wonder if there had not been a collective loss of constitutional scruples. In dealing with this issue, scholars turn to Abraham Lincoln, who casts a large shadow over the scholarship of the Civil War but especially over how the United States punished traitors. In most accounts, he acts as the chief arbiter of civil liberties. He was essential for executing policies on confiscation, conducting arrests of civilians in the loyal states, and defining treatment of Confederates who came within reach of the army. But to stop with Lincoln overlooks that various institutions and numerous people collaborated in constructing the rationale for the punishment of rebels and domestic traitors. While popular attitudes contributed to defining the parameters of liberty, the federal government also played its part. And although the interaction of the government's branches for prosecuting the war has not gone completely unnoticed, the axis of comparison most often runs between two branches—executive versus judicial or executive versus legislative—rather than trying to understand how all three performed their part.[1] In dealing with treason, whether in the Confederacy or in the states remaining in the Union, Lincoln hardly stood alone.

This is not to say that the three branches of government fell into complete accord. The *Merryman* conflict with Chief Justice Roger B. Taney in early 1861 vividly demonstrated that the judiciary could pose a challenge to the Lincoln administration. At least one scholar has made the case for considering the damage that the Court could inflict beyond this case. Eventually, Lincoln made enough appointments to the Supreme Court to help his cause, but even then the government faced opposition in state and municipal courts, specifically over the power to draft individuals and to conduct political arrests without civil trials. Over the course of the war, however, the Supreme Court generally upheld the administration on the very few cases it heard that involved treason, and the government allowed other potentially dangerous rulings on such things as habeas corpus to die at the state level without challenging them, thus limiting the damage. The legislative branch assisted by creating special legislation to protect federal agents from charges of false arrest. Even though significant friction existed between the executive branch and Radical legislators over numerous policies, such as the pace of emancipation, all three bodies reached a consensus—at least among the Republicans who were in the majority—over the nature of the war, the definition of the enemy, and the policies to apply against the rebels, including freeing the enslaved.[2]

Examining the three-branch approach to the war yields a number of insights. The government and its supporters assumed a position often described, in the words of historian James Randall, as embodying "the flexible principle of the double status of the rebels."[3] A closer look at the justification produced by all three branches of government shows that there was no double status, per se. Instead, a significant amount of international law and precedents smoothed over the contradictions and enabled federal authorities to treat the Confederates as public enemies who fell under the rules of war, while not forgiving them for treason.[4] America's Civil War was not new on the world's stage. U.S. authorities borrowed from international law to define what the president, the Congress, and the courts could do in regard to presidential powers and the confiscation of treasonous property by the courts and the military. The Constitution and federal statutes granted power to the chief executive to handle insurrection, but both were quiet about the nature of those powers. Union leaders reached for international customs and writing on the conduct of wars to legitimate the policies applied to the Confederates. The solicitor of the War Department, in fact, stated unequivocally in his treatise on war powers that "the law of nations [international law] is above the constitution of any government." Unlike what at least one specialist has argued, the Constitution was not "adequate" to meet the nation's greatest challenge but benefited from interweaving international law with domestic law.[5] International precedents from the mid-1700s had decided that rebellions could grow to the scale of a civil war. Once that occurred, the conflict became synonymous with a public war between nations, because it was considered the only humane thing to do. To treat rebellious citizens in a civil war as traitors, rather than public enemies, led to atrocities.[6]

Situating military and political thought within this broader context also makes the actions that have brought criticism of Lincoln appear as less extraordinary. Analysis has focused on whether he remained true to the founding principles of the United States without considering whether he adhered to the international rules of warfare. The precedents for making war that had matured in the Atlantic world gave ample justification for a leader to adopt stern policies to maintain the nation-state when facing a civil strife. This analysis also brings the judiciary back into having an impact on the war or, in the words of one scholar, as something other than "outside the mainstream of events."[7] In fact, it is not too far off the mark to say that the rationale for seizing goods through maritime law presented to Congress and the administration a justification for implementing similar policies on land until both Lincoln's Emancipation Proclamation and the code of war that came in 1863.

Finally, restoring the use of international practices, customs, and law reveals one more strategy by abolitionists in their battle to end slavery. Before the war, because of the widely accepted protection of slavery, antislavery men like William Henry Seward argued for considering a higher law than the Constitution. Similarly, antislavery proponents often found themselves relying on interpreting the spirit of the Bible rather than its literal writings on slavery. It should come as little surprise, then, that emancipationists looked beyond national borders and to the laws of war and nations to find the support they needed to press their claims for what one could do to a domestic traitor who was treated like an alien enemy. The logic revolved around the belief that the rebels had committed treason.

Of Ships and International Law

This journey begins on the ocean. It was action on the water that yielded the most important court rulings on treasonous behavior for the entire war. Legal historians have arrived before Civil War historians at an understanding that the cases involving action at sea reveal "most clearly how American statesmen, jurists, soldiers, and sailors of the time thought that the Constitution constrained or empowered their dealings with foreign nations."[8] These included rulings that defined secession as treason subject to civil punishment, that defined the Confederate traitors as enemies akin to alien belligerents in a public war, and that created the examples for the legal process for confiscating property not only on the sea but also on land. From coffee, tobacco, and other contraband hauled from

Confederate-owned or neutral ships captured on the ocean we can trace a line of logic to Union soldiers refusing to return slaves to their masters.

First, this journey requires a slight detour into the lexicon of international law. It can be confusing to encounter such terms as the law of nations, the laws of war, and the articles of war. They sound similar but contained subtle differences. All three rested on a foundation of legal and military practices built over centuries. But the first two—the law of nations and laws of war—dealt primarily with the international community and supposedly applied to civilized nations around the globe, even though the nineteenth-century context for this concept was decidedly Western-centric and, for the United States, dominated by English customary law.

The Articles of War represented the United States government's code of conduct for its own military. The articles of war were composed in the early Republic by the U.S. Congress and—during the early portions of the Civil War—were routinely read to troops by the Union officers to instruct their men. The Articles of War identified, for instance, punishment for desertion and established other standards of behavior, such as discouraging pillaging from civilians. Although important to the army, and especially to the officers who cared about inculcating discipline in volunteer troops, the Articles of War had a small influence in the larger debates about how to handle the rebellion.[9]

The laws of war and the law of nations dealt with rules of behavior that transcended national borders—the legal precedents and customary practices for the conduct of war among nations in an enlightened age. The term "law of nations" dates to antiquity. *Jus gentium* goes back to the Romans who created practices for dealing with multiple countries and subjects in their empire. By the seventeenth and eighteenth centuries, the term gained fresh life with the rise of modern nation-states. The modern law of nations had its roots in commerce, as well as war. The law of nations guided the ways that modern states were to interact, imagining countries and empires as living, social beings.[10] The pioneer of this thought was Hugo Grotius, a jurist from the Dutch Republic who in the 1600s laid the foundations for international law. As part of his body of work, he contributed a three-volume study, *On the Law of War and Peace*. Central to his treatise was the notion that nations were bound by common laws of conduct regardless of local practices. Nations conducted warfare by rules.

Grotius, however, did not have the most bearing on debates among nineteenth-century Americans. That honor fell to Emmerich de Vattel, a Swiss diplomat and legal expert. He compiled the ideas of writers such as Grotius and Samuel Pufendorf to produce a masterwork in the mid-eighteenth century titled *The Law of Nations, or the Principles of Natural Law Applied to the Conduct and to the Affairs of Nations and of Sovereigns*. The book dealt with more than warfare: it provided ideas concerning a code of conduct for a range of international relations, including commerce, the duties of sovereigns, the principles of good government, and even the responsibility of nations to encourage proper soil cultivation. The work found its way to America in time to find use among the revolutionary generation. By the advent of the Civil War, the *Law of Nations* was entrenched as the most widely cited text that influenced congressional debate and public discourse.[11]

Having rules and regulations rarely eliminates ambiguity, especially in a text as comprehensive as *The Law of Nations*. As a case in point, the Supreme Court decisions that set the precedent for confiscation of property in the Civil War arose from the War of 1812. In *Brown v. the United States*, an American citizen had secured timber that the owner was selling to the British. The cargo had started its journey from overseas when the embargo by the president of the United States came, causing its owners to head for Massachusetts. The ship and its cargo were seized as a prize of war, with the case brought before the district court of Massachusetts. In the meantime, the owners had offloaded the timber for storage when it was seized by authorities, a fact that became significant. Armitz Brown contested the confiscation. After winning in district court and losing in Circuit Court, Brown's case came before John Marshall's Supreme Court. Brown ultimately won, with the Court indicating that once the cargo had been discharged from the ship, it had landed. Even though war allowed for the capture of enemy property, once that property was ashore, confiscation required legislation from the Congress, a fact that would not be lost on the Civil War generation hoping to seize the property of traitors on land.[12]

The case showed the importance of international law for informing decisions on such affairs, but it also demonstrated that *The Law of Nations* could easily support contradictory positions. Chief Justice Marshall cited the text as part of his opinion for the majority, using the portion of the book that indicated that foreign property and persons were not to be detained if they found themselves on enemy soil at the outbreak of a declaration of war. On the other hand, Justice Story, who wrote a dissenting opinion, used different sections from the same book to argue the opposite point. He relied on Vattel's statements that authorities had the right to confiscate enemy property that fell into their hands once a war had been declared.[13] An incredible amount of flexibility existed within Vattel for anyone trying to support a particular position, which meant that even when United States officials tried to stipulate best practices, ambiguity existed.

However, the first opinions by jurists that emerged as the country broke apart in 1860–61 came not in actual cases but in statements made in charges to juries. It quickly became apparent that leading jurists supported the Union, not the Confederacy. In the nineteenth century, the federal court selected a grand jury to rule on whether enough evidence existed to hand down an indictment, or a true bill. In other words, the grand jurors did not render a verdict; they set the mechanism of justice in motion by declaring whether the government had enough evidence to warrant a trial. Often the charges did not deal with actual cases but alerted jurors to the situations that might arise from the broader political-judicial climate. One historian has indicated that the charges could serve as political stump speeches. In the secession crisis, the charges to grand juries revealed judges' positions on treason and the legality of the Confederacy.[14]

During the first seven months of the war, three charges to the federal grand juries in particular were noteworthy. They were not the only addresses to instruct the nation on the rules of treason. In fact, as one study indicates, federal judges "throughout the North hastened to deny the South's right to form a new nation." A judge in New York spoke out as early as January 1861. As spring came, more and more federal judges felt compelled to launch a discussion of the meaning of secession and to educate the public on treason in charges to grand juries. The practice did not end in 1861; throughout the conflict "federal judges in the North used addresses to grand juries as occasions to denounce the enemy and encourage support of the war."[15]

One charge that gained attention in the North came from the U.S. District Court in Massachusetts. Judge Peleg Sprague left no doubt what he thought about secession: he dismissed state rights and argued for the supremacy of the national government. He denied that the government of the United States was a confederacy and called this position "a fundamental and dangerous error." The country may once have been such an entity, but the relationship of states changed with the adoption of the Constitution of 1787, which Sprague said made the United States the supreme authority. Brushing aside ideas of Thomas Jefferson and John C. Calhoun, he stated that the laws of the United States could not be annulled or changed by a state.[16] The judge also captured the frustration about treason law that stymied prosecution of the rebels until after the war. He noted that "treason . . . can be tried only within the state and judicial district within which it was committed; and the accused has the right to a trial by jury in such state and district." Consequently, if a traitor committed his overt act at Charleston, the case had to be heard in South Carolina. And if the judicial tribunals of the United States did not function there, then the crimes committed "however atrocious, cannot be punished by the regular administration of justice."[17]

A second charge to the grand jury that stood out among the many at the time reassured those faithful to the United States about the loyalty of the remaining Supreme Court justices. Associate Justice John Catron made headlines in the summer with his charge to a grand jury in the Eighth Circuit Court that included Missouri, Tennessee, and Kentucky. One justice, John Archibald Campbell of Alabama, had resigned from the Court in April to join the Confederacy. Another justice, Chief Justice Taney of Maryland, had collided with the president over military arrests in Maryland. Justices Robert C. Grier and James W. Layne were from Pennsylvania and Georgia, respectively.[18] Catron's loyalty, if not suspect, interested northerners, who watched for which way the court leaned—and Catron might have been expected to lean in the wrong direction. The associate justice was known as "sound on the side of slavery" for writing a separate concurring opinion on the *Dred Scott* case. He had been born in Virginia and was from Tennessee. Instead of following his state, however, the justice remained in his position and used his office to excoriate secessionists.[19]

While in St. Louis on July 10, 1861, Catron delivered a charge to the grand jury of the circuit court that cheered the hearts of many Unionists and was widely reported throughout the North. District Judges Samuel Treat and Robert Wells had requested that the Supreme Court justice hold a session of the court; Treat had composed the address, which went out in the name of Catron. From the newspaper excerpts, it appears that the judges performed their duty of outlining with precision what treason meant and warning against "the frenzy of the hour," including the protection of a citizen's right to bear arms without being in league with a force hostile to the government and the protection of freedom of expression.[20]

However, the northern press most often picked up on the sections of the charge that supported an elastic definition of war making—in other words, a logic that could condone the use of "implied treason." Among the examples given were obstruction of U.S. officials in conducting their business, diverting food from the United States service to the enemy, detaining mail or destroying it, doing the same with newspapers, giving preference to pamphlets favorable to the enemy, and counterfeiting postage stamps. This section of the charge clearly meant to warn against the spreading of secession sentiments, as well as to prevent obstruction of federal agents or the progress of U.S. troops through Missouri.[21]

Emerging from these and other court pronouncements was the fact that a strain of Jacksonian Democracy existed within the federal judiciary: beliefs that supported limited government, but also a strong Union that did not allow for secession. Catron, a Democrat with ties to Andrew Jackson, was praised by both Republican and Democratic newspapers. Fully seven of the justices sitting when the war broke out had been Democrats, most of them appointed by Jackson and one each by Franklin Pierce and James Buchanan. This faithfulness to the Union by a man known to have southern tendencies came at a tense time in Missouri and just before the most significant battle in the eastern theater of war at Manassas, Virginia. While it was as yet unknown how a Democratic court might consider such policies as emancipation or conscription, at least at this moment in the war little sympathy came for secession.[22]

One more charge in 1861, this time by a justice to a regular jury, highlighted the importance of maritime cases in deciding whether the Confederates were enemies subject to the international laws of nations or rebellious domestic citizens eligible for treason. In many respects, one can see in these proceedings the desire to declare Confederates as both belligerent enemies *and* rebellious citizens. And we can see the judiciary making this work by meshing international with domestic law. In November 1861, Associate Justice Samuel Nelson faced in the U.S. Circuit Court at New York a legal situation that, if not handled carefully, could threaten the blockade and cause serious damage to a range of policies.[23] The justice presided over one of a group of cases moving through the system in various circuit courts that collectively became known as the *Prize Cases*, or decisions on privateers authorized by the Confederate government and ships owned either by foreigners or by people living in the Confederacy.

Of interest to Democratic newspapers like the *Harrisburg Patriot and Union* were the justice's comments that protected civil liberties. For Nelson, the knottiest problem that he faced involved defining behavior that aided and abetted the enemy. The clearest instances came when a citizen provided intelligence to the enemy, sent provisions or money, furnished arms or troops, or turned over a federal installation such as a military post. However, the justice drew a line on free speech. "Words oral, written or printed," he observed, "however treasonable, seditious or criminal of themselves, do not constitute an overt act of treason within the definition of the crime." He allowed for printed or spoken words to become evidence when an overt act had been committed, but only as a means of characterizing the intent of the accused and not as an act of treason in and of itself.[24] This position obviously resonated with Democrats who had faced arrests by both U.S. Attorneys and the military for treasonable language, both spoken and written.

The *Patriot and Union* and other organs overlooked the first sections of Nelson's charge that defined piracy and that cited the laws that allowed the United States to execute citizens who preyed on the nation's shipping. This section of the charge mattered a great deal because the justice had just presided over a trial that had blown up in the government's face. The case had involved the ship *Savannah* seized by the U.S. Navy. Twelve of the ship's crew faced charges of piracy. An eight-day trial ended on October 31 with a hung jury. Before it was impounded, the *Savannah* had captured a U.S. vessel, *Joseph*, carrying a cargo of sugar heading from Cardenas to Philadelphia. What made this a cause célèbre was the fact that the defense claimed that the men were privateers—commissioned by Jefferson Davis via a letter of marque which authorized a private vessel to attack ships manned by enemies of the Confederacy. Whether citizens or not, pirates were essentially rogues and criminals attacking ships for personal gain. Privateers, however, served as agents of a government. Recognized by the law of nations as enemies of the human race and codified by U.S. statute law of 1790, pirates could be executed as criminals. Privateers, however, had to be treated as prisoners serving a government at war with the United States. If the government executed the men, it risked acknowledging that there was no real Confederate States and the blockade thus did not have international sanction. If the trial found the men not guilty as prisoners of war, then the blockade stood, but the Confederacy could be considered as a de facto nation.[25]

Other factors not necessarily before the court had increased the sensitivity over this ruling. It was well known that Jefferson Davis had sent a letter to Lincoln dated July 6, 1861, that warned against trying the crew of the *Savannah* as pirates or traitors, rather than treating them as prisoners of war. Davis reminded Lincoln that the Confederate government had acted humanely and leniently whenever capturing Union soldiers, paroling some, allowing others to remain at large under their honor, and providing rations for all. "It is only since the news has been received of the treatment of the prisoners taken on the Savannah that I have been compelled to withdraw these indulgences, and to hold the prisoners taken by us in strict confinement." Then he threatened that the government would retaliate and kill Union prisoners in equal measure for the deaths of the crew.[26]

The jury for the *Savannah* trial deliberated for twenty hours without reaching a consensus, and it appears that the judge's refusal to define the war played a role in the deadlock. Part of the problem came with Nelson allowing so much evidence to be admitted by the defense concerning the existence of the Confederacy, such as the Constitution of the Confederate States of America.[27] One of the jurors sent word to the judge that a verdict depended on whether a civil war existed, or if the intent to commit robbery was in the minds of the prisoners. After consulting with the district judge, Nelson declined to clarify the status of the war. He gave an appropriate reason—that it was up to the legislative and executive branches of the Union to perform this task and not the judiciary. In essence, he left it up to the twelve men in the box to discern on their own the meaning of a civil war.[28]

The *New York Herald* suggested that two other factors contributed to the demise of the case. One was the precedent cited by the defense of Great Britain during the American Revolution, which had treated American privateers as prisoners of war, giving them the rights of belligerents versus traitors. Additionally, the reporter cited international law as condoning that "those who warred upon the ocean were entitled to the same humanities as those who warred upon the land." This had been a striking part of the defense's argument, which the reporter believed had registered on jurors.[29] A Republican newspaper in the city, the *New York Tribune*, fumed about the ruling. One column contained a rant about the impact of Great Britain's actions that ironically created "patriotic piracy" and that unfairly compared "the patriots of '76 and the pirates of '61." A separate item alleged that the city itself might have too many Confederate sympathizers to convict these men.[30] This case highlights how the country groped for a definition of the war, how international precedents through maritime law and practice worked their way into domestic concerns, and how some members of the public—the four jurors reluctant to convict—could influence even the case law's determination of disloyalty.

At roughly the same time the crew of the *Savannah* faced trial, another piracy case came before the U.S. Circuit Court in Philadelphia that had quite a different outcome, one favorable to the government. Supreme Court Justice Grier joined district judge Cadwalader to preside over the hearing for a man charged with piracy. William Smith had been part of the crew for the *Jefferson Davis*, a ship formerly known as the *Echo*, that had illegally carried Africans in the slave trade. After going through various hands, it had slipped out of Charleston Harbor in 1861 and then, after doing damage on the high seas to Union shipping, was captured and taken to Philadelphia. Grier, a Democratic appointee, used the occasion to give bold statements about the war. Smith's attorney took the approach, very common at the time, to assert that because of the allegiance of individuals to their states, the accused had no recourse except to capitulate once the state seceded. Grier had none of this. "You might, more justifiably, I think, plead the total insanity of the people in the South altogether. The question was once asked whether a nation could be insane, as well as an individual. I have no doubt that it can. You might as well set up national insanity."[31]

In the charge to the jury, Grier declared that considering the conflict as a Civil War was not tantamount to recognizing the Confederacy as a legitimate nation-state. The justice swept aside the notion that the raiders served as privateers authorized by an independent nation. Yet he reserved the right of the government to treat the conflict as if it were a war between belligerents. For Grier, the conflict was an insurrection or rebellion that had grown to the scale of a civil war. Every government was bound by the law of self-preservation to suppress insurrections "and the fact that the number and power of the insurgents may be so great as to carry on a civil war against their legitimate sovereign will not entitle them to be considered a state." He concluded: "Consequently, this court . . . can view those in rebellion against them in no other light than as traitors to their country, and those who assume by their authority a right to plunder the property of our citizens on the high seas as pirates and robbers."[32] This case, and the conviction of three of Smith's crew members shortly afterward, represented clear victories by the government to prosecute traitors in civil courts. The judge had declared the entire Confederate experiment as consisting of traitors trying to bring down the government.

Ironically, the government's success signaled the end of such prosecutions, revealing the true meaning behind seeking the sternest measures for such crimes. Grier did not want to move forward on any more cases. He announced in open court that he intended to leave such cases to the district judge and then gave a lesson on what he thought about splitting hairs between the treatment of prisoners on land and on water. "But why make a difference between those taken on land and on water? Why not try all those on land and hang them?" Then the justice answered his own question, which framed the difference between insurrection and a civil war. "That might do with a mere insurrection; but when it comes to civil war, the laws of War [international customs] must be observed, or you will lay it open to the most horrid reactions that can possibly be thought of: hundreds of thousands of men will be sacrificed upon mere brutal rage."[33] The prisoners in this case were transferred to military custody and were treated like prisoners of war, wholly in line with Vattel's prescription for such affairs.

The Union hunted down more than privateers on the ocean; its navy also captured merchant ships—blockade runners or neutral carriers of contraband for the Confederacy. From the start of the war, the handling of these cases in district courts piqued public interest for what the rulings said about the enemy and confiscation of property. Various owners of the vessels challenged the right of the government to seize the property. By 1863, a collection of these seizures had gone through the lower courts and came before the Supreme Court in what became known as the *Prize Cases*. The rulings on these four ships revealed a shift in thinking taking place throughout the Union toward treating everyone as enemies in an area considered in insurrection, regardless of individually professed loyalties. The decisions also leaned on international law to navigate the legal boundaries for the war powers of a president.

For these cases, timing was everything. The *Prize Cases* involved the seizing of four vessels *before* July 13, 1861, a date of some significance and yet one that rarely appears in the general narratives of the conflict. Until that moment, Lincoln had acted with somewhat debatable constitutional authority, even though most historians have excused him because of the emergency that faced the nation. Capturing vessels and declaring blockades typically involve a war between nations. Only the Congress, not the president, has the power to declare war. But the legislative branch was not in session when war commenced and was not scheduled to gather until December 1861, so there was no congressional action on these issues until the president convened a special session in July. Congress on July 13 passed what became recognized by the judiciary as the nearest thing to a declaration of war that could be found.[34] The legislation allowed the president to collect duties on imports in the states mounting insurrection, to interdict all trade, and to seize vessels judged to be in violation of the statute. The language was incredibly turgid and legalistic: it was hardly an act designed to inspire a public, but it did concede to the president the ability to define an insurrection and decide on the measures to take against the Confederacy.[35]

Once again Justice Grier provided the administration with a victory. Writing the majority opinion, the justice laid out the two questions germane to the situation. Did the president have the right to declare a blockade on the principles of international law? Could the property of people living on domestic soil be subject to capture as enemies? The second question came into play because two of the ships were owned by residents of

Virginia who had sworn oaths of loyalty to the Union. In the former case, he reasoned that the president had the power to act without legislative authority. It was his duty to defend the country against insurrection or invasion. "The President was bound to meet it in the shape it presented itself, without waiting for Congress to baptize it with a name; and no name given to it by him or them could change the fact."[36] To support his case, the justice cited the portion of Vattel that indicated a civil war created two distinct societies that functioned like two nations at war. As for the second question, he made the discussion of Unionism in the Confederacy moot as far as determining whose property could be seized. As long as people lived within regions considered by the president in rebellion against the government, they were enemies, although not foreigners. Grier reserved for the government the ability to prosecute traitors after the war.[37]

Beyond legal historians, few scholars have stressed the amount of international law that entered this discussion, and even legal historians have overlooked which justices on the Court embraced international law and which ones did not. In both the arguments of counsel and the opinions of the Court, references appear to Vattel's *Law of Nations*, but the *Prize Cases* also highlighted another authority: *Elements of International Law*. Compiled by Henry Wheaton, an American born in Massachusetts, the work first appeared in 1836 and was updated various times to 1845. It spread throughout the Atlantic world in translated editions. In essence, Wheaton tried to fill the chronological gap left between *Law of Nations* published in the eighteenth century and more recent cases, which he noticed had "greatly multiplied in number and interest during the long period which has elapsed since the publication of Vattel's highly appreciated work."[38] Both counsels in the *Prize Cases* used Wheaton, perhaps even more extensively than Vattel, because of the case law that had emerged in the early republic and antebellum period. They simply had more ammunition to work with in Wheaton's compilation. For instance, the government used a case decided by the U.S. Supreme Court in 1822 involving sale by a U.S. citizen of a ship to Buenos Aires, which then preyed upon the Spanish shipping as a vessel of war and brought captured cargo to a U.S. port. Typically, international precedents were used to justify expansive powers of a nation's leader to confiscate property in wartime.[39]

More interesting was the dissenting opinion rendered by Justice Nelson, which showed reluctance on the part of conservative justices to employ international law. The dissenters, who included Lincoln's familiar opponent, Chief Justice Taney, indicated that the president had the power to handle the insurrection, but he could not by himself declare a civil war, establish a blockade, or confiscate ships of foreign neutrals. Power was exercised by the chief executive under the municipal laws of the country "and not under the law of nations." In other words, they asserted the primacy of the Constitution over international law. Only the Congress could declare a war, Nelson asserted, but because of the militia acts passed in the 1790s the president had ample power to mobilize troops to put down an insurrection. But if he wanted to institute a blockade, the dissenters counseled that he should have called Congress into session earlier and waited until the legislature had declared war or given him the ability to interdict trade, which had occurred via the act of July 13, 1861. Once Congress declared war, then a blockade could be established and international law invoked. The more conservative justices were in no hurry to leave the boundaries of U.S. law.[40]

The *Prize Cases* affirmed important changes in thinking about the rebels and revealed the intriguing tensions that existed between domestic and international law. Maritime cases had been a subject of interest since the beginning of the war and informed congressional thinking about how to seize property on land. Especially after Lincoln appointed Republican justices, the Supreme Court stood ready to support the president on issues concerning secession and war powers. The *Prize Cases*, however, made it clear that the Union had crossed one noticeable divide. As far as the courts were concerned, no Unionists lived in the Confederate States. Grier had made that clear, indicating that treason had become identified less with individual persons than with territory. Yet he did not concede that this ruling recognized the Confederacy as a legitimate nation. After the war, Richard Henry Dana Jr.—who represented the government in these cases—understood the ruling as treating the Rebels "as belligerents in fact,—not as belligerents *de jure*,—by a policy revocable at any time."[41] The ruling thus contained a great deal of pragmatism and international examples in order to treat Confederates as enemies in war, while deferring whether to try them as traitors until after the conflict.

Conservatives and moderates adopted or avoided international law depending on how it suited their ideals. To put it another way, the U.S. Constitution was most often employed as a means of arguing for limited warfare or for holding off more radical measures. Whenever the country needed to push for a harder war or for expanded presidential powers, proponents sought international examples and skirted the civil court system in favor of employing executive authority. It is not the case that people were deeply interested in, or schooled on, international law: one historian's assessment seems accurate that few in the administration were concerned about it except in the practical way it could help national interests.[42] That they felt the need to resort to such ideas as the *Law of Nations* was, however, significant. The text played a role when it came time for the U.S. Congress to allow confiscation of the property of traitors.

The Ocean on Land: Congress and the Enemy

The first summer of the war featured an incredible outpouring of legislation intended to give the president what he needed to punish the rebels. Starting on July 10, or less than a week after Lincoln convened the Thirty-Seventh Congress in a special session, the representatives began to enact what amounted to no fewer than *sixty-five* public acts. This legislative flurry occurred in fewer than thirty days, with the last pieces put into place by August 6. To put this into perspective, historians justifiably rave over the achievements of the first hundred days of Franklin Delano Roosevelt's administration. In that time, the Congress enacted roughly fifteen laws that changed the nation. Under a similar deadline, given the output of the Thirty-Seventh Congress, it might have produced more than 200 laws. And it did not pad the legislative calendar with frivolous matters to achieve these totals. In looking over the list generated by the Congress from July 4 to August 6, it is striking how on point the lawmaking was. Although they might not have created a New Deal, the representatives dabbled in precedent-setting ideas that altered the landscape of what would be politically possible in the future.

In short, representatives in that special session put into place the mechanism for running a war against a domestic traitor who acted like a belligerent foreigner. The Congress expanded the militia, retooled each branch of the military including the navy and the marines, coordinated pay for all personnel, and authorized a national loan to pay for these expenses. Ironic because of today's party positions, the Republican-dominated Congress also enacted the first income tax in U.S. history, a progressive tax that took effect only after a person earned $800. More to the point, the Congress took aim at disloyalty and began creating additional tools to punish it. As covered previously, the legislators opened the way for the witch hunt that became the Potter Committee by establishing that government workers must swear an oath of allegiance or be fired. In the First Confiscation Act, the Congress clarified that slaves used to help the rebellion should not be returned, even though they left the status of those African Americans unclear. Congress also condoned Lincoln's decision to invoke a blockade and gave him the power to declare an insurrection in order to use virtually any means to put down the threat.

In these first important actions, the legislative branch conceded to the executive the power of defining the war and how to handle the insurrection. The special session of the Thirty-Seventh Congress condoned much of what Lincoln had done to this point in his interpretation of the Constitution. Throughout the conflict, representatives revised the laws in order to fend off attempts to thwart mobilization or conduct retaliation against public officials for cracking down on dissent. This does not mean that the Congress lacked contention. As is well known, the more radical Republican members pushed for greater changes at a faster pace than moderates and Lincoln were willing to go, and they were uncomfortable with letting the president have the lead on dictating policies against the traitors. But the story of restricting civil liberties and ferreting out treason contains a greater confluence of ideas than accounts typically stress.

The Union was as ill prepared legally as it was militarily for its Civil War. In 1861 the only crime that existed to punish rebels was treason. There was no crime of conspiracy in federal statutes. In the opening stages of the war, a convicted murderer of a United States marshal could, as a federal grand jury charge noted, "receive under national law a maximum sentence of one year in jail and a fine of three hundred dollars."[43] Not surprisingly, then, one of the acts of the Thirty-Seventh Congress came on July 31 when it passed "An Act to Define and Punish Certain Conspiracies." The law gave United States officials the ability to prosecute people who conspired to resist the government, who encouraged others to do so, or who blocked the enforcement of laws. Astonishingly, these actions had been out of reach of the existing laws as a major crime. With the new legislation, the federal government would try conspiracy as a high crime, although not a capital offense like treason. Judges could sentence the convicted to a fine of $500 to $5,000, or imprisonment from six months to six years.[44] Periodic trials occurred under this act, as well as the Second Confiscation Act. However, it was not resorted to in any great extent. More typically, the administration avoided the civil courts to stop treasonous behavior.[45]

In the midst of this legislative output, the Congress also exorcised some of its ghosts. The ritual had begun in March as the previous congressional session vacated the seats of six senators who had gone with the Confederacy, including Jefferson Davis. Resistance came from Democratic senators from the border states, who fought a resolution that called for expelling the members. Because of their efforts, the resolution merely recognized the reality that the seats were vacant and that the names of the absent members should no longer be part of a roll call. Senator James A. Bayard Jr. of Delaware did not want to impugn the men as traitors. He claimed that some of the absentees disagreed with disunion but felt compelled to remain with their states. Roughly a week earlier, an attempt had failed to expel former U.S. senator Louis Wigfall of Texas.[46]

The situation changed dramatically beginning July 4 with the special session of the Thirty-Seventh Congress as Republicans enjoyed commanding majorities in both houses. They needed a large edge in numbers if they hoped to muster the two-thirds vote required to evict representatives. Expulsion became the order of the day in the first summer of the war. On July 11, the Senate expelled ten of the missing members who had gone with the Confederacy, including Wigfall. They added to the list a member of the House, Representative John B. Clark of Missouri, who had taken up with the rebel forces in his state. Despite the fact that the men arguably deserved banishment and more, these first expulsions did not pass unanimously. The voting on the first batch totaled 32-10 in favor of the action. Among the dissenting senators was John C. Breckinridge of Kentucky, who had run as the Southern Rights Democrat for president and would leave the North to become a general in the Confederate army.[47] Within less than a year, half of the dissenting senators were expelled or resigned. Between the voluntary departures of southern congressmen and these actions, the Republican majority was solidifying its ability to forge one of the most activist congresses in American history.

When Congress resumed its regular calendar in December, the vote to banish the next six congressmen passed without significant opposition. Breckinridge was among them; by this time he was too tainted for sympathetic colleagues to save. Senators such as Bayard of Delaware had waged a rearguard action that depended upon divining the "motivations" of departing lawmakers, meaning whether they had opposed disunion. Motivations were one thing; actions another. That Breckinridge had donned a Confederate uniform made it spectacularly hard for sympathizers to find a moral high ground. When the resolution banning him from the Congress passed unanimously, it announced Breckinridge as a traitor. Lyman Trumbull of Illinois proposed the resolution that said Breckinridge had joined the enemies of his country and that he, "the traitor," should be expelled from the Senate.[48]

All told, Congress expelled seventeen members during the Civil War. For all of U.S. history, only three more have been added to this list. The Senate expelled fourteen and the House three. Arguably the most controversial case was that of Jesse D. Bright, a leading senator from Indiana. In March 1861, Bright had written a letter of introduction for a man hoping to show improvements in firearms to President Jefferson Davis, a former colleague. The judiciary committee at first recommended against the expulsion, but then one of the members changed his vote and Charles Sumner made an impassioned speech, demanding that the Senate purge itself of traitors. Even though he had supporters, Bright knew the numbers were not in his favor. The vote to expel totaled 32 to 14.[49] All of the expulsions were accomplished by February 1862, although both chambers attempted eight more abortive evictions through 1865.

For much of the first eight months that the Thirty-Seventh Congress conducted its business, various issues concerning loyalty confronted the legislative branch. What should the Union do about rebel property that came into grasp? Were the Confederates citizens subject to treason law, or enemies falling under international laws and practices? How should the country deal with its internal, domestic enemies? Which should be the originating power behind these efforts: Congress or the president, domestic or international law?

The debate over the Second Confiscation Act provided a legislative confluence of the concerns over loyalty, emancipation, war powers, admiralty law, and international practices. Although lawmakers had enacted the First Confiscation Act relatively swiftly in August 1861, the second one presented a much harder nut to crack. The first one was difficult to oppose because it allowed the military to seize property being used to aid the enemy's war effort. Few opponents could raise serious objections against an act that diminished the war-making capabilities of the enemy. But the second act, which took from December 1861 to July 1862 to pass, faced greater obstacles. The issues struck at the heart of the rebellion and the core of American political and personal ideals. They dealt with the protection of property, presidential and congressional powers, the right to free the enslaved, and how to punish the traitors. Although it is true that the opposition tended to be Democrats located in the border states, overlooked in the understanding of this act until recently has been the power of the moderate Republicans to thwart more radical measures.[50]

Ultimately, and largely because of the moderate Republicans, a highly flawed bill emerged that spliced together two different motivations: one to confiscate slaves as property and the other to constrain the punishment of rebels. The multiple identities of the bill were reflected in its title: "An Act to suppress Insurrection, to punish Treason and Rebellion, to seize and confiscate the Property of Rebels, and for other Purposes." Moderate

Republicans and Democratic allies influenced, and favored, the top four sections dealing with treason—not because they saw the chance to strike at the rebellion but because they hoped to limit punitive measures and encourage reconciliation. They were well aware that no court cases for treason in the rebel states were possible because the law required hearings to be conducted where crimes were committed, and this virtually eliminated prosecutions in Confederate territory. Radicals supported the bottom sections of the bill that allowed for the seizing of a wide range of Confederate property, including slaves. But radicals accepted the act somewhat grudgingly, and the originator of the bill—Senator Lyman Trumbull of Illinois—nearly walked away from it in disgust. Supporters of confiscating slaves had to swallow the more conservative sections in order to get their position through, even though it was far less than they wanted and contained ill-defined procedures for achieving their goals.[51]

In trying to decide the status of the Confederates and how to seize their property, the debate increasingly employed international laws and customs. Vattel became a chief resource, although Wheaton's *International Law* enjoyed select appearances. Radicals typically reached for international precedents; the opposition countered by arguing for the Constitution as the supreme law of the land.

That abolitionists sought precedents beyond the United States for seizing and emancipating slaves made sense because of the restraints in the Constitution. Literal interpretations faced an uncertain legal battle. Much as they had done before the war in advocating a higher law than the Constitution—and advocating for the spirit rather than the letter of the biblical statements concerning slavery—they favored an expansive interpretation of the fundamental law and the powers of Congress. Two things had changed, however, from the antebellum position. First, abolitionists shifted from stressing moral, humanitarian reasons for emancipation in favor of practical, "military necessity" as a means of winning the war and punishing the rebels. Ironically, even though continuing to recognize the enslaved as human beings, emancipationists found themselves arguing for slaves as property. They bolstered their position with the military experiences of history, the practices embodied in the law of nations, and the texts of such thinkers as Emmerich de Vattel.

Thaddeus Stevens, abolitionist congressman from Pennsylvania, was among the earliest to stake out this turf, doing so during debates over the First Confiscation Act in August 1861. He conceded that the Constitution protected property and did not allow for the liberation of the enslaved. He argued, however, that the time had come for the laws of war to rule, "when constitutions, if they stood in the way of the laws of war in dealing with the enemy, had no right to intervene." According to Stevens, constitutional protections were being invoked by the very people who intended to destroy it, as well as their sympathizers who remained in the Union. When challenged by the opposition, Stevens drew upon antiquity to suggest he was doing nothing more than following the precedents of thousands of years. He told his colleagues that the notion that war changed the usual legal life of a nation dated to Cicero, who had proclaimed "inter arma silent leges" (in wartime, the law falls silent).[52]

As for abolition, Stevens reached for a nearer precedent. He introduced the passage from Vattel that dealt with a "just war" and that became adopted as the mantra of antislavery congressmen in the months ahead. According to Stevens, the law of nations recognized the right of a "sovereign power" to use every means it could against an enemy. For the United States, Stevens claimed, that sovereign power resided with the Congress, which had the responsibility to declare war and not the president. He paraphrased a section from *The Law of Nations* that allowed for a sovereign who had conquered an enemy that had oppressed other people to liberate the downtrodden when rescued. The context of the passage was a little different from how Stevens presented it: Vattel spoke about a people conquered by an oppressor who subsequently was conquered. Slaves were not mentioned specifically, but one could interpret their presence nonetheless. The passage added a powerful argument that echoed in the halls of Congress for months. Depending on one's translation, it read that "we should certainly make use of our victory so as not merely to change its ruler, but to break its chains. It is a noble fruit of victory to deliver an oppressed people; and it is a great gain thus to win a faithful friend."[53]

In January, Radical Republican congressman George Julian of Indiana picked up the international banner in a speech to the Congress that was reprinted in abolition newspapers. Julian noticed that he had left behind the former abolition argument that stressed morality. Strikingly, he added in language that sounded like a future Lincoln: "I waive none of my humanitarian grounds of opposition to slavery, but I prefer to deal with the practical issues of the crisis. I am for putting down slavery as a 'military necessity.'" For the definition of military necessity, he turned to international custom. He stated that "the common laws which govern a war between nations apply to the conduct of a civil war." And for his authority, he cited Vattel, who proclaimed that a nation involved in a "just war" should use any measure necessary to weaken the enemy, provided the actions did not exceed the boundaries of morality.[54]

That Julian defined the conflict as a civil war was new. Previously, emancipationists had characterized the conflict as an insurrection or a rebellion. This had been a common interpretation among more radical people who operated from the mistaken impression that the position allowed for the maximum flexibility in punishing the traitors. But it would not, because of the constitutional restrictions that set high standards for proving treason and because of the impracticality of prosecuting it. Vattel had solved this problem more than a century before, offering men like Julian the possibility of having their cake and eating it, too. He had defined a civil war as occurring when a republic divides into opposite factions and both sides take up arms. "Civil War," he added in a statement widely quoted by Republicans in the Congress, "breaks the bonds of society and of government . . . ; it gives rise, within the Nation, to two independent parties, who regard each other as enemies and acknowledge no common judge." Unlike what one might expect from such a statement, Vattel argued for following the rules of war in order to preserve humanity and prevent a downward spiral into barbarism. "If the sovereign believes himself justified in hanging the prisoners as rebels, the opposite party will retaliate," he noted, adding later, "if he burns and lays waste to the country they will do the same; and the war will become cruel, terrible, and daily more disastrous to the Nation."[55]

The utility of Vattel's reasoning followed a paragraph later when he suggested that rebels in a civil war never relinquished their identity as citizens deserving punishment. And he espoused an idea that became popular among the northern men and women who wished to punish the rebels: the notion that leaders of rebellions deserved death while the masses could go free. "When the sovereign has conquered the party in arms against him, when he has brought them to submit and to sue for peace, he may except from the amnesty the authors of the disturbance, the leaders of the party, and may judge them according to the laws, and punish them if they are found guilty."[56] This interpretation was prevalent among supporters of the administration, who obviously overlooked that there was a U.S. Constitution that had been put into place between their time and that of Vattel. But in this view it was not the case that the rebels had dual identities. They were traitor-citizens, but the exigencies of war meant that it was better to deal with treasonous citizens when reunion came, not in wartime. This is why Julian felt quite comfortable telling the members of the House: "The friends of the Union need ask nothing more than the just application of the law of nations, and they certainly should be content with nothing less."[57]

One concern gave Republicans pause: how to integrate international law with the Constitution. Stevens's pronouncement about the law of nations superseding the fundamental law of the United States had few supporters. The position gave Democrats too big of a target. When Stevens was accused of declaring confiscation unconstitutional and that the war justified suspending normal municipal law in favor of the law of nations, he merely hemmed, "I say that it is constitutional and according to the law of nations in time of war," which provoked laughter in the chambers. The logic was not convincing just because Stevens said it was so.[58] Over the course of debating confiscation, Republicans modified their stance about the supremacy of the law of nations in these affairs and attempted to merge foreign with municipal law, trying to show how the two interrelated.

Further discussion over several months produced sounder reasoning that fused foreign and domestic law. By February 1862, Republican congressman Samuel Shellabarger of Ohio incorporated how jurists before the war, such as Justice Joseph Story, used international principles in defining presidential powers in wartime: "He cannot lawfully transcend the rules of war as established among civilized nations," Shellabarger quoted from the jurist, adding that the "modern usages of war are resorted to merely as a limitation to this discretion of the President." He and others were also fond of quoting from John Quincy Adams's statements to Congress in 1836, which constituted one of the few serious discussions of the war powers of the president prior to the Civil War. Adams was trying to provoke his southern colleagues by proclaiming that the president had the power to destroy slavery in times of national emergency—a situation that would occur if the United States annexed Texas. Adams said that two classes of power existed: the war power and the peace power. Adams suggested that the Constitution prescribed the limitations of the peace power, but he added the "war power is limited only by the laws and usages of nations," which meant international precedents. Nonetheless, he added that this war power was constitutional even though it broke down barriers erected "for the protection of liberty, of property, and of life." This caused Shellabarger to assert: "I conclude, therefore, that the law of nations is so incorporated into and so become part of the constitution law as to have become rules, limitations, and guides, controlling every department of the Government of the United States."[59]

Plus, they had the *Prize Cases*. Although the decision on the four cases awaited another year, the members had access to one of the important rulings in the lower court. In February 1862, Judge Peleg Sprague of the Boston District Court issued his opinion in the *Amy Warwick* case, one of the four decisions moving forward to the Supreme Court. Republicans seized upon the decision almost immediately because they saw how it fit with Vattel's interpretations. California Republican Aaron Sargent quoted a fragment from Sprague that reinforced Vattel: "In war each belligerent may seize and confiscate all the property of the enemy, wherever found, and this right extends to the property of all persons resident in the enemy's country."[60] David Wilmot, former congressman now senator from Pennsylvania famous for his controversial proviso during the Mexican War, adopted one of the more expansive uses of Sprague's ruling and Vattel. He characterized the Confederates in this way. "They are at the same time belligerents and traitors, and subject to the liabilities of both." Wilmot also drew on Wheaton's *Elements of International Law* to affirm that nations should maintain belligerent rights in a civil war, presumably to prevent atrocities.[61]

For the more radical Republicans, the conflict had left behind its origins and had become a civil war. Confederate rebels were public enemies, subject to the *international* rules of war making, which gave to the president the "sovereign power" to do most anything against enemies, within the dictates of morality. Confederates had not ceased being citizens and could face prosecution for treason after they were conquered—an interpretation supported by international authorities such as Vattel. They decided that this was also sanctioned in the Constitution, giving the credit to John Quincy Adams for saying that the war power is limited only by the law of nations. And they recognized the use of international law in Supreme Court decisions. The reasoning echoed in many places, but it could be heard in the rationale of Richard Henry Dana, who indicated that the *Prize Cases* affirmed the enemy as belligerents de facto, but not de jure.

The Democratic opposition noticed that emancipationists had adopted a new definition for the conflict and now eagerly embraced the term "civil war." And the Democrats could not resist a jab at their rivals. In June, Samuel S. Cox, a Democrat from Ohio, chided his antislavery colleagues for changing their tune. Many in the chambers had rejected Cox's desire in prior debate to call the conflict a civil war because it was understood as a strategy by more conservative men to assert a limited conflict with rules that shielded individual property from military confiscation. Cox now retorted: "Members who a year ago claimed that this rebellion was not a civil war, are now quick to find out that it is so," he said, adding, "when it will answer the purposes of vengeance and emancipation."[62]

The conservative critique first and foremost stressed the sovereignty of the Constitution. Charles A. Wickliffe of Kentucky was typical in asserting that the document was made to handle both peace and war and that its provisions were neither enlarged nor restricted by a state of war. He rejected Cicero's observation that in war laws are silent.[63] Additionally, Wickliffe and his colleagues detested the provisions allowing for the confiscation of slaves, not only because of racism but also because they were unhappy with the mechanism. Supporters of emancipation had borrowed from admiralty courts by allowing for *in rem* proceedings commonly used to confiscate ships. This meant that owners did not have to be present in court, which ruled on whether to seize and condemn property without hearing a defense from the owners. To anti-emancipationists, this smacked of ignoring due process. They also believed—quite rightly, in fact—that the treason sections of the bill offered an unconstitutional punishment. Confiscation of property hurt more than the individual owner by affecting family members and heirs, which was forbidden by the Constitution.

Just as Republicans backtracked to include the Constitution in their arguments, the Democrats scurried to Vattel and the law of nations to find passages that suited their position. They did so to prove that, even if one used international law, Vattel provided strong arguments for treating the enemy with clemency, which included respect for private property. Senator James McDougall of California cited passages from Vattel that indicated that conquerors could take public property but should respect that of individuals. Additionally, McDougall and his colleagues were fond of quoting from *The Law of Nations* about what happened when a sovereign took over the territory of the enemy. A conqueror acquired with a town or province all the rights of the disposed sovereign, with its limitations and modifications. Care should be taken to protect the liberties, privileges, and immunities of the conquered individuals within such a territory.[64] In sum, they tried to turn the law of nations against the emancipationists by asserting the limited and merciful treatment of the enemy and property.

The resulting bill was a mess: contradictory in intentions and confusing in form and process. The act featured both the disagreements of the moment and the consensus of the future when considering the definition of the rebels and how to treat their property. The first sections on treason reflected the desire of Democrats and moderate Republicans to keep the Constitution as supreme and to use its provisions for limited, restricted punishment to ease reunion and reconciliation. The language of the first segments of the act thwarted radical efforts by defining the rebels as citizens more than enemies. Republican supporters of emancipation, however, agreed strongly that the rebels remained citizens subject to future prosecution, but they had to be considered as belligerent enemies to maintain humanitarian forms of warfare and to allow for the confiscation of property. The final sections of the act allowed for seizure of slave property, based on judging the rebels as traitors, without, of course, due process of the law.

The importance of international law to the bill—and how much it irritated Democrats—becomes clear in a case argued before the Court of Appeals in Kentucky nearly a year after the Second Confiscation Act took effect. In *Norris v. Doniphan*, a resident of Missouri who supported secession had moved to Arkansas. A loyal man in Kentucky owed her $5,000. Courts used the Second Confiscation Act to deny her claim on the loan. Remarkably, the Confederate woman (a traitor) sued in a Union court to reclaim the money. Perhaps one reason that Rebecca Doniphan believed she had a chance at all was that the judge rendering the opinion was Joshua Bullitt of Louisville, a leading Democrat who would face arrest in 1864 on charges of disloyalty. The most important result of the case was not the findings, which had little impact, except for the bully pulpit it offered to a Democratic judge who hated the Confiscation Act.[65]

Bullitt considered the act unconstitutional, and one of the reasons he attacked it concerned its use of the law of nations. In line with the conservative position, he disagreed that international law applied. The law of nations may guide behavior in the absence of clear law, but such was not the case in this instance. The Constitution, to him, functioned well enough. Sounding like some modern legal scholars, he proclaimed that it was adequate. Like Democratic opponents in Congress, he saw an issue with having two authorities dictating the treatment of the rebels. He wrote that "the law of nations and the constitution of the United States are, in many respects, inconsistent with each other. Their co-existence and co-operation are, therefore, in many respects impossible, and would produce irreconcilable conflicts between different departments of the government." He added: "We do not perceive how that conflict can be avoided, except by holding that the constitution, alone, governs the relations between the parties to this contest." The judge stated that one cannot treat the Confederates as both alien enemies and as rebellious subjects.[66] The law of nations, he added, existed to handle foreign relations, and the seizing of contraband dealt with prizes captured at sea, not land. Taking the property of rebels without due process violated the Fifth Amendment to the Constitution. He turned the act aside, which had no bearing on the playing out of practical policy.

Even though opposition by Democrats arguably posed great challenges in the next two years, a consensus emerged over the treatment of rebel property, helped by the Supreme Court. In 1864 the Supreme Court heard a case with the quaint sounding title of *Mrs. Alexander's Cotton*. Troops under Union general Nathaniel Banks had seized seventy-two bales of her cotton during the Red River campaign in Louisiana. She filed a claim for reimbursement, which was denied. Her attorneys argued that she had taken an oath of loyalty and that Lincoln's Proclamation of Amnesty and Reconstruction (December 1863) had, in effect, pardoned her. The court ruled against her, using the Second Confiscation Act as one of the reasons. Chief Justice Salmon P. Chase ruled that there was no such thing as friends in a region judged to be in rebellion against the United States. He wrote "that all the people of each State or district in insurrection against the United States, must be regarded as enemies, until by the action of the legislature and the executive, or otherwise, that relation is thoroughly and permanently changed."[67] There was no such thing anymore as an involuntary rebel. As long as a state was considered in insurrection, the residents were treated by the courts as enemies whose property was vulnerable to the military.

Taken at face value, a decision like this from the Supreme Court challenged the pardon power of the president, a fact that no one seemed to notice at the time. In his Proclamation of Amnesty and Reconstruction in December 1863, the president had established a procedure for reunion of the sections. Known as the 10 percent plan, the policy allowed for a state to come back into the fold when 10 percent of its eligible voters from the 1860 election took an oath of loyalty. Chase's ruling did not recognize the bargain that Lincoln had struck with Confederates who took the oath. Constitutional niceties often took a back seat to practical matters, and Lincoln did not complain when policy served the needs of reunion.

So much for the traitors who behaved like foreign enemies; the Congress also dealt with citizens within the Union who threatened to disrupt mobilization, encourage desertion, or speak out against the government. In March 1863, legislators confirmed Lincoln's powers to suspend the writ of habeas corpus. That the president used this means to allow for political arrests and military commissions has been well known. Less represented by historians is how the act addressed a concern of the administration raised early in the conflict by Attorney General Bates: the tendency of people to fight back by attacking not the president or his powers but the marshals and other public officials on the front lines of implementing these policies. To protect against cases of false arrest, the fifth section of the

Habeas Corpus Act allowed for the parties in such action to file a petition to transfer the case to the Federal Circuit Court, where it was presumed that a ruling would be more favorable to the Lincoln administration.[68]

It would be hard to find a greater example of having one's cake and eating it, too. The act allowed for either party to petition to transfer the case *after* a ruling had been issued. And when the case arrived before the circuit court, judges there could treat the case as one of original jurisdiction, meaning not as an appeal but as an entirely new case. Practically speaking, the new law allowed for the administration to accept the ruling of a friendly lower court, or to hand over the case to a federal judge who would start the procedure over again as if nothing had happened.[69]

A case that displayed the challenges of filing charges of false arrest after the Habeas Corpus Act involved Governor David Tod of Ohio. The case began in Fairfield County, where a grand jury returned a true bill for the arrest of the governor. The action was initiated by Edson B. Olds, a Democratic politician and outspoken critic of the Lincoln administration. In early August 1862, orders from the War Department led to his arrest. Authorities took him to Fort Lafayette in New York, where he was held without charges for roughly four months. In the spring of 1863, Olds filed a civil suit against the governor and the arresting federal officer for $100,000 in damages. Tod was arrested, but he quickly sought refuge with the Supreme Court of Ohio. Under the provisions of the Habeas Corpus Act, he tried to transfer the case to the federal circuit court at Cincinnati. The court of common pleas in Fairfield County at first refused, challenging the constitutionality of the law. It took until December 1864 to effect the transfer, when the State Supreme Court issued a writ of mandamus. The transfer to the circuit court effectively made the case go away without heading to trial.[70]

Although it is true, as historian Jonathan W. White has observed, that the law failed to head off such suits, it was interesting to see the strong statements made by the State Supreme Court that upheld the constitutionality of the law. The Constitution, the state court observed, vested Congress with "plenary" war powers, without any limit on time, means, or manner for prosecuting a conflict or suppressing a rebellion. The president carried out the measures enacted by the legislature: "There is no limitation placed upon this grant of the power to carry on war, except those contained in the *laws of war*; and these powers, in their final execution, are all placed in the hands of the president." They added: "In time of war, a military commander, whether he be the commander-in-chief, or one of his subordinates, must possess and exercise powers both over the persons and the property of citizens which do not exist in time of peace."[71] Lincoln could not have said it better.

Executive Echoes

Two years into the conflict, after countless thousands of soldiers had died in battles and skirmishes, the United States announced the rules by which it conducted the fighting. These regulations took the form of a document bearing the nondescript title of General Orders No. 100, instructions for the government of the armies of the United States in the field, which was compiled by a professor at Columbia College. Francis Lieber was a German émigré, a classical liberal forced by political persecution from his native country. In his adoptive land, he had forged impressive connections: personally corresponding with Senator Charles Sumner, General-in-Chief Henry W. Halleck, and Attorney General Edward Bates. Out of frustration with guerrilla fighting and other unprecedented issues facing the nation, Halleck—certainly no amateur when it came to the international laws of war—had consigned his professor acquaintance to serve on a commission that would solve the problems facing U.S. soldiers in a domestic war—a war in which various definitions existed about the foe. Lieber happily obliged. In fact, he had lobbied his friends in the War Department for this opportunity. Although there were other men on this four-person commission, the German liberal wrote most of the text that resonated internationally by becoming the basis for the Hague Resolutions later in the century.[72]

But there is a puzzling side to this document that has gone largely unnoticed by historians and legal scholars. Why was it allowed to be created and adopted? One could argue that the process by which Lieber's code of war came into being contradicted constitutional principles and the established practices of the United States. The Constitution states that the power to declare war and, even more pertinently, to "make rules for the government and regulation of the land and naval forces" belongs with the Congress. When the nation created the Articles of War in 1806, it did so through *congressional* legislation, not executive fiat. With General Orders No. 100, the executive branch took a bolder step than many have realized, by assuming the right to determine the parameters of war making, especially the meaning of "military necessity," without these policies originating with Congress. As the compilation of military law and usages made its way through the bureaucracy, Lieber understood that at least a few paragraphs might benefit from "the assistance of Congress," but added that it "is now too late."[73] Even though he did not see the code until it neared completion, the president obviously found the document compatible with his views, especially his understanding of military necessity and how this interpretation supported his stance on emancipation. Lincoln signed off on the instructions, allowing the War Department to put them into place in April 1863. And the military went on about its business.[74]

Recent studies, however, have resurrected the boldness behind the code. Much of the emphasis had been on the benign, limited aspects of General Orders No. 100, but in truth the wording allowed for both restraint and fairly free interpretation of what kind of force to bring to bear on enemy soldiers and civilians. Numerous provisions of the code prohibited immoral or unjust actions, such as poor treatment of prisoners, torture, taking booty from slain enemies, or wanton destruction of civilian property. The key distinction, as John Fabian Witt has observed, came in condoning violence necessary to pursue a public war versus private violence for vengeance. Yet other sections gave the executive and his generals broad powers. The instructions allowed for the bombardment of civilians without warning if required; for herding civilians fleeing a siege back into towns so their suffering could force surrender more quickly; and for taking most of the property from an enemy based on military necessity. In fact, the instructions sounded remarkably consistent with the actions of a certain general named Sherman, who a year later argued that mercy in war meant punishing people hard enough so they capitulated. Once again, Witt has captured the dual nature of the code well in characterizing the treatment of civilians as a "mix of moral limits and unforgiving war" and military necessity as both a limit on war's violence and a "robust license to destroy."[75]

Perhaps nothing signified a new form of state power better than the portions of the code that supplied a rationale for the military's freeing of slaves. Lieber's commitment to emancipation—and to endorsing the president's power to free slaves as a military necessity—came through clearly in sections 42 and 43. The professor had not always been so inclined toward antislavery. Although saying throughout his life that he detested slavery, he owned a couple of slaves while living in South Carolina. As the war neared, his abolition sentiment grew. By midway into the war, he was an outright Radical. Not surprisingly, Lieber's instructions to the army supported the president's Emancipation Proclamation.

And here—as with federal court rulings, congressional interpretations, and abolition opinions on the matter—Lieber employed international precedents. "Slavery, complicating and confounding the ideas of property (that is, of a thing), and of personality (that is, of humanity), exists according to municipal or local law only." He added perfunctorily: "The law of nature and nations has never acknowledged it." He quoted from Roman law indicating that "'so far as the law of nature is concerned, all men are equal.'" And he cited the practice to recognize fugitives fleeing bondage or coerced labor from another country to be acknowledged as free in a different nation that did not recognize slavery. This reasoning had a legal basis in English law. In 1772, a British judge ruled in favor of freedom for a fugitive slave. James Somerset had been purchased by an Englishman and taken to England. Somerset escaped and was then captured, but abolition sympathizers pushed for his release through a court ruling. The justice obliged, establishing the principle that slaves taken to England, whose laws did not sanction slavery, could not be removed and sold by force. Lieber reminded military officers not to return fugitive slaves but to consider them as free people, adding that "a person so made free by the law of war is under the shield of the law of nations." Once again, abolition had sought precedents beyond national borders to rationalize freedom.[76]

This does not mean that Lieber adopted transatlantic ideals wholesale. He was an eclectic thinker by nature and borrowed from various sources, including the concept of military necessity expressed in Lincoln's proclamation.[77] Exactly which pieces of the document came from international law versus municipal or other sources is difficult to pin down because Lieber provided no authorities for his statements. International law, however, left heavy footprints on more of the document than the sections dealing with slavery. This was not new for Lieber. Decades before the war, in 1838, he had published *Manual of Political Ethics*. One of the chapters presented a treatise on war that provided important background on the laws of war and nations for his code of 1863. In this work he demonstrated a competent grounding in material from Wheaton, Vattel, Grotius, Bynkershoek, and even Cicero—the usual suspects in congressional debates on confiscation.[78] As early as August 1861, he went on record in a public letter to Attorney General Bates concerning why the government could treat Confederates as belligerents without recognizing their nationhood. He had seized upon the rationale that became commonplace in the administration—and that owed itself to international precedents—that humanitarian reasons dictated exchanging prisoners and operating under the rules of war. Following these procedures merely recognized reality.[79]

He also did not adopt prior works uncritically. He sniffed at the efforts of some of his predecessors, feeling that they had watered down the laws and usages of war. Most notably, he lampooned Vattel. "It makes me impatient to find old Vattel so often quoted," he told Halleck. That he made the comment at all underscores the influence of *The Law of Nations*. But, Lieber added, "He ought to be called Father Namby pamby," suggesting that Lieber adhered to a harder brand of warfare.[80] Perhaps the most significant element of Lieber's treatise that betrays the lack of attention to U.S. law comes down to this observation: there is no specific reference to the U.S. Constitution in General Orders No. 100. None of the powers granted to sovereigns or to the military in time of war was connected by him specifically to the fundamental law of the United States.

Reactions to these new instructions were predictable, with Republicans mostly supportive and administration opponents either ambivalent or hostile. The *New York Herald* digested the instructions for a day and then came out with a mixed review. It found some of the policy commendable, such as protection for noncombatants and restraint in seizing property. Predictably, though, the writer excoriated the provisions that freed slaves. And equally predictably, the conservative newspaper rejected the use of international law as a basis for determining freedom. The writer stated flatly that "the inhabitants of the Southern States are not alien enemies, but citizens of the United States in insurrection, and consequently the alleged law of nations does not apply." The *Herald* maintained that the Confederates had not left the Union but remained under the laws of the United States. Meanwhile, Confederate secretary of war James Seddon and President Jefferson Davis found nothing to praise in the instructions, pointing out how the definition of "military necessity" opened the door to barbarism. Seddon said the order was "the handicraft of one much more familiar with the decrees of the imperial despotisms of the continent of Europe than with Magna Charta, the Petition of Rights, the Bill of Rights, the Declaration of Independence, and the Constitution of the United States."[81]

Lieber was not the only influential thinker whose writings had a bearing on what could be done to a traitor-enemy. He was an external consultant to the administration. Within the War Department, another person worked at the task of defining aspects of fighting the war, especially the war powers of the president. Until recently, William Whiting had lurked in the shadows of the published histories of the Civil War. An attorney and future congressman from Massachusetts, Whiting served as the solicitor of the War Department. The job placed him in the midst of interpreting for public officials and the military how policy should play itself out on the ground. Whenever he issued interpretations of the conscription act or laid out the powers of the provost marshal, communities throughout the

Union paid attention and published his opinions.[82] Democrats detested him. On the other hand, Radical Republicans like Sumner considered him a friend and an "admirable lawyer *in the full confidence of the Presdt*" who was intimately involved with government policy. Secretary of the Navy Gideon Welles was less enchanted with the man, whom he characterized as conceited and inclined to intrigues. However, he also acknowledged Whiting's connections and influence. In July 1863 he remarked, "This Solicitor Whiting has for several months been an important personage here." He added, "My admiration is not as exalted as it should be."[83]

Whiting became a propagandist for the administration by issuing a tract that began as *The War Powers of the President and the Legislative Powers of Congress in Relation to Rebellion, Treason and Slavery*. He started dabbling with producing a pamphlet in the spring of 1862. Printed at first in Boston, it became adopted by the Union League of Philadelphia. The effort grew to enjoy a life of its own. Over the course of the war and Reconstruction, the original 143 pages ballooned to 695 pages when it reached its forty-third edition in 1871. It enjoyed wide distribution.[84] In March 1863 a newspaper indicated that the Union League of Philadelphia intended to print 30,000 copies. A month later the organization reportedly organized a second printing of 80,000 copies in newspaper form for circulation via mail. Even if these numbers are exaggerated, more modest estimates still make this a work of considerable attention. The report added that "true supporters of the government will rejoice to find so many of his boldest opinions sustained by the Supreme Court of the United States, in the prize cases recently decided at Washington."[85]

By 1864, *War Powers* had gone through ten editions as it made the case for expansive presidential war powers based on the Constitution, international law, court interpretations, and common sense.[86] The volume captured the consensus emerging among the majority in all three branches of government: to consider the rebels as belligerents but also as citizens whose treason could be prosecuted later; to give the president and the military broad discretion to seize property; to use international law in conjunction with the Constitution, but lean toward precedents outside of the United States to sanction freedom for the enslaved in the Confederacy; and to use the procedures and decisions of admiralty courts to guide the confiscation of property on land. One of the most compelling quotations from the work—and one that was part of the early editions—is downright irresistible, although potentially dangerous in how it condoned using whatever means available against an enemy no matter what a constitution says. Whiting said the United States was making war on the rebels; it was not waging law. "If the only way of dealing constitutionally with rebels in arms is to go to law with them, the President should convert his army into lawyers, justices of the peace, and constables, and serve 'summonses to appear and answer to complaints,' instead of a summons to surrender."[87]

Whiting interweaved the law of nations with the Constitution. He seemed perfectly at home with Thaddeus Stevens when issuing the incredibly bold statement "The Law of Nations is Above the Constitution," adding, "no people would be justified by its peculiar constitution in violating the rights of other nations."[88] However, he invariably drifted back to domestic law, claiming for instance that the Constitution allowed for confiscation of enemy property. Although he used a little bit of Vattel to support this contention, he borrowed heavily from U.S. case law and opinions of important justices, such as John Marshall in *Brown v. United States* from the War of 1812. In sum he said, "The army of the Union, therefore, have the right, according to the law of nations, and of the constitution, to obtain by capture a legal title to all the personal property of the enemy they get possession of, whether it consist of arms, ammunition, provisions, slaves, or any other thing which the law treats as personal property." In direct opposition to Democrat claims that confiscation denied due process, he flatly stated that no judicial process was necessary. And he provided not one whit of proof beyond his opinion.[89]

But when it came to freeing the enslaved, Whiting spent most of his time focused abroad. In answering the question of whether slaves could be liberated, he maintained "we must appeal to the law of nations" because "the constitution, having given authority to government to make war has placed no limits whatever to the war powers." The practice of nations set these boundaries. He then conducted a survey of the Atlantic world, dealing first with the British emancipation of U.S. slaves in the American Revolution and then again in the War of 1812. His examination included the Haitian Revolution, where he claimed that France had recognized the right, under martial law, to emancipate the slaves of an enemy. He even included Spain. He quoted from John Quincy Adams's speech on the war powers that slavery was abolished in Colombia first by a Spanish general. "'It was abolished by the laws of war, and not by the municipal enactments.'"[90]

So where does Lincoln fit in this story?

It is most convincing to consider him as someone prone to the practical and not inclined toward the abstract. One scholar has made the case that the president did not share the same views as Whiting on the logic behind the constitutionality of emancipation.[91] Lincoln looked for the means to end the war. He had at his disposal an incredible array of opinions that bolstered an interpretation for sweeping war powers of the executive and that kept returning to the same authorities: international sources such as Vattel and Wheaton, and native opinion in the form of John Marshall in *Brown v. United States* and John Quincy Adams's speech on the war powers. Even if he had not been aware of these before the conflict, he received a primer as he entered the constitutional-international thicket of enforcing a blockade, helping fugitive slaves, and exchanging prisoners. By the time he composed his thoughts on emancipation, it had become well known that emancipationists employed international precedents in arguing for confiscation and the early rulings had come out on what became known as the *Prize Cases*. But it is doubtful that he consciously sought the international dimension to make his case.

Yet he did use international precedents—in a more nuanced fashion than most. When employed, the international dimension came across as wearing plenty of homespun. The Emancipation Proclamation provides a telling example. He started by declaring his authority, by virtue of the war power to handle a rebellion (implying the Constitution), to order emancipation as a war measure. When he defended this act in an open letter to James C. Conkling, he elaborated in a way that suggested the commingling of domestic and foreign law. He challenged those who considered the proclamation unconstitutional, insisting that the document invested a commander in chief "with the law of war, in time of war." Again, like the abolitionists, he had to take the unsettling position that the enslaved were property. Then he posed the question: "Is there—has there ever been—any question that by the law of war, property, both of enemies and friends, may be taken when needed?" He added, "Armies, the world over, destroy enemies' property when they can not use it; and even destroy their own to keep it from the enemy. Civilized belligerents do all in their power to help themselves, or hurt the enemy, except a few things regarded as barbarous or cruel."[92] One can hear echoes of Lieber, not as someone who informed the president, but perhaps as a fellow traveler.

Ideas, and even stated policy, are one thing; practice quite another. Washington might set certain principles and condone the use of military necessity in both its broadest and narrowest definitions. How this definition played out as the army, civilian authorities, enemies, and citizens collided with one another presented more complicated stories. And it is to the communities away from the seat of government that we now turn.

4

THE PROVOST MARSHAL
CONFUSION

They were the men who pounded on a door in the middle of the night to roust a traitor out of bed and into military prison. They disrupted worship services, removed judges from the bench during proceedings, seized mail, and closed newspaper offices. They shut down taverns, closed brothels, and restricted the travel of civilians by issuing passports. They issued countless oaths of loyalty to people who had little choice but to sign their pledge of fidelity to the nation or remain confined under military jurisdiction without a hearing in civil court. Eventually, they administered the draft and dodged bullets from angry civilians whom they tried to enroll. Some of them died in this service to the nation. They assumed, in the words of one historian, the roles "both of a chief of police and of a magistrate."[1] Yet they have rarely appeared as a subject worth studying, despite their essential role in defining loyalty in the Union. The agents making arrests have been taken for granted as extensions of executive will: as a cog in the centralization of government, without considering their own problems and their own initiatives in determining the limits of disloyalty. They have not been examined for who made the arrests, under what authority, and for what reasons.

A variety of agents—a mix of special civilian and military authorities patched together over the years—policed the Union home front during the Civil War. They constituted a "system" that took shape haphazardly to meet needs as they arose, rather than emerging as a thoughtful, coordinated plan to protect national security. As the years passed, the provost marshals, a form of military police, became increasingly important. But even after 1863, when the federal government empowered military officers to control the draft and arrest deserters in congressional districts throughout the Union—a phenomenon that exists in the literature of the war as the penetration of centralized government into the lives of individuals—state and local power remained in play and mitigated the reach of national agents in certain communities.[2] The prevailing view overlooks the fuller evolution of this so-called internal security system and the fact that local and state agents other than the federal military engaged in the battle against treason before 1863. The Union's internal security and mobilization systems consisted of federal, state, and local officials who sometimes pursued competing goals. The surprise comes in that this alliance served its purpose for administering the draft and, to an extent, for combating treason. But fulfilling the national objectives presented challenges for the agents charged with their enforcement, especially if they supervised districts containing residents hostile to their mission.

Consequently, the phrase "provost marshal confusion" represents a dual problem. One concerned the chaos that often confronted the agents fighting treason on the ground. They faced situations that, at times, demanded the Wisdom of Solomon in processing arrests when they did not have Solomon's advantage of confronting two claimants. They also operated in a climate of heightened tensions. For instance, military authorities policing the home fronts of Missouri and Kentucky lived in a world consisting of active guerrilla warfare that fortified the morale and clandestine activity of civilians sympathetic to the rebels. In such an environment, it was not always clear how to cipher the loyalty of a man or woman who had spoken out in favor of the Confederacy. But a second meaning behind the "provost marshal confusion" describes the problem of contemporary historians trying to sort out who the arresting agents were in the fight against treason in the United States. This is not always an easy task. Depending upon the region, three different provost officials may have operated: civilian (or "special") provosts, army provosts, and departmental provosts. Add in the occasional state, such as Missouri, whose government maintained its own militia and arresting authorities, and the situation added a fourth layer to internal security—civilian-directed agents without federal oversight.[3]

Considering the enforcement of treason at the grassroots level in the United States reveals how the Lincoln administration could earn the characterization of showing restraint nationally while seeming arbitrary locally. Arresting authorities at the local level could become petty dictators who established their own rules over a community, until they did something that drew the attention of Stanton or Lincoln. Most often, they did their jobs as well as can be expected under considerable duress. Sometimes, they did not. And they faced additional pressure from below—or from the war hawks in communities who prodded them to go even further in abusing the liberties of traitors. Attention to the men in the middle of the hunt for treason reveals that the story of civil liberties and patriotism in the North was not only a tale of Democrats decrying actions by a tyrannical administration but also one of anxious Unionists pressuring for more abusive power by the government as they rarely pondered whether the policies they advocated pushed the country toward a constitutional precipice.

Lurching toward a System

As the military entered one of the greatest tests in U.S. history, the specified duties of the provost marshal seemed paltry at best and certainly incapable of meeting the crisis. In the *Military Dictionary*, published in 1861, the description of the provost marshal consisted of one paragraph with six lines. It described a person who had military oversight solely. The provost marshal was a glorified jailor, who assumed responsibility over prisoners. He was an officer "intrusted with authority to inflict summary punishment on any soldier, follower, or retainer of the camp, whom he sees commit the act for which summary punishment may be inflicted."[4] Contrast this description with that of 1865, when the duties of the provost marshal required six paragraphs over three pages. *The 1865 Customs of Service* indicated that there was more than one kind of provosts. It specified two, but actually hinted of more. One was attached to the army and functioned like military police. He had a wide range of duties including caring for prisoners, but also supervising order on the home front with the power to regulate trade and handle complaints from civilians. The other provost marshals were created by the Conscription Act of 1863, establishing agents in every congressional district to enforce the draft and to capture deserters. These men were appointed from civil life by the provost marshal in charge of a state. The description closed by indicating that, while in the field, provost marshals were selected by line officers and varied in rank from lieutenants to generals. "They were attached to brigades, divisions, corps, and armies, and often local Provost Marshals for cities, towns, and districts were appointed, and even detachments, operating independently for a few days." In other words, appointments were not made centrally, and provost marshals could come and go, drafted from the ranks of civilians if need be.[5]

Truthfully, though, the actual picture was even more complicated because of the way in which the country met the challenges of monitoring disloyalty. In the beginning of the conflict, the government used every resource it could find for this effort. The State Department employed civilian detectives. Additionally, U.S. Attorneys directed federal marshals to hold civilians. But these actions were not confined to the federal level. Despite the national government's attempts to clarify chains of command, grassroots policing of treason often determined the nature and pattern of arrests. Local police, constables, magistrates, and mayors performed this function and did not necessarily coordinate their decisions with Washington. Early in the war, states such as Maryland and Pennsylvania enacted new laws to combat treason and used their own personnel, rather than federal, to handle domestic enemies. These provisional measures often remained in place, even as the military apparatus evolved.[6]

The first provost marshals created by the U.S. Army were not intended to monitor civil liberties. Security of the army formed the paramount concern. After the Union loss at Bull Run, General George B. McClellan listed the responsibilities of Colonel Andrew Porter as prevention of straggling and suppression of gambling and drinking higher than political arrests. McClellan also cited as the priorities the monitoring of taverns, maintaining a passport system for travel, processing prisoners of war and deserters from the enemy, and investigating civilian complaints about the behavior of soldiers. One of the provost marshals at the lower levels of the army indicated to his wife as late as December 1862 that his first duty was to administer internal passports, but that he was also expected to arrest all drunken persons (whether soldiers or citizens), shut down grog shops, and attend to municipal duties generally.[7] This was hardly an effort designed to impose a military despotism on a civilian populace.

Although a military-first mentality undergirded this organization, it was only natural that civilians became affected. McClellan shared the concern among northerners about domestic traitors. By August 6, 1861, the general instructed Porter to use his men to conduct surveillance "on all persons in this city who are disposed inimically to the government." Under this charge, Porter screened the mails and employed State Department detectives to watch for suspicious persons. The next month McClellan cooperated with the orders to arrest members of the Maryland legislature, newspaper editors, and other public officials. There were rumors at the time that members of the legislature intended to pass a resolution for secession. McClellan served as a conduit for the orders, which were carried out by detective Allan Pinkerton in cooperation with local officials and the troops assigned to the area. There is no reason to doubt that this conservative officer considered such activity a valid use of his army. Ironically, this action by McClellan was revived by opponents to use against the general when he ran for president in 1864 as a means of undercutting Democratic complaints against the Lincoln administration for its heavy hand in civilian arrests.[8]

Quickly two kinds of provost marshals emerged: one that focused on behavior within the army and traveled with the troops as they fought; another that administered a fixed, geographic area, usually under the auspices of a military department. The first kind of official was referred to as the military or army provost; the second went by the various terms of civil provosts, local provost marshals, or special provost marshals. Both of these anticipated the creation of other provost marshals who would, via legislation of 1863, oversee the draft.

Concerning the military provosts, the senior official bore the title of provost marshal general of the army. These were men such as Porter and his more famous successor in the Army of the Potomac, Marsena Rudolph Patrick. Subordinate to them were provost marshals for the units composing the army: corps, divisions, and brigades. These men served two masters. Each provost marshal reported directly to the officer who led his particular command, such as the brigadier general. But he also reported to the provost marshal general of an army. It did not appear that the senior provost marshal reported to anyone in the War Department. In fact, Patrick refused to collaborate with Colonel Lafayette C. Baker, who became a special civilian provost marshal for the War Department and styled himself as heading a secret service. One student of Patrick's role in the army indicated that "his provost marshals remained independent of direction from Washington to the end."[9]

The military provost marshals focused on maintaining the moral behavior and fighting ability of the troops in camp and under fire. Unlike local provosts, military provost marshals found their jurisdiction constantly changing as they accompanied the army. Major General Irvin McDowell was among the first generals to concern himself with establishing this mobile supervision of his soldiers. In 1861, as his troops advanced from Washington toward Manassas, the general grew alarmed at the lack of discipline and looting reported among his men. He ordered that one officer and ten men from each regiment should act as a police force. These men watched over prisoners, guarded against stragglers, and protected roads, railroad depots, and telegraph lines.[10] They also, as Patrick did, might oversee the "moral health" of their charges beyond the usual police duties. In this regard, Patrick burned books that he considered obscene that had come into camp through the mail. Finally, there was an additional responsibility that set these men apart from the departmental or local provosts: they had a particularly tough duty during combat. The army provost assumed the necessary evil of organizing the guard that used their weapons to prod the men who ran from fighting to go back into line.[11]

The other kind of provost marshal established a longer-term posture in communities and functioned like a military governor, although he walked a fine line between imposing army discipline and respecting civil law. The men were appointed by someone within the military—army commander, department commander, or provost marshal general of the army—rather than from Washington. Or they could emerge from localities, such as citizens performing police duties in communities. One historian referred to these men as "rear echelon" provost marshals to differentiate them from those on the front line.[12] At least two terms were used at first to refer to this military agent: "civil provost marshal" or "local" provost. In Baltimore, it was common to see the term "civil provost" employed as a means to set this person apart from his military cousin.[13]

Early in the war, the civil marshals became the instruments for the civilian arrests that took place in politically charged cities. Wherever they presided—whether in Baltimore, St. Louis, or points in between—these agents set the day-by-day boundaries of citizens' liberty by authorizing commerce and trade, issuing passports for individual travel, restricting mail, supervising prisoners, and administering oaths of loyalty. They also cleaned up after the army by processing the prisoners from the battlefield or citizens who came within an army's scope.

Although the distinction between military and civil provosts sounds clear on paper, the coordination of these agents was much more complicated in the field. They often acted together or overlapped in duties. But another reason lay with the way the army organized its administrative control over various portions of the United States. The military divided the country into geographic regions called departments, with a general officer in charge of the headquarters, forts, camps, depots, and so on within a particular area. Departments formed the overall geographic administrative unit, which were further subdivided into districts and subdistricts, each with an officer in charge and each with its own provost marshals.[14]

The coordination among the different levels of provost marshals within geographic commands was far from perfect. Especially in the western theater, the local provost marshals began to exercise an independent power that raised complaints from army commanders in Missouri and Arkansas.[15] Major General Samuel R. Curtis, for instance, called the provost marshal "a spurious military officer which has embarrassed the service by including an extra wheel in a well-regulated machine." He added: "Everybody appoints provost-marshals and those officers seem to exercise plenary powers." What sparked such a reaction? Provost marshal generals, not the commander of the department, were appointing the subordinate provosts. This created a situation in which the men bypassed the commander in charge of a district in favor of reporting directly to the provost marshal general of the department, the larger administrative unit.[16]

Brigadier General John M. Schofield shared the concerns of his colleague and recommended that district commanders—his position—should appoint provost marshals instead of having these appointments dropped into their laps from above. The appointment system, he said, caused the provosts to act independently of their commanders, who inherited the complaints about military justice without being involved in decisions to arrest individuals. Schofield claimed he had little control over these arrests and complained to his departmental headquarters: "The officer commanding a district who is responsible to the general commanding the department for the condition of his district has nothing whatever to do with the disposition of prisoners captured by his troops, although at the present time in Missouri this is the most important question involving its future peace."[17]

Schofield raised valid concerns. There were more people involved in rounding up suspects than provost marshals. Zealous defenders of the country in the form of constables, mayors, police, State and War Department detectives, and citizen informants—many of them anxious over the possible dissolution of the country—did not create an environment that encouraged careful paperwork. And in Missouri, the problems were exacerbated by a state militia that answered to the provisional government and that had its own authorities making arrests in the name of the military, which was not the national force. The use of local police guaranteed that excesses occurred, especially in areas where local scores remained to be settled. As late as February 1863, Major General Horatio Wright warned provost marshals to use prudence whenever arresting citizens. "Old feuds, more recent dislikes," he said, "have an influence in controlling the judgments of the most loyal, and experience has shown that individuals entirely innocent of any disloyal designs may be arrested and imprisoned upon the evidence of the over-zealous patriot or of the designing enemy." He cautioned the provost marshals in eastern Kentucky to avoid conducting arrests based on hearsay, which indicated that such had been the practice.[18]

Military commanders tried to curtail excessive arrests, but with mixed success through 1862. Time and again commanders of departments and armies complained to officers within their jurisdiction to exercise vigilance against treason but to make arrests only when clear violations existed. Too often citizens arrived at holding areas without basic information such as the nature of the charges. Additionally, local officers acted too readily on the accusations of citizens, many of whom were not concerned with conveying accurate information. Supervising Baltimore and the eastern part of Maryland, Major General John E. Wool was one of many administrators who tried to curb these tendencies. In August 1862, he issued strict orders that persons arrested for disloyalty or treasonable practices "are to be submitted in writing and to be attested under oath by the person preferring them; and no such prisoner will be received for confinement by any provost-marshal, marshal of police or commandant of post unless accompanied by the charges above described."[19] The problem persisted. When Lieutenant Colonel Franklin Archibald Dick, provost marshal general at Saint Louis, tried to assemble a roster of civilian prisoners in February 1863, he found only one book that listed inmates' time of capture, the county, and place imprisoned. But even that testament to conscientious records-keeping in a civil war did not reveal the charges that caused the arrests. Dick had to assemble a military commission to sort things out.[20]

To state the obvious: the United States' internal security system required some fine-tuning.

Rehearsals and Final Roles

Provost marshals as a police force for the home front took an important step in the summer of 1862. Historians generally date the origins of the provost marshal general's office to the conscription legislation of March 1863, but this overlooks a first, unsuccessful effort to form this bureaucracy. After the reverses on the Peninsula of Virginia by the Army of the Potomac in the Seven Days' Campaign, the administration increased efforts to gain recruits for the army. It canceled furloughs and tried to bring officers back to the army. The government threatened a national draft if volunteer quotas from individual states went unmet. Not surprisingly, the number of deserters from the army earned more attention as public officials feared that residents actively discouraged enlistments. It is hard to pin down precisely, but it is more likely that the inefficiencies in the domestic security system played a greater role than subversion by civilians in allowing deserters to roam the home front. Efforts to find and punish wayward soldiers were notoriously poor and relied almost exclusively on the voluntary efforts of civilians in communities. In this regard, the government had undercut itself in September 1861 by slashing the reward for apprehending deserters from thirty dollars to five, lessening the financial incentive to turn in one's neighbor.[21]

Officials realized that they needed a force dedicated to rounding up deserters and investigating whether disloyal citizens sabotaged the recruitment drives. Secretary of War Stanton decided first to appoint a special commissioner to collaborate with state governors on the problems of mobilization. On July 31, 1862, he appointed Simeon Draper, a Republican merchant from New York, to this position. It took only a short time to discover that there was not enough muscle behind the new arrangement. The commissioner depended on the cooperation of state officials and used whatever police he scrounged from the home front. Stanton stepped up the pressure: on August 8 he empowered U.S. marshals and superintendents of police in any town, city, or district to imprison persons "who may be engaged by act or speech or writing in discouraging volunteer enlistments, or in any way giving aid and comfort to the enemy, or in any other disloyal practice against the United States."[22] What followed for the next month or so was a period that even scholars who defend the Lincoln administration consider "the lowest point for civil liberties in the North during the Civil War, the lowest point for civil liberties in U.S. history to that time, and one of the lowest for civil liberties in all of American history."[23]

The rehearsal for a provost marshal general's bureau took shape during this low tide for liberty. On September 24, Stanton defined the bureau by establishing a network of "special provost-marshals." These "special" marshals were primarily civilian officials given command of fixed regions in order to further the government's efforts to round up deserters and prevent treasonable behavior from interfering with mobilization. They also had the power to screen elections that fall, which was a crucial moment in the war as Democrats gained ground in the midterm elections. The special marshals were to bar from voting the men who had resisted the military draft by claiming they were aliens. On October 1, the War Department escalated the campaign against disloyalty by authorizing Draper to head this new organization.[24]

To some extent, the new bureau recognized a bureaucracy that had existed without the attention of Washington. When Draper assumed his more centralized command in October 1862, he suddenly realized that he had inherited twenty-two special provost marshals who had been appointed to oversee specific regions of the country. Some of them had been around for quite a while. Most of the men had control over cities, but a few had authority over a county. These special marshals had not yet appeared in Kentucky or in the occupied sectors of the states in rebellion. New York

State did not have as much as a single one, and Pennsylvania had only one such person stationed in a county near Philadelphia, a city with a troublesome cohort of citizens who spoke out against the government. Judged by the number of special provost marshals assigned, however, it was Ohio that led the list of sensitive spots in 1862. Well in advance of the controversial arrest of Clement Vallandigham in 1863, the state contained six special marshals posted at Columbus, Cincinnati, Cleveland, and a few smaller towns. All of these men had been busy expanding their control by appointing deputies, many of these positions filled after consultation with governors. This relationship with state officials had strengthened the local or regional control over these men, causing the local provost marshal system to function almost like patronage appointments that went to petty functionaries whose main concerns were particular rather than national.[25]

Where had these men come from and by whose authority did they function? This was a question raised at the time, one that revealed the confusing nature of General Orders No. 140 that had established the system. With the creation of the new bureau, authorities and military officers wondered if the civilian provost marshals should continue in their roles or be replaced. It was unclear who had appointed these civilian provost marshals: the secretary of war, the provost marshal general, state governors, or military officers at the scene. During the fall and winter of 1862, these questions rarely received answers. This much is certain: the patched-together nature of the domestic security system left in place police who allegedly served the nation but who maintained the locality as their focus. Once installed, they never went away, nor could they. In Missouri, Major General Curtis exposed this situation when he protested new orders in January 1863 to restrict provost marshals from regulating trade and commerce. They operated with police and militia, guarded public property, supervised prisoners, confiscated private property, and had become so much a part of the internal security system that to disband them could create even greater problems. "The provost-marshal system is not of my planting or growth," he told Stanton, "but is now so old, deep-rooted, and wide-spread it cannot be summarily disposed of without danger of losses and disasters."[26]

Maryland and Kentucky provided examples of the collaborative nature of national and local officials, both military and civil authorities, embodied within the provost marshal system. Baltimore had been in turmoil since the riot of April 19, 1861. The city was one of the first to experience the suspension of habeas corpus and occupation by the Union military. In late June, Major General Nathaniel Banks installed Colonel Kenly of the 1st Maryland Regiment as provost marshal "to see that the police laws are effectually executed. This he has to do with the aid of the subordinate police officers." Kenly used a person identified as Lieutenant Carmichael as his liaison with the civilian force. In August 1861, Carmichael was directing five policemen, presumably not from the U.S. military, during the arrest of a citizen.[27] In Kentucky, another key border state, a new provost marshal tried to create a civilian-military police force. When his assignment was announced in September 1861, Henry Dent made it known that he wanted "four hundred stout, able-bodied men, for infantry, and one hundred of a like kind for cavalry, to act as a Police force for the city."[28] This relationship never changed during the war; in fact, it served as one of the foundations upon which the government built its national system. It was a workable, although problematic, affiliation that left federalism very much a living organism alongside of centralization.

By following one such provost marshal for a brief moment, we can see how centralized government rested on a foundation of localism. On Draper's list of twenty-two special provost marshals that he had inherited was J. L. McPhail, provost marshal for Baltimore. McPhail, a hatter and furrier before the war, apparently had gained public experience as a fireman and an officer of the First Baltimore Hose Company. He gained his police powers the fairly typical way: through appointment by a military officer trying to stabilize a region. In 1861, when Major General Nathaniel P. Banks established security for the city under martial law, he named George R. Dodge as marshal of police and James L. McPhail as the deputy marshal. The local newspaper understood these men as being appointed under the power of the president, meaning executive authority, and indicated that they were paid from the federal treasury. Yet they were clearly not military personnel.[29] McPhail was vigorous about punishing secessionists, which made him troublesome at times to military commanders such as John Wool, who did not like to provoke the civilian population unnecessarily. Nevertheless, McPhail did his job well enough to keep advancing in responsibility.

When Draper assumed command of the new bureau in Washington, he found McPhail functioning as an important cog in the mechanism that supervised disloyalty on the home front. The local provost marshal had risen to command a large portion of the state of Maryland and had appointed twenty-one assistants (one for each county). Draper was not sure what his own powers were, especially if he could replace provost marshals currently in these posts. His communications reveal a man who was always looking over his shoulder. Plus, the bureau remained chronically underfunded, which increased its reliance on local officials and police. Draper's confusion about the appointive power and who should serve in these posts was shared by military officers in the field. Major General Horatio G. Wright, who commanded the Department of the Ohio from Cincinnati, interpreted General Orders No. 140 that established the bureau as confining the appointment power of special provost marshals to the secretary of war. He observed that the orders were unclear and, under the circumstances, left in place the incumbents, which meant men like McPhail.[30] Other military men who were sensitive about future reconciliation with the Confederate enemy had a blunt assessment of these men. When he heard about General Orders No. 140 that established the bureau, Marsena Patrick, provost marshal general for the Army of the Potomac, commented: "Look out, now, for Inquisition! I think trouble will grow out of the working of this Order."[31] It was an overstatement by a man who was a professed Democrat and who believed in conciliation of the rebels in order to ease the process of reconstruction. But Patrick's views reveal the suspicion that some of the army's military police held for their civilian counterparts.

Ultimately, this rehearsal of the Provost Marshal General's Bureau featured mixed results. Two historians have considered it "a step upward," even though they recognized that the system remained flawed and allowed for unauthorized arrests.[32] It certainly failed to achieve its mission to enhance the capture of deserters. The authority to appoint provost marshals remained confusing, and the underfunded effort resulted in too few personnel to make headway against desertion and other problems of mobilization. C. P. Buckingham, assistant adjutant general from the War Department, cited this lack of manpower as the top reason undercutting the effectiveness of the system. He believed that each congressional district should receive a provost marshal, which he believed would allow Washington to have a greater control.[33] Buckingham's assessment underscored that the main value of this first version of the bureau was allowing officials to have a better grasp on what was needed. With a few minor adjustments, he had predicted what was to come.

On March 3, 1863, the U.S. Congress enacted two pieces of legislation to extend and constrain the internal security system. In one of the acts, lawmakers in the North faced the mobilization problem head-on by creating a national draft, nearly a year after the Confederacy had taken this plunge. To implement and enforce the system, the law created a provost marshal general's office. The act empowered the president with the responsibility to place a host of new officers who would enforce the draft within congressional districts throughout the loyal states. Provost marshals, many of them civilians rather than military personnel, enjoyed the acting rank of captain of cavalry and were placed in each congressional district. They were aided by various assistants, including a civilian commissioner for the draft.[34] What took shape was a network of provost marshals supervising the draft in communities and having the power to arrest anyone who displayed the slightest inclination to interfere. To oversee this provost marshal system, Lincoln appointed James B. Fry.

Also on March 3 the Congress enacted a habeas corpus act, which did more than authorize the government to invoke martial law. One piece of the legislation tossed a bone toward the contemporary critics of the president over arbitrary arrests. Section 2 ordered the secretaries of state and war to furnish to the district courts of the United States a list of political prisoners held within federal jurisdictions. A variety of congressional resolutions that winter had foreshadowed this portion of the law, with various representatives trying to eliminate the shoddy practices of provost marshals, detectives, and local authorities who arrested without providing charges or describing the behavior that prompted the imprisonments. If political prisoners remained in jail without due process—even if a grand jury merely disbanded without handling the cases—the act empowered judges to discharge the prisoners. Furthermore, the law provided for fines and imprisonment of arresting officers who ignored the courts.[35]

The provost marshals created under the new bureau concentrated on putting conscription into place and arresting anyone who threatened to disrupt mobilization. They could arrest deserters, spies, and dangerous persons in general. And what "dangerous" meant was truly in the eyes of the beholder. These agents reported to the provost marshal general in Washington. They were unconcerned with maintaining order in the army, unless soldiers happened to create problems in communities. In the upper North and border region, they spearheaded the conscription effort and became involved in policing treason, while trying to meet a host of new regulations that required greater accountability for the arrests of political prisoners and the transferring of Confederate property that was seized by the army.

Thus emerged a system in which at least three, and sometimes more, provost marshals might operate in the same territory. One set belonged to the army, answered to the commander, and traveled wherever the soldiers advanced. Another set belonged to the military commander of a department and remained fixed in a geographic place. The last group of federal officials came during the spring of 1863 when the Provost Marshal General's Bureau placed officers in congressional districts to oversee mobilization. This manifestation of the domestic security system did not resolve all of the problems even though it improved administrative control and put more muscle behind the mobilization effort.

But the new bureau remained susceptible to patronage. Actually, the system depended on it. Although officials in Washington were empowered to appoint the provost marshals as well as the officials underneath them—such as the physicians, assistant provost marshals, and enrollment commissioners who operated in each district—practically speaking they could not have judged the abilities of applicants who were, of necessity, drawn from the communities. Washington relied upon the recommendations of governors, congressmen, legislators, and the like in order to fill appointments. After the war, one officer who was posted in Philadelphia revealed the problem with this situation: "But how is the government to know the good men, or those who vouch for them, except it is through the endorsement of men known to it by reason of their political prominence?" He added that everyone understood how worthless was "the endorsement of a politician, seeking votes to secure a position in the gift of a people, whom he proposes to represent, or trying to secure for the future what he may have already acquired." These recommendations inevitably put men into positions of power whose "familiarity with the people over whom their authority may have to be expressed, is not always favorable to an impartial discharge of their duties."[36]

In 1864, Thurlow Weed, a leader of the Republican machine in New York, recognized a similar phenomenon. In a letter to Supreme Court justice David Davis, Weed lamented that Stanton had deferred to Senator Edwin D. Morgan of New York concerning an appointment for provost marshal of the Eighth District. This was not a singular occurrence. Weed saw it as indicative of a broader phenomenon that underscored how local circumstances could dictate the nature of appointments. "Nearly all the office-holders appointed through our enemies, are now Mr Lincoln's enemies," he observed. Weed likely exaggerated the threat to the administration, but he described his own friends as left "out in the cold" from these appointments—and they most certainly were.[37]

Nor did the new bureau completely overhaul the prior system; instead, the Provost Marshal General's Bureau rested on the foundation that had been laid earlier. Missouri provided perhaps an extreme case but one illustrative of other parts of the northern home front that had an army present. When John Nicolay investigated the situation in the summer of 1864, he found "too many different and conflicting authorities." The secretary to the president identified at least three different arresting agents. Major General Rosecrans had established his provost marshals for the army, and General C. B. Fisk, in charge of the military district comprising the counties north of the Missouri River, presided over a separate provost marshal command for the department. Both acted independently of each other. "This is still not all," Nicolay observed. The governor of Missouri controlled militia that he used in a similar fashion; these were men who did not report to any federal officer. Nicolay was not even counting the men assigned and supervised by the Provost Marshal General's Bureau in Washington—a fourth element conducting arrests, these geared to mobilization.[38]

What had come into being was a system that could monitor disloyalty at the grassroots level. It did not stop excessive actions, but between a Congress demanding that all political arrests be reported to civil courts and the provost marshal's bureau providing new oversight, the mechanism was put into place to overturn the most egregious abuses. Most of the various police agents plied their trade faithfully and with the best of intentions. The problem was that, at the intersection between citizens and provost marshals, it was hard for the targets of arrests to appreciate that the actions were not arbitrary.

Policing the United States

Because of its strategic importance and volatile politics, the border region brought out the best and worst in the officials charged with monitoring internal security. Yet there were other places in the loyal states—New York City, Philadelphia, and Cincinnati to name a few—that featured similar conflicts over political arrests. A close look at the experience of these arrests highlights not only the improvisation that occurred but also the role that citizens played in influencing the parameters of justice. Self-described Unionists turned in their neighbors on the least evidence of rebel sympathies. And they singled out for social persecution the military officers who did not act vigorously enough. On the whole, the study of popular agitation reveals that the population was sometimes ahead of the government in asking for a harder war against not only the rebels but also the domestic enemies on the home front.

Conciliation and a respect for property among military officers marked much of the early portion of the war. Many of the army officers who led the opening campaigns shared conservative beliefs about military-civil affairs. Like many in the country, they were careful about inflicting property damage on the citizens who fell within their administrative control. Even though McClellan used military force to thwart secession, he hesitated to seize property or to consider everyone who lived in insurrectionary states as traitors who deserved punishment. Treatment of civilians by him, Don Carlos Buell, and Irvin McDowell—to name a few generals—tended to be selective, focused on leaders and known troublemakers. It was largely believed at the time that the rebellion had begun because a handful of planter-politicians had led their section out of the Union without having popular support behind them. A limited and targeted policy against treason seemed warranted to nurture the unionist sentiments within the Confederate population and encourage reunification.

The trouble was, the government's oversight did not allow for tight control of the military in supervising civilian affairs, and the public mood in certain areas supported a tougher stand against supposed secessionists than military commanders condoned. Both instances occurred in the arrest of a minister in Alexandria, Virginia. The city just across the Potomac from Washington came under almost immediate occupation and, for all intents and purposes, experienced similar activity as Maryland and Missouri. A famous incident occurred on May 24 as a young officer charged up the stairs of the Marshall House to take down a Confederate flag from the building. Colonel Elmer Ellsworth was killed by the owner of the establishment, James W. Jackson. A soldier shot and stabbed the assailant to death, and Ellsworth became one of the first Union martyrs of the war. Alexandria did not offer anything quite so spectacular for the remainder of the conflict, partly because the occupation encouraged the departure of the pro-Confederate residents. Even though it bustled from an influx of military personnel and business, the town's population declined steadily during the war until it left behind primarily Unionists or lukewarm loyalists (sometimes called lip loyalists).

One portion of the civil realm that came under military control, and that highlighted the conflicting nature of military oversight, was the churches. Officials closed down congregations that contained secessionists for the remainder of 1861, easing these restraints in early 1862. But one church in particular featured a conflict that provides insight into the pressures that occurred at the local level, especially the kinds of conflicts that could erupt within communities without the attention of higher authorities.

What happened on a Sunday morning in early 1862 showed the lack of coordination among authorities over political arrests as well as the public pressure that called for strong measures against traitors in Union-held territory. In this case, State Department detectives butted heads with a departmental commander with the arrest on February 9 of the Reverend K. J. Stewart. He was taken from St. Paul's Church during Sunday worship service. Soldiers from the 8th Illinois Cavalry—directed by a state department detective named S. W. Morton—waited for the minister to omit the prayer to the president. Stewart was notorious for speaking out in favor of the Confederacy and for defying orders to read the prayer. When he ignored the prayer this time, the detective commanded him twice to say it, but Stewart ignored him. An officer and some enlisted men went to the altar to recite the prayer, while the minister tried to continue with the liturgy. The soldiers eventually dragged the reverend from his kneeling position and announced his arrest "as a rebel and a traitor." The minister then grabbed the chancel rails to resist capture while promising his accosters they would answer at the "seat of the King of Kings and Lord of Lords for interfering by force of arms, with His ambassador, while in the act of presenting the petitions of His people at His altar." This response briefly caught the soldiers off guard, but someone broke the spell by ordering the soldiers to seize the minister. Two men grabbed him, forcing the prayer book from his hands, while another drew a revolver. Away from the action, a pistol appeared in the hand of "an old and venerated citizen within the chancel" who might have contested the capture or, more likely, got himself killed. Fortunately, cooler heads prevailed, and no one fired. Soldiers dragged the Reverend Stewart from the altar, down the aisle, and outside the church to imprisonment.[39]

With no facilities of his own for incarceration, the State Department detective had to turn the minister over to the military officer in control of the city. The minister thus entered a different jurisdiction, whose officer reported to the War Department and not the State Department. When Brigadier General W. R. Montgomery reviewed the case, he released the minister fairly quickly, which enraged the more passionate Unionists in the community. They announced their displeasure by having a small group of men at dusk nail a U.S. flag over the entrance to Montgomery's office. It was meant as an insult: an indication that the crowd did not believe Montgomery was loyal enough. When it became known that the officer took down the flag, it prompted a more extensive decorating campaign—this time aimed at all suspected secessionists. A newspaper correspondent proudly noted that the Stars and Stripes floated "from hundreds of buildings whose inmates, until yesterday, would have willingly yielded up life and property rather than repose a single night under its protection." A main target was the church in which Stewart ministered. Loyalists placed a small ensign at the peak of the roof and solicited funds for a larger flag on which organizers planned to inscribe: "Raised by the Union citizens of Alexandria. Death to the Traitor that dares to pull it down."[40]

General Montgomery acted no differently from many officers at the time, especially with conciliation dominating for the treatment of southern civilians. In a letter to Secretary of State Seward, Montgomery expressed his desire not to punish everyone, and he complained of the interference by the detective. He had known about the minister's behavior and had attended a service at St. Paul's Church in January, which had omitted the obligatory prayer for the president of the United States. He had reported the matter to headquarters, which had left a response to his discretion. He took no action, which angered the Unionists who hoped for harsher measures. "My own views and object in the performance of duty here," he told Seward, "has been to win rather than force back the affections and adherence of Southern people to the Constitution and its blessings. This I have and still believe the true policy to reinstate the Constitution in all its integrity."[41] The general's policies came under mixed reviews in the press, which reflected the divided opinions among northerners over how to treat the rebels. Ultimately, the *Philadelphia Inquirer* reversed its harsh position on Montgomery and conceded that the general had sought instruction from superiors, who allowed him leeway in the matter. The correspondent justified the release of Stewart because "the proof consisted of negative not active treason" and thus "a case could not have been made out."[42]

No hard and fast rules described similar situations for military commanders. They could be criticized by loyalists for arresting a minister as well as for letting one go. Major General John E. Wool learned this with the imprisonment of the Reverend Charles A. Hay, a Lutheran minister from Harrisburg, Pennsylvania. The reverend had traveled to Baltimore and written a public letter criticizing the administration for the poor care he had witnessed for wounded soldiers. He also complained that a woman of secessionist proclivities took into her home wounded Confederates, while the army prevented Unionists from doing the same with federal soldiers. A newspaper rose to the minister's defense, the congregation sent a delegation to meet with General Wool, and prominent people (including former governor Thomas Hicks) wrote President Lincoln for the general's resignation. The superintendent of the institution for the blind, Charles Keener, accused the general of being heavily influenced by secessionists, whom he called "Fence Men," or people who disguised their true sentiments.[43]

Wool and his officers were under assault in the press and from local Unionists for not waging a hard enough war against rebels. The general was being buffeted in the press for "losing" Harpers Ferry, technically under his jurisdiction, to the Confederates during the Antietam campaign. Local Unionists in Baltimore also had begun to conduct their own investigation of the military for alleged disloyalty, meaning being too lenient with rebels. They targeted officers who condoned conciliation toward secessionists or who safeguarded the rights of the accused. In response, on October 27 Wool's men seized a small group of Baltimore Unionists who had been conducting this investigation since the prior July, producing nearly a hundred affidavits. Among the arrested were an aide to the governor and a clerk of the criminal court. Wool felt strongly enough about his decision that he went to Washington to meet with Lincoln. He was supported by Johns Hopkins, the Baltimore merchant and philanthropist who founded the university that bears his name. Ultimately, the general survived the controversy, although he soon suffered a stroke and was transferred later to New York. Hay was released, and Lincoln reversed the arrests of the Unionists.[44] The situation had pitted hard-line Unionists, who favored removing the conciliatory gloves when it came to handling traitors, against military officers with more conservative war aims.

In general, churches were considered as possible spawning grounds for treason: places where congregants could engage in disloyal behavior while considering themselves shielded by sacred ground. But there was no sanctuary. Union officials, especially in the border states and occupied areas of the Confederacy, invariably watched these venues closely for signs of disloyalty, which usually meant professions of faith in the Confederate experiment or a lack of patriotic expressions. Small infractions gave officials the excuse to close down churches. In March 1863, stewards from the Central, Chatsworth, and Biddle Street Methodist Episcopal Churches in Baltimore complained to the governor that they were denied the right to worship by the Union military commander, Major General Robert Schenck. They had been turned out of their meeting hall and forbidden to conduct services unless they displayed the flag of the United States. The congregations had seceded from the General Conference of the Methodist Episcopal Church in 1860, which cost them their church buildings. They had been holding services in a public assembly hall since March 1862. On February 8, 1863, worshipers encountered two U.S. flags behind the altar, apparently left from an occasion the night before. Some of the congregants were outraged. When he learned about it, Schenck ordered that no service would be held without flying the ensign. The congregation refused, and its members abandoned the building rather than obey.[45]

Governor Augustus Bradford answered the congregants' request for his intervention with polite disdain, as he seized the occasion to lecture them on the fact that church did not supersede the state, at least in worldly affairs. The stewards of the congregations had charged that they were denied the American right of free worship. Bradford did not agree. He asked how, in God's name, "does the sight of our Country's Standard obstruct or impair the enjoyment of such rights?" He continued with obvious passion: "How is it, let me ask, that they have been so amply provided for? How is it that here, above all the earth besides, this religious liberty, this freedom of Conscience and title to equal protection, which you seem to think have been so outraged by the presence of the American Ensign, have all been so carefully secured to us? How but under the auspices of a free Government symbolized by that very flag, and which those who have shared most abundantly in its blessings are now treacherously striving to destroy."[46] The stewards fired off a reply in which they professed loyalty to the U.S. government. They argued that allowing Schenck to establish procedures for conducting worship could lead to him dictating other practices, such as a change in liturgy.[47] The protests fell on deaf ears. The religious principles were taken by Unionists as a cynical rationalization for treasonous behavior.

Not even public officials were exempt from the hunt for traitorous behavior. In 1862, James McPhail—the provost marshal who had risen through the ranks in Baltimore—served as the supervising officer in another of the controversial actions in Maryland, the arrest of county judge Richard B. Carmichael. The judge had asked the grand jury to issue charges against officers for the false arrests of political prisoners. McPhail arrested the judge, who was dragged from his bench as he ran a session of the court. During the arrest, one of the participating officers pistol-whipped Carmichael. The judge remained a captive in military custody from his arrest in May until his release December 4, 1862.[48]

McPhail in this instance had not acted arbitrarily: he implemented a targeted strike ordered by General Dix, who almost certainly had the blessing of superiors. This should come as little surprise. The judge had encouraged the prosecution of the agents who conducted political arrests. When a congressman from Maryland protested to Lincoln to free the judge, the president did not comply. He understood the danger in allowing prosecutions of potentially unjust arrests by federal agents. A verdict against the government could have hampered the effort to uncover disloyalty. Lincoln wrote his petitioner that "the Judge was trying to help a little, by giving the protection of law to those who were endeavoring to overthrow the Supreme law—trying if he could find a safe place for certain men to stand on the constitution, whilst they should stab it in another place."[49]

Yet it would be wrong to think of all targets of political arrests as victims. There were occasions in which arresting officers, particularly civil provost marshals, found themselves caught in the middle of a controversy. They did not necessarily lose their job or suffer punishment from superiors, but resistance by the accused could, at times, put members of the internal security network on the defensive. People living in communities with strong leaders who opposed the administration's conduct of the war had the best chance of winning these personal battles. And if they did not always create new precedent, or force the administration to reverse its policies, they at least made the government take notice and try to conduct damage control.

In late 1862, the detention of a Louisiana woman by Police Superintendent John Alexander Kennedy of New York City shows how local leaders, especially in Democratic Party strongholds, could mount a defense against a provost marshal. The case also highlights the confusion that existed over internal security and how political arrests sometimes could feature capitulation on the part of the administration. Isabel M. Brinsmade, a resident of New Orleans, was arrested in September as she traveled in Washington. She had left Louisiana with a pass issued by Major General Benjamin Butler. Reportedly, she had come East to visit family or acquaintances. No offense was specified for the action beyond the usual vague allegation of disloyalty, although newspaper columns hinted that she was suspected as a spy. After her arrest in the capital, Brinsmade was transferred to New York, where she sat for weeks at the 47th Street Station House. The provost marshal had to use the local precinct to house a federal prisoner because no federal facilities existed. The twenty-year-old married woman who had been cleared for travel by none other than the notorious Ben Butler sat in a makeshift prison with little recourse for securing her release.

The daughter of a prosperous merchant, Mrs. Brinsmade's plight proved too inviting for Democrats to pass. Victorian mores concerning gender presented critics of the administration's arrests with heavy ammunition. They used the case to mount an indirect assault on the nature of arrests by bringing male-female conventions into the argument. In this way, they could avoid a partisan tone as they focused on a scandalous abuse of power that defied common decency. Here was a woman, they argued, who deserved protection: a woman traveling alone and with the promise of national authorities (through her permission from Ben Butler) that she would remain unmolested. Yet the authorities acted in an unmanly fashion, showing little of the self-restraint expected of all gentlemen and men appointed to public duty. They compounded their sins by placing a woman of good standing in a common jail. The case presented a delicious opportunity to tarnish the use of political arrests in general by preying upon the concerns most men would have for the vulnerabilities of women. The *New York World*, for instance, trumpeted that anyone who had a sister, a wife, or daughter should come away from this case with the lesson "to what outrageous lengths the unbridled, unpunished exercise of unlawful domestic power will run."[50] Lincoln's minions, critics claimed, acted not only against constitutional principles but also against the basic duty of all men to protect women.

Leaders of this effort fairly quickly achieved the release of Brinsmade, but they proceeded seamlessly to a greater objective to hold the provost marshal accountable for his actions and, presumably, try to slow arrests that seemed to single out Democrats. At this point, Samuel L. M. Barlow stepped into the picture to mount a vigorous defense on behalf of Brinsmade. He was a lawyer in the city and a powerful Democrat who served as a confidante to McClellan. He used his connections to press Simeon Draper, the recently installed provost marshal general, to clarify and resolve the difficulty. In truth it was an embarrassing case for the government, for it quickly became obvious that Mrs. Brinsmade had done nothing to deserve her treatment, and no one could find any charges that were supported by evidence in this highly publicized case. Also embarrassing, neither Kennedy nor Special Provost Marshal Baker in Washington wanted to accept responsibility for the arrest; they pointed the finger at each other, further suggesting the lack of substance to the charges. Under the circumstances, her release seemed to be the only option, although this may have come anyway during a general easing of political arrests.

Barlow and his compatriots also pressured local authorities to conduct a hearing of the police commissioners to determine if Police Superintendent Kennedy deserved punishment for false arrest and imprisonment. Convened on November 20, the hearing lasted at least four days with numerous witnesses called from both Washington and New York. The proceedings received widespread coverage—undoubtedly more than what was deserved for the actual facts of the case—with opinions predictably falling along partisan lines. Democrats—at least those who were not War Democrats—were incensed; Republicans much calmer. Ultimately, the commissioners took a middle ground, trying to placate both sides. They found Kennedy innocent of false arrest, laying the blame on agents under Lafayette Baker in Washington for the original seizure. But they did not leave their local superintendent off the hook. They censured him for not trying to learn why Mrs. Brinsmade was held. Yet they confused the verdict further by giving Kennedy a vote of confidence in his overall performance.[51]

The controversy did not cost Kennedy his job, but the proceedings revealed the complexity of his position and the paradoxical values society ascribed to nineteenth-century American women. The hearing revealed that Kennedy served two masters and that at least the local ones were unwilling to relinquish control over him. He answered to local officials in his capacity as what we today would call a chief of police. Yet ever since the opening of the conflict he had been "borrowed" by the federal government to serve as a provost marshal to coordinate political arrests in the city. During the hearings, Kennedy temporarily lost his status as a federal provost marshal while the government waited for the results of the investigation. Later he resumed his powers as a federal agent, but the rulings by the commissioners indicated that they, at least, did not release him from the responsibility to follow civil law. Whenever lacking written orders from the government, they maintained, Kennedy had to obey civil procedures. Without that higher authority—which they believed needed to be confirmed in writing—the commissioners said he had no right to use the station house to hold Brinsmade, especially because the property remained under the Board of Police.[52] The commissioners attempted to indicate as much to the federal government, as to Kennedy, that they needed to be consulted if the national government wanted cooperation.

Additionally, the findings spoke to a complicated situation concerning how to consider women in wartime. The domestic often became the political. Women could be considered potential enemies of the state, capable of treason. Yet the commissioners also treated Brinsmade as a citizen who retained her rights to personal liberty, which included being notified of charges and having the right to a defense before civil tribunals. Although women were treated as political actors capable of committing treason, they were not the primary target of agents conducting political arrests. Women appear infrequently on the rosters of prisoners of state or in the newspaper columns as imprisoned for disloyalty. When the commissioners supervising the transfer of prisoners from the State to the War Department inspected the Old Capital prison in Washington, they recorded only a dozen females among 200 inmates, including the notorious Rose O'Neil Greenhow.[53] Gender afforded women some protection, or at least their sex deflected sterner measures against them—*if* they were white and hailed from the "respectable" ranks of society.

As for Kennedy, he did not get off completely, even though he remained the superintendent of police. The charges against him were part of a broader attack. Local people had created enough of a disturbance to cause the judge advocate general, L. C. Turner, to come to New York to investigate abuses relating to prisoners of state. The Democratic organ, the *New York World*, characterized the habits of Kennedy and his agents as contrary to the values of a republic. According to the newspaper, citizens "were taken off Broadway and hurried before the government official without a word of warning, or a whisper of what they were arrested for. Others were taken from their beds at midnight and compelled to visit police headquarters, there to learn for the first time the nature of the charges preferred against them. No warrants were exhibited by the officers, no explanation given, nothing but the announcement: 'The provost marshal has ordered you to be brought to his office.'"[54] Nothing suggests, however, that officials in the War Department considered Kennedy as anything other than a stalwart ally. They did not mind his tactics. He remained a partner with Washington for the rest of the war.

Even when the next layer of bureaucracy was added—the enforcement of conscription in congressional districts under the March 1863 law—provost marshals still had their share of frustrations. There was only so much of a federal mechanism that could be created in a short time. After the conflict, Provost Marshal General James B. Fry had provost marshals for states and districts assess how the bureau had functioned and suggest improvements. What became clear from these reports is that the collaboration with state and local people determined the success or failure of these officers. Almost no provost marshal ever said he had enough manpower to catch deserters; all had to lean on local people for assistance. To some extent, the Veteran Reserve Corps, composed of wounded or infirm soldiers unable to perform heavier duty, proved useful in catching deserters. But most of the loyal states did not have access to the troops. Day-to-day encounters depended on the special agents employed by individual provost marshals and the willingness of community members to turn in deserters either for patriotic reasons or to receive a reward. The federal government obviously could employ force when needed—and did, such as when it made incursions into portions of Pennsylvania in 1864 to capture deserters. But for the most part marshals needed cooperation from the community. Fry recognized this and added the innovation of establishing a provost marshal general in charge of a state, placing these men at state capitals so they could foster working relations with legislators and governors.[55]

Because of the need to conserve manpower, the provost marshals enforcing conscription were discouraged by their commanders from policing the home front for disloyalty.[56] That duty was left primarily in the hands of the special marshals, constables, police, and civil provost marshals who had oversight in a department. Conscription officers had enough on their plates in figuring out how to return deserters to the army or force drafted men to report. Depending on the political attitudes of citizens within an area—especially agricultural areas that were off the beaten path—they could find quite a few men lingering at home instead of rejoining their comrades. Conscription officer R. J. Barry wrote from Jackson, Michigan, that he found his district flooded with soldiers absent from commands. No one seemed interested in encouraging their return. Barry employed special agents whom he instructed to arrest every soldier who had no written authority for being there. This meant that even innocent men who had earned a furlough but lacked the proper paperwork would be arrested and branded as deserters.[57]

Not everyone was so effective. In St. Paul, Minnesota, the process of capturing deserters was "attended with too much expense and too little success." George H. Keith pointed out the disadvantage of having to rely on local people to use as detectives. "The deserter," especially when recruited from small towns or rural areas in which few were strangers, "knows and keeps out of the way of the detectives." Plus, if people in the area were against the war, it raised the prospect of future problems. He added: "Very few civilians are willing to arrest deserters for the reward of thirty dollars. . . . Nothing is made by the civilian, but he gets the ill will of the deserter and his friends for life."[58] In Missouri, A. H. Crane reported similar conditions—that agents were easy to avoid once they became known. But he highlighted an issue that concerned many of the provost marshals: the lack of incentive. Assistants hired by the provost marshals were not eligible to collect the thirty-dollar bounty for catching a deserter. Crane found his assistants more interested in going after nonreporting drafted men. "But the loss of the reward seemed to take away from them that sly and watchful vigilance necessary in the work of apprehending deserters, and except that the game was actually pointed out to them, special agents did not in this District answer expectations." Instead, he turned to using discharged soldiers and employees at military posts. They were familiar with popular haunts. Plus, the discharged soldiers had an extra incentive to see that others followed through on their pledge to service. Crane found this combination very useful.[59]

Using bounties to enlist citizens to the cause had its benefits, but it also created problems. The practice raised the incentive for neighbors turning on one another, but without establishing requirements for the kind of evidence needed for ensuring justice. Provost marshals encouraged residents to turn in their neighbors, such as A. C. Deuel in Urbana, Ohio, who asked his agents to use informants. They were to find "some loyal person who would at all times forward immediately to him any information that would lead to the arrest of deserters."[60] The practices increased the sense of urgency in looking for disloyal people, whether they were neighbors or strangers. In fact, it was better not to know the individual so the accuser could send someone to jail without fearing revenge from an angry neighbor. Under the circumstances, it was not good to be a stranger coming to town. The provost marshal stationed at Cincinnati made the observation that once the reward was raised to thirty dollars "no stranger (especially if roughly dressed) was safe from arrest." Men who had not even belonged to a militia unit found themselves in jail, only to be released once the facts became known. Additionally, some soldiers who had passes may have had them stolen by the vigilantes in order to cash in on the reward.[61]

The provost marshals had to clean up the resulting messes. Most often this fell upon the provost marshals of military departments, rather than the conscription and local provost marshals. The Military Department of Missouri with headquarters in St. Louis provides a few illustrative cases. The provost marshal for the military department (not the army or conscription provost marshals) usually ended up processing the prisoners, determining which to hold or let go. This work was complicated by the fact that the individuals deciding the cases were often not the ones who initiated the arrests. Housed in the National Archives in Washington, papers in Record Group 393 contain four boxes of arrests for the department. Boxes 1 and 2 cover 1863 and 1864. The majority of the files involve deserters and people suspected of bushwhacking or guerrilla activity. These individuals were processed fairly quickly. In these files also are the cases of people turned in for cheering for Jeff Davis or criticizing the war as one of abolitionist thieves stealing property from the South. This last exchange came between the owner of a dry goods store and a customer. The store owner had proclaimed his support for McClellan in the forthcoming presidential election and wished that peace would come. These kinds of cases invariably were dispatched easily, usually by requiring a suspect to take an oath of loyalty.[62]

One of the cases, though, reveals the problems that interrogators encountered in the campaign against treasonous behavior. Joseph Allison from Pike County was held on a general charge of disloyalty. Apparently, he had spoken in defense of bushwhackers who had taken goods from the community. On the trifolded case record appeared a notation that indicated the problem of learning the truth. To the question "What impression did he make?" an official responded, "Not very good." Then asked to rate the suspect's truthfulness, the respondent noted, "hard to tell."[63] Here was an officer who had to make a decision based on an interrogation of the arrested man alone, without the ability to discern the facts or to call others to testify. He suspected the worst of his prisoner. Allison might have been a dangerous man who consorted with guerrillas. In this case, Allison went free after swearing the oath and promising not to consort with known disloyal people. This kind of give-and-take occurred daily, with an arbitrary harvesting followed by more careful winnowing, even in one of the worst places within the Union for collisions among neighbors.

What conclusions can we make about the patterns of civil-military collisions in the loyal states via the provost marshals? First of all, it must be said that the effort succeeded in forcing more men into the ranks. Deserters were arrested when none might have been. But the federal government did not have enough manpower on the ground; local cooperation was needed, and sought, by the provost marshals. Avoiding the draft and arrest remained possible even under the heavier federal hand. Although some caution is warranted over blaming everything on political party positions, it is true that more Republicans tended to back the administration, while Democrats increasingly challenged the president and, in many communities at the grassroots level, could aid resistance rather easily, simply by remaining silent and doing nothing to help the agents trying to round up deserters.

It also mattered whether citizens resisting the draft lived in cities or countryside, communities that primarily supported or opposed the administration. The most succinct observation along these lines came from a provost marshal stationed in Warren, Ohio, who enjoyed a fairly routine time during the conflict. His district contained few deserters and he put his finger on the importance of the nature of the community in creating this circumstance. He mentioned that his region had no large cities and in the agricultural townships and villages "almost all strangers are closely scrutinized." The people performing the scrutiny, he added, were loyal, so "there was no chance for concealment."[64] Other communities had to become a considerable nuisance before invoking a response from federal military. This happened in the scarcely populated lumber region of Pennsylvania, which in December 1864 finally attracted squads of the Veteran Reserve Corps to clean out the deserters who had amassed there for years. But the federal government could not be everywhere, so it took a good while before it could mount this successful incursion into the hilly, wooded area along Pennsylvania's northern tier.[65] In general, provost marshals and the reserve corps had to pick their spots for bringing down the iron fist of federal authority.

The layers of overlapping provost marshals—and competing interests—within communities encouraged abuses in arrests even as they provided a mechanism for correcting them. The system allowed for, indeed stimulated, arbitrary arrests at the grassroots level. Local scores that had no connection to the broader war effort undoubtedly were settled. People of questionable abilities and moral fiber could find themselves rewarded with the power to determine the contours of everyday patriotism, primarily because they knew someone connected to the right political party. Especially in sensitive areas of questionable loyalty like parts of Missouri or southern Maryland, the system encouraged rash action, quick arrests based on flimsy charges, and preemptive strikes against behavior that had not yet become treasonous.

At the same time, we should acknowledge that committed Unionists did their jobs correctly, willingly, and judiciously, with enthusiasm for their duties. Fortified with a prosecutorial zeal to save their country, they nonetheless acted prudently either as cases made their way up the chain or as they had time to consider the circumstances. Egregious arrests were overturned and the suspects given their liberty, most often after taking a new oath of allegiance to the Union. It was a strangely effective system, even as it rarely achieved efficiency, and allowed for actions that may have made some of the founders squirm.

Treason, a charge leveled but not tried, served as the justification for all of this activity. And yet this was treason at home. What would be the nature of this civil-military conflict when it was carried into the Confederacy?

5

THE DOMESTIC IS THE PUBLIC

The Occupied South

In the occupied Confederacy, practices by Union soldiers underscore that a grassroots perspective complicates the task of generalizing encounters with enemy noncombatants. The hard war that historians reserve for later in the conflict seemed hard enough for the people experiencing it in the opening months. The Union's provost marshals were abusive, arbitrary, and anxious; they were also benign, judicious, and empathetic. At the level of human contact, one can find stories as variable as the individuals involved. Ultimately, though, one can say that the Union military generally established order and—except perhaps for a few cases—for the most part did not adopt a policy of devastation without rules and limits. While attention often has been on the criticisms of arrests, and the excesses of military oversight, provost marshals and the Union military offered stability, law, and charity even if the recipients of these "benefits" often found the experience fearful and degrading.[1]

Occupation of the Confederacy by Union soldiers, though, invariably broke down the ideological barriers between public and domestic worlds. A civil war, to use LeeAnn Whites's phrase, turned "the household inside out."[2] The private and the political merged whenever an army entered contested terrain. The job of occupying soldiers invariably caused them to violate the boundaries of the domestic world. Union soldiers foraged for food from farms, hunted spies in neighborhoods, rooted out guerrillas and their wives from homes, and tried to sever networks of provisions and other aid for the enemy—a good portion of it created through household production. Soldiers at various times also took slaves, another form of property generally considered to be private and untouchable by the prewar national government, yet essential to the same household production that provided foodstuffs and other goods. The traditional boundaries that had shielded individuals from the state became permeable as authorities looked into every nook and cranny for the human, material, and spiritual resources that aided and abetted the treasonous Confederate war.

Under these circumstances, officers recognized women as political actors capable of doing harm by sustaining the enemy through their prewar roles of provisioning, healing, and nurturing. It did not matter if they stitched a Confederate flag on their dresses, spit at soldiers in the streets, dumped chamber pots on those same soldiers, refused to take an oath of loyalty, counseled their men to fight, hid wounded soldiers, bit their tongue during the prayer to the president in church, gathered information on troop movements, or encouraged their children to toss stones at the enemy. Their actions large and small became viewed by provost marshals as behavior deserving monitoring. It might seem quaint today, and possibly as an overreaction on the part of Confederates, that so much furor occurred over Union general Benjamin Butler's infamous order that promised to treat females who harassed his soldiers as women of the night, plying their trade. Fortunately, recent works have taken a different approach, showing that the people on the ground understood these actions as more than charming nonsense. The war placed what might seem as harmless behavior into a context that made it dangerous. The whisper across the fence to a neighbor, a gesture once considered safe or domestic, could appear to the men challenged with keeping order as something dangerous and public.

More was at stake than a battle for control over domestic space; it was also a battle for the political will of the Confederate populace, whether male or female. Union officials used such things as charity and the right to work as leverage to compel Confederate civilians into accepting dominion by the United States. Loyalty became tied to provisions, to the ability to conduct trade, and to practicing professions such as ministers, teachers, and lawyers. Known Confederates who refused to take oaths faced taxation in order to pay for the support of poor people who had declared allegiance to the Union. They found their commerce restrained and a "free" market interrupted by soldiers if they did not declare loyalty to a nation. Property remained sacrosanct only as long as the owners swore fidelity to the Union, even if only symbolically by mouthing phrases that were not heartfelt. Slaves, cotton, and other "commodities" were seized because they were "tainted with treason." As the war lasted, it became more common to evict Confederate civilians from Union-held territory if they refused to take oaths of loyalty. For many Confederates, the situation forced them to pledge allegiance to an authority in which they did not believe in order to endure a situation that they almost daily regretted.

The Person in Charge

In the equation for the military's administration of enemy civilians, the commanders at the point of contact were a key variable. Officers in charge of departments served as de facto military governors. For a while, provost marshals, military officers, and soldiers in the South had to create their own policy for handling enemy noncombatants. Until 1863, and the adoption of the code of war embodied in General Orders No. 100, few guidelines existed for the administration of civilian affairs by the military. Generals sorted through the situations as they could and received correction from superiors when they strayed. Although early in the war the top military commanders tended to respect civilian property, the army contained general officers, many of whom—like John C. Frémont—brought to their work a passion for political causes, in this case what became a radical agenda that condoned freedom for slaves.

Most students of civil-military relations have portrayed a linear progression of increasingly harder policies against Confederate noncombatants as the war continued. Historian Mark Grimsley has noted that the Union higher command first adopted a policy of conciliation, meaning respect for enemy property and gentle treatment of civilians in order to nudge them back into the Union. This was followed by a period of pragmatism, which then gave way to a hard war that put more civilian property at risk.[3] There is much to be said for this description. It captures the big picture very well, especially the posture of the high command. But it does not account for the hard warriors who entered the conflict with a desire to punish the rebel traitors.

Although conciliation dictated the posture of soldiers toward unarmed rebels, the extent of confiscation and protection of civilian property depended upon the preferences of a military officer in charge of an area. Even early in the conflict, fugitive slaves could be kept from masters, should an officer be so inclined. Or, as historians know very well, before the presidential orders in the summer of 1862, fugitive slaves could be returned to masters, again if a military officer were so inclined. Similarly, goods might be taken if they were deemed "treasonable," which may sound strange to today's ear but was a fairly typical justification for taking a variety of goods. It should surprise no one that many Union officers considered cotton a particularly vile manifestation of treason, very much worth taking into custody. For instance, Major General William T. Sherman declared: "All cotton is tainted with treason, and no title in it will be respected." Even though he uttered this comment in 1864, when the war had taken a harder turn, he was hardly the first to make such a determination about a commodity.[4]

Considering the policy position of a particular commander requires taking into account more than his political party. Ideas about the Union, the role of government, and the punishment of traitors cut across party lines and informed War Democrats in their approaches to the property of enemy civilians. In other words, we must take into account their behavior as well as their party affiliation. To be sure, Union meant slightly different things to Republicans and Democrats. But there were intersecting values among Free-Soilers, old-style Jacksonian Democrats, and Young American Democrats who detested secessionists. Seizing slaves became one way to destroy the Slave Power, or the slaveholding oligarchy that dominated its section and seemed determined to spread slavery nationally. War Democrats who wore the shoulder straps of Union officers could act very similarly to colleagues from a more radical persuasion, even if they had different motivations and political philosophies for doing so. Union Brigadier General John White Geary, who enjoyed a political career before the war as a Democrat, became anathema to Confederate civilians as he allowed soldiers in 1861 to seize property in his sector near the lower Shenandoah Valley. Geary had no compunction about sending his men across the Potomac River to raid beef cattle and bragged when his men captured thirty-nine head. To him, turncoat citizens had brought this penance on themselves.[5] Like-minded Republicans and Democrats considered harsh measures against civilian property as punishment for the traitors who sought to sunder the Union.

The number of these kinds of seizures defies estimation. Studies of the confiscation acts have tended to dismiss the legislation as having little impact on Confederate property. Scholars point out that a total of only about $130,000 worth of confiscated property made its way into the federal treasury. They are correct in giving this picture of limited application of this legislation. However, as Sylvana Siddali has recognized in her study of confiscation, "military operations on enemy soil resulted in widespread seizure of land, cotton, livestock, and, of course, the labor of slaves." Much of this activity took place without relying on the confiscation legislation enacted by the Congress.[6]

Damage to civilian property also occurred despite the best of intentions of a commander. Large masses of men moving through a region wreaked havoc.[7] One soldier in the western army noted the destructive tendency of an army as he wrote home to Ohio. Near Oxford, Mississippi, in late 1862, Sam Evans "could scarcely believe, the damage done to a country that so large an army marches through. All the fence is burned; mules and horses taken, fodder, and corn besides a great many other things that could not be properly called confiscated." He added: "I would call it stealing if at home." Significantly, the soldier did not counsel return of the property or compensation for losses. He merely noted the trend. In fact, he helped himself to some rails to burn so he could see to write home during dusk and never thought about the contradiction his actions posed to his earlier statement. Like Geary, he was a War Democrat who believed that secessionists had brought this treatment on themselves.[8]

The most persistent collisions between the Union military and Confederate civilians came in what historian Stephen Ash has called the garrisoned towns, areas along the fringes of the rebel nation that sustained a longer-term presence of enemy soldiers. This does not mean that civilians living in contested zones where both armies roamed fared better than people under constant supervision. Residents in East Tennessee and the Lower Shenandoah Valley—the latter an area that changed hands numerous times—faced many anxious moments in trying to negotiate with the shifting commands from different armies. They faced reprisals when, for instance, a rebel army seized control of an area recently vacated by federal soldiers and now dealt with former citizens who had sworn loyalty to the Union. Garrisoned towns provided stability for residents, which ironically allowed for greater resistance on behalf of the Confederate citizenry. Opposition to authority, much of it conducted clandestinely, generally increased after the initial shock of occupation as the confidence level grew among civilians. This resistance could come through wearing certain clothing, shunning social contact with Union officers, refusing to pray for the president, or smuggling goods across the lines. Whatever the course taken, it raised the frustration levels of the military officers charged with keeping order.[9]

In other words, although the stated position of the administration early in the war favored the protection of the property of noncombatants—except for their use for military necessity—it did not always prevent the troops at the point of contact from overstepping these limits. This does not mean that the stance of public officials in the War Department or others among the high command did not matter. Until the policy started to change toward a harder war in the summer of 1862, the more conservative position concerning soldiers' treatment of Confederate property held sway. And the higher command operated as an anchor on how far soldiers and commanders could follow their own inclinations to drift from the stated position.

Lincoln occasionally stepped in to correct the actions of subordinates in the field. He became involved primarily when general officers stepped over the line of his own sense of constitutionality, especially if it created a political embarrassment. He was not divorced from stipulating what his officers and soldiers did in the Confederacy. He issued directives to his commanders in the field—such as his Emancipation Proclamation and his endorsement of Lieber's General Orders No. 100—concerning how to deal with enemy property. But this was an area that he did not micromanage. More often, he reacted to the more egregious situations. Most historians, for instance, know of his reversal of the emancipation edicts by Generals Frémont in Missouri and Hunter in the Southeast. But he also intervened in more situations than those involving slave property. He halted, as will be discussed shortly, the management of churches by the military or northern church organizations. He reversed the confiscation of a home of a Mary E. Morton in the Department of Arkansas in early 1865 because it was not taken strictly because of military necessity. And he overturned Grant's orders to evict Jewish residents from his department.[10] But he also let military oversight of enemy noncombatants enjoy a considerable amount of leeway, recognizing the right of officers to seize farms for a pasture, encampment, or fortification under the auspices of military necessity.[11]

Plugging into the equation of civil-military relations the variables of time, geography, and the tendencies of a military commander reveals portions of the Confederacy that fell under a brand of warfare that does not fit the current narrative. Some examples suggest how military commanders in the field complicated the description of moving from conciliation to hard treatment of the rebels under their charge. Geary already has been mentioned. The work of Noel Harrison on Alexandria and Fairfax counties in Virginia suggests that Geary's actions were not singular. The two counties sustained incredibly severe damage in the first year of the war. "Both consciously and unconsciously," Harrison noted, "their soldiers [from both sides] terrorized residents, devastated their property, and drove many from their homes. The counties' citizens, meanwhile, exploited one another's war-related misfortunes, collaborated with the military occupiers, and otherwise helped obscure the distinction between civilians and soldiers."[12]

Military commanders certainly ordered careful treatment of civilians and often chastised the wanton destruction of civilian property. But what mattered was the execution of these orders by subordinates. And here the story becomes a little more unpredictable. Small-scale operations conducted by bands of soldiers—similar to what John Geary conducted in the same region—"brought violent disruption to the lives of residents outside garrisoned areas." Officers justified these actions either as a military necessity to secure particular goods for soldiers (such as provisions) or as part of the campaign to punish disloyal citizens. As Harrison pointed out, the lines between military necessity and depredation blurred.[13]

Northern Virginia was not the only place feeling this kind of warfare early in the conflict. Missouri featured bushwhacking, destruction of property, and arrests for treason. Even though the border state remained in the Union, the divided sentiments of the residents often caused U.S. soldiers to treat it like an occupied zone littered with potential enemies. It is there that John C. Frémont tried to open his own brand of hard war by punishing treason through enacting a policy of emancipation, which Lincoln famously reversed. Officers like Henry Wager Halleck ordered soldiers to show restraint, but this did not work completely. Missouri to an extent represented the exception for nearly everything in the Union, yet it often served as the blueprint for how to handle the secessionists in the Confederate States. The fringe of Virginia along the East Coast also had its share of conflict between Union military personnel and Confederate civilians. On the Peninsula in 1862, it was still possible for civilians to receive a Union guard to protect a home. Even though the commander favored conciliation of rebels and control of his troops, the men considered all bets off if people had left their homes. The residents were considered traitors and plunder often followed.[14] Large chunks of the Sea Islands off the Carolina coast, much of it abandoned by planters, came under control of the U.S. Treasury by early 1862. Thousands of acres of private land were taken over by the government without historians classifying this large-scale confiscation and dislocation of civilians as a hard war. Similar to Civil War Unionists, scholars have accepted government control of private property as the consequences of treason, the just deserts for planters who fled, or one of the first experiments in Reconstruction.[15]

Few things, however, stand out in the conflict quite like the sacking of Athens, Alabama, by members of the 19th Illinois Infantry. The looting by soldiers, apparently tacitly condoned by Colonel John B. Turchin, illustrated how officers who made decisions that contradicted the orders of superiors could survive depending on the political context. During May 2, 1862, soldiers of the 19th Illinois Infantry stacked arms in the streets of Athens, Alabama, and in the presence of their commanding officer ransacked homes and stores of unarmed civilians. What they destroyed can hardly be classified as materiel falling under the definition of military necessity. Soldiers destroyed an inventory of Bibles and testaments in one store, tossed clothing into the streets from multiple homes, despoiled furniture and carpeting, stole money from homes and offices, carried off a microscope and geological specimens, chopped a piano to pieces with an ax, rifled bureaus for all manner of personal items (watches, jewelry, family silver), and vandalized a law office. Officials estimated that the destruction of property had amounted to more than $50,000.

The soldiers also violated women. White women appeared to get off relatively "easily" with only threats to their lives or the promises of molestation, most of which went unfulfilled. Even though there was no physical harm, these encounters were unsettling, to say the least. Black women were not as fortunate. The tribunal that heard the court-martial of Colonel Turchin specified that his men attempted the rape of a "servant" of Milly Ann Clayton and did rape the slave of Charlotte Hines. Sadly, the victims were not even dignified with their own names. These crimes presented clear, well-publicized cases of acknowledged sexual violations. No one tried to deny that the assaults had taken place.[16]

What came next seemed stranger still. Turchin's men finished their occupation of the town in a couple of weeks, and as time passed, the news of the looting created a firestorm that caused the colonel to resign his commission. He also faced a court-martial. After weeks of hearings before a military tribunal, Turchin was found guilty of various charges, including disobeying the policy set by General Don Carlos Buell, commander of the Army of the Ohio. Buell had issued orders that his men should let peaceful citizens remain unmolested, which the 19th Illinois clearly violated. The officers hearing the case ruled that Turchin should be permanently removed from command. Yet at the same moment that officer sat for his court-martial, a nomination promoting him to brigadier general worked its way through channels and was confirmed by the Senate. Six members of the seven-person tribunal asked for leniency after handing down the sentence. They obviously felt conflicted about punishing him, although they recognized that Turchin had not exerted proper oversight of his soldiers. Buell refused to overlook the situation and pressed to remove his subordinate in order to send a lesson to the rest of his command. Instead, within weeks Lincoln reinstated Turchin. From here, the irony only grew. By late 1862, it was Buell who was removed from office and who faced hearings on suspicion for being too lenient with the rebels, among other things.

The political situation obviously played in Turchin's favor. So did the timing of the act, which corresponded with the summer of 1862 when Union attitudes started to swing in favor of taking off the gloves and punishing the rebel traitors. He had strong supporters among Republicans in Illinois, including the governor and Joseph Medill's *Chicago Tribune*, which espoused a radical position concerning the emancipation of slaves. Significant portions of the public rallied to him. Continued resistance by southerners made it harder to espouse a position that treating them respectfully would coax them back into the Union. Instead of welcoming federal troops as liberators, or remaining neutral, Confederate civilians seemed to help partisans, cheer the demise of Union troops, and profess continued loyalty to the rebel cause. To historian Mark Grimsley, the reinstatement of Turchin provided evidence that the United States had lost its commitment to conciliation and highlighted how the war was taking a harder turn.[17]

Turchin's defenders at the time resented that the traitors (Confederate civilians) were allowed to testify against a military officer who put his life on the line for his country. More recently, two studies of the situation have excused him because he did not expressly order the looting and because he merely followed what was becoming a popular strand of thinking among many in the North to quit treating Confederates as if they were protected by the Constitution. The studies argued that no civilian was killed and that Turchin acted quickly to punish the men who committed rape. They also put him into a greater context of partisan activity conducted against Union soldiers in the region, suggesting that Turchin's men acted out of retaliation for the poor treatment of comrades. When members of the 18th Ohio were chased from Athens prior to May 2, citizens reportedly taunted the men, called them "D—d Yankee Sons of Bitches," and cheered for Jefferson Davis. Women spit at them. These are not, in their own right, dangerous gestures worthy of the kind of retaliation that took place.[18]

The point here is neither to praise nor to blame Turchin—or to deny that he benefited from a time when conciliation seemed increasingly bankrupt—but to note that civilians facing an army quickly learned a hard, cold reality. The individual commanders who stood in a Confederate town and directed soldiers in their duty mattered more than the commanders of departments or the policy makers who lived in Washington. The dialectic of action, retaliation, and negotiation became a pattern in the daily interchange between soldiers and enemy civilians. Smaller cases that did not command the notoriety of Turchin's undoubtedly occurred. It is also absolutely true that the army did play by unspoken rules even in outrageous situations, such as the pillaging of a town. In this case, the soldiers stacked arms before committing their depredations. They did not murder indiscriminately, torture the residents, or torch the town. However, it is doubtful that the residents of Athens, Alabama, took comfort from this fact as they stared at their personal goods littered on the sidewalks alongside the tattered remains of Bibles.

Yet it is also true that this hard war remained constrained, as both Grimsley and Neely have observed. Grimsley has argued that even such a practitioner of hard war as William Tecumseh Sherman still envisioned a "trinary division of the Southern population," into openly hostile, neutral, or loyal. Each type of citizen called for a different approach. Sherman, however, did not speak for everyone. And the actions of civilians formed another crucial variable in the equation of civilian-military relations.[19]

Loyalty of the Stomach

As the Union military advanced through Confederate territory, the soldiers brought with them an organization for combating disloyalty similar to the one that had evolved in the Union. One enormous difference, however, characterized the Union military's oversight of Confederate territory. It was expected that officers would supplant civilian rulers and take control of civil society. Domination by an army collapsed a community's legal, political, and economic infrastructure. Commanders of military departments and their provost marshals had to ensure that life functioned as safely as possible, although it was the security of the army that formed the top priority. The federal occupiers sorted out who could be trusted in towns and countryside to collaborate with them. They decided who preached in churches, taught students in schools, tried cases in court, sold goods to local people, and traded with buyers beyond the region. As biographers of Secretary of War Stanton have observed, provost marshals determined "who among the Southern civilians in their control should remain free or go to jail, stay at home or face exile, get scarce food, clothes, seeds, and tools, travel on the railroads, receive mail, or practice professions and trades."[20]

Although the broader picture of occupation is known, historians have not featured prominently enough the link between livelihood and loyalty in the occupied South. Military commanders and their provost marshals insinuated themselves into most aspects of local exchange, including household domestic production. In this hypercharged political climate, nearly every commodity became scrutinized for its support of treason. Provost marshals stopped the use of Confederate script and tightly monitored all cash exchanges. They restricted trade, offered supplies only to those who took loyalty oaths, and even ran banks. As the war lasted, eviction of the "secesh" from Union-held territory became part of the battle against treason in regions experiencing either long- or short-term occupation.

In the occupied South, the army typically needed to dispense relief for noncombatants. Nearly five months after the fall of New Orleans in 1862, Ben Butler reported expending roughly $50,000 per month in food for the white inhabitants, "and more is needed." He also used the military's commissary stores to feed slaves.[21] The occupying army became instrumental in holding together the local economy. It was not unusual for a departmental provost marshal to collect fees for the trade in cotton or to regulate commercial exchanges with the army.[22]

Consequently, charity served as a form of coercion. It was common for fees and other assessments on the secession population, but not Unionists, to be used for the benefit of specific needs on the part of loyalists, such as funds for a Union hospital or for the benefit of the poor. Predating Andrew Johnson's Reconstruction policy to target rich men, Benjamin Butler in 1862 levied assessments against the wealthy in New Orleans to alleviate the "middling and working men" from shouldering the burden of making a living. Butler referred to the nonplanters as men who "have never been heard at the ballot-box unawed by threats and unmenaced by thugs and paid assassins of conspirators against peace and good order."[23] It was an appeal specifically designed to exert pressure along the fault lines of class.

The Union general found an easy way to select "the traitors" who should pay for the hardships suffered by less fortunate southerners. He secured the names of residents who had contributed a total of $1,250,000 for the Committee of Public Safety in the city. This was a local organization popular in many southern communities that raised funds to benefit the Confederate war effort. In August 1862, Butler's staff created a list with three columns: the first naming an individual or business that had donated to the committee; the second "Sums subscribed to aid treason against the United States" (the donations to the Committee on Public Safety); and the third "Sums Assessed to relieve the poor by the United States" (the "tax" assessed against them). Butler justified his actions on the grounds that, in his judgment, the affected individuals had committed treason. It probably did not mollify the "donors" in this coerced subscription that Butler did not try to recoup the entire amounts that they had contributed to the Confederacy, but assessed only one-quarter of the amount they had given. Even that was not enough. By December 1862, Butler charged an additional assessment because the needs of the poor had increased. When the fund ran dry in 1864, a new commander of the department repeated the initiative and levied another round of assessments.[24]

Butler's prescription for helping the poor by punishing disloyal citizens may not have occurred everywhere in the occupied South (we simply do not know enough yet), but it was far from unique. The blueprint for the process had appeared in Missouri in 1861–62 and was developed by the scrupulously legalistic Henry Wager Halleck. Rebels driving loyal families from southwestern Missouri provided the impetus for his action. What emerged was a progressive tax on disloyalty. The Union military decided to raise funds for the relief of Unionists by punishing Confederate sympathizers who remained within federal lines. The tax defined three kinds of disloyal persons: those who had joined the Confederate army and held property in St. Louis, those who had given money or other aid to the enemy, and those who had published or had declared their support of the rebellion. The amount of money owed was based on the degree of disloyalty, with service in the Confederate army earning the greatest penalty. If individuals failed to pay, Halleck allowed their property to be taken. The system was administered by the provost marshals attached to the Department of Missouri.[25] Similarly, when Andrew Johnson sat as military governor of the conquered portions of Tennessee, the town of Pulaski was assessed money by the provost marshal to compensate a Union merchant for goods seized by Confederate raiders under John Hunt Morgan. Ash's work on the Confederate home front has argued that assessments for reparations became common on secession families in communities where guerrilla attacks occurred.[26]

Even if they were well off, Confederate civilians needed supplies that Union officers controlled. Early in the war, Brigadier General Egbert Viele noticed the dilemma, indicating that he had to make food available to the people under his charge, whether they could purchase the provisions or not. In making his report, he cast himself in the role of a jailor responsible for the care of his captives: "We are . . . holding here in custody about 20,000 people; we must either let them feed themselves or we must feed them. . . . Food must be allowed to come in or the people will starve."[27] Later, occupying forces used this dependency to their advantage by forcing men and women to take oaths in exchange for the right to acquire merchandise. One member of a Massachusetts regiment indicated that his provost marshal had opened an office "where he is exchanging salt and amnesty for allegiance oaths, and as this is the fishing season, he is driving a right smart business." He added: "There are probably some honest men among them who would like to do about right if they dared to, but the whole thing looks ludicrous, for there is evidently not one in a hundred of them who would ever think of taking the oath were it not for the hope of obtaining a little salt. The boys call it the salt oath."[28] Similarly, a woman referred to Memphis in 1863 as featuring a "perfect reign of terror," adding, "Not even a spool of cotton can be purchased without registering your name and address, and 'swearing['] it is for personal or family use, and no *number* of articles can be taken from the store without, after selection, going with a list of them in your hand, to the 'Board of Trade' accompanied by the clerk of the store, and there swearing an oath on the Bible that the articles mentioned are for family use and not be taken out of the United States."[29] This was not the only case. In January 1863, Ellen Renshaw House reported similar circumstances in East Tennessee. She noted: "An order came out yesterday forbidding any one from buying any thing except those who take the oath as Loyal citizens, not even a dose of medicine or a spool of thread."[30]

Provost marshals consequently intruded into most areas of Confederate life, including domestic production, to uncover dangers to the national state. They considered something as mundane as a cotton spool as a possible weapon of war—as generating clothing for the enemy and as suggesting a treasonous leaning on the part of the owner. More important, they considered access to these goods as a means of coercing loyalty oaths from the population. Coerced patriotism based on provisions was becoming one of the bases for creating the reunion of the country.

This was one of those moments when the people involved in these engagements understood that oaths served primarily ritualistic, political functions—that they did not signal the real sentiments of the people. Federal authorities knew they were purchasing loyalty (rebels would say coercing). They realized that the commitment to the relationship was rather shallow and likely feigned. Securing provisions and other goods became a goal for many of the people who pledged themselves to the Union. One Arkansas planter with the unfortunate name of John Brown captured the motivations of neighbors who took the oath in this way: "They would obtain protection for their families and something to eat."[31] The Federals referred to this as lip loyalty, recognizing that the commitment to Union was skin deep at best. In Missouri, a colonel was so vexed by the civilians in his northwestern district that he commented: "They take loyalty like gin and sugar and pass it off just as easy."[32]

In 1864 a New Hampshire newspaper highlighted this fact by running an interview between Benjamin Butler and the Reverend George

D. Armstrong, a Presbyterian preacher in Norfolk. The interview reportedly appeared first in the *New Regime*, a journal obviously pledged to the Union side. It undoubtedly represented a biased account, true in the facts that the minister was arrested and imprisoned but with details of the interrogation possibly distorted. No matter the veracity of the report, the account showed that officials recognized that oaths could only go so far and that they believed it useful to publicize transgressions in the hopes of quelling similar behavior. Under examination, the reverend reportedly stated that he considered Norfolk a conquered town and the United States "to be 'the powers that be.'" He took the oath with the intention of keeping it "so far as my actions were concerned. *My feelings, of course, I cannot control.*" After a longer exchange, and further pressing, the minister admitted that his sympathies lay with the Confederates and that he would not say prayers for the United States. He considered the oath "an oath of amnesty," which referred to the president's proclamation of December 1863. The story ends with Butler lecturing the reverend and placing him in the guardhouse.[33]

As Butler's cautionary tale suggested, ministers were targets of the occupiers—more than most scholarship has noticed until recently.[34] It was understood that clergymen had enormous influence with their congregations; that they served as community leaders, molders of opinion, and people who could help citizens overcome loss of loved ones and flagging morale. If they omitted the prayer for the president from worship service, mouthed support for the Confederacy from the pulpit, or became known as ardent Confederate sympathizers, preachers faced harassment, arrest, or worse. The extent of these arrests has not been counted and, as with most of these situations during the war, likely cannot be pinned down precisely. But they appear enough in newspapers and government records to indicate that authorities watched churches closely. And, as the Butler item revealed, they publicized these cases of disloyalty as a demonstration of what faced those guilty of the same behavior.

Lincoln did draw a line for preserving the boundary between church and state. The case that caused him to declare his position involved the arrest of a Presbyterian minister in St. Louis. Late in 1862, authorities seized the Reverend Samuel B. McPheeters and banished him from Union lines. More conservative members within Lincoln's administration, particularly Attorney General Bates of Missouri, interceded on the reverend's behalf. McPheeters had an interview with the president, who concluded that the minister was indeed a Confederate sympathizer, but said he had taken the oath and promised to say the prayer of the president during worship services. Lincoln at this time favored keeping hands off of ministers who, even if southern in inclination, did nothing overt in sympathy with the rebels. He directed the Union general in charge to reverse the eviction and indicated that he supported arrests if they netted open secessionists. However, he wrote that "the U.S. government must not, as by this order, undertake to run the churches. When an individual, in a church or out of it, becomes dangerous to the public interest, he must be checked; but let the churches, as such take care of themselves."[35]

The man who had initiated the action against McPheeters once again highlighted that the political inclinations of the men on the ground proved influential in the kind of actions taken against civilians. In this case, the provost marshal in charge of the area was F. A. Dick. He had strong, personal connections with members of the Blair family and followed them on their path from Democratic Free-Soilers to the moderate side of the Republican Party. Like his political cohorts, Dick remained a committed Unionist and often expressed private beliefs that the administration moved too cautiously against rebels. Unlike officials in Washington, he saw the need to purge the region of secessionists. He clearly considered McPheeters only the tip of the iceberg and stated in a letter to Montgomery Blair—intended for the president—that all clergymen were disloyal. He favored shipping every one of them out of the state. It was not an idle threat and undoubtedly might have happened if superiors had not intervened. In this case, the political situation did not support the desires of the provost marshal.[36]

Even Lincoln's delineation of church and state, however, could be abused until the actions by officials in occupied areas became politically volatile. Less than a year after the McPheeters flare-up, subordinates completely ignored the president's guidelines for church affairs. A government crackdown on preachers put the administration in the position of running churches, or the very situation that Lincoln wished to avoid. Apparently without consulting him, the military began to oversee the removal of ministers. Secretary of War Stanton issued the orders in November 1863 that empowered Bishop Edward R. Ames of the Methodist Episcopal Church to remove preachers he considered disloyal and to replace them with clergy of his own choosing. The orders—which covered the departments of Missouri, the Tennessee, and the Gulf—gave him complete authority to act as judge and jury. Stanton justified the action by claiming, "It is a matter of great importance to the Government, in its efforts to restore tranquility to the community and peace to the nation, that christian ministers should, by example and precept, support and foster the loyal sentiment of the people."[37]

Military officers seemed only too happy to enforce the order. A general in Memphis, Tennessee, threw a reverend out of Wesley Chapel, allowing Bishop Ames to replace him with a clergyman from Indiana "who was right on the slavery question." Similar actions were reported in New Orleans. And in St. Louis, commanding officers received orders to gather data for the bishop and assist him in his duty. Baptists apparently faced this intrusion as well. The American Baptist Home Missionary Society took over vacant churches found in the South and installed its own preachers, although it is unclear how vigorously it moved and how many of the southerners were retained, if any.[38] Major General Benjamin Butler apparently liked the idea enough that he decided to adopt the order for his own department in Norfolk and Portsmouth. As usual, he took measures to a new height by failing to discriminate among denominations. His provost marshals were to assume control of *all* places of public worship, not just Methodists, with instructions to "see the pulpits properly filled, by displacing, when necessary, the present incumbents & substituting men of known loyalty of the same sectarian denomination either, military or civil, subject to the approval of the Commanding officer."[39]

This went too far for Lincoln. He put a stop to Bishop Ames's assault against the Confederate Methodists, which presumably halted all such actions. But his stand was not particularly forceful. His communication with the secretary of war pointed out the contradiction of his position concerning the McPheeters incident with the more recent sanctions against ministers and asked Stanton, "What is to be done about it?" Whatever exchange happened in private, no one knows, except that Lincoln's position won. Orders went to General Rosecrans in St. Louis to stop the meddling with churches. However, Rosecrans received the message at the end of February, or more than three months after Stanton had initiated the policy. The general was confused by the reversal and sought clarification, suggesting that the attention to this by Washington was less than adequate.[40] It is possible that Secretary of War Stanton and others in the War Department had been emboldened to adopt such a measure because Lincoln had looked the other way on many occasions when preachers were arrested in the Union and Confederacy. The president did not mind it when a minister went to jail for expressing Confederate support. He drew the line, however, with denominational leaders or generals installing ministers without congregational approval.

Ministers were not the only important people in Confederate communities. Provost marshals suppressed newspapers and arrested editors who refused to retract their rebel claws, but they also deprived people of the right to practice their professions. Missouri adopted such a course early in the conflict. In 1861, the constitutional convention that served as a provisional government adopted the policy of a test oath necessary for suffrage. Citizens had to swear past and present loyalty to the state and the nation. By 1862, Unionists expanded the practice to determine who sat on juries, served as officers of corporations, and functioned as ministers and teachers. Military officers adopted similar practices in the Confederacy, with one study concluding that citizens in Louisiana and Tennessee experienced these practices the most, but that Norfolk and Portsmouth followed suit as Butler moved to the East Coast and supervised civil affairs there. Ministers, physicians, lawyers, merchants, and store clerks had to take the oath of loyalty before doing business along the Virginia coast. The practice was common throughout the occupied Confederacy, yet it seemed to be a policy that received impetus from commanders on the ground rather than directives from Washington. Once again, the picture that emerged was one of an administration more focused on winning the war than consumed by the subtleties of civil-military relations.[41]

Taking loyalty oaths could leave Confederate civilians in a precarious position. They had to worry about neighbors who refused to play by the Union rules. Some people like the planter John Brown might shake their heads and understand that citizens did what they had to do to survive, but others might hold it against the turncoats, considering their swearing loyalty to the United States as a traitorous act against the Confederacy. Sarah Morgan Dawson had fled with parts of her family into Confederate-held Louisiana as Union forces moved into New Orleans. The mail brought word that a brother who remained behind had sworn an oath to the Union, probably prompted by General Orders No. 76 of September 1862 that required enemies of the state, whether male or female, to register with the government. The brother in this case prospered. Neighbors of Sarah, meanwhile, taunted the family by saying the brother was no better than a Yankee. In regions of consistent occupation, such as garrisoned towns, the consequences of this community pressure might be restricted to social ostracism, refusal to conduct business, or shame. But in contested areas that changed hands, or where guerrillas operated, residents were aware that taking an oath might bring reprisals from the next group of armed men who came to town, resulting in confiscation of property or loss of life.[42]

Although Union authorities recognized that the ritualistic lip service of oath-taking might not really reflect the true beliefs of the swearer, the procedure did have consequences if one failed to perform. Sherman's policy to let obedient Confederates alone was not always followed by the military in occupied regions. The longer Union officials supervised an area, the more they became motivated to rid themselves of suspicious noncombatants. Often they suspected these individuals of encouraging bushwhackers or guerrilla fighters. Increasingly in these regions of long-term occupation provost marshals did not allow people to remain in the middle. From 1863 on, Confederates within Union lines faced a varying degree of persecution, with provost marshals having the power to evict them from their homes. This practice, however, has made only a spotty appearance in the narrative of the Civil War, usually tied to a few large-scale actions such as Sherman's eviction of citizens from Atlanta as he launched his March to the Sea in November 1864 or to the Union order that caused the evacuation of two counties in Missouri. Historian Stephen Ash has identified the practice as taking shape toward the end of the war, indicating that it had become common by 1865 to send citizens who refused to take the oath from their homes.[43]

Discrete studies of particular areas, such as Louis Gerteis's book on St. Louis, have shown civilians facing danger of government-sanctioned removal as early as the spring of 1863. The triggering mechanism came in General Orders No. 100, the code of war created for the administration by law professor Francis Lieber. It is ironic that something intended to control military actions against civilians, or to limit what the military might do, also allowed for greater hardships. Article 156 instructed commanders to throw the burden of war on disloyal citizens as much as possible. They could demand that residents swear an oath of allegiance to the government, and if they refused, commanders could "expel, transfer, imprison, or fine the revolted citizens who refuse to pledge themselves anew as citizens obedient to the law and loyal to the government."[44] It was not, however, a mandate: the code gave permission for certain kinds of actions against civilians. Implementation remained decentralized.

Field commanders and provost marshals received their copies dated April 24, 1863, and used the code to justify expulsion of civilians who refused to cooperate. Some officers had been itching to get rid of the Confederates in their midst. Major General Robert H. Milroy, who was about to find himself in the way of Lee's Army of Northern Virginia on its way to Gettysburg, had become frustrated with bushwhackers in the vicinity of his garrison at Winchester, Virginia. In May 1863, he wrote his superior officer, "What do you think of the policy of requiring all persons to take the oath, or move south of our lines immediately? I am very tired of living in the midst of treason." He did not have to wait long for an answer. Major

General Robert Schenck stated the same day: "Yes. Put the traitorous and mischievous beyond our lines."[45]

Toward the end of the conflict, toleration toward enemy civilians plummeted further still, even in the eastern theater of war, which has generally been recognized as the scene of more limited warfare, although not without harshness. Military and political leaders appeared to watch closely the response of Confederate civilians to Lincoln's proclamation of amnesty of December 1863, which promised leniency and restoration of political rights on fairly easy terms geared toward oaths of loyalty. However, as the autumn arrived, it became more typical to treat Confederate civilians with greater severity. By May 1864, a soldier in Memphis wrote his father that the commanding general was coming down on "Citizens of secesh Proclivities," sending many of them to the South for the remainder of the war. In the meantime, their property was forfeited.[46] Provost marshals supervising the Norfolk-Portsmouth area of Virginia seized the abandoned property and homes of disloyal persons who had traveled to the rebel lines. In this case, they used confiscation as a novel way to aid the poor families. They rented out the abandoned structures and used the proceeds for the relief of destitute families. Later, provost marshals began to target property owners who remained in their homes. By September 1864, Marsena Patrick with the Army of the Potomac in Virginia had launched a registration of all civilians within his lines in order to banish those from the area who refused to take the oath.[47]

In January 1865, Union officer Robert H. McAllister witnessed the eviction of one family from its sizable farm near the Weldon Railroad in war-scarred Virginia. A provost marshal for the Army of the Potomac supervised the banishment with the help of a few cavalrymen. The farm in question was owned by a man referred to as "Colonel" Wyatt, apparently a prewar honorific, not a Confederate one. A wealthy man who was well known in the area, Wyatt had refused to take the oath of loyalty from the provost marshal. He claimed to be a Unionist—as did nearly everyone—but protested that he lived in a region that could fall back into Confederate hands. If he avowed his loyalty to the Union, it left him open to hanging by the rebels who lurked nearby. Union soldiers did not accept the rationale. "But the stern rules of war never argues [sic] the question long," McAllister told his wife. "He had the offer to take the oath and declined." Wyatt's family was allowed one wagonload of goods, which meant they left behind the bulk of their furniture and other goods too bulky to fit. The remaining items were boxed by the provost marshal and sent to Norfolk to be sold by the government. Snow fell as the family loaded its remaining belongings, adding a somber chill to the occasion. Even on such an occasion that seemingly called for sympathy for a helpless enemy, McAllister refused to do so. Just as he seemed ready to give himself over to sympathizing with the family, McAllister pulled back and said that as "sad as this was, it is nothing to what I have witnessed on fields of battle when *life*, not property and comfortable homes, were sacrificed. They cry out: 'Vengeance! Vengeance on the traitors of our land!'"[48]

These actions against civilians lacked a central, guiding hand that applied a consistent course of action.[49] In fact, it was easy to become confused about what Lincoln favored. He could take contradictory positions. In October 1863 he counseled John Schofield, who had charge of Missouri, against interfering with freedom of speech without cause. Yet he added: "With the matter of removing the inhabitants of certain counties *en masse*; and of removing certain individuals from time to time, who are supposed to be mischievous, I am not now interfering, but am leaving to your own discretion." However, when Hunter applied a similar policy to expel citizens in the Lower Shenandoah Valley and portions of Maryland in 1864, the president suspended the order.[50] Hunter operated in a region that presented a political problem for Lincoln. In Maryland, Unionists like Senator Reverdy Johnson leapt on the situation to point out the faults of the administration during a coming election. Still, the two situations illustrated how military officers who fell into the habit of acting very independently suddenly found themselves reined in by the administration.

The merging of loyalty with livelihood, and the patchwork nature of supervision, reinforced at the local level a constant negotiation between military officers and civilians in which the rules of behavior were established by daily interpersonal exchanges. Union officials operated within limits, to be sure, and had to obey certain conventions of gender, military customs, and legal codes. Next to security, their main purpose was to try to train the Confederate population into becoming citizens again or, failing that, to show respect for the representatives of their former country.

The Confederate Household Turned Inside Out

With the breaking down of the sanctity of the home in order to fight traitorous behavior, gender and race became crucial elements in the confrontations between soldiers and noncombatants. Union soldiers had to figure out what to do with white women; planters and their wives had to develop strategies to protect their person and property; slaves had to decide which side to favor; rebel men had to choose whether to take an oath or not, with consequences for the family. White women and the enslaved—what scholars have called dependents, and another has defined jointly as the disfranchised—increasingly became factors in the political, national realm. The ideological and legal boundaries between private and public realms blended in ways that became significant to military officers, Confederate men and women, and the enslaved.[51]

The solicitor for the Union War Department captured the point in a public treatise that he began to write in 1862 and revised during the conflict. William Whiting began his project to justify how Lincoln could employ powers under the Constitution to attack slavery by considering the emancipation of slaves as part of the effort to combat treason. As he put pen to paper in 1862, Whiting laid out a legal rationale for allowing the executive department to seize slaves on the basis of the war powers granted to the chief executive. A central tenet was that the household was not safe from federal intrusion. He asserted that

> when the institution of slavery no longer concerns only the household or family, and no longer continues to be a matter exclusively appertaining to the domestic affairs of the State in which it exists; when it becomes a potent, operative, and efficient instrument for carrying on war against the Union, and an important aid to the public enemy; . . . when slavery has been developed into a vast, an overwhelming *war power*, which is actually used by armed traitors for the overthrow of government and of the constitution; . . . then indeed slavery has become an affair most deeply affecting the national welfare and common defense, and has subjected itself to the severest enforcement of those legislative and military powers, to which alone, under the constitution, the people must look to save themselves from ruin.[52]

Whiting hoped to dismiss the philosophy that argued that slavery remained primarily a domestic institution, regulated by the master at the household level. The solicitor claimed that the actions by planters had changed these conditions by turning slaves into a weapon for treason and making them a threat to national security.

Most attention has been paid to the impact of this kind of reasoning on freedom for slaves, but those sharing in Whiting's rationale saw it as an opening to the military to apply it to the entire household, not just the person of the enslaved. This household included the land, crops, livestock, structures, and dependents within a space defined not only by property lines but also by loyalty.[53] Whiting's treatise shoved aside the ideological shield that proslavery southerners had raised against abolitionists and others who struck at the peculiar institution. The key argument had been that slavery was a domestic institution, regulated no higher than at the state level. The Civil War changed these terms. Congress also validated that a traitor's property could be taken via the Second Confiscation Act in 1862, which linked the loss of goods and slaves to an owner's position in relation to the Union. According to Whiting and a host of like-minded northerners, the Union military could ignore the traditional barriers of the household in the Confederate States.

Wherever soldiers went, they encountered white women helping to protect the domestic front, using gender to their advantage as much as possible. New studies of gender and occupation have argued that the Union military took women seriously as political actors and that Confederate sympathizers may have shifted their strategies toward more covert means, rather than direct confrontation of soldiers. For example, they supplied provisions to guerrilla fighters as well as mounted other forms of opposition. They opened, in the words of one scholar, "an unanticipated second front, where some civilians—many of whom were women—continued resisting what they perceived as illegitimate domination."[54] Provost marshals and Union military officers in the slaveholding states daily confronted the fact that white Confederate women presented a problem because of their ability to encourage and participate in resistance at home, as well as to support the continued service of their men in the military through letters.

Various factors put women at the forefront of contact with military officers. One of the most obvious came from the accidental result of mobilization. Women constituted a majority in communities where the demands of war stripped them of military-age males. Confederate mobilization by the first quarter of 1864 was approaching roughly 80 percent of the men between ages seventeen and fifty. Men at home tended to fall outside the parameters of conscription age, or they were recuperating soldiers, political leaders, exempted professionals, slaves, and agriculturalists excused in order to maintain food production for the military. Also, the peculiarities of a "modern" army that still based much of its activities on traditional forms of supply caused soldiers to come into conflict with women. The army needed forage, horses, mules, and even buildings in order to conduct the business of war. Centralized supply chains existed, but they worked far better for the Union than for the Confederacy. Even the federal side could experience times when there were not quite enough goods or buildings, especially when it came to supplying such things as bandages and hospital space. For instance, a woman in East Tennessee encountered a Union officer who sought bedding from the home to start a hospital. Plus, the men naturally sought out homes for "purchasing" such things as home-cooked meals and experiencing other reminders of home, such as the entertainment of women who played piano or sung popular melodies.[55]

In contested areas that experienced the sudden appearance of Union armies, another element contributed to the lack of men. When residents received word that the federal soldiers were coming, men fled with the livestock or other valuables, leaving women behind to treat with the soldiers. There was concern over what the enemy would do to civilian men: especially whether they would imprison them under suspicion of helping the enemy. In December 1864, Union General McAllister told his wife about one such instance in Virginia when soldiers visited one rebel farm. "The father and son had fled to the woods for fear that they would be taken prisoners because they belonged to the home guard, or rather guerrilla band."[56] The home guard was not necessarily a partisan band, but the civilians had no idea how their membership in the unit would be interpreted. Because Union soldiers sometimes worked their way through the countryside in unauthorized raiding parties, it behooved southerners to act cautiously. By fleeing, the men protected their own labor for the household and the commodities that helped the family to sustain itself.

It is perplexing that males apparently felt comfortable with abandoning farms and plantations, leaving women behind to meet enemy soldiers. Women were just as essential as men for maintaining the household economy, if one wants to reduce love and companionship to the level of crass materialistic concerns. Why did men, even if we concede the strain they were under and their value to production, not consider taking their wives along with the livestock? One reason might be the impact of rumor, which spread the impression that unoccupied property would be pillaged and only occupied homes might be spared destruction. Indeed, this seemed to be a customary, often unspoken rule among soldiers for violating property. One young lady in Louisiana recorded in her diary that Benjamin Butler decreed that "no unoccupied house shall be respected."[57] Another possibility is that Confederate men may have believed that the soldiers, even if they were crass and barbaric Yankees, might contain enough humanity to make them think twice about employing violence against women.

This begs the question: to what extent did gender provide a shield for women in civilian-military encounters? For a while historians have considered that civilian women—at least white ones of a certain class—could employ their womanly position within society as a form of protection. A recent study of Gettysburg's encounter with the Confederate army, for instance, affirmed that women "used and abused prevailing gender norms as a means of providing military assistance and assuring self-protection." Domesticity was "a powerful tool of negotiation, and frailty . . . a shield for safety." In these interpretations, helplessness becomes a means of resistance—a survival strategy or a way to exercise "symbolic politics" through etiquette.[58] These practices were more effective among elite or middle-class women, whom the Yankee soldiers appeared to give more discretion than working-class women and enslaved females. Even in the area of sexual assaults, the class position and racial background of women seemingly set the boundaries of behavior among soldiers.[59]

Scholars, however, have chipped away at this edifice, and it is probable that the narrative will undergo a significant revision. A new study of rape in the Civil War, for instance, indicated that women, whether black or white, may have faced violence and personal assault more than previously considered. Hundreds of women in the occupied South and the border states filed charges of rape. Union military courts prosecuted approximately 450 such cases. The scholars make the argument that sexual crimes occurred against white and black women of all classes. One instance in a published account provides an example. Provost Marshal General Marsena Patrick reported from Virginia in 1864 on the trial of two men, presumably soldiers, "who had committed a crime upon the body of a Mrs. Stiles living near Prince George's Court House." He did not specify the race of the victim, but the context suggests that she was white.[60] Another project under way forecasts results that will support this new interpretation. Historian Crystal Feimster believes that thousands of women may have been raped during the Civil War, with the shame over the crime causing it to be severely unreported.[61]

Other kinds of assaults were frequent, especially affronts to women that one scholar has called "symbolic rape." It was common for soldiers to break into bedrooms, open drawers, defile clothing, or wear the women's garb over their uniforms as they paraded outside. One woman's account of Sherman's men in North Carolina has captured the menacing nature of encounters that ended with the mistress being unharmed physically but undoubtedly shaken. One woman reported how federal soldiers treated a woman and her daughter in Lenoir, North Carolina: "[The daughter's] hat and garments were placed on the floor and loathesomely polluted. . . . [W]hen there was nothing more to break and steal, one of them approached [Mrs. Clark] and thrust his fist into her face. As she raised her head to avoid it, he struck her forehead, seized her by the throat, cursing her furiously . . . seizing the neck of her dress, tore it open, snatched the gold watch, which hung by a ribbon, tore it off and left her." The despoiling of clothing, whether or not cross-dressing followed, and threats to women in bedrooms sent a strong message: Confederate men could not protect their women. This message began with the entrance of soldiers into bed-chambers. If they did nothing more than paw through clothing or strip valuables from a person, the gestures reinforced women's vulnerability, announcing that these men could go anywhere, especially into spheres usually protected by the norms of common decency.[62]

Ultimately, civilian and military leaders never viewed rape or assaults on women as an acceptable practice. Lieber's Code specifically addressed the issue, forbidding the use of force against subdued civilians and ac-knowledging the sexual violation of women as a capital offense. Within the Conscription Act of March 1863, lawmakers put teeth to this posi-tion by giving to courts-martial and military commissions the jurisdiction over a range of felonies, including rape.[63] Conventions about how to treat women did define a substantial portion of the rules of behavior between soldiers and civilians, but those conventions may have disappeared at the level of personal confrontations. Scholarship to date probably has under-represented the extent and nature of sexual assaults.

Taking goods from a household was commoner yet, even if the belong-ings did not meet the definition of military necessity. Women confronting an enemy army negotiated to save goods from forage parties, vandals, or soldiers looking for extra subsistence. Disloyalty, no matter how defined, became one of the justifications that soldiers used to seize or destroy prop-erty. One day might feature the loss of a pony; another might find soldiers entering the home, searching it, and taking a substantial portion of the family's food. Or a lone soldier might pick through drawers and take a necklace. In confronting the soldiers, women had to act cautiously for they faced the consequences if they acted too forcefully.

One of the first instincts of Confederate women was to induce the enemy's men to live up to their roles as protectors of the opposite sex. They petitioned officers for protection of property. Upper-class women especially reminded authorities that they deserved such consideration be-cause of their sex. For instance, a plantation woman in Mississippi sent an appeal that circumstances "demand my rights of protection as a *lady*." Soldiers had searched her house for arms three times and taken nearly all of the household's provisions.[64] This appeal to gender norms worked best in the early stages of the war. Yet protection could be granted even later in the conflict, at least to certain kinds of property such as structures or valuables. Once again, the sentiments of officers on the ground mattered the most in securing guards for homes.

Although guards posted outside a home were the first choice, it was not unusual for women to seek military personnel as boarders. The theory was that having a Union soldier billeting in a home would prevent others from stealing or destroying personal goods. For instance, a Mrs. Cain in East Tennessee had a captain from the provost guard boarding in her home, with a neighbor commenting that she "has taken him for protection." Soldiers had been stealing her wood, and by having a Yankee stay with her, clearly she hoped to stop the practice. She did not.[65] Other women, however, found themselves with permanent intruders imposed upon the household as soldiers became nightly "guests" for dinner. The situation proved to be a mixed blessing for the women who recognized that they faced some protection yet had to buy it with close contact that did not always feel comfortable. A Missouri woman known to be southern in her leanings wrote that she had to play host to "ignorant soldiers" and added: "Home was no longer a safe asylum, a sacred place." Other Confederate women grasped the irony. Emilie McKinley was pleased that a soldier decided to stay for a day to guard her household with a gun. "Did we ever think we should be so very glad to see, and persuade a Yankee to stay with us?"[66]

Writing and Talking Treason

Along with the battle over provisions, civilians waged a daily struggle with the enemy over the flow of information and speech. Union soldiers recognized that information was a valuable commodity, one that could aid and abet the enemy. Social scientists, psychologists, and historians have analyzed rumor and gossip as a means of exploring cultural values and shared beliefs. And masters in the Old South recognized the problem of slave communication networks as a means of resistance. Rumor might touch off panics concerning supposed slave plots.[67] What worked for the slave could work for the master in times of occupation. However, one scholar's conceptualization of prehistory perhaps best captures the way rumor, fact, conjecture, gossip, and information of all kind flowed through the home front. Civilians and soldiers lived in what Stephen Cushman has termed "prehistoric" moments, or before the present and past could be sorted out and verified for accuracy. The term described the moment when "present, or recent past, still has no name, and official records have not yet tagged and labeled it for future use by historians."[68] People under occupation sought information—hungrily—often second only to the twin priorities of securing provisions and personal safety.

Historians have demonstrated how rumor, gossip, and other forms of information affected the emotions or morale of the Confederate populace. Civilians were "whipsawed" by false reports on the war or uplifted by hopeful signs, whether verified or not. One scholar of this phenomenon for the Confederacy has suggested that rumors provided "tangible evidence that made continued resistance seem reasonable."[69] But the same held true for Union soldiers. Civilians grasped this as they watched the impact of reports from the battlefield on the enemy. Mississippian Emilie Riley McKinley noted that the community learned of the failed Mine Run Campaign by the Army of the Potomac. She added: "When the Yankees are victorious they are domineering, but when they are whipped they are humble."[70] Knowing this, she and other civilians deliberately employed information to try to provoke guards. In June 1863, before Vicksburg had fallen and during a season of increasing unrest in the Union over conscription, McKinley asked one of the soldiers she encountered (an Ohioan) if he would like to see Clement Vallandigham, the gubernatorial candidate from the Buckeye State who had been banished to the Confederacy for disloyal speech. The man grumbled that should he encounter Vallandigham he would shoot the disloyal politician. The women also alluded to the New York City draft riots so her enemy could ponder the effect of that violence on the Union war effort. Did they know what they were doing? "Of course," she noted, "we do all we can to demoralize them."[71]

Information did more than influence moods or the psyche: it had an impact on people's actions and on policy making. The most obvious benefit involved civilians providing the disposition of enemy troops or other sensitive knowledge about the military situation. It was not unusual for noncombatants who crossed between the lines to be quizzed by a military officer to see if they had any intelligence that could reveal weaknesses and strengths of the enemy. Women were often "profiled" by provost marshals as the persons to watch for transporting mail or for carrying other contraband in their clothing, such as quinine. This placed men in the sometimes uncomfortable position of searching the persons of Confederate women, a violation of conventional morality.[72] But the rumor of troop movements could influence a range of behavior—even if the news was incorrect. Reports of advancing Yankees sent Confederate men scurrying for the woods. Wherever the army's contact with civilians appeared to be threatened, even in the lower North, it touched off repercussions. One Ohio resident wrote his son that war rumors made an impact on the local economy. "Those little raids & rumors are interfering most terribly with farmers' work, hands are very scarce, & to take all them, and keep them from their work for a few days now will cause terrible losses in seeding and cutting fodder &c."[73]

The actions of Union soldiers reinforced that they considered information a cause for concern. It was easiest to control printed materials. Because of their visibility, newspapers often were shut down in a particular locality or tightly monitored. One soldier traveling through Tennessee verified for his Ohio family that his general drew the strings tighter on secessionists and suspended two Memphis newspapers "for publishing contraband news."[74] However, the war opened private papers to the examination of soldiers who entered households looking for damning information in letters. In 1864 an officer from the Missouri State Militia complained about the amount of treason he found in the supposedly loyal border state of Missouri. In Saline County, he had arrested several women that he promised to send along and was holding "several of the worst rebels" as hostages to protect Union men. He and his men did search a few homes. The private papers of the occupants sickened him. "You can't pick up a letter about any of their houses but you will find treason in them," he remarked, without further explanation. He obviously figured that his readers understood what he meant. Similar patterns occurred in other areas where bushwhacking occurred or the military situation appeared to be unstable.[75]

Oral transmission of news was tougher to curtail, yet Union authorities attempted to restrict this as well, including the most seemingly innocuous speech. Ellen House of Knoxville, Tennessee, had become used to visiting Confederate prisoners held by the Union soldiers in the town. One day, the access to their friends and loved ones was abruptly halted, with new instructions informing visitors that they needed a permit to speak to the prisoners. They tried their luck anyway and went to the jail without the paperwork. The guard refused to let them in. "That is something entirely new," she observed about the policy. But she quickly put two and two together, connecting the restriction to actions on some battlefield. "There is good news for us," she reasoned, "and they are afraid that someone will tell the prisoners."[76] The same game was played in reverse, too. House noticed that Union foragers who passed by her place in November 1863 remarked that Lee was whipped and Richmond evacuated. This time, they overplayed their hand. "I cant tell how many times they have reported the same thing since they have been here," she said. "They must get something of the kind out to encourage their soldiers."[77]

A far more common tactic by Union authorities was to prohibit "disloyal" speech, defining everything that hinted of criticism of the United States or support for the Confederacy as treasonous. Because no one defined the term, provost marshals acted on flimsy reports, and the inhabitants were inclined to test the limits of the occupiers' patience. The experiences of a Missouri woman illustrate various themes concerning the contact between soldiers and civilians in occupied territory—especially the tendencies of an officer to be instrumental in shaping that experience. Even though Missouri was supposedly loyal, many policies for civil-military relations first emerged there and in other parts of the border region. Missouri was one of the rare places in the Union that exhibited tendencies similar to the deeper, Confederate South. (Another of the places to share these characteristics in the loyal North was southeastern Maryland, especially Cecil and Kent counties.) More to the point, Union authorities treated it as a place that contained secession sympathizers and people enmeshed in suspected guerrilla networks. On the other side of the coin, some residents thought of themselves as more Confederate than Unionist and referred to the provost marshals and soldiers as if they were the enemy.

Elvira Scott of Miami, Missouri, kept a record of the conflict with one particular Union provost marshal named Lieutenant Adam Bax. In July 1862, tensions grew in this small community in Saline County, located in north-central Missouri. Bax tried to curb behavior that he considered to be helping the Confederate war effort. Through the diary of Scott, we encounter a man who appears to be in over his head: petty and possibly vindictive. He appeared to rely too readily on unscreened intelligence from members of the community: Unionists who sometimes held a grudge against a southern sympathizer. Yet the exact context of the situation in which Bax lived and operated cannot be resurrected. Missouri was notorious for guerrilla activity, so it might be that Bax acted rationally within a tense situation where it was better to assume that people were guilty first before determining innocence. No matter what the quality of his thought process, his decisions shaped policy and the nature of civil-military relations at the ground level, forcing civilians to acquiesce or push back, and sometimes to do a little of both.

One summer's day a soldier handed Scott a document whose contents startled her. It was notice of her arrest for treasonable language and for exciting men to rebellion. She was ordered to report to the provost marshal every Friday morning at eleven o'clock. The appointment remained in force until Bax was convinced that she had changed her ways. The offense was never clearly laid out, but she seems to have avoided attending some kind of Union display, such as a parade of soldiers. Bax did say in his order that a lady's place was "to fulfill her household duties and not to spread treason and excite men to rebellion." To make sure she understood the consequences of failing to obey, Bax warned her that transgressions would cause the arrest of her husband, sending him to the prison at Marshall, Missouri, for the remainder of the war. As expected, Scott was *"indignant, outraged."* But she also was not alone: she learned that at least three other women faced similar charges and treatment.[78]

The evening she received the order, Scott faced the unwelcome prospect of feeding and entertaining the Union soldiers who regularly secured their meals at her household. Her husband, John, warned her not to talk with them or to play the piano, as was her custom. She did respond to their inquiries about whether she had any news to share. When she mentioned her arrest, she hinted that conversations she had with them might have been the reason for the reprimand. It was not, but Scott clearly could not miss the chance to let them think they might share in some of the guilt. She claimed that one looked amazed and said to a comrade, "Jim, don't that get you, arresting women? Lieut Bax must be a damned fool & will get himself in a scrape." Despite her vow to herself not to play for them, she did, claiming that she felt "no animosity to the poor, ignorant soldiers." She added: "Home was no longer a safe asylum, a sacred place."[79] Scott may have been playing more than the piano; she may have been playing up to the soldiers to see if she could elicit sympathy for her position.

The next day, the situation escalated with an exchange between her husband and a Unionist that drew a crowd. Someone fired a pistol. Elvira ran to John's workplace, where she found the front porch covered by armed and excited soldiers. She tried to push her way through to her spouse, but soldiers blocked her. In the meantime, Bax rushed up and thrust a hand into her face with pistols, saying, "Madam, you shall not insult the flag of my country." She protested that she had not done so but could not resist adding, "but I have neither country nor flag to protect me." She then sought comfort in a friend's store and tried to elicit sympathy from Unionist neighbors. She was finally ordered home by the soldiers as they took her husband off to a makeshift prison on the fairgrounds.

It turns out that the precipitating incident was a clash between John Scott and another man who apparently had taken the oath of loyalty. Scott had criticized Bax, calling his order disrespectful; the military had no right to tell women how to behave. Scott then impugned the character of his listener, who apparently had once been an uncompromising secessionist who had flown the rebel flag on his house and business, but had signed the document of loyalty that allowed him to maintain his store. The newfound Unionist—a switch based on self-interest, Scott alleged—had made himself "a pusillanimous sycophant." The man went to military authorities, reported the incident, and said he had been threatened by Scott, who had used treasonable language. He also reported that Scott said Bax "was a contemptible puppy & deserved to be kicked out of town."[80]

With accusations hanging over her husband's head, Elvira Scott and the other ladies faced quite a remarkable interview when they reported as ordered for examination before the provost marshal. They were not exactly cowed by the experience. One of the women, a Mrs. Lewis, insisted that Bax should define what treason was. He apparently ducked the question. Instead, he accused Mrs. Lewis's children of calling his soldiers abolitionists. She and another woman accused of hurrahing for Jeff Davis, a fairly common phrase that landed people into trouble, played it coy and blamed the episode on their children, claiming the youths were goaded into the pronouncement by soldiers. Emboldened for some reason, Scott began to criticize the policies of the government, claiming that poor decisions created factions within the Union and presumably blocked the ability to have peace. Bax interrupted, "Madam, you be talking treason now, blaming the government & speaking against it." Instead of backing down, Scott declared that the South would win independence. The officer again told her that the remarks constituted treason.[81] Eventually, matters calmed down. Bax gave up on persecuting the Scott family. John had been sent to another town to have his case adjudicated. In the process, he finally confronted Bax, claiming that the officer would be embarrassed to take such a paltry case to his superiors, especially considering the language that was used against women. The captain apparently had had enough and decided to cut his losses. The case never went forward.

What do we make of such an incident? First of all, this small affair was likely one of hundreds, if not thousands, that took place beneath the attentions of superiors at higher levels. Unlike Butler's edict in New Orleans, it generated no "woman order" that incurred widespread wrath beyond upsetting the local community. It is not even clear if it would have been recorded in official records, indicating that quantifying such occurrences would present a very dubious endeavor. Yet to the people involved, the collision with federal authority loomed large, with repercussions to a family's ability to sustain itself by losing a key provider to prison. Women's speech and possibly other behavior triggered reactions from Union provost marshals. In this case, the women had fallen under suspicion for failing to support a celebration, for failing to show respect for a Union flag, for jeering at Union soldiers, or for talking in a garden. These gestures, which in peacetime would be considered harmless, were in wartime interpreted as political acts—in fact, treasonous ones. Once again, treason was defined by one officer and maybe a few his cronies. From the high ground, the case certainly could not be sustained by officials, at least in civil courts. But even from the low ground, prosecuting John Scott before a military commission undoubtedly seemed like more trouble than it was worth.

The series of events in Miami, Missouri, also revealed the daily acts of resistance that occurred in occupied territory and wherever Union soldiers functioned as the main arbiters of disloyalty. Reading between the lines of texts such as Elvira Scott's suggests that women in particular pushed the boundaries of behavior to see what might be considered treason. They were not beyond poking the bear to see if it slumbered, snorted, or attacked. Once it became clear what course the officers chose, civilians either backed down or staked out new ground for resistance. To halt offensive behavior, Union provost marshals were not above targeting a family's livelihood. Controlling the behavior of women by putting their men in jeopardy made good sense—and effective policy.

Yet, as usual, the situation eventually calmed. Soldiers more often than not were less interested in punishing than in training their charges not to make a nuisance of themselves. Also, they were interested in securing with the least trouble the material goods that they needed from a potentially hostile population. Through such small and large collisions, civilians and soldiers drew the parameters for a treasonous act. It took a perfect dunderhead not to notice, for instance, that hurrahing for Jeff Davis or wishing for the success of the Confederacy brought the provost marshal to one's door. Or to realize that the best way to conduct business and maintain provisions was to take an oath of loyalty. Or to understand that a previously private act—like a conversation between neighbors—had become something riskier.

Interestingly enough, these definitions followed almost identically the terms being set in loyal states; however, the differences were important. Far more property was seized in the Confederacy—slaves and other chattel liberated. An uncounted number of Confederate civilians faced eviction from homes. Banishment was not unknown in the border region, but it became more common deeper into the conflict in the occupied South. Organized political opposition to these practices rarely materialized or created the same level of controversy as in the Union. And why should it be otherwise? Confederate civilians were, after all, considered as traitors.

6

THE MILITARY IN POLITICS,

1861–1863

When the Democratic Party wrote its platform for the 1864 presidential election, it summoned the most potent complaint it could muster against the Lincoln administration: interference by the military not only with personal liberties but also with elections. In the first resolution, the delegates pledged their faithfulness to the Constitution, which indirectly attacked Lincoln for failing to do the same. Then they got down to business by accusing the administration of abusing its powers through the doctrine of "military necessity," which allowed for the trampling of rights and the impairment of justice. This resolution also contained the most famous plank, in which the Democrats advocated a cessation of hostilities to forge a peace that could restore the Union. Third in the list of concerns came the allegation of tampering with elections as a "shameful violation of the Constitution." This part of the platform has received little attention in accounts of the convention, but at least half of the planks—arguably the heart of it that spanned resolutions two through four—dealt with military arrests of civilians and interference by the soldiers in elections. Perhaps more striking was the absence of discussion about racial issues. In the fifty-some odd pages of the convention's proceedings, the word emancipation appears no more than a few times: once to deny that George B. McClellan was a closet emancipator, which was hardly necessary.[1] The Democratic cry for peace and repugnance for emancipation have been the messages stressed most by historians, while the military's influence on elections has remained in the background of the partisan use of treason and loyalty in the American Civil War.[2]

The scholarly debate about the Democrats centers on whether they represented a loyal or disloyal opposition. Did the peace wing of the party constitute an effort to commit treason or was its impact exaggerated by Republicans? Opinion has swung on this question. Studies in the 1960s reclaimed the reputation of Democrats as conducting an honest opposition to Lincoln, suggesting that Republicans overstated "treason" in order to win elections. Today, the Copperheads have returned to a position in the literature of representing a dangerous movement, if not being intentionally treasonous.[3] Additionally, Democrats have been characterized as racist, differing from their Republican colleagues by employing the color bar as a vivid, important, and ugly part of political campaigns.[4] There are problems with stopping with this more recent presentation, primarily for what it leaves out. It is true that the party used racism as a central rhetorical strategy; however, the consideration of the loyalty of the opposition party, and its racial views, has kept scholarly attention on the validity of the Republican lament, rather than on the substance of the challenger's critique. This focus has prevented taking seriously the broader charges by the Democrats, especially Republicans' use of coercive military power on the loyal citizenry in the United States.

Shifting the focus to the Democratic complaint exposes that the military, an arm of the executive branch controlled by the Republican Party, left a heavy footprint on northern elections, although primarily in the border states. This represented more than the rhetorical battle of parties that most scholarly treatments feature when dealing with the partisan use of treason. Beneath the rhetorical surface, soldiers and the executive played hard politics justified to the public by the stated desire to prevent disloyal people from disturbing the democratic process—in other words, guard against treason. Troops supervised test oaths that determined the eligibility of people for voting, and they were deployed by the War Department to oversee the ballot in Maryland, Missouri, Kentucky, and Delaware. One historian of political rituals in the nineteenth century has argued that this intrusion by federal arms into the democratic process, especially during state and congressional races in 1863, may have made the difference in the outcome of the war by bringing to Washington supporters of the administration from the border states who could protect the Republican majority in the Thirty-Eighth Congress.[5] If we consider other forms of involvement, such as officers allowed to campaign for the Republicans in problematic precincts and soldiers furloughed home by the War Department to swing votes, then the activity extended to most corners of the Union. To Democrats, the arrest of Clement Vallandigham and the prosecution of the Indiana treason trials by military commission constituted related practices within the general context of the military attempting to stifle political opposition.

This use of the military should not resurrect the trope of Lincoln as dictator. Republicans played the game within the norms of nineteenth-century

American political culture: had Democrats been in control, they would have resorted to the same methods. Both parties used the rhetoric of treason to demonize the opposition and win elections. In fact, next to condemning the rebels in arms, treason as an epithet occurred most often in political campaigns. Manipulation of every factor within one's legal means remained a technique of even the fairest-minded partisan.[6] And, ironically, if being dictator meant using the mechanism of state power to chill a political opposition, then Lincoln proved wanting in this area. Rather than silence the Democrats through military arrests that included politicians and newspaper editors, the president handed his rivals the ammunition for attacking his policies deep into 1864. It was ammunition that, at least in the first two years of the war, quietly troubled Republicans behind the scenes, who sometimes worried that the chief executive used excessive measures that may not have been necessary.

From Underground to Overt Partisanship

In August 1861, Democrats from northwestern Pennsylvania gathered in St. Mary's Borough to express their hostility to the conduct of the war. They came from Clearfield, Jefferson, Elk, and McKean counties. These portions of the state constituted a corner of the lumber region, a fairly isolated area stretching across the top tier of the state near the New York border that even today retains a wilderness distinction by the Keystone State's bureau of tourism. The assembled delegates attacked the "fanaticism" and sectionalism of the Republican Party. The delegates deplored the slaughter of men in Virginia at First Bull Run. Peace reared its head as an objective. Resolutions favored a speedy settlement of the conflict through compromise and urged protection of freedom of speech and the press, adding that Lincoln deserved rebuke for running the government contrary to the Constitution.[7]

These resolutions were striking because they came during a period in the war considered as the height of nonpartisanship, when the call for unity dominated the usual political rhetoric. It was a time in which leading politicians on both sides warned against their followers placing party ahead of nation. And it was a time in which taking positions described by political parties invariably brought on the allegation of treason. Republicans in particular became especially adept at trotting out the charge of treason to condemn an emerging opposition, although Democrat Stephen Douglas set the precedent first when he said: "There are not but two parties, the party of patriots and the party of traitors."[8] The St. Mary's resolutions appeared as a counternarrative to this story of partisan unity. They also served as a precursor to what became Democratic standards by 1863 and carried through to the presidential election of 1864. The resolutions—with some editing—foreshadowed the party's platform for the presidential contest. What should be made of this seemingly inconsequential gathering of delegates in an isolated section of an important state? St. Mary's was hardly New York City or Washington, two recognized centers of political power and influence. We could easily dismiss this activity by a small group of people from a wilderness region. Was this meeting a singular event—a strike of a match within a much larger conflagration?

New York and Philadelphia exhibited similar activity. In late June 1861, a few editors from Democratic newspapers met in New York City to adopt resolutions that condemned the war, denounced the administration, expressed horror at the expense of the conflict on the public treasury, and weighed in heavily against the Republican Party. In another part of the Union, well before anyone fired a shot at Bull Run, the State Democratic Convention of Ohio launched a salvo against the administration, calling it "incompetent" and proclaiming that corruption dominated public affairs.[9] In Philadelphia, an election to fill an empty seat in Congress on July 2 resulted in a victory for Democrat Charles J. Biddle. It was a narrow victory of a couple of hundred votes, helped undoubtedly because Biddle served as an officer in the Union army, which suggested he supported the prosecution of a war for reunion. By August, Sidney George Fisher, a Republican, looked at events in his city of Philadelphia and determined that Democrats were organizing a peace party "to divide public opinion and weaken the efforts of the government." He considered such a party "in alliance with the rebels of the South."[10] Similarly, in the middle of June unanimity existed only on the surface among the electorates in Ohio, Indiana, and Illinois, with collisions coming especially in the fall campaigns.[11] The partisan game was afoot well before the more recognized moments in 1862.

However, it could not yet become a widespread trend. Partisan expressions remained nascent, confined to local or regional movements, and without a national voice primarily because these positions were easily marginalized as treasonous. The meeting of the Democratic editors in New York earned scorn from many parts of the Union, including from newspapers dedicated to the party of Jefferson. Political expression varied according to the peculiar nature of communities, even while the overarching, national dialogue stressed abandoning parties as a show of patriotism.[12] Early in the conflict, partisan debate at the national level often took place indirectly by employing the rhetoric of loyalty. Treason provided the lexicon for condemning rivals without compromising one's own patriotism. According to moderate and conservative Republicans, as one historian has argued, the war demanded abandoning the usual tolerant positions; "anything less was treason."[13]

Commentary on the progress of the war gave partisanship the means to cloak itself within the banner of patriotism—to allow both sides of the congressional aisle to advocate their agenda without appearing to follow the goals of party. Much of the "nonpartisan" wrangling occurred over the army: its action, its lack of action, and its effectiveness in stopping the traitorous secessionists. The outcome of battles, if the results were poor, invariably sparked a partisan critique of Lincoln's judgment. The federal loss at Bull Run emboldened critics of the administration who chastised the war effort without appearing to be treasonous. The other side understood the situation quite well. In Boston, a Republican wrote his friend who served in the army that the election results in the fall of 1862 were due to a lack of progress by the military. "With the Administration military success is everything," wrote John C. Ropes, "it is the verdict which cures all errors."[14]

The Radical Republicans in particular assumed a so-called nonpartisan stance that barely masked political goals. They seized upon a disastrous reconnaissance by Union soldiers at Ball's Bluff, near Leesburg, Virginia, to convene an investigative body known as the Joint Committee on the Conduct of the War. Formed in December 1861 because of the discontent with Union reverses since First Bull Run, and with the restricted brand of warfare that protected slaves and rebel property, the committee held nearly 300 secret sessions. The members enjoyed unrestricted scope and broad powers to conduct their business. Although it investigated a number of issues, such as potential corruption in military supplies, a large portion of the committee's efforts centered on trying to condemn more conservative Union generals as sympathizers with the Confederacy.

The committee first turned its attention to the reasons for the failure at Bull Run, which brought before it Union General Robert Patterson, a known Democrat. He had been criticized for allowing the Confederate army under Joseph E. Johnston to slip away from the Shenandoah Valley and support General Beauregard at Manassas. Although the inquiry did not result in further actions against Patterson, it derailed his military career.[15] As the focus next turned to Ball's Bluff, treason became an increasing refrain. The scapegoat became Charles P. Stone, the general in charge of the operation that had resulted in the death of more than 200 federal soldiers. Unfortunately for Stone, one of those fallen soldiers was a sitting U.S. senator, Edward Baker, who served as a colonel of infantry. Baker was a personal friend with the Lincolns and the namesake for one of their children who had passed away in the 1850s. Admittedly, Stone had not handled his troops well; however, it was outrageous to think that he had deliberately sacrificed his men. Yet such was the indictment against him in the Republican press and among members of the committee.[16] In New York, Democrat George Templeton Strong noted in his diary: "That there has been treason somewhere in high quarters is certain, and if Stone be guilty, I hope he may be speedily hanged."[17] Stone suffered imprisonment for six months until winning exoneration in the spring of 1863.

Stone and Patterson served as the vanguard of a procession of generals ordered to Washington to defend themselves from suspicion of treason. This included Irvin McDowell and George B. McClellan, both of whom were considered by Radicals as soft on the rebels. Radical congressmen used the conciliatory actions of generals toward rebel traitors to create support for a harder brand of warfare. In June 1862, the joint committee conducted hearings that were eventually published under the title of "Protecting Rebel Property." The report by the committee revealed that a healthy amount of confiscation occurred under the auspices of the War Department, especially through the Quartermaster's Bureau run by General Montgomery Meigs. A citizen employed by the bureau told the committee that he had been charged by the bureau with collecting abandoned rebel property along the railroad line that ran through Manassas Junction.[18] However, military policy remained ambiguous, if not contradictory. The bureau might counsel its men to function in one way (take all property needed), while the commander of a department laid down more restrictive regulations (protect property of peaceful noncombatants). Such was the case with McDowell, who also came under scrutiny for his command of troops in northern Virginia in the spring of 1862. As he came before the Joint Committee, the general learned that he had to defend allegations that he had stationed guards over rebel property that could have been used by the military.

General Abner Doubleday provided some of the more damning testimony concerning the Union's conciliatory policy. He told the committee that, upon arriving at McDowell's command in late May 1862, he "received a long lecture on the necessity of doing my best to conciliate these secessionists; the people about there, who were said to be all secessionists." He had tried to commandeer the home of a Dr. Carmichael for his headquarters near Fredericksburg. The doctor, who had abandoned the property to relocate to Richmond, had a son in the Confederate army, but Doubleday said that McDowell's orders prevented using the property.[19] A few weeks after the general's appearance before the committee, Provost Marshal General Marsena Patrick noticed the impact. McDowell remained unhappy with Doubleday, who "has been the cause of more evil to him than any one else, having made the matter of his guarding rebel property a test of his loyalty." Patrick noted that orders came down from McDowell to withdraw guards from the rebel home, adding: "He is frightened by the attacks of Newspaper writers & the Tribune, & Pope's Order for political purposes." This last item referred to the promotion of Major General John Pope to lead a newly organized Army of Virginia and the general's orders that his men use the property of rebels to feed the army.[20] In addition to his appearance before the Joint Committee, McDowell faced a court of inquiry over his behavior in late 1862. In this session, a frustrated general read into the record what he thought was really going on with the investigations: "The question which stands forth prominently in this case, and which may be assumed as the charge to which all the other can be regarded as specifications, is that of treason."[21]

As the midterm elections approached in the fall of 1862, a number of ingredients allowed for more partisan opposition to the Lincoln government. Although many studies cite the Emancipation Proclamation, there were more elements. This is not to say that emancipation played no role: obviously it did. One of the more incendiary Democratic newspaper editors in the North, Peter Gray Meek from the hometown of Pennsylvania Republican governor Curtin, proclaimed, "Abolition has triumphed," suggesting that treasonous antislavery proponents had destroyed the American Union, murdered a million American citizens, and "beggared the whole American people," and that it now sought "a continuance of this war, to crown its infamy by dragging the white man down to a level with the negro."[22]

The racial anger, however, took place in the broader context of a stalled war effort in the Virginia theater and as the Congress enacted monetary policies that burdened the population with new taxes. The political impact of the financial crisis cannot be overstated. By December 1861 the country faced bankruptcy. By the summer of 1862, congressmen authorized the formation of the Internal Revenue Service and placed taxes on a range of items such as liquor, tobacco, playing cards, billiard tables, jewelry, newspaper advertisements, and even licenses on professions. The policies irritated Democrats, who viewed them as consolidating power in a financial class and who hated paying taxes to support an increasingly unpopular war. In Boston, antislavery Republican John Ropes believed the election results "have nothing to do with the nigger question." He added that it was the loss of life on the battlefield, coupled with anger over new taxes, which mobilized rivals.[23]

And the government escalated military arrests. The militia draft had awakened resistance on the Union home front, which had the unintended consequence of steeling the resolve of supporters of the administration. The Democratic enclaves that manifested early expressions of partisanship provided fertile ground for preaching against mobilization. In Pennsylvania, the south-central, southwestern, and northeastern regions captured the most attention of federal agents. Anxious supporters of the war wrote Curtin about the treason they saw around them. A man from the Philadelphia area cited a newspaper from Selinsgrove that urged resistance to the draft. He hoped the government would crush this treason promptly. Another man reported a "rebellious element" in Luzerne County "equally better and the same in spirit to that in the rebel States." They uttered threats that they would resist the government with arms if it resorted to drafting, and they vowed to resist the tax collection "even to the death."[24] Although the protest was avid, so was the support for the government. Republicans and War Democrats considered any attempt to discourage enlistments as treason that should be punished. This included *expressing the desire that the campaigns should fail*. Implied treason was very much alive in popular and official attitudes.

Increased arrests came through an order issued by the War Department on August 8, 1862, which empowered marshals, their deputies, and military officers to arrest anyone attempting to leave a state or the country to avoid enlisting. A different order published the same day broadened the activities that came under inspection. Authorities were to imprison anyone who disrupted recruitment by actions, speech, or writing. Once again, federal officials employed an expansive notion of criminal behavior that echoed the English definition of constructive treason. It allowed agents of the government to define treasonous behavior. They were armed with the authority to conduct arrests outside of civil legal channels and without having to announce charges. On September 24, 1862, Lincoln later sanctioned the practice already in place as he proclaimed a general suspension of habeas corpus. Democrats often referred to "The Two Proclamations of 1862," indicating that the suspension of habeas corpus enjoyed an equal reference with emancipation.[25]

The petty behavior of officials commanded the attention of public discourse, partly because Democrats made it an issue and partly because the actions looked excessive even to Republicans. In New York, George Templeton Strong, a supporter of Lincoln and leader of the Sanitary Commission, privately called the arrests "imbecile, dangerous, unjustifiable." Strong believed that the arrests brought to the surface the leaders who had labored underground for eighteen months in their efforts against the war. Now, they could cause a national calamity. "If it come, it will be due not so much to the Emancipation Manifesto as to the irregular arrests the government has been making. They have been used against the Administration with most damaging effect, and no wonder. They have been utterly arbitrary, and could be excused only because demanded by the pressure of an unprecedented national crisis." In Philadelphia, Sydney George Fisher sounded a similar refrain as he looked back at these and subsequent arrests from the vantage of the summer of 1863. "The government has made a great mistake in this matter of arresting & sending off to prison men charged with treasonable language & opinions, and has thus attacked the most sensitive part of the American character. Many of the arrests were wholly unjustifiable and they have been made by military authority instead of civil, which has given them a more odious character."[26]

The fallout from the arrests aided the Democrats in the midterm elections, in which they realized significant gains. Lincoln scholar David Donald has suggested that while the president understood that his party would take a hit from emancipation, he was "surprised" by the impact of the critique of the suspension of habeas corpus. It caused him to pay closer attention to military arrests and to develop a stronger rationale for suppressing the domestic traitors in the Union.[27] Illinois attorney and Lincoln supporter Orville Hickman Browning—who lost his bid to retain the Senate seat vacated by the death of Stephen Douglas—conferred with moderate Republican senator William Pitt Fessenden of Maine about what had gone wrong. Fessenden was surprised that the "proclamations" had been issued. Note that he spoke in the plural, referring to the preliminary emancipation *and* the habeas corpus pronouncements. Concerning slavery, the senator from Maine thought that Lincoln could have forecast a policy shift—that he would ask the army to begin seizing slaves in the insurrectionary districts come January 1—without issuing an official proclamation. He considered the invoking of martial law in the loyal states "an exercise of despotic power which he did not possess, and very dangerous." A day later Browning conveyed similar sentiments to the president, claiming that "the proclamations had revived old party issues—given them a rallying cry—capitol to operate upon and that we had the results in our defeat. To this he made no reply."[28]

Shortly after the elections, the administration began releasing the political prisoners held in federal installations, causing relief among Lincoln's supporters and indignation among his detractors. The *New York Times*, a moderate Republican organ generally supportive of the administration, applauded the order by Stanton to release political prisoners and those in confinement for having discouraged enlistments. "We are very glad this order has been issued," noted the writer. "It will put an end to much clamor against the Government, some of which has not been wholly without foundation." This was telling. The author continued: "There can be no doubt that the power of arbitrary arrest, which has been asserted by the Government as a necessary precaution during this rebellion, has been exerted, in very many instances, with harshness, and in nearly all without that careful regard to the requirements of justice which should have been inseparable from its exercise."[29]

Democrats seized upon the clemency as proof that the administration had imprisoned people to control the elections. Stanton's order was taken as a tacit admission that the restrictions on liberty had not been necessary but had swept into prison innocent people who could be safely released without creating danger for the nation—once the political campaigns had ended.[30] Newspapers throughout the loyal North noticed the release of inmates from Old Capital Prison in Washington and reminded readers this gesture had occurred *after* the elections. The *Dubuque Herald,* for instance, mentioned that a candidate for Congress was discharged once the polling had ended. And the *Chicago Times*, an important Democratic newspaper in the Midwest, made the link more clearly, in accusing the government that the stifling of liberty of speech was "being actuated by partisan malice, rather than the desire of subserving the public weal."[31]

Once tossed onto the table, the arrest card remained in play for the next couple of years. New York governor Horatio Seymour, a conservative Democrat, criticized the administration's abuse in his first message to the legislature in January 1863. He demanded that free expression of opinion be respected. Seymour refuted the idea that the war had come because of an unavoidable contest about slavery. He claimed the origin was rooted in a lack of respect for the Constitution and "local prejudices," which he left undefined. The governor attacked Lincoln's Emancipation Proclamation, but spent far more of his message disputing the president's positions on martial law. According to Seymour, the imprisonment of citizens in the loyal North had been "glaringly partisan" and ignored the right to free discussion. The government treated with contempt the fact that the courts operated freely in the North and that the judicial system contained ample powers to protect the country from treason. He denied that his attack on the government constituted a desire to appease the South with the result of creating two separate countries. He made it clear that he wished to restore the Union. Obviously looking over his political shoulder, he called for people to support the army in the field and to use every possible means to end the war, but he included the possibility of a negotiated peace.[32]

At relatively the same time, Union troops began to escalate their presence at polling precincts, especially throughout the border region. But it was more than a border state problem: it was a problem in Indiana and Ohio and Tennessee. It was a problem, indeed, that Democrats tried to use to their advantage.

Soldiers "Mingling in Politics"

Ironically, the past haunted McClellan: the conservative general and future Democratic challenger to Lincoln, whose party accused the sitting president of abuse of power. In the fall of 1861, the military left its imprint on one election in particular. Throughout the war, Maryland remained a sensitive strategic and political region. Lincoln created controversy by ignoring a ruling by Chief Justice Taney that the president had no right to suspend habeas corpus in the arrest of John Merryman. As autumn approached, reports indicated that the Maryland legislature—which had relocated from Annapolis to Frederick—was considering a resolution supporting the right of secession. The legislature had held a special session in August that denounced the "tyrannical acts" of the president and promised to reconvene on September 17. In response, the administration used troops to arrest thirty-one public officials, including the mayor of Baltimore, imprisoning them until the election of a Unionist legislature.[33] For added security, it placed the army at election precincts to ensure a Unionist victory. Screening for voters who supported the administration was fairly easy to accomplish in mid-nineteenth-century America because voting was conducted publicly, often through color-coded tickets placed into different boxes or bowls clearly indicating the party vote. The secret ballot awaited until well after the war.

Major General George Brinton McClellan shut down the legislature of Maryland. Then he sent troops to screen precincts. The repression of the lawmakers came after consultation with the president and the secretaries of state and war. McClellan clearly supported the decision and did more than operate as a functionary. In his note to Major General Nathaniel Banks of September 12, 1861, he urged care in handling the legislature, adding: "If it [the plan for arrests] is successfully carried out it will go far toward breaking the backbone of the rebellion."[34] More than a month later, he contacted Banks again concerning fears that citizens favoring disunion intended to interfere with the election on November 6. Rumors had come from "the chief of the Secret Service" (presumably Pinkerton) that secessionists who had gone to Virginia now plotted to return with arms to influence the forthcoming contest. McClellan directed that Banks "send detachments of a sufficient number of men to the different points in your vicinity where the elections are to be held, to protect the Union voters and see that no disunionists are allowed to intimidate them." The order empowered Banks to throw secessionists into prison and clarified that habeas corpus had been suspended. Three years later, McClellan did not apologize for what he had done, despite military arrests serving as a consistent part of the Democratic critique. To a political supporter, he explained that at the time of the arrests he had considered the army weak and remembered that rumors suggested the Maryland legislature would invite the Confederate army into the state. The only thing to do was to "nip the whole affair in the bud."[35]

Even so, these actions at the time raised remarkably little criticism. One has to look hard to find Maryland's suspected secessionists evoking sympathy in the periodicals of the North, although they did give southern editors something to rail against. Fear of domestic traitors created a common ground for people from both parties. Republicans and Democrats alike could hate secession and hope that their country was not ripped apart by the maneuvering of state legislatures. John Forney's *Philadelphia Press*, a moderate organ that gravitated from Democratic to Republican positions and back again, saw the danger of state rights and declared that a legislature "has no more right to pass a bill designed in any way to destroy the political connection between any State of this Union and the Federal Government than a township meeting or a justice of the peace."[36]

Delaware makes the point that some interference in elections did not provoke partisan reaction, even after Stanton's order on August 8 sent a stream of civilians to military forts. On November 4, Election Day, troops guarded the polling places. According to one account, the soldiers barred the way and "raised their drawn swords to permit the passage of voters who carried Unionist tickets."[37] William Cannon—who later protested the use of troops in a different election—won the gubernatorial seat by 111 votes, indicating that the campaign was close enough to warrant the concern. Few Democrats protested the swords that guarded the electoral "purity" of the gubernatorial race in Delaware. Cannon was a Democrat—albeit one who supported emancipation—who ran on a Unionist platform rather than as an outright party man. And the Democratic press was enjoying a season of success, celebrating the gains in congressional campaigns and the election of Seymour as the governor of New York.[38]

A little more troublesome were the patterns emerging in other parts of the border, especially Kentucky and Missouri. During the summer of 1862, Kentuckians experienced an escalation of military oversight under Brigadier General Jeremiah T. Boyle. The state had tried to assume a position of neutrality, which failed. Lincoln treated Kentucky carefully because he feared losing this strategically positioned state with resources for war making. However, once it became clear that the support requested by the Unionists would not push the state into the arms of the Confederacy, the administration allowed for an increased level of military oversight. An antislavery Republican, Boyle entered the state in July 1862 and served as a de facto military governor until 1864. Earning a reputation for acting capriciously, the general moved on a number of fronts to consolidate the state for the Union. Although he promised to exercise caution in arrests, their frequency escalated under him. One of Lincoln's friends, Joshua Speed, thought the general did harm by saying one thing and doing another. "This fickleness is injuring us," he said, adding that Unionists needed to encourage loyal sentiment rather than rely on the bayonet.[39]

Boyle conducted arrests widely, targeting newspaper editors and members of the judiciary alike, so it was only natural that he paid attention to polling precincts. August 1862 featured elections for governor, legislature, and state officers. Boyle issued a warning against people of Confederate sympathies. On July 21, he threatened to arrest and charge with treason anyone running for office who criticized the national government. He allowed the formation of an election precinct with as few as three voters—a concession to areas in which the Confederate population had fled, leaving behind a handful of Unionists. This policy made every possible Union vote count. Other actions that may have been taken by the military remain less clear, such as whether soldiers restricted voting. Yet something must have happened. A year later, as the state faced the election of a governor and the legislature, a Kentuckian asked the president to consider allowing Burnside to adopt the tactics of Boyle to prevent the state from being carried into the rebellion. He referred to "interposition" in the election but did not specify what that meant.[40]

Next door in Missouri, residents faced what one historian has termed a "rough-and-tumble" political culture that also proved, once again, that many hands beyond the federal government contributed to the campaign against disloyalty.[41] To a great extent, repression of the franchise and other liberties was imposed by local Republicans. In October 1861, Missouri's acting government passed an ordinance requiring public officeholders to pledge their allegiance to the state and the U.S. Constitution. Quickly the policy expanded to require the oath to practicing professionals, such as teachers, professors, lawyers, jurors, city officials, clergymen, and officers of benevolent associations. Eventually, the Missouri State Convention required citizens to take the oath to vote as well as serve as judges of elections. They had to state that they had not taken up arms against the United States or the state of Missouri since December 17, 1861. If election judges did not perform their job, they faced arrest and trial by military commission.[42] The practice occurred beyond Missouri. In April 1862, an editor lamented the requirement for a test oath for the qualification of electors in Georgetown and Washington in all municipal elections. Other states did the same.[43] As one scholar has demonstrated, screening disloyalty through oath-taking became a principal way to affect elections in Missouri.[44]

Complicating the story of military interference in elections was the existence of a state militia. Union soldiers did not need to police polling precincts for a couple of years because it was being done for them by the state's military apparatus. In late 1861, the governor of Missouri had negotiated with the Lincoln administration for the creation of the Missouri State Militia. This special military force was not to serve outside of Missouri. It answered to the governor, operated from garrisons throughout the area, and established itself as the chief enforcer of loyalty, including at elections. It functioned as a military arm of the state Republican Party, so whatever repression it conducted was homegrown. Even though it lost recruits to this organization, the federal government benefited from the arrangement because the militia allowed for troops of the United States to be deployed against Confederates rather than against civilians in the rear. But its members did not differentiate between maintaining order at elections and influencing how they turned out. And General Orders No. 24 of this Missouri State Militia forced disloyal people—as defined by its own criteria—to register themselves, which invariably was used against them at elections.[45]

In May 1862, James H. Birch—a candidate for governor—was arrested allegedly for proclaiming he would withdraw support for supplying troops to the Union if Lincoln emancipated slaves. He was quickly freed but later harassed by a captain of a Missouri militia company. Birch had opposed secession and could be considered loyal, but he drew this attention because he was no fan of emancipation and openly criticized Lincoln. Although Birch continued his campaigning, more serious interference came during the autumn elections. Benjamin F. Loan, who served as a general in the Missouri State Militia and later as a Republican U.S. congressman, ordered arrests of people he considered to be disloyal. He banished some and imprisoned what one scholar has estimated as roughly 200 more. One of the men targeted was Sample Orr, a former candidate for governor in 1860 who gave a speech a few days before the 1862 election that was considered inflammatory. Orr was dedicated to the Union but, like Birch, opposed emancipation, while also attacking the policy of military arrests of civilians. A military commission acquitted Orr of the charges in June 1863, meaning he spent more than half a year behind bars before release. Loan had not stopped there, however. His soldiers turned away people from at least 8 of 150 precincts, and in St. Joseph soldiers entered the courthouse and destroyed the poll books.[46]

In 1863 the mood among Democrats openly soured against both military arrests and the presence of troops in elections as soldiers interfered with either the campaigning or the balloting in Ohio, Kansas, Kentucky, Missouri, and Maryland. With the arrest and trial before a military commission of Clement Vallandigham, former congressman and future candidate for the governor of Ohio, the government no longer appeared to target primarily secessionists in the border states and occupied Confederacy. Even if they did not think that Lincoln was an actual dictator, they used the assaults on free speech and the supervision of voting by the military to rebut the charge that *they* were the ones who were traitors to the nation's principles.

To see the building blocks for this interpretation first requires considering the place of soldiers in elections, not as guards but as citizens exercising their civic rights. Allowing soldiers to vote via absentee ballot was not the norm. When the war began, only one state allowed soldiers to vote when outside of their election districts. By the 1864 presidential election, that number jumped to nineteen. Democrats usually opposed this change. In New York, Governor Seymour vetoed a bill allowing for absentee balloting by soldiers, holding off the measure until the spring of 1864. Valid reasons existed against having soldiers vote while in the ranks. Because there was no secret ballot, people worried that fraud was easy to accomplish and that enlisted men faced intimidation by officers.[47]

If the truth be told, though, Democrats feared the soldiers' vote less for ideological reasons than for practical ones. Especially after 1861, they thought they would lose elections. Both sides held the impression that most men in the military were either Republicans or War Democrats who supported the administration. Republicans complained in print that the military had stripped districts of men loyal to the government, leaving behind communities containing Confederate sympathizers.[48] One historian's analysis of the soldiers' vote provides a striking statistic that makes the point. "In 1862 voting-in-the-field soldiers gave a four to one majority to the Republican candidates for the state legislature," noted Frank Klement. He added: "In 1864 the ratio was fourteen to one. Voting-in-the-field helped to keep Republicanism in control of the state governments."[49]

Given the conspiratorial bent in American politics, it did not take much effort to consider that conscription—enacted in March 1863—represented one more tool for Republicans to force Democrats into a nonvoting army. Contributing to this impression was the way the War Department acted as the head of a political machine involving the military. The army obeyed a Republican president, whose subordinates authorized generals to go home to campaign for him or who released soldiers on furloughs to help in problematic districts. There is no doubt that this happened. Writing nearly fifty years after the war, Assistant Secretary of War Charles A. Dana unapologetically recalled that during the 1864 presidential campaign "all the power and influence of the War Department . . . was employed to secure the re-election of Mr. Lincoln." He had witnessed a flow of telegrams from all over the country requesting leaves for officers and furloughs for privates who were needed in close districts. Apparently they were granted.[50]

From such actions and commentary, Democrats built an argument that conscription provided a way not only to revitalize the army but also to control the balance of political power on the home front. Common impressions held that the volunteers of 1861 tended to be the most supportive of the administration and likely were Republicans or War Democrats. A person from a small town in southwestern Pennsylvania commented on this to Governor Andrew Curtin, saying that the lack of a strong volunteer drive—supported by a state draft—would prove disastrous. Most of the men volunteering from Fayette County had been Republicans. A draft could correct this imbalance by placing more Democrats into the army. Similarly, a Pittsburgh Republican asserted: "*We must have a draft or we are lost. Nothing short of it can prevent an utter and entire defeat of our party in October.*"[51]

The Democrat who made the connection between conscription and military arrests was Clement L. Vallandigham, well before he provoked the Union military into arresting him for disloyal speech. He was a casualty of the congressional election of 1862, defeated by Union Major General Schenck. On February 23, 1863, he delivered a farewell address to the Congress titled "The Conscription Bill—Arbitrary Arrests." Representatives at the time were crafting the legislation for conscription. Vallandigham thundered against the seventh and twenty-fifth sections of the bill, which placed provost marshals in congressional districts and empowered these military officers to arrest citizens who interfered with enlistments. The address characterized conscription as denying free speech. Vallandigham did not exaggerate: the act established that critical speech (i.e., words that affected enlistments) could result in imprisonment. Counseling a person against reporting was considered an offense punishable by imprisonment and fines. Vallandigham considered the draft an escalation of government powers to prevent peaceable assemblies, to deny the right to bear arms, and to limit the right of suffrage.[52]

He was not alone in professing such thoughts. A man identifying himself as "Seventy Years" told a Democratic newspaper in Columbus, Ohio, that the pattern of arrests and the draft represented "a deep-laid plan to crush the Democrats and their principles." He claimed that the names of Democrat voters eligible for the draft had been *especially marked* and were designated to fill up old regiments, which spread them thinly to diminish unity of action.[53] Was this true? Probably not. The names for the draft were chosen through a lottery wheel, which meant that election officials, even if they wished to control the outcome, had to stuff an untold number of Democratic names into the bin to have an effect. A recent study also has proved how easy it was for those who were selected to avoid the draft, especially in cities, so it is doubtful the end would have been achieved.[54] The rumor of such a campaign, rather than its actuality, resonated with Democrats.

Vallandigham's final address to the Congress made a plausible case that the bill resurrected the traditions of the English monarchy concerning constructive treason. In fact, a section of his speech came across as a treatise on the subject. He reminded that treason had a specific meaning in the U.S. Constitution; that it required an overt act—not uttered wishes but an actual armed assault, confirmed by two witnesses. Constructive treason, banned by the U.S. Constitution, did not involve an overt act. It included, among other things, calling the king names, impugning his supremacy, and refusing to disperse when ordered. Foreshadowing his own arrest, Vallandigham pronounced: "Whoever shall denounce or oppose this Administration—whoever may affirm that war will not restore the Union, and teach men the gospel of peace, may be reported and arrested, upon some old grudge, and by some ancient enemy, it may be, and imprisoned as guilty of a treasonable practice."[55]

His critique overlooked one issue—the difference in executive power between peace and war. Supporters of Lincoln cited *Luther v. Borden* to justify the use of martial law and military arrests in wartime. This U.S. Supreme Court case from 1849 involved Dorr's Rebellion in Rhode Island, in which citizens attempted to overthrow the state government by military force.[56] Vallandigham pleaded for recognizing the Union and the Constitution as it existed before the war. He argued cogently for a particular understanding of governmental power, but it was a power most appropriate for a country at peace. Lincoln considered what the Constitution enabled when a country was at war, especially if that nation faced an internal rebellion, a fact that Vallandigham and his followers rarely mentioned. The stage was set for a confrontation that reverberated throughout the Union.

The seeds for trouble were sewed in the town of Mount Vernon, Ohio, on May 1, 1863. On this day, the town pulsed with excitement. Partisans had the chance to honor their political champions, who, they hoped, had Abraham Lincoln on the run. These heroes included not only Vallandigham but also Ohio congressmen George S. Pendleton and Samuel S. Cox, as well as the editor of a local newspaper. The size of the gathering, estimated at 15,000, required multiple speaker stands. A large U.S. flag served as a canopy over the main platform on which sat Vallandigham, Cox, and Pendleton, the future Democratic candidate for vice president. The cumulative effect screamed patriotism. National flags proliferated, as did Democratic hickory poles in honor of Andrew Jackson and Copperhead liberty pins. On a large wagon drawn by six horses, thirty-four young ladies representing the states of the Union waved to the crowd. It was a moment of fun, of partisan community, and of confrontation.[57]

As Vallandigham rose to speak, a man leaned against the speakers' platform off to one side, scribbling notes. Was it a reporter? No, it was Captain H. R. Hill of the 115th Ohio, who made himself less conspicuous by wearing civilian garb. He settled himself about six feet to the side of the speaker during the two-hour address, while a comrade—Captain John A. Means of the same regiment—stood about ten feet in front of Vallandigham. Means also did not wear a uniform. Both men tried to capture the gist of the politician's comments. They dutifully recorded—Means scribbling his "minutes" down hurriedly after he returned to his hotel room—that Vallandigham decried the war as unnecessary and cruel, that he accused Lincoln of prolonging it for the purposes of abolition and for waging a campaign to deny people of their liberties. Vallandigham did not advocate violent resistance; he asked his listeners to obey the law. Because he was aware of the investigators, he stressed channeling their protests through the courts and the ballot box. Clearly, he offered nothing more than political speech.[58]

The military commander of the district, Ambrose E. Burnside, had issued orders prohibiting such speech. On April 13, he had published General Orders No. 38 in which he outlined the behavior that earned a military trial for treason. "The habit of declaring sympathies for the enemy will not be allowed in this Department. Persons committing such offenses will be at once arrested, with a view to being tried . . . or sent beyond our lines into the lines of their friends." He added: "It must be distinctly understood that treason, expressed or implied, will not be tolerated in this Department."[59] Burnside had invoked the rationale of implied treason, similar to the British doctrine of constructive treason that Vallandigham had criticized in Congress. It was an order that arguably contradicted the principles of free speech.

Burnside waited a few days before sending the military to Vallandigham's door. About 2:30 A.M. on May 5, the usual nighttime visit for politically sensitive arrests, soldiers arrived at the Democrat's home and demanded that he surrender. Captain Charles G. Hutton led a handful of men who cordoned off the structure in case of an escape attempt. After Vallandigham refused to surrender himself, an attempt to break down the front door failed. The soldiers then attacked the rear door with axes and ramrods. Vallandigham went to a window and fired his pistol three times into the air to alert potential allies. (A few appeared later but offered no resistance to the soldiers.) He retreated deeper into his home as the soldiers entered, forcing them to crack open the panels of bedroom doors with rifle butts. As they surrounded him, he kept the pistol in his trouser pocket but did not reach for it. Instead, he surrendered to the men, gave his wife a brief hug, and went off to prison in Cincinnati.[60] There, facing a hearing before a military commission, he maintained his innocence and rejected the right of the panel to try him while civil courts functioned. The military convicted him and sentenced him to imprisonment in a fort for the rest of the war. Lincoln stepped in and changed the sentence to banishment to the Confederacy, whose officials let the Ohio politician make his way to Canada.

Vallandigham's arrest and banishment triggered a riot in Dayton that destroyed a newspaper office, sparked protests by Democrats across the North, and elicited a frightening missive by President Lincoln that became known as the Corning Letter. In May, shortly after the incident,

Democrats at Albany, New York, passed resolutions that professed support for a Union victory—not an immediate peace such as the Copperheads vouchsafed—but resolutions that censured the president for his use of military arrests. Governor Seymour could not attend the meeting presided over by Erastus Corning, a railroad and iron magnate, but sent a strongly worded letter that decried Vallandigham's arrest as bringing "dishonor upon our country" and raising potentially great danger to individuals and homes. The action had involved "a series of offences against our most sacred rights," including free speech, security of homes, and right to trial. Continuing down this path would lead to military despotism. The committee's resolutions could not have agreed more, although its wording was more temperate. After asserting the group's loyalty and desire to defeat the rebels, the committee chastised the seizing of Vallandigham for "no other reason than words addressed to a public meeting." It also reminded the president about the laws for treason and how the Constitution intended to protect the rights of citizens against arbitrary power, "especially in times of civil commotion." The committee urged that Lincoln abandon the policy of military arrests of citizens, which would "divide and distract the North, and destroy its confidence in the purposes of the Administration." And they hoped that he would reverse the decision of the military tribunal and release Vallandigham.[61]

Lincoln did neither. Instead, he responded in a public letter that was widely circulated and that advanced a rather startling proposition about arrests that should still raise eyebrows. The first portion of his letter assumed a careful, reasoned rebuttal against the Corning Letter's characterization of military arrests coming under the auspices of treason. The arrests were made, he asserted correctly, on different grounds from a capital crime defined by the Constitution. He also offered a strong defense concerning the suspension of habeas corpus. He reminded his readers that the Union was in the midst of a rebellion and that a condition of war rendered civil courts powerless to handle offenses against the government. The Constitution specifically stated that a rebellion or invasion allowed for circumventing the normal channels of justice in peacetime.

Then he entered slippery terrain. He posited that *preventative* arrests were allowed to be conducted by him. In other words, he condoned imprisoning people *before* they had done anything wrong. He added that in this civil war *doing nothing* could earn a visit from the military. "The man who stands by and says nothing, when the peril of his government is discussed, can not be misunderstood. If not hindered, he is sure to help the enemy." He added: "Much more, if he talks ambiguously—talks for his country with 'buts' and 'ifs' and 'ands.'" Instead of backing down, the president had expanded his powers and bluntly said it was likely that "I shall be blamed for having made too few arrests rather than too many." Lincoln had solidified a new rationale for seizing people that in some ways was more plausible by not leaning on treason law; however, preventative arrests—imprisonment for possible actions or for saying nothing— represented a very dangerous doctrine in the wrong hands. Lincoln, as historian Mark Neely has noticed, had targeted the Democratic opposition in a "hair-raising" document. He is one of the few historians who have understood the potential damage that this position of preventative arrests contained for civil liberties.[62]

The concept had done damage. From the opening of the war, "preventative arrests" had happened hundreds of times under the banner of "implied treason." The doctrine expressed in the Corning Letter had informed the actions of officials on the home front since 1861, and it continued to do so after conscription was put into place. Roughly the time Lincoln composed his letter, the solicitor of the War Department, William Whiting, advised a provost marshal on what should cause detention for interfering with the draft. He claimed that more ways existed to do this beyond physical violence or flight. Echoing Lincoln's position that silence might not be golden, Whiting wrote: "*Standing mute*, in civil courts, is under certain circumstances a punishable offence, and so if a person, with intent to prevent the draft, refuses to give his true name when lawfully requested so to do by an officer whose legal duty is to *acertain* and *enrol* it, it is an obstruction of that officer in the performance of one of his duties in relation to the draft." A year later, General Banks issued General Orders No. 23 that stressed a similar interpretation for Confederate sympathizers in occupied New Orleans. The orders indicated that neutral behavior should be interpreted as disloyalty. "Indifference will be treated as crime," the orders stated, "and faction as treason." Faction, by the way, referred to opposition politics. The commander added: "Men who refuse to defend their country with the ballot-box or cartridge-box have no just claims to the benefits of liberty regulated by law."[63]

If Democrats hoped for federal action to criticize, they had their wishes amply fulfilled in campaigns in Delaware, Kentucky, Missouri, and Maryland. After the Vallandigham affair, Burnside remained active in his surveillance of potential subversion. Although the general supervised the Department of the Ohio, the name is misleading. The "Ohio" encompassed a much broader area that incorporated the states of Michigan, Indiana, Illinois, Wisconsin, eastern Kentucky, and eastern Tennessee. By July 1863, rebel raider John Hunt Morgan raised a stir in the region that ended with his capture, but that also allowed officials to justify greater restraint on liberties. On July 31, Burnside issued General Orders No. 120 that used the invasion of the state to declare martial law for the elections on August 5. Burnside said the rebels intended to intimidate the loyal voters, "forcing the election of disloyal candidates." He indicated that civilian election judges would administer the balloting, but they would be backed up by soldiers to protect the rights of loyal citizens and maintain "the purity of the suffrage." ("Purity of the suffrage" became the metaphor offered by the supporters of federal intervention at polling precincts.) In western Kentucky, a military commander went further in preventing from voting persons under arrest or imprisoned "for uttering disloyal language or sentiments."[64]

In Lexington on August 3, a woman noted that Election Day passed "unusually quiet" and resulted in a large Unionist victory. Thomas E. Bramlette crushed the Peace Democrat candidate for governor by 50,000 votes. The state senate contained only Unionists and the house only a handful of Peace Democrats. The same woman noted in her diary that she believed that fewer than half of the state participated in the polling.[65] Intimidation at the polls had occurred and military officers at times adopted Draconian measures. General Boyle, the radical Republican, had set himself up as a candidate for Congress and jailed his opponent; he also declared that anyone voting for the Peace Democrat would be considered a Confederate sympathizer whose property could be seized.[66] Boyle did not win election, revealing the public's distaste for his aggression, but the Union Democrats more compatible with Lincoln's policies gained majorities in both branches of state government, as well as the governor.[67]

The Union ticket might have won handily without this interference. About half the number of voters turned out for this election as did in 1860 (85,000 compared to 145,000). Detractors explain this falloff as coming from the interference of soldiers. While partly true, the judgment requires modification. If we subtract 41,000 Kentuckians in the Union army (even though a portion was in the state and could vote) and the 25,000 to 30,000 white males from the state who joined the Confederate army, we can easily account for 65,000 or so votes, getting us nearer to the turnout of 1860. While hundreds of voters may have been discouraged by the federal measures—a bad enough situation for civil liberties—a Cincinnati newspaper had the best assessment of Burnside's proclamation. "It had no more effect upon the election than would have been produced by a small boy whistling 'Yankee Doodle' at the State capital, at six o'clock in the morning." But the writer added: "It was unwise to issue such a proclamation, as the only effect it has produced is in giving a color of plausibility to the pretense made by the Wickliffe [peace] party, that they were defeated by bayonets. The proclamation didn't influence the election, but it has impaired, if not destroyed its moral force."[68]

To be fair to the Union military, Kentucky's Democrats to some extent brought this federal oversight on themselves. In January, a minority of members of the legislature introduced a series of resolutions that excoriated the Lincoln administration for unconstitutional actions, including interference with justice and tampering with the elective franchise in a variety of states. It was a manifesto worthy of the Democratic presidential platform for 1864, although this effort lacked the support to pass. Not so for another set of resolutions, prompted again by military interference. On February 18, as Democrats met in convention, the military commandant of the post in Frankfort sent soldiers to harass the members on the pretext that the meeting contained rebel spies. Colonel Gilbert apparently closed the proceedings and warned that anyone nominated as a candidate faced arrest. The incident fortified the opposition. Later that month, on February 27, the assembly pushed through resolutions that portrayed the state as "assailed by an armed rebellion on one side, which can only be met by the sword; and on the other by unconstitutional acts of Congress, and startling usurpations of power by the Executive, which we have seen by experiment can be corrected by the ballot-box." The proclamation was not as inflammatory as the first set of statements, but it did list emancipation, the imposition of martial law, and the elevation of military over civil authority as some of the sins of the government. Because the fall election involved the first change in state officials since 1861, these positions by Democrats obviously captured the serious attention of the administration's supporters.[69]

In Missouri, the government took a surprisingly evenhanded approach, given the guerrilla activity and the fact that it was, after all, Missouri. Before the November 1863 election, Lincoln received letters from citizens in the state requesting that he protect the political process and enforce the election laws. The president said he did not want soldiers to interfere with balloting but to ensure that the eligible, loyal voters exercised the franchise. Whether he was giving soldiers on the ground the cue to do what they needed cannot be determined. Union General Schofield warned his subordinates not to affect the ballot or they faced punishment. But he also told commanders that they should place troops at precincts that might feature guerrilla action or intimidation of voters. Once again, the instructions left discretion for interpreting the situation to subordinates on the ground. By all accounts the balloting proceeded peacefully. More to the point, Missouri had in place the loyalty oath that allowed judges of elections to disqualify voters suspected for holding sympathies for the rebels.[70]

Maryland and Delaware provide more interesting stories. In Maryland, the government clearly affected at least one congressional race as well as some minor political offices. The military commander of the region, General Robert Schenck, issued General Orders No. 53, which called on provost marshals to arrest disloyal persons who approached polling places, to support judges of elections in requiring an oath of loyalty to the United States, and to report election supervisors who did not administer an oath. When called on to explain his actions by Lincoln, Schenck made a beeline for Washington. As he told Stanton, "If it [Order. No. 53] is revoked, we lose this State."[71] Lincoln apparently listened. He did modify the order, rewording the first paragraph to eliminate the phrases that encouraged the military to arrest disloyal people at the polling places. With his editing, the order instructed the military to maintain the peace and did not make an issue of arresting the disloyal. But he let the overall policy stand, allowing Schenck to post his troops at election precincts.[72]

The decision irritated Governor Augustus Bradford, to say the least, and caused him to trade words with the president. Bradford, a Unionist who had benefited from federal intervention in his own election in 1861, considered the orders by Schenck offensive and unnecessary. He claimed that most of the candidates were loyal men so the elections were likely to result in a Unionist victory anyway. In making his point, Bradford took a mild jab at Lincoln over the Vallandigham affair. Ohio, he suggested, was allowed to hold its gubernatorial election without such conditions despite having a candidate "considered so hostile to the Government that for months past he has been banished from the Country." Because of this, interference with loyal candidates in Maryland would be seen, by comparison, as objectionable.[73]

As he had with Vallandigham, Lincoln defended the meddling of a general in politics, in this case offering statements a little more entertaining, and a lot less provocative, than the Corning Letter. The president indicated that Schenck believed that violence would come at polling places unless prevented by the provost guards. The general had asserted that Unionists were wary of heading to the polls without protection. As for imposing federal rules on a state election, Lincoln reminded the governor that the state of Maryland, unlike Missouri, had no test oath in place.

Consequently, one could imagine a scenario in which a Confederate General like Isaac Trimble of Maryland—who was captured after leading a segment of Pickett's Charge at Gettysburg and who remained home recovering from his wounding—found his way to a precinct where he demanded to exercise his right to suffrage without "recanting his treason." Without a federal oath, Trimble could cast his ballot as a legal voter. Even Schenck's order, the president reminded, allowed Trimble to vote if he took the minimal action of swearing loyalty to the government. "I think that is cheap enough," Lincoln maintained. If Bradford could not resist a poke for the Vallandigham election in Ohio, Lincoln could not withhold his own jab. "Nor do I think that, to keep the peace at the polls and to prevent the persistently disloyal from voting, constitutes just cause of offense to Maryland. I think she has her own example for it." Wait, here it comes. "If I mistake not, it is precisely what General Dix did when Your Excellency was elected Governor." Ouch. Bradford had been hoisted on his electoral petard. Could someone who had benefited from federal interference in an election hold the moral high ground on this issue?[74]

Impressively in the face of a presidential chiding, Bradford tried. Concerning the methods that got him elected, he told the president that that was then and this was now: that a state that appeared on the brink of secession in 1861 now contained substantial Union support and did not need extreme measures to ensure its fidelity.[75] To his constituency, Bradford issued a counterproclamation that stated his repugnance over the use of troops in the election. He addressed his comments especially to judges of elections, noting that Schenck's order had been issued without consultation with state officials. With the exception of one person, Bradford claimed that the congressional candidates in the state were loyal. By military edict, provost marshals had become the judges of voter eligibility as well as the persons who determined whether to conduct arrests. This represented to the governor an arbitrary power that was potentially dangerous, especially since two of the five provost marshals of the state were candidates for office. Bradford reminded the judges that they could summon executive officers of the county to preserve order at the polls and that they should report to the state's attorney infractions of the election laws. Bradford maintained that the judges alone had the ability to determine the qualification of voters, not provost marshals. Overall, it was a strong assertion of state over federal supervision of elections, civil over military authority.[76]

But it caused an immediate, and unfortunate, response. Schenck found the proclamation so detestable that he prohibited the telegraph lines from sending it and the editors of the *Baltimore American* from publishing it, revealing additional ways that the army interfered with political affairs and civil society. Still, the governor's proclamation found its way to the public, published in a Washington newspaper among other places.[77]

What impact did this intervention by the federal government have on the election? Concerning averting potential violence, no significant unrest manifested itself, but it is hard to believe that disruptions at the polls presented a real possibility in the first place or that the military was needed in this capacity. That portion of Schenck's anxieties should be discounted. Concerning controlling the vote, a different story presents itself. Four out of five of the congressional candidates considered favorable to the government swept into office. At the least, the military enhanced the margin of victory in one of these races. The most egregious interference occurred in the First District, especially in Somerset County on the southern tip of the eastern shore of the Chesapeake Bay. The area below Baltimore made up the plantation region of the state, in which resided a black majority and the white men most likely to sympathize with the Confederacy or create problems for the Lincoln administration. In the election for Congress from this district, John Creswell, Unconditional Unionist (translation: emancipationist) defeated John W. Crisfield, Union candidate (translation: Union without emancipation). After the election, Crisfield protested his defeat to Lincoln, claiming that the military had refused to let men vote even when they tried to take the oath of loyalty. Crisfield knew what he was talking about: he was intimately acquainted with events at the poll in Princess Anne on November 4, 1863, when a cavalry officer named Captain Moore shut down the election after exactly one person voted in a precinct that had traditionally featured more than 300 voters. Crisfield witnessed the intervention. More interesting, the person who triggered Moore to act was the second man to step up to cast his ballot—the congressional candidate's son.

Arthur Crisfield had tried to vote legally, but the military prevented him from submitting a ballot on behalf of his father. Captain Moore, the cavalry officer overseeing this district, grilled the younger Criswell on his political beliefs. The interrogation resembled a Catholic priest's use of the Baltimore catechism against a suspicious penitent. Moore asked him whether Crisfield was loyal. Yes. Had he ever taken arms up against the United States? No. Did he consider the rebellion an unholy war that ought to be put down? Yes. Would he sacrifice his property to put down this rebellion? Yes. It probably frustrated the officer that Crisfield seemed willing to take an oath that others found insulting. Finally, an election judge stepped in to protest, proclaiming that the officer's questioning slowed the balloting so much that it might jeopardize finishing within the allotted time. This was not a problem for Captain Moore. His troops arrested the judges of elections and shut down the polling place, leaving on record the one vote cast.[78]

The elder Crisfield had served as a Whig in the Thirtieth Congress with Lincoln, but he was not on the right side now. Nonetheless, the president found grounds for allowing an investigation into this election. He endorsed putting Captain Moore on trial before a court of inquiry for exceeding the parameters of General Orders No. 53. Not surprisingly, the commission quickly exonerated the captain, saying the judges of elections had brought the arrests on themselves by refusing to administer oaths, thus disobeying the order from Schenck. The election stood. And the man more favorable to the administration went to Washington.[79]

Another investigation, this time by a Maryland legislative committee in January 1864, provided evidence of additional meddling on the part of soldiers. A day before the election, federal troops staged demonstrations and reinforced the troops' desire to support Schenck's Order No. 53. Election Day arrived with three different tickets in circulation. The ballots for Unconditional Unionists (supporters of Lincoln) were printed on yellow paper, Conservative Unionists (not total supporters of Lincoln) on white paper, and Democrats (definitely against Lincoln) on . . . it does not matter, because they had virtually no presence in this campaign. This election came down to a choice between yellow tickets (good for Lincoln) and white tickets (bad for Lincoln). If the tickets did not immediately reveal one's vote, judges of elections or the military tore them open to discern the color of the paper. Without a secret ballot, controlling an election was rather easy in the Civil War era. Quickly, it became clear that the soldiers allowed yellow tickets to be cast—sometimes without requiring an oath of loyalty—while white ballots provoked a challenge, initiated a test oath, or caused voters to be sent home without casting a ballot. The governor's proclamation did have an impact; it fortified judges of elections to resist the Union soldiers by reading the state executive's wishes aloud at precincts. But they may as well have howled into the wind. The judges had Maryland state power on their side but that gave them little help in countering the federal troops. The federal military ignored the proclamation of the governor and obeyed the order of an army officer, supported by the president, to regulate the election.[80]

In another incident, soldiers arrested citizens in Anne Arundel County who refused to swear loyalty to the government before the election judges.

Among the roughly dozen people listed by a provost marshal as taking this stand were three candidates running for office and various members of the bar, some of whom later went to the grand jury to have the judges of elections punished. When a contingent of these men wrote Bradford about their plight, he defended the soldiers, saying that he could not fathom that only the refusal of an oath had sparked their arrest, "for I cannot believe that it is the intention either of the President or the Commander of this Military Department to arrest or furnish any one for simply declining to take the oath as prescribed in . . . the aforesaid order." The loss of one's vote was the penalty for refusing the oath; an arrest, Bradford said, indicated that other objectionable behavior existed. This reasoning could not have soothed Thomas G. Pratt as he sat in prison. A former governor of the state, he refused to swear an oath in order to receive a parole and remained a captive through the end of the month.[81]

Even military repression could not control the outcome everywhere. In the Fifth District of Maryland, a region nearest Washington that contained numerous critics of the war, the electorate chose Democrat Benjamin G. Harris. When he took his seat in Congress, Harris distinguished himself by casting the only dissenting votes on resolutions pledging the resources of the country to support the war and thanking the soldiers for their devotion. These were incredibly obnoxious stands. An attempt to expel him from Congress for uttering treasonable sentiments narrowly failed in 1864, but he was removed from office in May 1865 through the unusual mechanism of a court-martial before a military commission on charges of harboring two Confederate soldiers at the end of the conflict. Both soldiers had been paroled by Lee's surrender. The congressman encouraged them against taking an oath of loyalty to the United States. Clearly the government wished to get rid of him through whatever means possible. But the point is, despite the increased scrutiny at the polls in 1863, a fish like Harris still could swim through Schenck's net.[82]

In the neighboring state of Delaware—also under the jurisdiction of General Schenck—one of the congressional campaigns took a strange turn because of what had happened in Maryland. Peace Democrat Charles Brown, referred to by detractors as the anti-emancipation candidate, opposed Republican N. B. Smithers for Congress in a special election to fill a vacancy created by a death. In the antebellum period, Brown had served posts in Philadelphia as a customs collector and as a congressman, but had since moved to Delaware. The Democratic press confidently predicted victory for its champion. To say that the Republican won in a landslide does not quite capture the strangeness of the picture. In more than thirty precincts spanning three entire counties and the city of Wilmington, the Democratic candidate captured a measly 13 votes to his opponent's nearly 8,000. Only four precincts reported any votes for him at all, meaning that about thirty precincts posted: zero, after zero, after zero, after zero. Did these figures reveal more tampering by the military?[83]

The answer was both yes and no. The army posted itself at election precincts. Schenck handed down the same directives to judges of elections and provost marshals that he had in Maryland. However, the army had very little work to do because of the unique reaction among Democrats to protest the use of the army to screen elections. Just a few days before the polling, the Democrats in Delaware learned that Schenck intended to have his soldiers "support" judges of elections in the qualification of voters in order to ensure the purity of the ballot. They responded by encouraging members of their party to stay home. Brown withdrew as a candidate just before the election. Party leaders in New Castle County issued a public statement that hoped voters would boycott the polls. The members listened. The Republicans earned a victory that was virtually unopposed.[84]

Predictably, opinions varied about the need for this gesture of protest. Lincoln's party crowed that the tactic showed the opposition had no support and withdrew before the electorate could certify this embarrassment. Democrats countered that Brown would have won handily, but the handwriting was on the wall for a different result because of the posting of soldiers at precincts. "Nine thousand freemen, in the State of Delaware," one account noted, "voluntarily refused to exercise the elective franchise rather-than recognize the right of a military commander to prescribe the terms upon which they might vote! We repeat, no action could be more sublime. . . . To-day, every Democrat, conscious of rectitude of purpose, holds up his head a freeman; he has not surrendered his manhood at military dictation nor done aught in violation of the Constitution and laws of his State."[85]

This was not the only time that Democrats faced restrictions at the ballot box. Historian Frank L. Klement noted that the situation in Indianapolis during 1863 sorely tested the resolve of Democratic voters. Federal soldiers stationed themselves near polling places at Indianapolis. Intimidation at the polls caused an immeasurable number of Democrats to remain home rather than vote. When Republicans refused Democrats representation on boards of elections, an entire slate of Democratic nominees for city office withdrew. Indiana represented a trouble spot for the administration in general. During a campaign rally in May 1863, soldiers rushed the speakers' platform of Democrat Samuel R. Hamill of Sullivan County. Fights broke out. Troops arrested Democrats for defiance, for carrying concealed weapons, and for uttering disloyal sentiments.[86]

On the one hand, the administration's interference in these elections seemed excessive, especially in the face of sweeping Unionist victories. In Maryland, Bradford probably was correct that the state was safe for the Union. The congressional candidates most akin to the administration's goals appeared destined to win.

But more than an election for the Union was on the table. Bradford was correct; this was not 1861. Antislavery was growing as a policy, not only on the battlefield through the limited emancipation in the Confederacy but also as the subject of intense lobbying by certain Republicans for slavery's general eradication in the nation. Authorities within Maryland, supported by Washington, pressed for a new state constitution to legislate abolition for slaves. Planters in the southeastern portions of Maryland resisted this change to their constitution. Republicans looked upon the congressional election as the state inching its way toward antislavery.[87]

When considering the elections in the border states in 1863, it becomes clear that the military served the cause of an antislavery Union, not civil liberties. Favorable congressmen joined the Thirty-Eighth Congress from Maryland and Delaware, as well as from Ohio. They remained stalwarts in Lincoln's corner when it came to supporting the Thirteenth Amendment, voting for the administration in three of the crucial votes in the House, the first coming in January 1864 or just a couple of months after Maryland's election.[88] Radical Republican Whitelaw Reid felt confident that the returns signaled congressional support of Lincoln's policies.[89] Republicans enjoyed a majority in Congress; it was not enough in early 1864 to overcome the constitutional regulations that allowed Lincoln and his supporters to drive the knife into the heart of slavery. But as one scholar has noted, the Unconditional Unionists elected from the border states gave the Republicans the working majority needed to back the government's prosecution of the war. "Without the support of the Unconditional Unionists," Bensel observed, "the Republicans would have fallen short of a majority by five votes when the Thirty-eighth Congress convened."[90] Five congressmen favoring emancipation had won Maryland's and Delaware's elections "supervised" by the army.

Soldiers rejecting the ballots of unfavorable candidates in Kentucky, Missouri, Maryland, and Delaware helped pave the way for the outcome, although it is unclear if the elections would have returned favorable results to the government even if they had run their course without military oversight. The more important result may not lie with the tally at the ballot box but with the impetus provided to the Democrats who—weathering a winter of discontent with political reversals and the military success of Grant in the West—seized upon arbitrary arrests and the military's interference in elections to articulate what was wrong with the administration and with the country. And they did so with their eyes on the White House.

7

FREE ELECTIONS OR

A FREE FIGHT

Touring America in 1864, Frenchman Ernest Duvergier de Hauranne encountered a startling scene in St. Louis. The state of Missouri struck him,
as it did Union officials, as not a loyal state for the Union but as a rebel
region that endured occupation by a Union army in which southern sympathizers seethed with repressed rage. Unionists overreacted "by treating
as a traitor anyone who offers resistance—even if it be perfectly legal—to
their policy." On September 15, he encountered a riot that revealed the
passion behind the debate over loyalty. Two political meetings took place
a short distance apart: one to launch a Republican club and another to
honor George Brinton McClellan, the Democratic challenger for president.
Each party tried to outdo the other with bonfires and fireworks. Speakers stood on platforms surrounded by banners, placards, and lanterns
that projected slogans. Suddenly, the event turned ugly. Laughter in the
Democratic crowd turned to shrieks as placards and lights disappeared.
In the confusion, de Hauranne made out what he thought were uniforms
among the attackers. Bayonets flashed and civilians froze against walls as
if fearing to be shot. When the situation settled, they moved away slowly.
What was the meaning of the fistfights, the rock throwing by soldiers, the
rifle-butts rising and falling, the officers walking with swords among the
populace? He answered his own question: "The military had decided the
meeting would not take place." Down went the lamps, posters, speaking
stand, and banners bearing the name of McClellan. A gang of boys directed by men in uniforms smashed "the Rebels'" platform into splinters.
A sullen crowd moved on, mumbling "'Those damnded soldiers!'"[1]

Such was a presidential campaign during the Civil War. In 1864, political rallies in areas such as St. Louis were hardly for the timid as they
underscored the tensions that could wrack communities, especially in the
border states. Missouri was somewhat exceptional, to be sure, and there

were discrepancies about who tossed the first stones at whom in this riot: Democrats or soldiers.[2] Violence during the 1864 campaign reared its head in various corners of the loyal states, reflecting an intensified level of the "normal" kinds of rough play that constituted politics in the nineteenth century. Before the war, Democratic gangs in Baltimore and New York had salted the political process with violence by stabbing at the legs of opponents who stood in precinct lines or bumping their shoulders. In the Civil War, the presence of the national state introduced a wild card to elections—especially because it was not always controlled from above but gained its impulse from below, such as in this story. Lincoln hardly directed this St. Louis riot from Washington. In this case, the signs point to a spontaneous confrontation from an unknown igniter.

The presidential election remains a marvel among historians—not for its results, but for why it happened at all. The Civil War featured one of the greatest trials in the history of the United States. The country fought for its existence. Civil strife had cost hundreds of thousands of lives and had bled the nation's treasury, mortgaging the monetary cost of the war to a future generation. The Republicans faced internal divisions as a more radical wing endorsed John C. Frémont as a candidate for president against the incumbent. Democrats, derailed temporarily by the battlefield victories under Grant in late 1863, had their train heading back down the track against the Lincoln administration, charging him with abrogating free speech, ignoring the Constitution's protection of property, conducting arbitrary arrests, and interfering with the ballot box in state and municipal elections. Despite this—and despite a pronounced proclivity to bend the Constitution to suit the emergency—few Republicans suggested that the nation should suspend the forthcoming election. Instead, they worked to portray the Democrats as traitors belonging to secret societies that sought the triumph of the Confederacy.

The Democrats mounted an aggressive counterattack with a compelling argument that highlighted military arrests of loyal civilians and election tampering. Nonetheless, they lost the presidential election. One of the reasons, but not the only one, involved divisions within the party, with anti-Lincoln Democrats uncomfortable with the peace wing and recognizing that a national election faced problems if the solution for the war resided in a peace that might not create reunion. But they found agreement around the issues of military arrests, repression of freedom of speech, and suppression of the free ballot. When it came time for announcing their platform, Democrats warned that the president might not let the election proceed without using the military at the ballot box. They made the suppression of the ballot an explicit point in their party's presidential platform, warning that these efforts in the coming presidential campaign would be considered "revolutionary, and resisted with all the means and power under our control."[3] What form that resistance might take was left unsaid.

The election did not feature only a rhetorical contest over the meaning of loyalty and treason. Both sides tried to shape legislation to their advantage. Soldiers had an impact as Republicans mobilized their absentee ballots, through furloughs, balloting away from home, or the usual fraudulent voting. Both parties tried to portray themselves as the friend of the soldiers. The campaign centered itself squarely on the issue of loyalty and treason, with Democrats and Republicans doing their level best to condemn the other as traitors to the principles of a democracy. Although the Republicans enjoyed the upper hand, the Democrats did not enter the battle unarmed.

Free Speech, Free Press, and Free Ballot

The Democrats opened the year aggressively, determined to depict the Republicans as traitors to the nation's principles by their use of the military to influence balloting. They harped on this point for various reasons: to prevent—if there were any such intentions—the rigging of the presidential contest, to cultivate independent voters, and to deflect the criticism aimed at themselves as traitors. Democrats put forth this message through public speeches, tracts, and congressional legislation. They also conducted investigations by committees of the state legislatures of the balloting in Maryland and Delaware. In December 1863 and January 1864, Democrats from the border states introduced a bill in the Senate to block soldiers from interfering in elections. Barely a month after the fall campaigns had ended, Lazarus Powell of Kentucky notified the Senate on December 9, 1863, of his intention to create a bill that prohibited soldiers from stationing themselves at election precincts. In 1862 the Senate had tried to expel Powell, unsuccessfully. In 1864 he remained very much present in the Senate chambers, thank you, and had a fire in his belly that obviously was stoked by the coming presidential campaign.

The bill took shape rather quickly, coalescing in early January. It banned the placement of troops within one mile of a polling precinct. Europe provided a precedent: the legislation borrowed the distance from English law. Closer to home, the state of Delaware contained such a precedent. In this latest example, the penalties for transgressions were steep. Fines ranged from \$200 (nearly the annual wages of a laborer) to \$20,000 (roughly \$275,000 today), and imprisonment from two years to twenty. The bill allowed for soldiers to appear at precincts to exercise their rights to suffrage as citizens, but they could not be placed there in order to screen who participated.[4] Democrats hoped to keep military justice, which rarely served their party, out of the picture. As was the case during the entire conflict, civil law involving treason supported the conservative cause much better than radicalism.

In pressing for enactment, Powell and Willard Saulsbury of Delaware cited the electoral transgressions in the border states of 1863, especially the controversy over Crisfield in Maryland. The policies put into place by Schenck, policies they indicated that Lincoln had allowed, provided material for an opposition's message. Democrats repeatedly questioned the constitutionality of a president's decision to allow for national power to override a state's authority to define the electorate and to establish practices for balloting. Additionally, Saulsbury proudly revealed that he had not voted in the last election. His confession represented less a surprising lack of patriotism than an admission of sympathy with the thousands of Democrats who had boycotted the election in Delaware. "When the exercise of the right of suffrage ceases to be free," he said, "I do not wish to go through the mockery of attempting to exercise it."[5]

Republicans, mostly Radicals, tried to scuttle the bill. First, they contested which committee would supervise the proposed legislation. Democrats argued strenuously that the responsibility for the bill belonged with the Judiciary Committee, since the law defined infractions that fell under civil justice. Republicans said no, the Military Affairs Committee deserved this duty because soldiers were the subject of the legislation. When looking at the composition of the committees, the reason behind the fight becomes clear. The Judiciary Committee contained Powell of Kentucky and Reverdy Johnson of Maryland, both safe for Democrats on the question of soldiers interfering in elections. And although a majority of the committee came from the Republican side, it was led by Lyman Trumbull of Illinois, a moderate who had been known to criticize the Lincoln administration. On the other hand, the Committee on Military Affairs featured Henry Wilson as chair. A Republican senator from Massachusetts, he kept close company with the more radical members of his chamber such as Charles Sumner. The Radicals won this early battle, sending the bill to military affairs. A Democratic newspaper judged this result as "strangling the thing in its birth."[6]

Republicans certainly tried to strangle the legislation. By early February, the committee issued a fifty-two-page report by the majority that dismissed the charges as groundless and the bill as unnecessary. Heading the effort was Senator Jacob Howard of Michigan, a Radical who often advocated for the toughest measures against the traitorous rebels. He authored the report, which characterized interference in elections as "wholly imaginary" and recommended against passing the proposed law. Howard and his supporters argued that the elective franchise existed only for the friends of the government and that soldiers stationed at the polls guaranteed the "purity" of the balloting by protecting it from "contamination of disloyal votes." In the report, Howard collected orders from military officers and other documents from 1861 through 1863, especially concentrating on the polling in Missouri, Kentucky, Maryland, and Delaware. The report found guilty anyone who opposed the government's policies, calling them traitors, secessionists, and anti-emancipationists. Such people, in Howard's opinion, deserved losing the suffrage. The committee's majority echoed Lincoln's logic of preventative arrests as necessary policy in war. And it offered the rationale of constructive treason for justifying harsh measures, without calling it that by name. Anyone who "desired" the overthrow of the government (meaning they had not done anything yet) deserved restrictions by federal authorities. According to the logic of the dominant Radicals on the committee, political dissidents were enemies, and handling enemies in a war between two belligerents naturally came under the jurisdiction of the military. In conclusion, the majority argued that "blind party rage," by which they meant Democrats, encouraged the rebel insurgents by feeding their morale.[7]

If ever the moment existed to use a word like "balderdash," this was it. Howard's report spun a fabulous tale of the "purification" of elections by military force necessitated to hold off suspected, but not yet encountered, treasonous activity that may have (but perhaps not) resulted in intimidation of loyal people. The logic did not convince everyone, even some members of Howard's own party. The attempt to quash the bill failed, and moderate Republicans like Trumbull joined the effort to allow the debate to continue. The Democrats played a high-stakes political game and cannot have their words taken completely at face value. It seems reasonable to assume that they were nervous about the coming presidential election and tried to do everything possible to tilt the scales a little in their direction. However, this report by the Committee on Military Affairs, engineered by a key Radical in the Senate, gave cynics a reason to get up in the morning. It was a blatant political attempt to whitewash what had happened at the polls.

The report did not cause Powell to back down. On the contrary, he led the rebuttal in an address that took two days to deliver before the Senate on March 3 and 4. In his lengthy comments, he pointed out the amount of interference and intimidation witnessed by voters throughout the border states during the 1863 elections. He mentioned the British legal tradition that informed the bill he had crafted and reminded his listeners that there were examples closer to home. According to Powell, the state of Maryland and at least half a dozen other states had laws on the books that prevented soldiers from appearing within view of precincts on election days. He talked about the abuses in his own state of Kentucky and turned to Maryland, which served up the most clear-cut examples of tampering in an important election as well as a governor who had protested the process.[8]

From the floor of the U.S. Senate, Powell took the dramatic step of accusing the president of the United States of tampering with the most sacred ritual of popular government. He targeted the interference with the reelection bid of John W. Crisfield in Maryland, which he said failed because of the interference of soldiers, but he chose to draw a higher power into the picture. He did not blame the generals administering the military oversight of the polls. "In this Maryland case you cannot throw off the responsibility upon Schenck, nor upon Colonel Tevis, or other subordinates," he said. "You have the President most directly implicated. Here he is upon the record, violating the Constitution of his country by interfering with elections in States in order to return menials and miserable creatures to Congress who would do his bidding; and I arraign him before the Senate of the United States and the American people. I brush away the trash and come right to the Commander-in-Chief himself, and charge him, upon the most indubitable testimony, with trampling under foot the most inestimable right of free suffrage and free election."[9]

Furthermore, Powell charged that Lincoln's Proclamation of Amnesty and Reconstruction, the Ten Percent Plan, influenced elections. Issued in early December 1863, the executive order considered a rebellious state government as reconstructed when 10 percent of the voters from 1860 swore loyalty to the Union and agreed to abide by emancipation. Powell alleged that this proclamation put the president in the position of qualifying who should vote in a state. He had a point, although his thesis of a conspiracy did not wash. The proclamation established the wording for the oath of loyalty that decided who voted. Powell said that the order did a disservice to Unionists who had supported the government all along. Even if they were inclined to take the oath, it required them to support emancipation, which Powell called unconstitutional. But he also reminded listeners what had happened in Delaware. He predicted that many Unionists would not take the oath.[10]

Privately, Democrats expressed worse fears about the amnesty proclamation. An Illinois Democrat wrote McClellan in the summer of 1864 that some considered the maneuver a way for the president "of gaining quick votes that he could control." He asked the general that if victory came because of these new voters, "would you permit Lincoln to hold on to power by the electoral votes of the seceded States obtained by his one tenth System or would you be inaugurated and fight if necessary for your lawful right."[11]

Powell continued to fight this battle whenever he could, and he was joined by Democrats who stressed themes that made their way onto the presidential platform. In late May, the senator used the debate over the Thirteenth Amendment to answer criticism of the party as embracing traitors to the cause of union. He stressed that the main mission of his cohort remained to preserve free speech, free press, and a free ballot. One can discern whom he considered as the audience for this part of his message. It was not the president. One part of the speech revealed an underlying motivation to find common ground with conservatives regardless of party. At one point he said, "I tell the conservative men, the Democracy, the old Whigs, the honest Republicans everywhere—and I wish to God my voice could extend to the remote parts of the country—to be of good cheer; and if those in power attempt to enslave them, to put chains upon their limbs, to prevent their free tongue from wagging in words of honest and burning censure against those who are striking down their liberties, if the minions of power attempt to interfere with the freedom of the press, I would advise the people throughout the length and breadth of the land to *insist on freedom and give their lives in its defense.*" He added that he hoped for a free election during the coming campaign. If not, he added in words that gained currency throughout the Union, "I shall advise the Democracy and the conservative men in every State of the Union to fight for them; I do not mean to go out of the Union, but I mean to fight for the ballot, and to fight under the Constitution and laws of their country."[12]

Democrats maintained their barrage against Republicans' meddling in elections throughout the winter and spring, although they did so as part of an overall critique of Lincoln designed to portray him as a traitor to the Constitution and to democratic governance. They showed a remarkable consistency of message across newspapers, congressional debates, governors' messages, and political tracts that carried into both their presidential convention and the election. The party at this time suffered from divisions between those favoring an armistice and those looking to continue the war for union. The concern over "fraud and force"—a phrase that became something of a slogan—provided the possibility of a bridge between these differing factions and raised hopes that such a thrust could appeal to moderate and conservative men of any partisan background. Emancipation lurked around the edges of this refrain but within a broader constitutional lament. Governor Seymour of New York provided a good example in his annual address to the legislature in early 1864. He opened with the charge that Lincoln intended to destroy state rights and expand powers beyond the Constitution. Later in the address he stated: "The proclamation of emancipation at the South, and the suspension of the writ of *habeas corpus* at the North; the confiscation of private property in the seceding States, and the arbitrary arrests, imprisonments, and banishment of the citizens of loyal States; the claim to destroy political organizations at the South, and the armed interference by government in local elections have been cotemporaneous events."[13]

In other words, for Democrats these attacks did not represent separate instances but a grand design to redefine their free speech as treasonous for the purpose of controlling elections. Benjamin G. Harris of Maryland, the man who had slipped through Schenck's net in the 1863 congressional elections, put it in these terms in a long-winded speech to the House in May in which he raised the question of why treason seemed to be punishable only during election season. Was it not interesting, he posed, that traitors lived in freedom the remainder of the year, when balloting was not conducted? But whenever elections came, then treason was found. He explained: "This charge of treason is a wide-spread net. It has entered the Halls of Congress and been used for the purpose of arresting free debate and stifling the warning voices which will reach the ears and warm the hearts of the American people. For the bold utterances of my political sentiments, this charge of treason has been called from the 'vasty deep' in order to proscribe me."[14]

It is tempting to dismiss this talk as politics as usual and claim that the allegations were duplicitous, exaggerated, and intended only to keep a constituency in tow. Some of it undoubtedly was. However, evidence suggests that opponents of the Lincoln administration did worry that the election might not happen, that tampering by the government would mar the balloting, and that officers in the army would screen which soldiers could vote. Examples continued to present themselves that the government used the charge of disloyalty to attack political opponents, especially in the western portions of the Union. To be sure, speeches in Congress lend themselves to excess on the part of representatives who postured for reelection or who fought for a particular agenda. However, there is a strong reflection of these public expressions in private correspondence among Democrats, lending credence to the authenticity of their beliefs, if not to the validity of the allegation.

One of the men writing McClellan during the presidential campaign reported to the general that "all the croakers are croaking about *force & fraud.*" William Prime remained a key investor with the *Journal of Commerce*, which had transformed during the war from an abolition newspaper to a Democratic organ. Yet despite his tone that at first comes across as dismissive, he told the candidate that complaints about interference or tampering should be taken seriously. He fretted that the Democrats had not done enough to mobilize the vote of soldiers in the field. "I greatly fear that the army vote has not been taken care of by the committees in the several states."[15] A person from Maryland told McClellan that the true Democrats of the state will stand by him, adding, "for three years we have had no Free Ballot Box." In a second letter from the same man, J. C. Clarke noted, "All we ask is a free ballot." He promised that McClellan could "be assured nothing but fraud, perjury and Bayonets can give the electoral vote of Maryland to Lincoln & Johnson in November next." Clarke also alluded to the test oath that Maryland had enacted as a requirement for voting on the state's new antislavery constitution. He claimed the oath was meant "to disfranchise us, thereby hoping to bind us hand & foot to the Abolition oar, of that Springfield abortion, now in the presidential chair."[16]

Taking an oath of loyalty to vote caused general consternation among Democrats. Some wondered what to do if the practices of military commanders in Maryland were extended to their communities. If orders came from the executive branch concerning test oaths, should Democrats swallow political principles and submit to the humiliation at precincts of being singled out as disloyal? Remember, not everyone had to go through this examination: only those suspected of being potential traitors. The procedure was open to interpretation by judges of elections — men from the locality who had their own feelings about the character traits of their neighbors. And even if the suspicious traitors pledged their faithfulness to the Union, the judges still could decide against qualifying the voter. Nonetheless, Charles Lanman, a government official, artist, and writer who wrote the general from Georgetown weeks before the election, referred to this issue in the context of a congressman stumping for votes in Maryland. "The Democrats there," he observed, who "have concluded to face the music, will come forth and take Lincoln's oath and thus be privileged to vote."[17]

Louis C. D'Homergue, an agent for the Manhattan Fire Insurance Company in New York City, indicated in a letter to McClellan that New Yorkers deliberated over how to react to loyalty oaths to cast a ballot. Democrats planned a mass meeting in October 1864 at which one of the items under discussion concerned a response if additional test oaths were imposed. "I am in favor of voting," he said, "but if on the contrary oaths not required by the Constitution are exacted, then I am in favor of not voting, so that our friends in the Electoral College can contest the right of Louisiana of representing an electoral ticket there." He even had crafted a resolution in anticipation of such an event: "That while we consider it the imperative duty of all American Citizens at all and every election, and especially at this crisis to express their opinions through the ballot box, we consider it an equally imperative duty resting on the part of the Administration to provide that such expression be free and unrestricted by test Oaths, not required or recognized by the Constitution."[18]

The private letters to McClellan contain additional evidence that gives reason to take the public concerns about election tampering as genuine: the correspondents believed that their communications faced interception by the government, and they took pains to create secure delivery systems or to write in code. They had reason for caution. Since the opening of the war, the mail had been fair game for the attention of government agents as a carrier of treason and had been confiscated by detectives hired by the State Department. The Post Office operated on the basis of patronage appointments, not civil service, and the correspondents to a presidential candidate indicated that both sides played a game of cat and mouse that involved spying on each other. Randolph B. Marcy, a Union general and father-in-law of McClellan, felt sensitive enough about his position in St. Louis to create a cipher and sent his son-in-law the key for unlocking the code. He matched letters of the alphabet with different letters for his code and indicated he would throw in a random letter after every five to throw the enemies off the track.[19] Benjamin Rush from near Philadelphia took advantage of submitting his letter through the Post Office Registry because he thought his message otherwise could be compromised. By taking this course, his letter was recorded and assigned a number, lessening the chance that someone might "lose" an envelope addressed to the famous general. Others sent material first to third parties to have them delivered by hand.[20]

But espionage did not belong to one party. Late in September, a Democrat from Pittsburgh sent a ciphered package of materials to McClellan, apologizing for having no time to translate the code. He asked the general not to reveal his name or that of a compatriot, because they both worked with the telegraph company in Pittsburgh. If their complicity with the candidate became known, the superiors at the company "would take our heads off and thereby put it out of our power to *watch* hereafter." In other words, these men guarded their jobs so they could continue to intercept Republican communications about political strategies. Spying on each other was a routine part of the political process. Once again, speech was not quite free, or at least had a different meaning in America's Civil War.[21]

Ultimately, the Democrats won the battle to protect the ballot from the bayonet; however, the triumph warranted not so much as a single toast for the success. The bill did become law—but not until February 1865, or well after Lincoln's reelection and well after the law had any meaning for the Civil War. It was a hollow victory and could be considered a slap in the face of the Democrats who had fought for the passage. You can have what you desired, Republicans might have said, but you have gained nothing that mattered except to highlight our joint wishes to preserve a free ballot—well after it had been cast. In the meantime, opposition Democrats received more alarming proof during 1864 that the legislation was needed—that the Lincoln government, as well as community rivals far from the political centers of Washington, continued efforts to define a political opposition as traitors and then to act on that supposition of latent treason with a hard hand.

Traitors, Conspirators, and Politics

In selecting a time in the Civil War that may have caused the Union to worry if the republic could be saved, the period spanning spring through late summer of 1864 ranks near the top. In these six or so months, various twists and turns on the battlefield lifted the spirits of the Republican Union, then shook them, then raised them again. A new general commanded all the U.S. military and provided a sense of momentum, which diminished as he lost some 60,000 casualties in six weeks of fighting in Virginia as offenses in the western theater stalled. Throughout this period the northern public heard of conspiracies among domestic traitors especially in the Old Northwest, in which citizens allegedly conspired with Confederate agents to liberate rebel prisons to create uprisings in the Union. One such plot led to the conviction in Indiana of four men by a military commission on charges of disloyalty and fomenting insurrection. Democrats, especially those of the peace persuasion, saw these so-called treason trials and other arrests as simply more of the same behavior by a government that had resorted to the military to eliminate free speech and a free ballot. On the other side of the political aisle, Republicans interpreted the events as proof of traitorous intentions hiding behind the guise of conservative constitutionalism. The more someone cried about tyranny, the more they raised suspicion of their loyalty. In the words of one Republican-oriented Unionist in Kentucky, "Conservative and traitor mean the same thing."[22] This was a sea change from the antebellum period, when radicalism—in the form of antislavery—earned the epithet of treason. Now, conservatism was on the defensive.

Interference by the military at the polls eased a little in the eastern border states in 1864, but Democratic concerns about free elections gathered additional impetus from events in Indiana and Kentucky. Other parts of the Union contained confrontations—political riots like the one in St. Louis that opened this chapter or lesser jostling in communities such as when Republican city councils denied Democrats meeting space in public halls. And there were quieter methods of making a ballot less free than resorting to such drama. Everyone knew the importance of the soldiers' vote in the reelection attempt of Lincoln, and everyone was very much aware that two-term presidents had been a rarity, with Andrew Jackson as the last executive elected to his second four-year stint in 1832.[23]

Despite history leaning in their direction, Democrats found themselves in a difficult situation. First, they had to prove that their complaints about the government, as real as they were, merited consideration as a matter of high principles rather than low partisanship, proving that they did not mask disloyal intentions. Second, without the ability to dictate the kind of protective legislation advocated by Senator Powell of Kentucky, they could only raise sound and fury against the potential of election tampering, while hoping that their protests signified more than nothing. They had no legal force to deploy, no troops to bring to bear against the situation. They did, however, threaten to conduct an unspecified "revolution" should the free ballot not be respected—a murky, ominous vow that did not reconcile this potential action with constitutional scruples, yet it was a pledge that found its way into the Democratic platform. And it was a pledge that, to detractors of the Republicans, appeared to negate the charges of disloyalty. But it was a pledge that likely held little real consequences beyond the hopeful bluster of a party reaching out for anything that gave it a toehold in the uphill climb for the presidency.

Adding to the nervousness of Lincoln's opponents was the rise of the Loyal Union Leagues, Republican clubs formed in many cities of the North to bring to bear every possible support for the president, including serving as a watchdog against treason. Two kinds of leagues existed, even though they appeared to be similar. One branch of the leagues, as noticed by historian Melinda Lawson, was popular in nature, sprouting in hundreds of communities throughout the North and open to anyone willing to undergo the secret initiation rituals. These emerged by 1862, with members distributing pamphlets and other literature, supporting the raising of troops, helping fund-raising efforts, pledging their primary loyalty to the national government rather than to their state, and forming vigilante committees to patrol their towns for treasonous behavior that they then reported the U.S. government. Rabid Democrats like the editor of the *Democratic Watchman* in Bellefonte, Pennsylvania, said about these organizations: "They use the word *Union* as a cover for their treason. There can be *no good* in a secret political organization. They desire merely to betray and enslave democrats." The elitist Union League held similar goals but recruited people from upper ends of the socioeconomic scale who joined gentlemen's clubs that then put their economic wherewithal behind the Union war effort. Boston, New York, and Philadelphia had particularly strong organizations.[24] These exclusive clubs in major cities produced an impressive amount of propaganda for Lincoln. They also used their financial resources to help with fund-raising drives, such as the Sanitary Fairs, and furnished bounties for the mustering of soldiers. In the six weeks before the presidential election, the Philadelphia Union League circulated 560,000 copies of its *Union League Gazette*. From December 1863 to November 1864, the board issued documents in both English and German. In its 1864 annual report, the Philadelphia league noted that its military committee had sent into the field two full regiments: one for 100 days and another for a year. That made nearly seven regiments the league had helped recruit at an expense of more than $100,000.[25]

Put the popular and elite wings of the leagues together and the government had a formidable ally, and the Democrats—especially the peace wing of the party—a resourceful, dedicated, and partisan enemy. It was an enemy who wore the face of neighbors, of generals in the army, of lower-level judges, of scholars like Francis Lieber, of newspaper editors, of financial barons, of clergy, and of people from many walks of life. The Democrats also had friends in high places and had printing presses that churned out partisan dogma, but the Union Leagues had one thing going for them that the opposition did not: the full force and support of the national government.

For years abuses had occurred in the military arrests of civilians that appeared to be aimed at free speech and political activism. The Republican press, politicians, and eventually the leagues combined to justify the arrests as necessary to fend off a constitutional conservatism that intended to undercut the war effort rather than protect liberty. One newspaper columnist decoded for his readers the kind of behavior that constituted disloyalty. The people who took cheer in news of rebel victories "we may safely class as traitors at heart and enemies of their country." The writer provided an additional primer on how to decipher speech and behavior alleged to be patriotic but that hid treasonous intentions: "Whenever you find a man talking all the time against the Government, and saying nothing against the Rebellion; who denounces the administration of Lincoln but is silent as to that of Jeff. Davis; who speaks of the habeas Corpus, suppression of the press and the hardship of the draft, and says nothing of rebel conscription, despotism and cruelty, you may set him down as disloyal." Later, he added: "Whenever you hear a man say 'that he is as loyal as any man in the State,' that he 'observes the laws' and 'pays his taxes,' and at the same time withholds his moral support and sympathy from the government, you may know that he is, what in his heart he knows himself to be, disloyal."[26]

Two well-known pamphleteers for the league stressed similar messages. Francis Lieber, the Columbia College law professor who compiled the code of war, produced an aptly titled missive, *No Party Now; but All for Our Country*. He had read the speech before the Loyal National League in New York on April 11, 1863. This was the time when Republicans smarted from the gains by the opposition in the elections of the prior fall. "When we are ailing," he said, "we do not take medicine by party prescription. We do not build ships by party measurement; we do not pray for our daily bread by party distinctions; . . . nor do we eat, drink, sleep, or wake as partisans." He concluded that there were only the loyal and disloyal.[27] Similarly, the president of the U.S. Sanitary Commission, Henry W. Bellows, published a tract titled *Unconditional Loyalty* in September 1863. He argued that citizens of the Union could not criticize the man without criticizing the office. Opponents of the administration had done just that: tried to separate the Republican Party from the government. "The office is so much larger than the man, that any abuse directed at him, hits it in spite of the marksman."[28]

As always, buried within the allegations were kernels of truth about treason. When B. H. Hill, a provost marshal assigned to Detroit, submitted his final report in 1865, he remembered the sensitivity surrounding the 1864 election and the fears of Confederate incursions along the Canadian border. This was not a reaction cultivated in the hothouse of paranoia. Agents of the Davis government operated across the border to instigate such plots as torching hotels in New York City, raiding banks in Vermont, and liberating prisoners of war to create chaos on the Union home front. They even hoped to control the Great Lakes by seizing Union ships. Conspiracies and plots against the Union existed as more than the mutterings of feverish persons. To guard against this possibility in Detroit, Hill cooperated with the Union League to organize a private militia that would rush to his aid in times of emergency. Each lodge selected an officer who reported to the provost marshal. Hill claimed that 4,000 loyal men could have assembled in half an hour in Detroit. The state had 1,000 stands of arms with ten rounds of ammunition for each. Could he have raised so many men so quickly? Probably not. But this partnership represented a public arm of the state reaching out to a private, secret society whose members were encouraged by federal authorities to be nervous, although they would have defined their posture as vigilant.[29]

Small wonder that events in Kentucky and Indiana unfolded as they did in 1864. Kentucky comes first in this story because it earned the chronological honor for Union interference. Scholars have spilled a lot of ink in trying to figure out why a state that remained in the Union "became" Confederate *after* the Civil War—or, to use the famous phrase of historian E. Merton Coulter, the state "waited until after the war was over to secede from the Union." Yet the conversion from Yankee to Rebel identity was very much under way during the war, with the Lincoln administration and the military superiors who ruled the state supplying ample reasons for supporters of the Union to wonder if, during the fracture of the nation in 1861, they had made the right choice after all.[30]

In March 1864, Colonel Frank Lane Wolford chose to make a bold political address as he accepted a presentation sword from admirers. A professed Unionist, and someone who had raised a regiment of soldiers for the United States, Wolford and his colleagues had grown increasingly disenchanted with the raising of black soldiers in their state. The process was supposed to occur voluntarily through masters, with the government compensating slave owners $300, thus giving a nod toward local rule. Instead, recruitment agents from other states flooded the area to attract— Kentuckians would say "steal"—black recruits for their units. The procedures undercut masters and meant in many cases that they received no compensation. Tightening regulations to prevent this abuse of the system invariably increased the presence of federal soldiers and agents, further eroding the authority of masters.[31]

Into this situation stepped Wolford, whose speech in accepting the honor "stirred up a hornet's nest," as he vowed resistance by Kentuckians to black recruitment. Additionally, officers of regiments who enjoyed an easy time patrolling the state rather than fighting Confederates apparently decided that they would refuse to go to the front if ordered, raising the specter of a band of unhappy military men who had arms and influence on the home front and who supported a man who professed open defiance to the Lincoln government. Wolford then charged Lincoln "with wantonly trampling upon the Constitution, and crushing, under the iron heel of military power, the rights of the people governed by that instrument." The president, he claimed, had violated his pledge that the war was about reunion. His methods for attacking the rebels would prolong the war. Lincoln was a tyrant and a usurper.[32]

The problem was, in addition to being an alleged tyrant, the president was also Wolford's boss and the Articles of War frowned upon subordinates chastising their superiors. As was often the case, local authorities acted without waiting for clearance from Washington. General Stephen G. Burbridge, the commander of the military district, had Wolford arrested and sent to Knoxville, Tennessee, where he remained confined without charges. Eventually Lincoln interceded, granting a dishonorable discharge for the officer for disloyalty and conduct unbecoming an officer and gentleman. This let Wolford out of prison, for which he showed his gratefulness by further antagonizing the government. He accepted the nomination of anti-Lincoln forces as a candidate for an elector in the next presidential election. On May 25 he addressed the meeting in Louisville, where he warned, according to an informer, that if the military attempted to interfere with the election, "*Bayonet* would be met with *Bayonet* & he counseled his friends to prepare for the conflict & it was highly applauded." The informer also noted that Wolford had authority to raise a regiment of six months' troops, which would be filled with men hostile to the administration. He hoped that the president would stop the recruitment effort, but if not, he warned that Kentucky would erupt in civil war.[33]

Within days of this meeting, J. H. Hammond, an assistant adjutant general in charge of the camp and draft rendezvous in Louisville, wrote George McClellan with news that seemingly confirmed the intensity of the situation. "I am greatly exercised as to the next Presidential Election," he noted. "I fear that the Administration will exert undue influence & that bloodshed will follow. Any outbreak at that crisis will precipitate Revolution at once. In such an event too a cavalry officer at the head of a good Regiment, well disciplined, would be of more weight in the body politic than an Asst. Adjt. Genl."[34] This kind of planning did not seem worthy of a republic.

During the summer, the Union military stepped up a campaign against such a scenario. By late June, Halleck in Washington authorized General

Burbridge at Lexington to impose martial law. He indicated that disloyal persons were giving aid and assistance to armed rebels and sought insurrection. Among these "aiders and abettors of rebellion and treason are distinguished officers of the State government and members of the Congress of the United States." Burbridge was to arrest and send to Washington anyone suspected of this activity. "Any attempt at rebellion in Kentucky must be put down with a strong hand, and traitors must be punished without regard to their rank or sex."[35] Included in this sweep were about twenty-five people—Judge Joshua Bullitt of the state Court of Appeals, the president of the Democratic Central Committee, the chief of the fire department, a water company president, a jailor, a doctor, and others suspected as being part of a subversive, secret group known as the Sons of Liberty. These arrests came just before the state elections on the first Monday in August. Also just before the election, General Burbridge issued an order to strike the name of a candidate from poll books in the race for the Court of Appeals.[36]

One of the military men who condoned taking a hard line against Kentuckians was Major General William T. Sherman, who in the process revealed the frustrations of the practical, day-by-day determination of loyalty. As another series of arrests began on August 11—arrests that resulted in the expulsion of perhaps forty citizens from the region—Sherman told a colleague at Frankfort, Kentucky, "I am aware that military power, unchecked by the forms which in peaceful times surround the citizen, may do wrongs, grievous wrongs, but how is it to be avoided? Shall we sit down and trust to grand juries in these days of revolt?" The general then articulated his frustration with trying to separate the loyal people from the traitorous ones. Few paper trails existed for this important duty. Most of the determination of treason came outside of courts, outside of documentation, and outside of corroboration of stories beyond the personal assessment of someone who sat in front of the adjudicator and who invariably professed that he or she was innocent, so help them God. According to Sherman, the state of Kentucky contained "such a bundle of inexplicable family and State factions, that the veriest murderer, and horse-thief, and dirty dog, if arrested can forthwith produce credentials of respectability that I could not establish or you either." Most often, the determination of loyalty came down to a gut-level judgment based on incomplete information, leavened by political leanings, and assisted by information from local informants.[37]

Missing from the story so far is the horrible guerrilla warfare that disrupted the western border states, causing the federal government to care less about civil liberties than about security. When Bramlette became governor in 1863, he moved aggressively against the terrorism in his state. He enlarged his militia and established a policy of holding five suspected rebels hostage for every one seized by the irregulars. He also enacted reparations against rebel citizens for damage to Unionist property and announced fines for people who assisted the rebels. Burbridge picked up where the governor left off, but in a grander way. On July 16, he issued General Orders No. 59 that specified retaliatory measures against the harassment of Union citizens. Sympathizers living within five miles of the scene of an outrage faced expulsion from the U.S. lines. More grisly, he promised that for every Unionist murdered, four guerrillas would be chosen from a pool of prisoners "and publicly shot to death in the most convenient place near the scene of outrages." Possibly fifty executions took place.[38]

A supporter of tough measures against guerrillas, Bramlette parted company with Burbridge when it came to soldiers meddling with elections. Killing enemies was one thing; denying traitors, real or imagined, the vote was quite another. The governor did not appreciate a federal general sticking his nose into the ballot box and disqualifying a candidate for office, especially a sitting incumbent for the state's highest judicial office. Bramlette complained to Lincoln that the government treated Kentucky as though it were a rebellious, conquered province, declaring it under martial law and allowing a military commander to interfere with an election. The military also restricted trade and levied assessments on citizens without hearings, even though the courts functioned. And the men of his state were unwilling to lay down their lives for the enslaved. He added: "The course pursued by many of those intrusted with Federal authority in Kentucky has made to your Administration and re-election thousands of bitter and irreconcilable opponents, where a wise and just policy and action would more easily have made friends."[39]

The appeal had virtually no impact. When the presidential election arrived, Burbridge arrested both Wolford and Richard T. Jacob, the latter person no less than the lieutenant governor of Kentucky and president pro tempore of its senate. The prisoners concerned federal authorities because they held key positions for recruiting troops and both had gone on record as opposing black enlistments. For Wolford, this represented his third arrest since March. He also had been targeted in July, this time as a citizen and not a soldier, for speaking out against the government at the Democrat convention on May 25—a meeting at which he became a presidential elector and uttered the phrase that Kentuckians should meet interference at the ballot with the bayonet. Federal intervention should have been anticipated. After the second arrest, a delegation of congressmen from Kentucky that included Senator Powell and Representative Robert Mallory visited the White House to condemn arbitrary arrests. They demanded charges and a speedy trial for Wolford or his release. In Mallory's account, Lincoln claimed not to know why Wolford was arrested but reckoned it was "for making speeches calculated to prevent men from enlisting in the army." The meeting apparently did not end the way the Kentuckians wanted.[40]

The circumstances paralleled that of Vallandigham a year earlier, although Wolford may have been less cautious with his words than the former congressman from Ohio. As with Vallandigham's address at a political rally, friends of the administration established themselves in the crowd, heard the inflammatory comments, and then reported the speaker to the army commander. A military commission, not a civil court, launched the case against Wolford, invoking in the first charge the same order that had secured Vallandigham's arrest and conviction. Burnside's General Orders No. 38 was still very much alive and continued to prove useful to Republicans. The difference from 1863 in Ohio is that Wolford apparently lived something of a charmed life and escaped a trial and banishment to the Confederacy. Burbridge, for reasons unknown, was a bit surprised to see the man in Kentucky again; he had received no word of Wolford's release. It was as if the federal government either lost track of him or lost interest. However, as to be expected with a man who performed stubbornness as a high art, Wolford continued to rail against the administration and provoked his third arrest in November, just days after the presidential election, in an action that jeopardized his ability to vote as an elector for McClellan. Wolford went free before January; it was more trouble than it was worth to push him through a military commission and truly unnecessary. The election had been decided.[41]

Jacob, the sitting lieutenant governor, enjoyed less good fortune than Wolford. Like Vallandigham more than a year before, the military banished Jacob to the Confederacy, except without a hearing. Jacob had criticized Lincoln for emancipation and the enlistment of black soldiers and campaigned vigorously against his reelection. Federal authorities in the state apparently lumped him in with the reputed activity of secret societies, but it appears that Jacob's primary faults lay in opposing Lincoln, opposing emancipation, and opposing the recruitment of African Americans for the U.S. military.

Witnesses before a subsequent congressional investigation described the lieutenant governor as delivering bombastic speeches in Kentucky and

Indiana in which, if true, his statements did sound like an insurrectionist. One man reported a hearsay account in which Jacob allegedly said, "There is no possible chance for the election of Mr. Lincoln to-morrow, but by bayonets; and I am ready, in the event of his election, to shoulder my musket and join you (the audience) in overturning the government." It seems questionable that a politician in a sensitive state, knowing the scrutiny that the government maintained, would utter such statements; however, such was the rumor that appeared in a Cincinnati newspaper, suggesting that Kentuckians wished to inaugurate a second revolution for independence from the government. Jacob denied the account as foolhardy.[42] Whether or not he actually tried to incite rebellion, private correspondence to Lincoln from two Kentuckians indicated that popular attitudes considered violence at the polls a possibility. An elector who stumped a congressional district, Charles Eginton, said he had heard of violent denunciations of Lincoln and advice given to avowed rebels to "go to the Polls with arms in their hands, and use violence if necessary to put down the 'Minions of the Administration.'" W. C. Goodloe supported this impression, adding that the speeches of Jacob, Wolford, Bramlette, and others "have so aroused the bad passions of the opponents of the Administration as to require severe measures of repression." He believed that Kentucky had become more disloyal than Tennessee and that only military force protected Union sentiment.[43]

Whatever the actual case, soldiers seized Jacob at his country home twenty-five miles from Louisville. He at first thought that guerrillas had come to call and had buckled on his revolvers to greet his visitors. When he saw instead a federal captain accompanied by armed soldiers, he went with them peacefully. Like Vallandigham, he was expelled from federal lines, not to return under penalty of death. "Seized as a felon," Jacob wrote Lincoln, "not permitted to talk or consult with my friends, not confronted, no charges preferred, and no trial permitted, I am hurried through the lines to accept the hospitality and protection of a people that I had fought against." He admitted opposing the president's reelection and using all of his energy to defeat Lincoln. But his time in exile was far shorter than Vallandigham's. Jacob received permission to return to Kentucky by January 1865.[44]

In New York, French tourist de Hauranne heard people debating the arrest and banishment of Jacob to rebel territory and came to some incredible conclusions about the use of arbitrary power. The Frenchman was not sympathetic to Jacob, considering him as long engaged in traitorous activity. For de Hauranne, though, the main lesson conveyed by the arrest concerned the defects of a democracy. In America, the laws left the government powerless. At first, that causes one to do a double take, but he meant that the government in a democracy had to adhere to written rules, which provided less flexibility in responding than is available in other systems. In a democracy, public opinion entered the picture in determining how far executives could go in interpreting what the law allowed. "The authority of the government is, so to speak, elastic, and provided that public opinion supports it, acts of arbitrary authority can come to be accepted on the plea that the defense of liberty requires them." Such a situation the law had not foreseen. Instead, he claimed, the Americans had to improvise answers to meet pressing needs. Additionally, state laws existed often in contradiction to national goals, establishing conflicts between state and federal law that "make the use of the police power illusory and in troubled times actually make impossible the use of this complicated instrument. Each case must then be treated as an exception. There are neither fixed principles nor generally enforced regulations, no consistency in the use of force; society lives by expedients from day to day."[45]

Just over the line from Kentucky came more examples of disloyal behavior that by now seemed destined to provoke, contrary to the outcome in Kentucky, what had become a predictable use of force by the military. The Indianapolis treason trials have been well known and reported by scholars as part of a so-called northwestern Confederacy, a conspiracy of an alleged 500,000 members of secret societies intent on creating insurrection in the loyal North. The Union woke up to the news in late August of gun shipments received by Copperheads in the region, especially Harrison Horton Dodd, referred to by historian Frank L. Klement as "a second-rate politician with a printing plant at his disposal." Dodd had been the cause of controversy in 1863 when the military arrested him for inflammatory speech and Indiana Democrats clamored for his release. He had built an organization later called the Sons of Liberty, a secret organization designed to combat the propaganda by the Union Leagues, turn out the vote, and prevent the nomination of McClellan. The organization had generated a constitution, rituals, and rules of operation, all of which could be construed as establishing an organization in opposition to the U.S. government. But Dodd struggled to launch an actual overt act, and if the group had a plan to conduct an uprising, its leaders showed very poor initiative, to say the least.[46]

What is not ambiguous is that Dodd had done the unthinkable. He consorted with Confederate agents who operated out of Canada to encourage various plots against the U.S. government. Jacob Thompson, the former secretary of the interior under Buchanan, served as one of the principal agents funded by the Confederacy. Some of the activities promoted by Thompson and his colleagues included seizing U.S. warships on the Great Lakes, rigging the gold market, burning boats on the Mississippi, burning down New York City hotels with Greek fire, and conducting raids on banks at St. Albans, Vermont. But the main plot—one linked to the capture of ships on the Great Lakes—involved freeing prisoners of war in various northern facilities (such as Johnson's Island, Ohio, and Camp Morton, Indiana) to join with the Sons of Liberty in Illinois, Indiana, Ohio, Kentucky, and Missouri to conduct armed insurrection in the hopes of bringing on an armistice. Dodd had met with the Confederates and accepted perhaps as much as $10,000 for establishing a new steam press. Union detectives directed by the departmental commander of Indiana, Brigadier General Henry B. Carrington, shadowed Dodd and his compatriots, seizing in one raid materials that revealed the organization of the Sons of Liberty, its constitution, and some of its members. Carrington also planted a detective who infiltrated the organization and figured prominently as a witness in the resulting prosecutions. More papers seized by Carrington from the Terra Haute office abandoned by U.S. congressman Daniel W. Voorhees contained statements from a parallel organization known as the Order of American Knights (to which Dodd had belonged) that expressed support for secession, for the servitude of the African to the white race, and for the duty of the people to expel "by force of arms" the authorities of the United States. These were strong, imprudent, dangerous words.[47]

Authorities acted once the news came of 400 arms shipped to Indiana for Dodd's use. Events then unfolded rather quickly. Dodd and five others were charged with various offenses and brought before a military commission at Indianapolis, rather than a federal court. None of the charges involved treason, even though this allegation became the popular way to depict the matter then and to remember the trials later. The government had grown increasingly reticent to try people with treason under the constitutional definition. The burden of proof was too high. It was better to rely on the newly created charge of conspiracy, as well as inciting insurrection, conducting disloyal practices such as urging people to resist the draft, and pretending to be a peaceable citizen. During the trial, the mercurial Dodd escaped and fled to safety in Canada, discrediting him and allowing the commission to find him guilty of a capital offense in absentia. The five other accused conspirators, including Lambdin P. Milligan, whose name became associated with a later Supreme Court ruling, were also found guilty and sentenced to death. Lincoln delayed the executions, and the men eventually received vindication when in 1866 the U.S. Supreme Court determined that military commissions could not try such cases when civil courts operated.

Lost in the more recent studies of this matter, although present in the work of Frank Klement, have been the fears that these Democrats shared about sham elections supervised by the military as one of the motivations behind forming secret societies. Klement, in fact, argued that Kentucky provided a lesson for them and a reason for extremists to argue for arming themselves to protect their political rights.[48] Indeed, they had evidence of interference in the border states. Interestingly, the concern over free elections appeared in the negotiations with Confederate agents and in the Indianapolis trials. Jacob Thompson, the U.S. cabinet officer turned Confederate terrorist, reported to Richmond about the Sons of Liberty, "In the month of June last [1864] the universal feeling among its members—leaders and privates—was that it was useless to hold a Presidential election. Lincoln had the power and would certainly reelect himself, and there was no hope but in force." And during the argument in defense of Milligan, attorney John R. Coffroth mentioned that one of the allegations against his client was that he had "advised resistance to any encroachment upon the elective franchise." The attorney added, "Suppose he did; who would not and be a man?"[49]

Although the military intervened because of legitimate concerns about 400 revolvers in the hands of a possible revolutionary—a revolutionary who had demonstrated minimal aptitude for good judgment—the arrests and prosecutions contained political value, especially for Governor Morton. Many of the conspirators were rivals and Morton, who was running for reelection, pressured the provost marshal to find evidence of misbehavior. A Jeffersonian Democrat, Milligan had tried to enter the gubernatorial campaign to unseat Morton but did not win the support of his own party—which probably speaks volumes about the leadership qualities that he lacked and the unlikelihood of him mustering enough followers to launch an uprising. Morton hoped the trial, starting in September, would influence the elections in October and send strong signals across the Union about the government's intolerance for treason. The tribunal also resisted an attempt by counsel to separate the trials of the remaining men from one into individual hearings after Dodd had fled. It was beneficial to the Union to move the trials along as much as possible before the election in order to discredit the opposition to the Republicans as traitors.[50]

In short, the exploits of the military during 1863 and 1864 could be interpreted by opponents of the administration as repeated measures to harass political rivals in order to ensure a victory for the president in November. This does not mean that the administration intended to do this. Lincoln and his Washington colleagues had bigger problems consuming their attentions, although it is also likely that people in the executive branch did not object to the actions of Carrington, Morton, et al. Added to the interference of troops at the polls throughout the border states in 1863, the arrests in Kentucky of political opponents and the military trials of citizens in Indiana in 1864 reinforced for Democrats a pattern that dated back to the fall of 1862 and that manifested itself most dramatically in the arrest of Vallandigham. In fact, military authorities like Carrington tried to link the Ohio politician with the conspirators in the Indianapolis trials in order to discredit him and diminish his voice in the coming election. The party of accused traitors fought back, charging Republicans with looking for excuses to shut down the presidential election. Whether a columnist truly believed in this possibility, or just thought it was the best line of attack against Republicans, a Democratic newspaper in Indiana alleged that Morton might void the October elections if his party lost. "Old Abe will then issue a proclamation declaring Indiana in a state of rebellion, and proceed by force of arms and the proclamation aforesaid to subdue, conquer, and crush the same, giving us a military instead of a civil government."[51]

Just before the presidential contest, Judge Advocate General Joseph Holt added more reason to judge Democrats as traitors. Using information secured by Carrington, Holt reported to Secretary of War Stanton a threat posed by secret societies, primarily in the western portions of the Union but also with some representatives in New York. Known variously as the Order of American Knights, Knights of the Golden Circle, and the Sons of Liberty (among others), these societies, according to Holt, conducted secret rituals and organized themselves like an army with leaders given rank as officers and caches of weapons traced to their various headquarters. There was some truth to the depiction. The goals of the members clustered around discouraging enlistments, aiding the enemy with information, speaking out against the war, and even occasionally running guns to Confederates. Holt produced a hair-raising document that warned of an expansive conspiracy that could spill over into further outbreak of arms and violence.[52]

Issued in October, the report received wide circulation and has been debated ever since for its accuracy. Republicans seized the document and made the most of it, with Union Leagues and the party distributing copies that condemned the secret societies. To them, it served as gospel.

Democrats dismissed the threat as patently ridiculous and downright insulting. To them it was political manipulation. They attacked the report as, in the words of one newspaper writer, a "partisan electioneering document." If these societies were so dangerous, the writer asked, why did the government fail to nip them in the bud when they formed in 1862? According to this writer it was ludicrous to consider a violent uprising staging itself with a bunch of revolvers and no muskets, likening these weapons to "paving stones" in the face of organized soldiers.[53] Historians have taken similar positions, ranging from disparagement of the report as a myth designed to affect voting to more recent interpretations that take the underlying threats of violence more seriously.[54] Lincoln brushed off the secret societies, indicating to one of his secretaries that he "treats the Northern section of the conspiracy as not especially worth regarding, holding it a mere political organization, with about as much malice and puerility as the Knights of the Golden Circle."[55] Holt also claimed that these groups mustered at least 500,000 members, an estimate he attributed to Vallandigham. These estimates seem about as accurate as McClellan's miscounting of the Confederate troops while he led the Union army. In the key states of Indiana, Illinois, Ohio, and Missouri, judged as having the most conspiratorial activity, Holt's estimate constituted, at the low end, more than 50 percent of the Democrats who voted for McClellan from those states; and at the high end, nearly 80 percent. It seems a stretch that these "treasonable" societies attracted such support.[56]

The government perhaps feared insurrection less than the impact of these secret societies in deterring enlistments. Republicans needed success at the polls to sustain the war effort; opponents of conscription needed to be held in check so that new recruits came to the army; the army needed troops in order to continue the fight for reunion. Even free speech protected by the Constitution became a problem if it hampered the military's ability to put men into the field and win the war. Letters to Francis Lieber from Henry Wager Halleck, who served like a chief of staff for the army, underscored this point. By August 1864 the Union's war effort looked glum. The army melted away from deaths, wounds, sickness, and expiration of service. Stalemate appeared to be the best one could discern from military action in Virginia, Georgia, and other parts of the United States. And the army needed more men. The Union decided in the summer of 1864 to stage the third of its four drafts. Halleck bemoaned the fact that 100,000 men lay in hospitals, "and the number is increasing." Then he learned of the Chicago convention that selected McClellan as the presidential candidate. "The effect of this platform on military affairs is already felt. Before the convention we were receiving over *two thousand* recruits daily; since the nomination of MacClellan we have received less than *six hundred* per day." He also heard that "armed organizations" had formed in Indiana, Missouri, Ohio, and Pennsylvania to resist the draft.[57]

Was the threat of violent upheaval on the part of treasonous societies in the Northwest exaggerated? Undoubtedly. Was it believed to be real? Not by everyone in the administration—perhaps not even by Lincoln. However, Holt's report supplied more ammunition to the eager Union League supporters and, more importantly, registered on a number of significant people in the War Department. The Union diverted manpower from the battlefield until authorities could assess the nature of the national security picture. Halleck wrote just after the report became public in October that he had "serious apprehension" over the possibility of armed resistance in the loyal states. Referring to a prior letter from early September, he added, "I was then satisfied that we were almost on the brink of a revolution in Ohio & Indiana, and we were compelled to send additional troops to guard the arsenals & prison depots, at the very time that Grant & Sherman needed them most in the field. No one who saw the evidence we had could doubt the intentions of leading copperheads to plunge the whole north into anarchy & thus secure the complete success of Jeff. Davis' rebellion."[58] Military authorities like Halleck may have hoped the report was overblown, but they certainly gave it their attention.

On the basis of these tensions—the specter of armed insurrection revealed in a government report, arrests and trials of political figures, the vow of radical Democrats to protect a free ballot with bullets if necessary, and a government trying to pacify a rebellion that threatened its existence—it truly was a wonder that the election came off, after all. And it was perhaps more of a wonder that it did so within the parameters of the traditional, riotous antebellum political culture, with the additional presence of a government that held the advantage of controlling an active military in wartime.

And the Election Came

Federal actions in Kentucky and elsewhere remained a central part of the Democratic political lament as the delegates convened in Chicago in late August. Early in the proceedings the members heard letters from two of their number whom the military had arrested and put into prison at Louisville, preventing them from participating in this election ritual. One of the men, J. R. Buchanan, said he was arrested under "vague suspicion," that he had no chance to defend himself, and that he saw new prisoners brought in every day under the same circumstances. "In the last Gubernatorial and Congressional election," he observed, "the voice of Kentucky was silenced by these means (terrorism and robbery), and it is needless to hope for any better treatment at the ensuing election." He called the times truly alarming. The opponents "with their secret societies"—a reference to Union Leagues—might attempt anything. They controlled the national wealth, national arms, and national soldiers. They deployed "hordes of negroes" and "detective spies." They disregarded the laws. They had little respect for the oaths they took to protect the Constitution. Overall, the convention's *Proceedings* maintained a running thread on the administration's alleged abuses of the Constitution on free speech and other liberties, as well as the concern over whether the presidential contest would unfold without military intervention. If a free election did not occur, the platform considered such an event "revolutionary" and, as numerous speakers like Wolford had vowed ahead of this meeting, one that deserved resistance "with all the means and power under our control." Toward the end of the meeting, Charles A. Wickliffe of Kentucky, who had lost his congressional seat in 1863 from what he characterized as military interference, proposed that the first act of a newly elected democratic president should be to open Abraham Lincoln's prison doors and let the captives go free.[59]

The passionate commentary against arrests, free speech, and constitutional violations in general, as well as hatred for Lincoln, created a semblance of common ground for a contentious party. The delegates were not only unhappy with the incumbent president but also had serious problems with each other. They entered the meeting disagreeing over both the policy for ending the war and the candidate who best represented the constituency. In fact, it is more accurate to think of three factions composing the democracy at the time: the War Democrats who supported Lincoln (and were not necessarily at the convention), the Democrats who advocated pushing forward with the defeat of the rebels with McClellan as president, and the Democrats who favored seeking an armistice with people like Vallandigham as leaders. The members who pressed for peace detested McClellan as the candidate because they saw only more lives lost, more taxes enacted, more debt amassed, and possibly more unconstitutional abuses of power based on his performance in Maryland in 1861. The supporters of the general considered Vallandigham and his backers as out of touch with reality because most citizens and soldiers in the army saw victory through war as the only means to restore the antebellum country. And the peace men demeaned the sacrifice of soldiers. This was not the stuff that won elections in wartime. Both sides struggled for control at the convention. Both tried to characterize themselves as patriots rather than traitors. Both left the convention failing to achieve all they wanted. The peace faction won the platform; the war-for-reunion faction won the candidate.

Although historians occasionally have chided the Democratic Party for allowing the peace wing to control the platform, the criticism ignores the rising momentum of this faction spurred by the carnage on the battle-field and the return of Vallandigham. As despicable and marginal as he appears today, he was less marginal for many Democrats who opposed Lincoln. And he was more moderate in his public expressions than people like Dodd or Wolford. He was, if there is such a thing, a centrist-extremist, more calculating than the less cautious ideologues. Tired of his exile that kept him from family and out of political affairs, he had left Canada to re-turn to the United States on June 14. The military shadowed him, keeping the president apprised of the politician's movements. He was not about to hand them something actionable. In speech after speech, he led listeners to the edge of implied treason but provided the spies sent to listen to him with nothing useful. Arrest and exile had taught him the limits of free speech. Meanwhile, politicians and editors gave contradictory advice to the president about whether to rearrest him or let him go. Lincoln chose to wait and watch. If Vallandigham had learned to be more cautious in his utterances, Lincoln had learned to withhold fuel from the fire. Instead, the president adopted a coy, public response that appeared periodically in newspapers over the next months: that he had not been officially notified of the facts and would not know anything until the Ohioan did something objectionable.[60] The choice empowered Vallandigham, to be sure, but less so than making him a martyr twice over.

Throughout 1864, the clamor for peace increased to the extent that it threatened to splinter the party. The signs came early—in fact, preceding the election year. In December 1863 the Ohio State Central Committee nearly succeeded in calling for a convention in January to put forward Vallandigham as a presidential nominee. The call failed by one vote. A political crony of McClellan and chair of the Democratic Party, George W. Morgan, warned the general against trying to shut out Vallandigham men from future meetings. In Ohio, the peace faction was stronger than the general's supporters. By August, Morgan, who became a delegate to the convention, reported the peace sentiment had become a "torrent which no man can check," but he believed it could be channeled. Although Ohio and the Northwest harbored the most critical mass of Peace Demo-crats, the region was not the only place of concern. A correspondent from

Philadelphia reported that he had toured two or three counties in Pennsylvania and claimed to have consulted with hundreds of Democrats. Among them he found only one man not in favor of a peace candidate. Many of the rest, he told McClellan, favored the general's nomination, but even those supporters would not necessarily back a war candidate. Later in the letter he counseled that adopting the peace policy party offered the possibility for the "overthrow of the treasonable dynasty at Washington."[61]

One Lincoln supporter who covered the convention as a journalist noticed the discord within the opposition, as well as how McClellan held the key to unlocking the White House for Democrats in November. The reporter singled out Samuel S. Cox as an example. Cox was a fellow Democratic congressman from Ohio with Vallandigham, but there the similarities ended. Cox constituted one of the anti-Vallandigham clique writing to McClellan, a group that included people such as August Belmont, a Wall Street financier who had risen from ties with the Rothschild family and served as a chair of the Democratic Party; Manton Marble, editor of the *New York World*, the leading opposition newspaper in the Northeast; and Samuel Tilden, future New York governor and presidential candidate. Cox was one of many maneuvering to put peace on the platform but to control the nomination. In August he counseled editor Marble to tell the general to write something on the necessity of using all honorable methods for peace and union. The position was needed not for his election but for his nomination. Conservatives, he said, would stand for the plank, and McClellan could win "if we don't insist on war in our platform." It was not a pretty fight in convention, however. As the more extreme members offered resolutions excoriating the president for his tyranny and asking that the draft be postponed until after the election, Cox attempted to refer the drafts to a committee without being read. He was hissed at and received the following less-than-kind greeting, "Sit down and shut up, you war democrat."[62]

The more pragmatic politicians won the battle of the nomination, but the struggle exposed the vulnerabilities that McClellan faced in the campaign. In an attempt to hold off the inevitable victory and damage the candidate, peace men dredged up the general's role in the arrests of Maryland legislators in 1861. Benjamin Harris of Maryland charged that McClellan was more of a tyrant than Lincoln; that the general had inaugurated the usurping of state rights among Union civilians. Chiming in with a similar critique, an Ohio delegate asked the participants what it was that they had complained about for the past three to four years. Why, of course, an abridged freedom of speech, arbitrary arrests of citizens, and interference with free elections. Yet, he observed, the convention intended to promote a man for president who had gone further than Lincoln in attacking liberties. To him, the delegates took a hypocritical stance, overlooking that the leading candidate had done more than arrest a citizen here and there; he had taken down an entire state legislature. In sum, critics alleged that McClellan had abridged all three freedoms—speech, habeas corpus, and free elections—by jailing duly elected officials who had honest differences with the government.[63]

They had a point, these anti-McClellanites, although their rationale overlooked the context of the historical moment of 1861. Lincoln, not McClellan, had initiated the arrests then, and the public largely favored the action during a hypercharged moment when loyalty and national security remained uncertain and treachery seemed to travel with the wind. For many in 1861, traitors lurked in every nook and cranny of the Union, and the Potter Committee was purging the government of supposed Confederate sympathizers. That a general followed the orders of a Republican president to shut down a state legislature can be forgiven in such a climate. In 1864, McClellan remained assured he had done the right thing. But the Democrats against him used this example to level supposedly nonpartisan criticism against what they considered to be the general's poor service to the Constitution and to civil liberties.

On the positive side for Democrats, McClellan had been a warrior, no matter how tepid of one by contemporary judgment. His background as a commander of men in battle gave him the gravitas to carry the convention and sweep aside the delegates who called for an armistice. Those within the party who saw him as a weak candidate nevertheless understood, no matter how reluctantly, that McClellan gave the Democrats the greatest hope among their number for securing the voting by soldiers, which was a concern of both parties. A Vallandigham candidate presented an easy target for Republicans to condemn as a traitor who was unsympathetic to the soldiers in the field and disloyal. And the soldiers' support mattered. Under the circumstances, a former general offered the better chance of attracting the support of the army because he had led soldiers into combat and, in his acceptance letter, promised no peace without reunion— otherwise he could not look into the faces of the survivors who had lost so many brethren, potentially in vain.[64] So the question begs: Given this background, could McClellan be portrayed as a traitor . . . convincingly?

Some of his political rivals tried, although it was not the most prevalent line of attack because it lacked solid evidence and, more to the point, plausibility. Edgar Conkling, a railroad magnate and brother of one of

Lincoln's acquaintances, urged the president in late September to put a detective on the track of McClellan to gather proof that the general had been a traitor. Rumor had it that a family physician of the general had become offended that his patient had expressed sympathies for the South and a housekeeper allegedly proclaimed that while living in Chicago he had been visited by Jefferson Davis and Confederate general P. G. T. Beauregard. Ridiculous. But the more persistent speculation involved a rumor that McClellan had conferred with Lee at midnight after the battle of Antietam to allow the Confederate army to recross the Potomac without harassment. Beyond this were accusations that the general had leaked to the enemy sensitive information about troop movements. "If yourself & friends would set parties at work putting Macs failures & concessions to rebels, and the many mysterious incidents together," Conkling told the president, "it would impress the Country at least of his disloyalty, and thus defeat Peace Party." He added: "I boldly proclaim he was *then*, and is *now* a *traitor*, and . . . I want to see the proper parties prove it for good of Country." The next month he told Lincoln he intended to send "thousands" of copies of the allegation across the country printed in pamphlet form. Lincoln did not answer, indicating that he did not see much merit in investing in this pursuit.[65]

The Democratic convention had reinforced the most important themes for the election: the administration's infringement of civil liberties, free speech, and free elections with a hint of anti-emancipation sentiment. Although the Emancipation Proclamation upset many in the ranks, and motivated the grassroots members, party leaders gave up on it as a strategy for national politics, except as it supplied more evidence of the president's disregard for the Constitution. When Senator Powell of Kentucky had an admirer nominate him as a possible presidential candidate, he refused, flatly proclaiming "that the candidate for the Presidency at this awful crisis in our country's history should come from one of the non-slaveholding States." Party leaders apparently considered that anti-emancipation, as a primary part of the campaign, offered less chance of winning than focusing on the administration's breaches of the Constitution and civil liberties, as well as incompetence with defeating the Confederacy. William Allen of Ohio gave a rousing speech after McClellan's nomination in which he prided the Democratic Party on its history of holding the nation together, and then hoped that the election proceeded fairly. "We have not a musket; We don't want any—we don't need any. We have the ballot box, we have tickets, we have human reason, and all we ask of Mr. Lincoln is, that he will keep the road to the ballot box unobstructed by fraud or force; that he will keep that road open to the people; give us a clean ticket and a fair count."[66]

At first, the signs were not good, as violence greeted Democratic meetings in parts of the Union. Delegates at the convention had called for party members to stage their traditional mass rallies to ratify the nomination of the candidate during the anniversary of the adoption of the Constitution in Philadelphia, September 17. Obviously, the date sent a strong statement of which party cherished this founding document. But it also put Republicans on the alert about when their rivals intended to flood the streets and town squares. What followed was not out of the ordinary for antebellum cities that had their full measure of riots and tempestuous political meetings. However, the stakes for national life enhanced the usual rough politics that Americans played at the local level in the nineteenth century. Whatever interference with political rallies took place typically had nothing to do with orders from Washington. The collisions arose among men, women, and children who confronted each other during the outdoor spectacles that drove American political culture.

Judged by the play they received in the newspapers of both parties, the significant political violence erupted in St. Louis; Cincinnati; Pottsville, Pennsylvania; and Philadelphia. Soldiers figured prominently in only the St. Louis and Pottsville rallies. In St. Louis, a ratification rally for McClellan touched off, as we have seen, a confrontation with soldiers whose origins may not be pinned down precisely. Some said soldiers threw the first stones and damaged political paraphernalia. Others said that Democrats pitched stones at the troops and called them cowards, a story reinforced in an investigation by General Rosecrans. This particular riot received the most play among newspapers, with Democrats relishing their righteous outrage.[67] At Pottsville, party members gathered to commemorate the passage of the Constitution on September 17 by staging a procession and listening to speeches for about four hours. As the meeting disbanded, an estimated twenty cavalrymen rode into the crowd with sabers drawn. Momentarily surprised, the participants gathered themselves, turned on the soldiers, and began pelting them with stones. For a few minutes it appeared as if the situation might escalate into a full-blown riot; however, the troopers disappeared as quickly as they had come. Six people were wounded, including a soldier who had just come home after three years of service. The soldiers were reported to belong to a one-year regiment raised at Chambersburg that was camped near Pottsville. Moderate Republicans helped ease tensions, as they urged the military commander to keep his men in camp.[68]

Cincinnati witnessed the most costly encounter that claimed the lives of three people, one of them a woman, and caused the suppression of a newspaper in Baltimore. This time, Republicans conducted the rally. Their concluding procession came at 11:00 P.M., touching off violence in the Fourth Ward. As usual, both sides blamed the other. The *Cincinnati Enquirer*, a Democrat newspaper, featured within its pages witnesses from the coroner's inquest favorable to its political views. According to this testimony, as the Republicans marched by, one woman hallooed for McClellan and a young boy tried to seize a torch from another boy marching in the procession. Men described as mounted grand marshals—one of them wearing spectacles and the other a military style uniform with shoulder straps—took umbrage, and one in particular pulled his pistol and wheeled the people around to head into the crowd shouting about the "sons of bitches" and yelling for his followers to "clean out the d——d Irish from the 4th Ward." In the melee Margaret Connelly, twenty-six-year-old mother of one, yelled that she had been shot and staggered to the ground. By the time the doctor arrived, she had passed away. In Baltimore, Major General Lew Wallace heard that the proprietors of the *Baltimore Evening Post* had placed a clipping of the Cincinnati riot on its public bulletin board. Threats had come in that a mob planned to storm the newspaper office. On September 30, he ordered the newspaper to discontinue publication as the "surest means of preventing your office being made the subject of violence." But this surely looked very bad. The action occurred a couple of weeks before Maryland voted on its antislavery constitution, and the *Post* was an opposition newspaper in the city. Appeals to Lincoln to reverse the order came to naught.[69] These were not the only fatalities during the election. Several soldiers entered a Methodist church in Troy, Missouri, which housed a Conservative meeting, struck an old man in the head, and shot one man fatally and wounded two others.[70]

Minor destruction and brief skirmishes over politics occurred in other places around the Union. The ratification meetings and mass rallies touched off infractions by both parties against each other. A McClellan Club in Massachusetts saw its national flag torn down; Republicans broke up a Democratic meeting at Covington, Kentucky, as former U.S. senator George Ellis Pugh of Ohio spoke, compelling him to leave the hall; a Democratic torchlight procession in Philadelphia "ended in a row," and someone broke windows of the party's headquarters on Chestnut Street, destroying images of McClellan and Pendleton; soldiers in the crowd listening to speeches in Madison, Wisconsin, roared, cheered, hissed and tried to disrupt the meeting, then stormed a cannon used for a salute until fended off by the governor of the state; and in New York City the "'free election or free fight' rowdies" assailed some Republicans with stones and brickbrats.[71] Hardly blameless, Democrats initiated some scrapes. They twice assaulted Major General John A. Logan, who eventually surrounded himself with armed friends when helping with the canvass. "Copperheads" in Washington "made sundry riot demonstration" which nearly provoked a fight but the crowd kept its temper. In San Francisco, as a Republican meeting broke up, a band of persons cheering for McClellan and groaning for Lincoln formed a procession and marched through the crowd until police stepped in to stop it.[72]

Democrats made political hay of these situations by asserting that *they* had become victims of a government-sanctioned attempt to deny the right to free assembly. As in the platform and through the speeches of extremists like Wolford, they warned of possible violence. For instance, "The Democracy are too powerful to plead the baby act," the *Cincinnati Enquirer* observed. "They are not non-resistants. They must either discontinue their meetings, or go prepared for a fight in their behalf. We advise the latter." The columnist concluded: "Protect your meetings by force."[73] Strong words, indeed. And they seemed to offer a forceful course of action for a party on its heels because of the turnaround in Union fortunes on the battlefield.

The threats, however, proved to be more bluster and bombast than a true call to arms, partly because the government did not mount a concerted effort to shut down political rallies and because Republicans in numerous communities called for moderation and calm. And it probably occurred to many a Democrat that it was not the safest course to mount resistance against determined, disciplined, armed soldiers ordered to break up public meetings, if that were going to happen. Kentucky was one of the exceptions for highly sensitive political arrests by the military deep into the presidential campaign, but for the most part the canvass proceeded with the usual bumps and taunts characteristic of the political culture, except perhaps with Democrats glancing over their shoulders to check for soldiers. The revolution prophesied in the Democratic platform did not happen.

The absence of violent conflict over the right to vote did not make what happened any less unusual. The bulk of election chicanery occurred less publicly and less dramatically than through riots or overt intimidation of civilians by the Republican-controlled military. The difference in the use of soldiers for the 1864 election came less in stationing them at precincts, as they had the year before throughout the border, than in mobilizing their vote through absentee balloting and furloughs.

The executive branch played politics with government positions, both civilian and military. Under the banner of purging the disloyal from sensitive positions, coercive measures included firing civilian employees and demoting officers who openly supported the Democrats. Informed that quartermaster clerks endorsed McClellan, Secretary of War Stanton let twenty of them go. A protest from one of these men drew little sympathy from the secretary, who answered: "When a young man receives his pay from an administration and spends his evenings denouncing it in offensive terms, he cannot be surprised if the administration prefers a friend on the job."[74] A military agent for the state of New Jersey reported to McClellan that pressure existed within the army to vote for Lincoln and Johnson. "A democrat or 'McClellan man' is denounced as a traitor; if a soldier he is pursued with abuse and continuously, is persecuted in every way a petty but bitter tyranny can devise, and is a *marked* man."[75] Charles S. Tripler who worked in the Medical Department in Ohio observed, "From one fact within my own knowledge, I feel sure Mr. Stanton is now engaged in removing officers, who are suspected of opposition." John H. Ferry, an officer in the Quartermaster Depot at Louisville, believed himself a victim of this pressure. Promoted to colonel in August, he attended the Democratic convention while on business in Chicago. "Spies were in the Convention to report all officers in attendance upon it, or in the city at the time," he alleged. "I fell under their notice, and received an order revoking my commission as Col., reducing me to a Captaincy, and ordering me to report to Memphis for duty. My offense being of purely a political character, and no charges having been made against my integrity or capacity, now pointed but to one course, that of resigning my position, which I have done." He added that five officers were relieved at his post on the same day for similar circumstances. A staff officer with Meade in the Army of the Potomac told his wife about the unfair political situation. A Colonel Collis sent letters to newspapers and dispatches to Stanton about the enthusiasm for Lincoln among the men; nothing happened to him because he held the correct opinion. Meanwhile, Lieutenant Colonel McMahon openly talked about his preference for McClellan. "What is the consequence?" Colonel Theodore Lyman asked, answering, "He is, without any warning, mustered out of the service!" He also believed that three officers had received brevets as brigadiers because they came from Pennsylvania and the promotions were intended to seal their political support and those of their friends and acquaintances.[76]

Also, public officials in the executive branch, including President Lincoln, shifted the pieces on the military chessboard to favor the Republican Party at the polls. During October, the president requested that General

Sherman furlough soldiers so they could vote in the state elections in Indiana. The military commission was in the midst of conducting the disloyalty trials that resulted in the *Milligan* decision just as the state featured campaigns that could put into power officials who opposed the national policies. Indiana was one of the so-called October states—Pennsylvania and Ohio also among them—whose elections of state officials became interpreted as how the presidential election might unfold the following month. Moreover, Indiana was the only important state voting in October whose soldiers did not have the legal ability to vote in the field. Indiana mattered too much to adopt a laissez-faire policy and Lincoln secured what he needed from his general. Additionally, the October 11 voting for Congress and state legislature in Pennsylvania caused Lincoln to realize that he needed to ensure more of the soldier vote from the Keystone State. Although Republicans had won handily in the October state elections, McClellan had Philadelphia connections, and it was unclear how many soldiers from the state supported their former commander. Lincoln also wanted victory to appear as if it came from the home voting because the army balloting was vulnerable to criticism as resulting from the bayonet rather than free will. Consequently, Meade and Sheridan received requests from the president to furlough roughly 5,000 Pennsylvania soldiers from each of their commands, adding 10,000 more people to the appearance of "citizen" voters. It provided him with a face-saving victory of 5,000 or so votes of the people at "home," although he carried the state by a margin of 20,000 with the vote from the field included.[77]

One such maneuver failed. In late October, or a little more than a week before the presidential election, Grant received a request to send troops home and responded at first hesitantly—not because he did not agree with the policy but because he needed the soldiers to break the siege at Petersburg. In a message sent in cipher to protect secrecy, Stanton had asked the general to send home three Delaware regiments because the vote of the state depended on them. "Troops are now very extended," Grant responded, "but if possible I will give the furloughs you ask for." It was not a huge commitment, perhaps a little more than a thousand men. And Grant sympathized with the political situation. Eventually, he ordered Meade to send the 1st, 3rd, and 4th Delaware regiments to Washington where they were furloughed home to vote.[78] In this case, however, the authorities had accurately gauged the threat to election. Delaware was one of three states that gave electoral votes to McClellan.

Lincoln obviously saw nothing untoward in these uses of executive power. The election game was played differently then. In an essay produced decades ago, David Herbert Donald argued for considering Lincoln as a politician, but he did not use the term as a pejorative. The president clearly used patronage, believed in party discipline, and leveraged whatever advantage he held if it remained within customary practices. For instance, he allowed the fund-raising technique employed by the Union National Executive Committee to squeeze a percentage of salaries from government workers to cover the expenses of publishing tracts and printing tickets. Employees in the War, Treasury, and Post Office departments, no matter their political affiliation, found their pay lightened by anywhere from 2 to 10 percent.[79]

Not everyone supported the practice. Navy secretary Gideon Welles stubbornly resisted pressure from Henry J. Raymond, chair of the Republican Executive Committee and editor of the *New York Times*, to remove men from the Brooklyn Navy Yard who interfered with the assessment of the workers. In a strange meeting conducted in the White House in front of a silent Lincoln, Raymond instructed Welles to remove the commandant of the yard and allow for the collection of the funds, which were needed to support the campaign in Indiana. Raymond indicated that prior administrations had done similar things, but the secretary refused. Welles considered it "inexcusable and indefensible; that I could make no record enforcing such assessment; that the matter could not stand investigation." He next faced a visit from Seward's son, Frederick, assistant secretary of state. The party had tried to station a man next to the paymaster's table to collect the fees, but the commodore forbade the practice, which Welles refused to overturn. It appears that more powerful men simply went around him. Senator Edwin D. Morgan, who chaired the Republican National Committee, put the fund-raising in place without objection from Lincoln. An unknown number of McClellan men were dismissed from the yard.[80]

It was not open season for political pressure, however. There were limits to such intrigues, despite the routine invoking of the epithet of traitor. Lincoln did not force Welles to change his position and apparently never spoke to him directly about the matter. And when it came to the election itself, the president condoned no forms of intimidation. On their way to take absentee ballots to the soldiers in Grant's army, election commissioners from the important state of Pennsylvania enjoyed an audience with Lincoln. One of the men wrote home that the president instructed: "I want to get all the votes I can of course, but play fair, gentlemen, play fair. Leave the soldiers entirely free to vote as they think best. All I ask is fair play."[81] Grant followed suit. The general hated the idea of civilian commissioners entering army camps to deliver party tickets. He considered this procedure disruptive and better administered through the provost marshals of each army. But if practicality demanded their presence, he intended to limit their influence. He prohibited political meetings or canvassing of regiments for votes. "Their business should be, and only be, to distribute, on a certain fixed day, tickets to whoever may call for them."[82]

Fraud happened, with two agents from New York arrested for forging the names of fictional soldiers to help the Democratic Party. News of their arrests, their trial by military commission, and their conviction spread across the Union during the canvass.[83] And the intentions of higher authorities—at least their professed desires—did not always match the behavior of people on the ground. A soldier in the 20th Michigan, George M. Buck, claimed that Democrats faced obstacles in exercising their ballots. Noncommissioned officers and privates, according to him, were bribed with promotions if they voted for Lincoln. Otherwise, they faced "reduction to the ranks or 'a place in the front during every engagement' if they chose to vote for you [McClellan]." Buck alleged that hundreds voted for Lincoln under protest, and he claimed that more ardent supporters of the general did not vote at all. As proof, he cited that his regiment produced 188 total votes polled in a unit that contained 300 potential voters.[84]

Similarly, military commanders who favored Lincoln sometimes kept information from soldiers and from election commissioners. It was a common accusation by Democrats that the War Department interrupted the distribution of party materials, especially Democratic newspapers, which very likely occurred under the auspices of individual military commanders.[85] Election commissioners encountered either cooperation from officers or some stonewalling. To locate soldiers from their states required commissioners to gain the information from generals like Ben Butler. Otherwise, they had no clue about where to find the men they needed to contact for their votes. That intelligence was furnished promptly or slowly, depending on the general's interests and the commissioners' political persuasion. But lower-ranked officers sometimes dragged their feet when understanding that a commissioner represented the opposing party. David McKelvy, an election commissioner from Pennsylvania, gathered returns of the 58th Pennsylvania Infantry, whose officers "were mostly democratic, and the other officers were perfectly indifferent as to the election, and it was with some difficulty that they were urged into opening the polls yesterday and with more difficulty that they were to-day urged into the task of finishing out the forms and necessary papers appertaining to it." But after briefly resisting, they fulfilled their duty.[86]

Despite exposing the dark underbelly of the political culture, the voting within the army came off more orderly than the usual balloting on the home front. Scholar Richard F. Bensel has observed, "Military discipline usually made elections held in the field more orderly than those in civilian communities." Polls opened. They kept regular hours, with notices of the times posted in advance. Commissioners tallied votes. Officers signed off on the poll books as witnesses. This is quite extraordinary, especially given that some of the men had to march to polling places directly from coming under fire just to exercise their civic duty. And if their states required it, they had to remember to carry with them proof of paying their poll taxes. But if peer pressure, as Bensel has argued, factored into the social cohesion of regiments, it also may have affected casting ballots. There is not enough published evidence to judge. But it does make sense to question whether soldiers cast a vote contrary to the wishes of the bulk of the regiment, knowing that they needed those men in battle. But it makes equal sense to think that, unlike Bensel's model, men who had been under fire together created other bonds that superseded politics. The social context of camps added additional pressure to vote Republican. Or it made little difference, especially if a Democrat had saved a Republican's life, or vice versa. One thing is certain in the grand scheme of things: accounting for this pressure only marginally alters the picture of the army's majority support for Lincoln.[87]

When the home vote for president was cast on November 8, Democrats found they did not need to fight in order to have a free ballot. Remarkably—given the Indiana disloyalty trial, raids across the Canadian border on Vermont banks, news of other black flag operations in the works, and jostling in communities at election rallies—neither riots nor anything more than minor disruptions broke out at election precincts. Possibly the Democratic lament made an impact. Perhaps federal officials listened to the fierce proclamation of Governor Bramlette of Kentucky, who a few weeks before the election ordered sheriffs to arrest soldiers who screened balloting and vowed he would call off the election in the face of such interference.[88] Perhaps news of arrests in Kentucky and Indiana, and the habit of soldiers stepping into the picture, counseled for caution. Perhaps the administration realized it did not require a military presence at the polls in order to win; rather, the soldiers' vote protected the Union. Or perhaps the public at large, including soldiers, interpreted the fall of Atlanta on September 1 and the victories by Sheridan over Confederates in the Shenandoah Valley in October as signifying that the Lincoln government had the momentum on its side, foreshadowing a successful conclusion to the war that undercut hopes for a Democratic triumph.

Whatever the case, the behavior of the army at election precincts was noticeably different from that in 1863. The orders of Major General Lew Wallace, who had replaced Schenck in charge of the Middle Department that spanned Maryland and Delaware, testified to the altered posture of the military in the election of 1864, especially in the eastern border states. On October 4, Wallace ordered the military to avoid interfering in elections. He dealt with Baltimore first, saying that soldiers could not approach precincts in the city unless two things happened: civilian police were overwhelmed, and the mayor asked for help. Outside of the city, judges of elections had to ask for assistance *in writing* for soldiers to come. Under Wallace's instructions, the troops obeyed civilian authorities, reporting to the judges of elections and following their lead in screening for disloyalty. And if they were not asked to intervene, they could not station themselves within one mile of the precincts. This was a remarkable turnabout. Minus the penalties for infractions, these protocols matched the intentions of the bill that Powell had promoted in the Senate.[89]

Despite less interference by the military in 1864, not every balloting proceeded purely. The test oath remained in place in Missouri, reinforcing the sense of the Republicans managing the election. In Unionist Tennessee, Andrew Johnson, as military governor, invoked an oath for voting that considered opposition to Republicans as treason. The oath taker specifically had to repudiate the Democrat platform. Kentucky had its problems with the arrests of a lieutenant governor and a recruiter for white troops. And in Ohio, Samuel S. Cox, the anti-Vallandigham representative, lost his reelection bid. He told McClellan that the administration "put their machinery to work. They closed the polls at Camp Chase at noon, because it was going for me; & at Tod Barracks they drove me out & my friends, for distributing my tickets to my friends & yours there, who were literally hungry for our tickets." He accused an army officer of blocking his distribution of the tickets.[90]

Tensions over the election existed, and these tensions affected the deployment of troops. New York concerned federal authorities and caused them to transfer infantry to handle potential riots or terrorism. Sixteen months had passed since the city faced one of the worst riots in U.S. history, and the reports of Confederate agents in the Northeast hatching terrorist plots riveted attention by the government. Rumors of trouble on the Great Lakes diverted a small militia force to Buffalo, New York, to investigate, and others warned of Confederate insurgents along the Detroit River. Nothing came of those accounts. Other unconfirmed reports raised the specter of Confederates infiltrating the polling places to cast fraudulent votes and of possible discord in Jersey City. Once again the War Department tapped Grant for troops. To keep the peace, Ben Butler was dispatched to the city to oversee the election with roughly 5,000 soldiers from his Army of the James. This was in addition to 1,250 soldiers that Grant had sent. They maintained a careful watch, some of them placed on board tugboats for quick transport to sensitive spots. Butler also stationed soldiers at telegraph offices to monitor communications. A dense fog greeted Election Day morning, but the weather did not hamper participation. "In spite of the apprehensions of many persons that the election in this city would be attended with tumult and violence," a columnist noted, "it proved to be one of the most quiet and orderly elections ever held in New-York. The pretended fears of the Copperheads that there would be military interference with the freedom of the ballot turned out to be entirely groundless, and consequently their threats of a 'free election or a free fight' found no occasion for their execution."[91]

These kinds of requests from the people at home frustrated military commanders. How could they stretch a finite number of men to cover not only the major armies against them but also the political and police problems away from the battlefield? Grant crept to the edge of testiness but never exploded over the requests to send infantry to serve political ends. And he almost always tried to help. Henry Wager Halleck revealed how difficult was the dual role of securing an election while trying to win a war. When told he should send soldiers home to monitor elections, Halleck told his friend Francis Lieber that the past year featured an almost incessant application for troops: at New York and Philadelphia against rebel privateers; on the frontiers of Vermont, New York, and Michigan against raids from Canada; in New Mexico, Indian Territory, Kansas, Colorado, Nebraska, Dakota, Idaho, and Minnesota against Indians; in Missouri against bushwhackers; in Illinois, Ohio, and especially Indiana against disloyal agents; in Kentucky, Tennessee, West Virginia, Pennsylvania, and Maryland against rebel raiders; and everywhere to enforce the draft and to keep peace at elections. He observed that "if one half of these applications & appeals were granted, we would not have a single soldier to meet the rebels in the field!"[92]

The margin of Lincoln's victory was so wide that manipulation by the military played only a marginal role in the outcome. Lincoln won handily with 55 percent of the popular vote and an overwhelming number of electoral votes, 221 to 21. One message from the election that screams out concerns the states that did go for McClellan. Two of the three were the border states of Delaware and Kentucky—places that had grown increasingly disenchanted with the government's policies and had felt the heavy hand of the military on elections. Kentucky featured a whopping victory for Mc-Clellan, who captured nearly 70 percent of the vote.

In 1865 the Republicans followed their victory with two pieces of legislation that rubbed salt into the wounds of their opponents. During February, legislators finally adopted the gist of Powell's bill to restrict the military from elections, adopting the distance of a mile as the closest to precincts that they were to be posted. Of course, this came after the law could make a real impact. The second bill, adopted on March 3, 1865, denied citizenship to soldiers who had deserted. Men had a grace period of sixty days from a presidential proclamation to return to the ranks forgiven or, after the time period, face the loss of their rights as citizens. The law intended to disfranchise Democrats. It was not true that all Democrats were deserters, but many deserters were thought to be Democrats. Eliminating deserters from the voting roster was viewed as helping the Republicans. Yet the bill looked innocent enough. It punished dishonest men who had betrayed their oath to serve their nation.[93] Lincoln subsequently issued the desertion proclamation. It was an application of punishment that had support within communities. Andrew Evans, a local politician and a War Democrat from Ohio, told his son during the presidential canvass of 1864 that he had in mind punishment for local fellows who had absconded after entering the army. "They are unworthy to live among a patriotic people," he told his son who was in the infantry, adding, "I pledge you my honor, that if I live to get into the next session of the Legislature, I will report a bill, and use my utmost endeavor to have it passed into law, to for ever disfranchise them in the State of Ohio."[94] Undoubtedly, Lincoln intended the bill to encourage men to rejoin the army, increasing the odds of ending the war, rather than putting a practice in place that affected elections in peacetime.

But he could not foresee the end of the war, its aftermath, or especially his own death at the hands of an assassin. The fighting ended in 1865 after Lincoln had died, but it did not end the laws that the war had spawned. The deserter legislation empowered election commissioners to disfranchise on the spot at polling precincts anyone they considered to be a wartime deserter. The federal government provided rosters to local officials upon request. But there were no guarantees of the information's accuracy. And there was no due process of law or further examination. Opponents of the law criticized it as unconstitutional because the fundamental law of the land forbade passing *ex post facto* laws, or legislation that criminalized prior actions that were not illegal at the time. Additionally, Missouri's test oath was still in place, denying the ability of lawyers, ministers, teachers, and others to practice their professions or vote unless they swore a stringent oath of loyalty to the Union. With the war's end, Republicans had not relinquished their power to determine loyalty and treason. The same laws and attitudes carried the nation into peacetime in a questionably constitutional way.

8

THE POLITICS OF MERCY
AFTER APPOMATTOX

As the soldiers of the United States paraded through the streets of Washington during the Grand Review in late May 1865, thousands of northerners lining the dusty streets of the capital cheered their champions and, in the words of one spectator, found it "strange to be so intensely happy and triumphant, and yet to feel like crying."[1] Victory brought mixed emotions. It had been a tragic four years. Northerners were exuberant that the fighting had stopped, but they also realized that the rebel traitors who had caused so much loss of life might return to the Union with few consequences. Were the men who had waged the insurrection traitors subject to trial and execution? That question had been deferred until after victory was achieved, with international precedents allowing for the Union to treat the Confederates as public enemies while the fighting raged, and then try them as traitors afterward. The time had arrived to tackle the issue. Should the rebels be punished? Should at least some of them hang or be expelled from the country? More than a few people on the winning side advocated that trying the worst of the leaders would send a message about how a strong republic dealt with insurrection: with mercy for the many, but with malice toward some.

However, despite cries for vengeance from various corners of the Union, the United States government hanged none of the traitors. Henry Wirz, the commandant of Andersonville Prison, suffered execution—but for war crimes, not treason. Similarly, the national state hanged the Lincoln assassins and conspirators. But by the time a general pardon was issued by President Johnson in 1868, John Brown remained the only person in U.S. history executed for treason since the adoption of the Constitution.

Why did the North refuse to hang any of the traitors? During the conflict, treason had been central to northern conceptualizations of the insurrection. Plus, the war had featured atrocities that inflamed northern passions. Guerrillas had operated in portions of the loyal states such as Missouri and Kansas; terrorists had tried to burn down hotels in New York City; Confederate jailors, so the common impressions went, had mistreated prisoners of war at hellish places such as Andersonville; and an assassin sympathetic to the Confederacy had put a bullet into the head of the president. Hatred of the enemy and outrages have a firmer place in the present-day narrative of the war, which now estimates the butcher's bill at well over 700,000 dead.[2]

People in the United States did advocate punishing some of the rebels; historians have charted a surge in treason indictments in 1865 and 1866 as Confederates came under northern control and finally could be prosecuted. East Tennessee was particularly active, with more than 2,000 cases on the docket for treason and giving aid to the enemy. The state produced one conviction in a county circuit court that was quickly overturned. Missouri had another 4 cases for treason and 142 for conspiracy. In Maryland, military authorities wanted to prosecute everyone who left the state to join the rebel army. More than 4,000 names were submitted to a grand jury, but it quickly became apparent that the public supported trying only the more prominent of the Confederates.[3] In the movement for prosecuting the rebels, however, passion failed to overcome leniency as the order of the day.

The reasons offered by historians for this clemency favor several lines of thought: American exceptionalism based on democratic ideals, emotional bonds of a people who were more alike than different, and racism that inclined white people to clasp hands across the bloody chasm. There is very little published on the topic of treason and leniency, but what exists contains the implicit position that the United States enjoyed the mildest end of any nation to a fratricidal conflict, and did so because of its beliefs in the Constitution and popular rule. The strands of mercy lead back to Lincoln and his proclamation of amnesty and the resounding message of his Second Inaugural to display malice toward none and charity for all. Another tendency in the literature of Reconstruction has been to characterize those who pushed for harsh punishment as Radical extremists blinded by hatred of slave owners or filled with political ambitions that made them duplicitous in their support for black people and out of touch with broader northern society. Perhaps the most accurate depiction of the literature on this subject, however, is that the failure to prosecute treason has not been considered as a problem to be explained, but simply either noted or celebrated.[4]

However, practical, political-legal issues influenced clemency toward traitors. Democrats in the North needed Democrats in the South to defeat their rivals and regain national power. Republicans in the North struggled to reconfigure their party's principles and mission, with some of the most famous antislavery leaders advocating leniency as a way to gain enfranchisement of black people. In fact, a case was made by leading abolitionists that executing rebels potentially jeopardized suffrage for the freedpeople by hardening white resistance. For their part, black people considered other issues more paramount, such as solidifying their claims on citizenship and gaining the suffrage. Plus, even with the fighting ended, the civil courts offered uncertain prospects for gaining the decisions that supported executions and upheld national sovereignty. Finding a jury of peers in the former Confederacy where the crimes were committed presented quite a challenge, to say the least.[5] When all was said and done, experts advising the Johnson administration concluded that it was too dangerous to try someone like Jeff Davis, because it was not preordained that the government would win. Even if it did, the trial might backfire by creating a martyr. It remains to be seen how treason in the postwar world did not, despite Andrew Johnson's professions to the contrary, become odious.

The Problem of the Confederate Veteran

If any group had a right to feel safe from prosecution for treason, it was the Confederate veteran who participated in the surrenders of the armies at Virginia, North Carolina, and the trans-Mississippi. Most historians have removed these men from the table of postwar retribution because of the paroles that characterized these ceremonies. Considering the bloodbath that had just concluded, the terms were indeed lenient: if the men put down their arms, went home, and obeyed the laws of the United States, the federal government was to leave them alone. The officers and enlisted men interpreted this as a blanket amnesty. So did many of the officers and civilians loyal to the United States. However, they were about to learn otherwise: that the paroles could have been ignored and the leaders prosecuted for treason—if the political will had existed to do so.

The chipping away at the protection of Confederate veterans began with a ruling on how to prevent them from returning to their homes in the loyal states, particularly the Maryland-Washington corridor. Shortly after the Lincoln assassination, Secretary of War Edwin Stanton asked Attorney General James Speed for clarification on several points. Former Confederates who had once lived in Washington tried to come home. The secretary did not want them back. Nor did he appreciate it that rebel veterans wore their uniforms in the public thoroughfares of loyal states. At this point—April 22, 1865—the war was not over. Two Confederate armies remained in the field. Having remnants of the rebel army walking the streets of the nation's capital in military garb struck northerners as downright offensive and, as one newspaper columnist wrote, represented "an act of hostility to the national government."[6] The attorney general was asked if the government could intercede.

Speed's opinion did not deal with the paroles, per se, but portions of it hinted that they had a limited function. Grant, he maintained, had acted in the capacity of a military officer. He could grant paroles but the terms encompassed only military actions and did not secure an amnesty from civil prosecution. Military actions lasted only during the war, not in peace, much as a prisoner exchange system became void once hostilities ceased. More to the point, Speed indicated that only the president could issue a pardon. He maintained, with a good deal of constitutional support: "His power to pardon, as a civil magistrate, cannot be delegated; it is a personal trust, inseparably connected with the office of President."[7] Grant acted in accordance with the wishes of Lincoln, but there was no official declaration by a president. The paper trail of clemency ended with an order of a general officer employing a procedure for forgiving prisoners in wartime. The attorney general followed this ruling with another clarification on January 6, 1866, concerning Jefferson Davis, in which he again asserted that the paroles did not protect ex-Confederates from prosecution.[8]

Speed was not alone in constructing this position. Northern columnists pointed out that Francis Lieber, the Columbia College professor who had composed the code of war, advocated this position. E. L. Godkin's *The Nation* endorsed Lieber's proposition that "any cartel or military agreement remains military in its character, and the general to whom an army surrenders cannot go, or be considered to go . . . beyond his own military power." It added "that so soon as rebellion is at an end, the power of parole ceases with it, and the paroled person becomes again simply a citizen or subject, with undiminished responsibility to the law of the land." The columnist gently tweaked Grant, calling the paroles "unfortunately and unskillfully worded."[9] Much later in the year, in December 1865, the Union arrested Admiral Raphael Semmes, the Confederate commerce raider notorious for sinking Union merchant ships. Secretary of the Navy Gideon Welles itched to have him prosecuted despite Semmes's claiming he fell under the immunity of the paroles. Welles consulted with Lieber, who, he said, "thinks Lee and the whole of his army liable for treason, notwithstanding

Grant's terms." The only question in Welles's mind was whether to hold the trial in military or civil court.[10]

Speed's ruling at first caused only minimum inconvenience for Confederate veterans. Stanton acted quickly to restrict their movement. From April to June, they were banned from traveling into loyal states, even if they were trying to return to their own homes. People in Carroll County, Maryland, enthusiastically supported this policy. A meeting of Unionist citizens there resulted in a resolution proclaiming "we will not tolerate their presence among us at any future date, and if they should return they shall be notified to leave."[11] However, the policy was short-lived. All restrictions were lifted by President Johnson in early June. Although travel eased, the Union army that occupied the former Confederacy enacted prohibitions against the wearing of military garb by its enemies. When some claimed that poverty forced them to wear their gray, Union authorities allowed the uniforms but forced the removal of military insignias and buttons. Signs of rank and government were unceremoniously stripped from the wearer by Union soldiers.[12]

One such case led to a military trial of a well-known Confederate staff officer on a variety of charges, including treason, for wearing his uniform in public. Henry Kyd Douglas had served as a staff officer with Stonewall Jackson during Antietam. He had grown up in the area near that Maryland battlefield and returned to Shepherdstown, West Virginia, after the surrender at Appomattox. On May 5, 1865, he and a lady friend strolled to the photography studio of Thomas L. Darnell to have their portraits taken. Douglas wore his military pants and a civilian coat, carrying the rest of his uniform over an arm. After the photo session, he saw that the room and antechamber of the studio had filled with ladies awaiting their sittings, which he claimed made it impractical to change before returning to his quarters. The military officer in command of the region, Brigadier General John D. Stevenson, had Douglas brought up on three charges before a military commission: violation of his parole, violation of military orders, and treason. The military orders in question were General Orders No. 28, issued by Stevenson on April 26, which prohibited wearing Confederate uniforms, which he considered a violation of Grant's terms of parole. Douglas pleaded his case to no avail. The military commission that convened on May 10 found him guilty of violating the general's orders, although it absolved him of the charge of treason. He was sentenced to two months' imprisonment at Fort Delaware. General Stevenson approved the ruling, claiming that the "wearing or display of any badge of treason within the United States, proceeds from a spirit of hostility to the established Government. The purposes of the Government, and the whole purposes of the war, are to utterly eradicate such feelings in the country."[13]

Another example revealed that the paroles offered at Appomattox and elsewhere could be set aside if the people in charge had determined that it made sense politically to punish the rebels. In the spring of 1866, the federal Circuit Court, Western District of Tennessee, rendered a decision in a proceeding that mirrored the popular rationale offered by such thinkers as Francis Lieber. On April 6, Brigadier General E. W. Rucker came under indictment for treason. Rucker, who had served under Nathan Bedford Forrest in the western theater of war, protested the arrest by raising the paroles granted to soldiers serving under General Joseph Johnston during the surrender to Sherman in North Carolina. In *United States v. Rucker* the judge ruled that the president of the United States could not delegate his pardon power. The agreement fashioned at Durham Station constituted a military parole that terminated with the end of the war. And he believed that the men understood this. As proof, the judge cited the overwhelming number of paroled soldiers who also sought a pardon from the president rather than leave their fates in the hands of the paroles. According to the judge, "These applicants must have understood that the conditions of their surrender had no other or greater effect than we have herein given to them. For, if they had thought differently, they could scarcely have deemed it essential, and have been so eager to obtain the additional pardon of the President." A federal judge had given the executive branch a court-sanctioned rationale to support a quest for vengeance.[14]

In June 1865, action by the federal court sent a wake-up call to the military leaders who thought they had been paroled. The U.S. District Court of Virginia that sat in Norfolk handed down indictments against former officials and military officers for treason. Judge John C. Underwood, a Virginian who had remained loyal to the Union, issued a stirring charge to the grand jury that demanded the trials of "the authors and conductors of the most gigantic, bloody and unprovoked crimes that ever cursed our world." He reproduced two arguments common in public discourse. First, he absolved the hundreds of thousands of Confederate soldiers who technically had committed treason but whose "universal prosecution would be unreasonable and impossible." The masses of people driven into rebel service "are not morally responsible for the Rebellion." This, by the way, contradicted case law that stated otherwise—that treason allowed for no accessories; that all involved remained principals. If Davis were guilty, according to legal precepts, so was the common foot soldier. However, that fact remained noticeably absent from the judge's charge. Second,

Underwood swept aside the paroles granted to Confederate soldiers. The judge claimed this protection "was a mere military arrangement, and can have no influence upon civil rights or the status of the persons interested." Here he replicated the arguments of Speed and Lieber, whether consciously or not.[15]

The results came swiftly. By the middle of the month, the grand jury handed down indictments charging thirty-seven ex-Confederates with treason. The list included generals Lee, James Longstreet, and Jubal Early, as well as two of Lee's sons and a nephew. Also on the list were former Confederate governors and other political figures.[16]

Lee was stunned. He wrote personally to General-in-Chief Ulysses S. Grant. For a proud man like Lee, it had to be a hard task to beg for the help of the man to whom he had surrendered. Lee had been thinking of petitioning for a presidential pardon. The treason indictment forced his hand as it appeared that Grant's parole might not be enough to protect him. On June 13, he sent the request for a pardon from the president via Grant with a cover letter indicating his belief that the paroles granted in the surrender terms had protected him. Even if his interpretation was correct, he wished to gain exoneration from the commander in chief. On June 20, Grant wrote Lee back that the government would honor the paroles.[17] The fact that Lee sought a pardon remained unknown to historians until 1970, even though it was widely reported in newspapers at the time. It turned out that Lee had to file another piece of paper—the oath of allegiance—in order to receive a pardon. He apparently fulfilled this step in September, but the paperwork was lost in the bowels of the National Archives, where it remained until discovery 105 years later. Lee received his pardon, courtesy of President Gerald Ford in 1975.[18]

Lee owed Grant a very large debt, which rarely has been acknowledged then or now. The decision to uphold the paroles had not come easily; the Union general had to lobby the president personally. Johnson had enamored himself with northerners by declaring that treason would be made odious, a position that cheered certain Radicals and War Democrats. His actual position on the treason trials is difficult to tease out of the documents because he announced no clear policy. And although the public then, and historians later, have criticized Johnson justifiably for what became a ludicrous show of leniency through the pardon power, in the summer of 1865 he appeared to be serious about prosecuting some of the rebel leaders and was certainly farther out in front on this issue than his top general. At the very least, he seemed to want the possibility to remain alive, perhaps to make the men who had come under the state's power sweat a little while longer. Additionally, Benjamin Butler had gotten the president's ear and reinforced that the paroles were a military convention, convincing Johnson that top generals remained open to prosecution for treason. The Judge Advocate General of the Army was on board, as was the attorney general. Public opinion and expert opinion coincided, giving the government the justification to set aside the paroles and prosecute the leading rebel traitors.[19]

Grant did not agree. He expressly wrote the War Department on Lee's behalf, claiming, "In my opinion the officers and men paroled at Appomattox C. H. and since upon the same terms as given to Lee, can not be tried for treason so long as they observe the terms of their parole." He added: "Bad faith on the part of the Governm't or a construction of that convention subjecting officers to trial for treason, would produce a feeling of insecurity in the minds of all the paroled men. If so disposed they might even regard such an infraction of terms, by the Government as an entire release from all obligation on their part." Johnson did not cave immediately. He was a stubborn man, too, and tried to convince Grant that Lee and others deserved prosecution and loss of their property. But Grant believed that Lee's example set the tone for reconciliation and enhanced the possibility that ex-Confederates would not resist any further. His own honor, as well as that of the nation, was at stake. When Johnson remained unconvinced, Grant played what historian Brooks Simpson calls the general's most powerful card: he threatened to resign his commission. This early into his administration, Johnson could ill afford to lose the support of the nation's military hero. On June 20, the word went out to the district attorney at Norfolk to hold off on arrests. On the same day, Grant dashed off his letter of good news to Lee.[20] It is not clear that the Union general received a thank-you.

It would be tempting to stop here and say that Grant foiled the prosecution of rebels beyond Lee and allowed for an easier reunion; however, there are pieces that do not fit this interpretation. Nor does it capture the whole story to, like one historian, give all the credit for leniency to Lincoln and Grant for their magnanimous spirits.[21] Grant certainly delayed a movement against the rebels under parole until it became politically unviable as other Reconstruction issues took precedent. But Grant cared only about *his military* figures; Confederate politicians and anyone else beyond his paroles remained fair game for losing their lives. When it came to civilian leaders and guerrilla fighters, he leaned toward sternness during the war. Partisan rangers such as John S. Mosby who had conducted guerrilla-style warfare in northern Virginia did not qualify for mercy. For

Mosby, Grant offered a bounty of $5,000 for anyone who hunted the man down and brought him before authorities. He also took a hard line against political leaders. As the war wound down after Appomattox, he pushed Major General Henry Wager Halleck to order the military arrest of Confederate politicians in Virginia, including former senator R. M. T. Hunter, former governor John Letcher, "and all the other particularly obnoxious political leaders in the State." Soldiers arrested Hunter and placed him in prison in Richmond, where he remained without charges for a little more than two months. Similarly, Letcher was arrested and imprisoned in Washington from May 20 into July. Orders also went out on May 8 for the arrest of Zebulon Vance, wartime governor of North Carolina, who spent forty-seven days in prison without charges or trial.[22]

Later in 1865, more arrests came without apparent murmuring from Grant. The president in September ordered the federal marshal in west Tennessee to call Nathan Bedford Forrest to the courthouse in Memphis to face a presentment against him for treason. He had raided supply lines, and soldiers under him had executed black soldiers who had tried to surrender at Fort Pillow. Raphael Semmes, commander of the Confederate States vessel *Alabama*, was arrested in December. Semmes could be considered a guerrilla of the high seas as he used a British-built ship to prey on United States merchant ships. As captain of the *Alabama*, he sunk more than sixty U.S. ships, angering federal officials who also filed claims after the war against Great Britain for its complicity. Welles, who ordered the arrest, found Semmes's behavior deeply obnoxious. "He did not belong in the Rebel region and has not therefore the poor apology of those who shelter themselves under the action of their States." He considered it reprehensible that a man trained by the U.S. government made it his business to destroy the ships of unarmed countrymen engaged in peaceful commerce. Semmes had tried to include himself under the paroles of Joseph Johnston's men in North Carolina, where the sea captain had fled after the fall of Richmond.[23]

Another situation shows how Grant could exercise, as historian Simpson has noted, a "double standard" when it came to protecting or punishing the rebels. In September 1865 the grand jury of the U.S. District Court in Baltimore returned indictments against four men including Bradley T. Johnson, a Maryland cavalry officer elevated to brigadier general of infantry in the Army of Northern Virginia. He was indicted for levying war against the United States for actions in Washington County, Maryland, on June 18, 1863 (during the Gettysburg campaign) and for burning and destroying property during Jubal Early's Raid on Washington in July 1864.

It took a while for Grant to intercede, but on March 30, 1866, he asked President Johnson to release the ex-Confederate from the bonds under which he was held, claiming that Bradley Johnson fell under the "convention" between Sherman and Johnston at Durham Station. Once again the president honored the request, ordering the attorney general to discharge the former enemy.[24]

Clearly, Grant was not squeamish about military arrests and the possible prosecution of certain kinds of rebels. And his reasons for punishing a few contained the same goal as that of asking for lenience for the enemy soldiers in the conventional forces. He wanted the war to end without provoking guerrilla action, renewing conventional fighting, or causing alliances to be made by defeated Confederates with the French in Mexico. The situation south of the border was an especially sore point with the United States; many officials were concerned that harsh treatment of former Confederates might chase them into the arms of the French and Mexican monarchists who conducted a civil war with the liberals under Benito Juárez.

The monarchists knew this and tried to woo former Confederates to their side. Possibly no more than 5,000 settlers went to Mexico (maybe fewer), and most did not last there for very long. Yet, at the time, the flow of these few thousands across the Rio Grande caused serious discussion. Northerners read in their newspapers that Confederate generals such as Jubal Early, Jo Shelby, Edmund Kirby Smith, Sterling Price, John Bankhead Magruder, and Cadmus Wilcox headed over the border. Former governors Henry Watkins Allen and Thomas O. Moore of Louisiana, Pendleton Murrah of Texas, and Isham Harris of Tennessee went along, too. Maximilian encouraged immigration by offering land grants and providing tax incentives to those who had no financial means. He also designated Matthew Fontaine Maury, famed oceanographer and naval agent for the Confederacy, as his imperial commissioner of immigration. Rumors were published in the *New York Times* that 10,000 Confederates were to be armed and paid by the empire to remain in the states of Sonora, Chihuahua, Durango, and Tamaulipas to serve as a buffer between the monarchy and the United States. Those numbers never were achieved, but the northern public at the time had no way of knowing otherwise.[25]

After the flurry of activity surrounding Lee and others indicted for treason in the summer of 1865, it became clear that the Confederacy's top public official, and not former soldiers, would determine the course of possible prosecutions of traitors in the post–Civil War United States. The case of Jefferson Davis became the focal point for the government deciding whether to prosecute even so much as a few of the insurrection-ists. The debate over his fate provided a window into the various elements factoring into leniency.

To Try or Not to Try Davis

With the capture of Jefferson Davis in May 1865, and his confinement in Fort Monroe under military authority, letters flowed to President Andrew Johnson from most corners of the North demanding that the rebel leaders pay the ultimate price for their actions. The letters contained understand-able cries for vengeance from people who had suffered personal loss of loved ones during the war. Levi Alger, a carpenter from Wisconsin who had lost a brother, offered to build the gallows for Jefferson Davis and even provided a sketch for the device. Thirty women from Northampton, Mas-sachusetts, sent a petition stating: "We the undersigned are very anxious that Jeff Davis—that traitor who has already lived too long—*should be hung* up by the neck. Do you not think our wishes just and right? *Let him be hung! Is the cry of the daughters of the Bay State.*"[26] Soldiers threw their lot in with civilians. A petition from six people in Lancaster County, Penn-sylvania, identified the signers as men who had served in the army for three years "and met the conscripts of Jefferson Davis, on many a bloody field." They wanted Davis to be hanged so high that it established a new American idiom: people would say that criminals should be "hung as high as *Jeff Davis* the great American Traitor."[27]

The writers of these letters held Davis culpable for the losses on the battlefield and the poor care that cost Union prisoners of war their lives in places like Andersonville, Georgia. They considered him representa-tive of the men who were trying to destroy the government. Many re-ferred to Davis as the "Arch Traitor" or "Arch Rebel," clearly considering him guilty of treason against the United States. They wanted him and other Rebel leaders tried for war crimes and for disloyalty to the nation. Time and time again they reminded Johnson of his famous comment about making treason odious, begging him to live up to his statement so that punishment of the traitors would not only provide justice for their transgressions but also serve as a warning to those who might consider the same course of action against the United States.[28] The intentions expressed in this correspondence were not always bloodthirsty, despite being written in the heat of a crisis rife with rumor that Confederate leaders were complicit in the assassination of the president. The letters, in fact, often coolly made distinctions between those southerners who should be tried and those who should be left alone, revealing a commonly held class bias. For instance, although outraged at Lincoln's murder, the attorney general for Michigan did not propose blanket prosecutions. "The honest masses, including the deceived and misled, South as well as North, may, no doubt, be safely trusted; but perjured souls, steeped in treason, acting a *leading* part, never. . . . Hang the very worst of them, expatriate many more, and disfranchise a still larger class than the second, thereby teaching that Treason is a crime that must and will receive . . . punishment."[29]

A sermon delivered in Brooklyn, New York, reinforced the tendency to consider higher officials more to blame than the masses. The Reverend Samuel T. Spear of the South Presbyterian Church asked his congregation in late April 1865: "What shall we do with the rebels?" The South, he maintained, consisted of slaves, middle-class white people, and aristocrats. The slaves should not be punished. The middling whites had been drawn into the rebellion by treacherous leaders and then paid for their fealty with their lives. It was the high officers of the army and state who should bear the price. To Spear, the government should indict a select number, try them for treason, confiscate their property, and hang a few. In this group he included Davis and Lee. Again betraying a class-defined sensibility, the minister said the general represented "one of your highborn and high-bred Southern traitors." He had been trained by the government at West Point and then deserted the flag in time of peril. "General Lee is conquered, but not converted."[30]

Within a few months after Appomattox, then, arguments to execute at least some of the leaders of the rebellion had coalesced into a fairly consistent refrain. They differentiated between the guiltiest and the masses who were allegedly misled into seceding from the Union. The reasoning continued an emphasis from the antebellum period to view the South as dominated by a Slave Power that exercised its power undemocratically. The southern oligarchy, in this view, deserved the hardest treatment for fostering the bloodshed, although disfranchisement came up about as much as executions as a means of punishment for these ex-Confederates. Commentators forgave the mass of southerners owing to the ideal of state sovereignty, which remained a strong undercurrent in discussions of what to do about the rebels. A majority of the Confederate states had seceded through actions of state conventions without submitting the result to a popular referendum. Once a state seceded, so the reasoning went, its citizens had little choice but to follow and obey its laws else they might face charges of treason against their state.

In late July 1865, President Johnson brought before the cabinet the question of how to bring to trial the former president of the Confederacy. Davis sat in Fort Monroe, Virginia, in legal limbo as a prisoner of war held by the military. He was not yet charged in court. Johnson's advisers had different positions on the situation. Seward believed that no conviction in the civil courts was possible and favored a military tribunal. Treasury Secretary Hugh McCulloch preferred a civil trial but argued for postponing the case. James Harlan, secretary of the interior, did not want Davis tried for treason unless winning a conviction was certain; if there was doubt, then a military tribunal should handle the proceedings. He added that it was better to pardon Davis rather than to lose a trial. Welles argued that it was best to move forward with a civil trial, stating, "If our laws or system were defective, it was well to bring them to a test." After failing to hear a consensus, Johnson put the question on the table: Shall Jefferson Davis be tried for treason? Yes. Unanimously. Now came the next question. Which court should hear the case? Five of the seven advisers favored civil court. Seward and Harlan voted for the military.[31] In sum, they all supported treason trials but disagreed over which method to use and the timing.

One other revelation emerges from this cabinet discussion: the Civil War, technically speaking, was not over. Finding the precise date when the government recognized a state of war—July 13, 1861—is easier than uncovering the end point. Perhaps the best date is April 2, 1866, when Johnson issued a proclamation that the insurrection had ended. Nonetheless, in the cabinet discussion of July 21, 1865, Attorney General Speed doubted that a civil trial for treason could proceed, in the words of Welles, "until the Rebellion was entirely suppressed." To Speed, the former president enjoyed the condition of a prisoner of war entitled to rights of a belligerent. In an earlier opinion concerning arresting paroled officers in Louisiana, Speed had counseled delaying the arrest of Confederate officers who had been paroled "until the President has officially proclaimed the suppression of the rebellion, and announced that the war is at an end."[32]

These were cogent issues. A military commission offered the best hope for winning a conviction against the former president. Unlike a civil trial, only a simple majority was required to convict, rather than a unanimous verdict. Different rules of evidence applied. The government could select the military officers who presided, virtually ensuring sympathy with the national position. And they could hold the trial virtually anywhere, rather than needing to adhere to the constitutional dictates for holding civil trials in the area in which crimes were committed.[33] However, if the case became a matter for civil courts, then that begged the question: where to hold such a trial? Davis had been charged in various locations. An opinion by Attorney General James Speed in January 1866 narrowed the choices—and not necessarily in favor of the government. The opinion came in response to a Senate resolution on December 21, 1865, that demanded to know why a Davis trial had not been initiated. Speed responded that issue of jurisdiction played a factor. "I have ever thought that trials for high treason cannot be had before a military tribunal," he wrote. "The civil courts have alone jurisdiction of that crime. The question then arises, Where and when must the trials thereof be held?" He did not specify which court should hear the case, but his reasoning indicated that it should take place in Virginia. At the time of the opinion, the federal courts in the former Confederate states remained a work in progress with none of the justices of the U.S. Supreme Court holding circuit courts since hostilities ceased. It became an accepted fact that any civil trial that occurred would come before the U.S. Circuit Court in Virginia over which presided Underwood and the chief justice of the United States, Salmon P. Chase.[34]

The cabinet's preference for civil courts to decide these issues mirrored that of public opinion, some of which hungered for military trials, but more of which had lost its appetite for them. Four years of arrests without habeas corpus and with military tribunals overseeing civilian cases in the loyal states had taken a toll. The use of a military tribunal to convict the Lincoln conspirators turned opinions against traveling down this road any longer. It is no surprise that Democrats—with their suspicions of concentrated power, fears of government encroachment on liberties, and persecution during the conflict—had qualms about military commissions, especially when they were conducted by Republicans. But even supporters of the government had issues. Former attorney general Edward Bates followed the proceedings of the Lincoln conspirators and asked an acquaintance to explain "how the govert fell into the blunder of insisting upon trying the conspirators, by a military court." Bates, a conservative Republican, stewed on this issue for days, and supplied what he saw as the central problem with military trials: "It denies the great, fundamental principle, that ours is a government of *Law*, and that the law is strong enough to rule the people wisely and well; and if the offenders be done to death by that tribunal, however truly guilty, they will pass for martyrs with half the world."[35] Another man wrote the president from Cincinnati that he should not put Davis before a military commission. "They are a wide departure from the old, familiar ways in which we have been educated and to which we are attached. Trial by jury is esteemed to be a strong bulwark of liberty and, life, and Military Commissions are associated with tyranny and despotism. Our people do not wish to get accustomed to them. On the contrary, they want them put away."[36]

This sentiment cut across party lines. At least several Republican newspapers—the *Philadelphia Public Ledger*, *New York Evening Post*, and *New York Tribune*—echoed these comments, as did Republicans across the country. Significantly, because he would judge such a case shortly, Chief Justice Salmon P. Chase wrote in a private letter in July 1865: "I sincerely hope we have seen the last of Military Commissions." In Massachusetts, attorney John C. Ropes wrote his friend in the judge advocate's office in South Carolina that the trial of the Lincoln conspirators was "outrageous." He added: "Had the prisoners been tried before a respectable Court-Martial I might have judged the Government more leniently. But to try them before [Maj. Gen. David] Hunter and those other weak and prejudiced men is monstrous. The great offence however is trying them at all before a Military tribunal." He also mentioned that Governor John Andrew of Massachusetts, a stalwart Republican during the war, said he would fight the prosecution were he not holding public office.[37] Even more striking was John C. Gray's position. Gray served in the judge advocate's office at Hilton Head. He was mortified by the trial of the conspirators. "I am not entirely sure that the trial of the assassins by a military commission is absolutely illegal," he noted, adding, "but it is on the very extreme verge of the law, and of course ought never to have been adopted and the secrecy of the proceedings was a burning shame." He hoped that Jefferson Davis would hang, but was skeptical it would come about. "Judge Holt [who tried the Lincoln conspirators] has certainly done more to shake the foundations of the law than any one lawyer in the country." For all his dislike of Greeley, Gray appreciated the editor's advocacy for conducting fair trials.[38]

There were certainly some prominent advocates for the use of military trials. First and foremost was Joseph Holt, who had used military courts to try a number of cases, including the Lincoln conspirators. He told Stanton that the commissions were good for "bringing to justice . . . a large class of malefactors in the service or interest of the rebellion, who otherwise would have altogether escaped punishment."[39] Stanton had few problems with trying traitors before military commissions. When Benjamin Butler was called in to provide Johnson advice on the way to handle the Davis trial, he recommended a commission of senior major generals (not surprisingly he nominated himself) to hear the case and find the ex-president guilty. Once a decision had been rendered, Butler said the president could suggest that the Supreme Court rule on the proceedings to give them the stamp of legality.[40] Congress also had its supporters, although it would be more accurate to think of these men as advocating for a conviction, no matter the location of a trial. This included Senators Jacob M. Howard and Zachariah Chandler of Michigan and Representative George W. Julian of Indiana, to name a few. In the House, Thaddeus Stevens doubted that a civil court could find Davis guilty, but he spoke in favor of a military tribunal for Davis, not necessarily for treason but for war crimes by a belligerent.[41]

Another obstacle to a civil trial was Chief Justice Chase, who would oversee the proceedings with Judge Underwood in the U.S. Circuit Court that sat in Richmond. Chase did little to push the Davis trial forward. In fact, he impeded its progress, either from a desire to protect his chances of running for the presidency or from understanding that legal constraints and public attitudes risked supporting the legality of secession.[42] In explaining his position, even in private letters, the chief justice claimed that he followed the law and did not wish to put the former president on trial until civil authority had been restored in the former Confederate states. These were not inconsequential factors. As long as the military occupied the region, and the president or the Congress left it unclear if habeas corpus had been restored, the chief justice said the court could not function. Johnson had issued a proclamation of peace, but that was not enough for Chase. "I am not willing," he wrote his former law partner in May 1866, "as a member of the Supreme Court to hold Circuit Courts where martial law has not been abrogated or the habeas corpus restored. Some think that these things are accomplished by the proclamation of peace; but the fact that military commissions are still held & other like facts bring this conclusion into doubt." He thus shifted the blame for any delays in the prosecution of traitors to the executive and legislative branches.[43]

Many at the time, however, concluded that Chase wanted nothing to do with the prosecution of Davis. The justice's caution in this affair did have merit legally, and perhaps because of the stature of the accused and the possibility for setting an unfortunate precedent, he deserved to err on the side of caution. And he did, in the words of a biographer, see "constitutional and legal problems of a formidable nature that would hamper if not foreclose a trial."[44] Winning a unanimous opinion of jurors from Virginia, even with African Americans empanelled, was not a foregone conclusion. But one can easily imagine a different person, say Judge Underwood—who was much more aggressive in his statements about punishing deserters— adopting a different posture that pushed the trial forward. Both cabinet insiders and the public interpreted Chase's behavior as demonstrating less enthusiasm for indicting and prosecuting Davis than that of President Johnson, the man considered to be too lenient.

One indication of his lack of enthusiasm for presiding over the case came in the summer of 1865, after Johnson had polled his cabinet for their thoughts. The president was anxious to hear Chase's opinion. In late August, he invited the chief justice to the White House to confer about Davis. Chase dutifully answered the invitation; however, one can imagine the uncomfortable manner in which the meeting unfolded. The justice may have thought the president wished to consult with him about his acclaimed trip to South Carolina, but it quickly became clear that Johnson had other intentions. He asked Chase about the time, place, and manner of the trial, which the justice declined to discuss because "this did not seem to me a proper subject of conference between the President & Chief Justice & so I respectfully told him."[45] The president pressed him but, according to Secretary of the Navy Welles, "Chase [put] himself on his judicial reserve." Johnson was a proud man and likely felt rebuffed. An attempt by Chase to discuss other subjects, especially to impress upon the president the need to include black voting as a part of Reconstruction, found no enthusiasm. Welles added that Chase "little understands the character of President Johnson if he supposes that gentleman will ever again introduce that subject [to him]." Welles concluded: "I have seen no indications of a desire on the part of the Chief Justice to preside at the trial of Davis."[46]

Further actions underscored a lack of enthusiasm for bringing Davis to trial. When Johnson finally proclaimed martial law ended in the South—a situation that Chase previously had declared would allow for a trial—the chief justice raised two more obstacles. First, he pointed out that Congress had reduced the size of the Supreme Court from ten to seven but had not set the jurisdictional boundaries for the Circuit Courts. So he held off on the case until the Congress clarified who presided over a particular District. But then he claimed to have scheduling problems. His calendar was too full with Supreme Court business that he could not to travel to Richmond at the times most convenient to government prosecutors. Yet at relatively this same moment, the summer of 1867, he did his duties in that portion of the circuit that encompassed North Carolina. Throughout this time, Chase's actions, or lack thereof, raised the frustrations of government prosecutors, whom he tried to blame for delays by claiming they were not adequately prepared. Whether to avoid a case that could hurt his political future, or to protect the government from a potentially disastrous ruling, the Chief Justice undoubtedly served as an obstacle to the trial of Jefferson Davis and to the possible prosecution of the rebel traitors in general.[47]

Within a few years, the government came to the conclusion that no trial was better than one that could result in an endorsement of secession and state sovereignty. In between had come the transfer of the case to civil court, to set the bail of Davis, on May 11, 1867. Richard H. Dana Jr., prominent Boston attorney who served as a government attorney, in 1868 advised his client against proceeding with the case. Attorney General William M. Evarts read a letter from Dana to the cabinet that stated, "By pursuing the trial, the Government can get only a re-affirmation by a Circuit Court . . . of a rule of public law settled for this country in every way in which such a matter can be settled [*i.e.*, by war], on giving to a jury drawn from the region of the rebellion a chance to disregard the law when announced." Dana reminded Evarts that it took only one juror to set aside a conviction. "The risks of such absurd and discreditable issues of a great state trial are assumed for the sake of a verdict which, if obtained, will settle nothing in law or national practice not now settled, and nothing in fact not now history, while no judgment rendered thereon do we think will be ever executed."[48]

The longer the issue lasted, the less likely it would result in punishment of the leader of the rebellion. Reconstruction involved more critical problems: peace and security in the South, protection of the freedpeople and white Republicans from terrorism, issues of citizenship and rights, and struggles for power to determine the answers to these questions. It became less probable as time went on that President Johnson would bite one of the only hands that could feed him politically—that of white Democrats in the South—by making Davis into their martyr. And there were serious reservations even among those who wished to prosecute that the outcome would serve the interests of the nation. And so Davis and the rest of the Confederate leaders under indictment for treason never went to trial.[49]

Leniency among White Abolitionists

On his way to learning whether he remained in military custody, Davis assured a U.S. marshal that he wished to avoid a third autumn inside prison. He need not have worried. On May 13, 1867, the courtroom of the District Court of Virginia in Richmond was, predictably, packed. Because of the small size of the room, Judge Underwood had restricted admission to the media, members of the bar, and other essential people, regulated by tickets. The moment had to seem a little surreal for the former president. The building was the one that had housed the Confederate Treasury and his own executive office during the late rebellion. Then, he had held the reins of power; now, he was a stranger in his own edifice where he awaited what others decided for him. Underwood conducted the legal ceremony quickly and without fanfare. The *New York Times* reported: "The whole proceeding appears to have been as quiet and as brief as the arraignment of a petty offender in a Police office." And with the government saying that it was not ready to begin proceedings—to begin proceedings, mind you, after two years of debating among itself what to do about Davis with the help of the best legal minds in the country—his fate was to go free on bail.[50]

Then came the truly interesting part, something perhaps equally surreal for Davis himself. Called forward to sign the bail papers of Davis were roughly twenty people, including Horace Greeley and Gerrit Smith. They were longtime abolitionists: the very group whom the states that formed the Confederacy in 1860–61 blamed in their secession ordinances for bringing on the war through agitation against slavery. Greeley, editor of the radical *New York Tribune*, was known as an extremist to moderate people in both North and South. Among conservatives, he was known with more unkind adjectives and nouns. Someone familiar with his positions before and during the war would not have thought this man would provide bail for Jefferson Davis. More strange, Smith had helped fund John Brown's raid on Harpers Ferry in 1859, for which he faced a congressional investigation to see if he, too, should face charges of treason or inciting insurrection. Although never prosecuted, he had been the South's worst nightmare as an instigator of a potential slave insurrection. Yet here they were, two of the old antislavery ultraists stepping forward to pledge $5,000 each toward the $100,000 bail for a case that most people by this time believed would not come to trial. Greeley and Davis met for the first time, exchanging comments whose content we will never know. Davis went with his family to Niagara Falls, Canada, promising to return to the United States for further hearings the following year. The night of the proceedings, Greeley and Smith went on to an African American church in Richmond to explain themselves, and then returned to their respective places in the North to defend themselves.[51]

If any faction within the United States had the argumentative weight, the access to newspapers, the passion, and the organization in the Congress to kill a few of the rebels, it was the Radicals. No other coalition so forcefully advocated executions of traitors. Democrats hoped to forge new alliances with the white South, and moderate Republicans wanted former rebels to accept defeat, the end of slavery, and peaceful accommodations with African Americans as free laborers. Yet, as the Greeley-Smith episode highlights, a portion of the old abolitionist vanguard had gone over to the enemy—at least when it came toward reconciliation. Joining Greeley and Smith on the side of clemency were such antislavery luminaries as Henry Ward Beecher, Lydia Maria Child, William Lloyd Garrison, and Lysander Spooner. They did so for a variety of reasons, humane and political. But one of the goals for their pursuit of leniency was to promote universal amnesty of the criminals against the United States in order to achieve universal suffrage, freedmen included. They believed that a reasoned approach would meet with a reasoned response. And they retained a faith in the ballot as the means of achieving equality for black people by giving them the ability to protect themselves through political power.

The behavior of these leading lights of abolition modifies the typology of historians who consider the postwar world as consisting of emancipationists, reconciliationists, and white supremacists. The current story of how northerners and southerners clasped hands across the bloody chasm posits that the white people who supported emancipation eventually forsook their African American colleagues to forge an alliance with former Confederates in order to create reconciliation between the sections based on white supremacy. From the very start of Reconstruction, however, the people who focused on emancipation—the Radicals—contained within their orbit people who espoused clemency for the rebel traitors, to the point of embarrassment from others in their ranks as well as the discomfort of African Americans. Yet they did not relinquish remembrance of slavery as a cause of the Civil War, and they celebrated emancipation as a resounding achievement of the conflict, even if some of them could not rise above the mistaken paternalistic notions that the white race might have been a little more advanced than the black one.[52]

The differences among white abolitionists became apparent during the war in the debates over whether emancipation meant that the American Anti-Slavery Society should disband. At a meeting of the Massachusetts Anti-Slavery Society in January 1864, the question arose as Garrison continued to ponder whether the society had achieved its goals. With the president's proclamation of emancipation, he considered the victory had been won. Wendell Phillips led a contrarian segment of the society that believed that the goal had been only partially reached—that full equality encompassing suffrage and the ability of black men to sit on juries, walk where they pleased, or associate with whomever they liked served as the real end of the quest. Also, the government had to find a way to prevent former Confederates from coming back into power. This fear had grown with Lincoln's announced Reconstruction policy that favored a quick restoration of states whenever 10 percent of the voters from 1860 had sworn their loyalty. With such a reconstruction of the Union, Phillips warned, a significant segment of the slaveocracy would populate the Congress, perhaps even dragging out the general end of slavery.[53] The meeting in Boston displayed a rupture between Phillips and Garrison that forced abolitionists to choose sides even in the presidential contest. Phillips rejected Lincoln and supported John C. Frémont as the Republican nominee because of his more aggressive posture concerning emancipation. The Union at this point still had no certainty of full emancipation with the Thirteenth Amendment still a year away, much less a clear policy for black rights. In fact, nothing could have been muddier at the time than policies concerning voting and civic rights for black people.[54]

As the war ended, the disagreements among abolitionists over how to punish the rebels grew more apparent. The leaders of the "hang them" faction tended to be the most radical of the Radicals in Congress, such as Senators Zachariah Chandler and Jacob M. Howard of Michigan; Congressman George W. Julian of Indiana; and Congressman Thaddeus Stevens of Pennsylvania. Julian, in fact, introduced one of the most laughable resolutions in the Congress when, on January 29, 1866, he proposed the speedy trial of Jefferson Davis for treason, "and his prompt execution *when found guilty.*" When challenged, he did agree to a change that acknowledged that the legal system should presume innocence until proven guilty.[55] Senator Charles Sumner was more pragmatic and had given up on hanging Jefferson Davis. Privately, he wished Davis had escaped because he entertained little hope of ever convicting the man. Sumner did, however, favor exiling perhaps 100 to 500 of the Confederate leaders. The senator targeted R. M. T. Hunter, a former U.S. senator from Virginia, as his first choice for banishment.[56] At first, these Radicals supported Johnson, who had remained loyal when his state left the Union. He also had talked tough about making treason odious and seemed to be the right man in the right place at the right time—that is, until he pardoned more than 90 percent of the former Confederates, many of whom resumed their former positions of leadership in public offices.

One of the most single-minded proponents of vengeance was Howard, a man in the background of histories even though he played an influential role in the Joint Committee on Reconstruction. On the Senate floor, Howard agitated for punishing traitors because he believed that the rebels had not accepted defeat. "It is true the war has ceased to drench the earth with blood; the rebels have laid down their arms; they are conquered, but with a supercilious sneer at their conquerors, kindly and condescendingly assure them that they 'accept the situation,' that southern independence is a failure, and that they are willing and ready again to be represented in Congress; but we all know that at heart they hate and detest the Government they betrayed four years ago, and which now holds them in the iron grip of conquest." He was only warming to the task. "They hate it, and hate the loyal people who uphold it, for the same reason that any criminal who has sought the life of an innocent man hates the man who has brought him to justice. They hate it because their failure to shake off its authority had deeply stung their pride and brought a total eclipse upon their vainglory and their vanity; because, seeing among themselves the desolation of war, and the poverty, starvation, and beggary it has brought to their own doors, they recognize in these the lasting, the unanswerable evidence of their own folly, weakness, and madness."[57]

As a primary inquisitor on the Joint Committee on Reconstruction, Howard examined a substantial portion of the people who appeared before the committee, including Robert E. Lee. It was during the interview with Judge Underwood in January 1866, in fact, that the committee heard the unwelcome news that it would be "idle" to think that a jury would convict a former Confederate of treason. "They boast of their treason," Underwood said, "and ten or eleven out of the twelve on any jury, I think, would say that Lee was almost equal to Washington, and was the noblest man in the State, and they regard every man who has committed treason with more favor than any man in the State who has remained loyal to the government."[58]

Howard and his colleagues looked for evidence of the damaging effect of clemency. They had become alarmed by President Johnson's free use of the pardon power and by the easy restoration of traitorous rebels to public office. Alexander Stephens, vice president of the Confederacy, won election to the U.S. Senate but was not allowed to take his seat, along with other rebel traitors. Howard especially wanted to know whether the administration's leniency with pardons had encouraged resistance by former enemies, allowing the spirit of the rebellion to continue. Again, these hard-liners saw forgiveness as requiring repentance, which seemed to be in short supply in the former Confederacy. Invariably, Unionists or friends of the government told him what he wanted to hear: that disloyalty reared its head because of Johnson's policies; that leniency begat greater confidence within the traitorous element for persecuting loyal citizens, meaning white Republicans and African Americans. Howard used this forum to try to prove to the northern public why ex-Confederates deserved punishment, including, where applicable, execution.[59]

The problem was that not enough of his colleagues felt the same way, and it was particularly problematic that the naysayers espoused a faith in

clemency that moderates shared. A significant portion of the abolitionists not only rejected executions but also actively preached forgiveness of
the insurrectionists to accelerate the restoration of the Union and gain
black rights. Horace Greeley became an open supporter of lenience by
the summer of 1865. In Brooklyn, New York, one of the leading church-
men of his age preached reconciliation from his pulpit. By the fall of 1865,
Henry Ward Beecher—the man who had helped supply guns to abolitionists in antebellum Kansas—openly endorsed the Reconstruction policies
of President Johnson. "Men at the North are disappointed," he told his
congregation in November, "because prominent men at the South are pardoned, when they do not give up their theory of secession. I should not
respect them if they did. Let them accept the fact of union from this time
on, and they can have their theories. A man who too readily gives up his
theories and doctrines cannot make a desirable citizen."[60]

A rationale for opposing treason trials emerged publicly in Greeley's
Radical newspaper less than a month after the surrender at Appomattox. An article titled "The Abolitionists for Clemency" identified Phillips,
Smith, and Beecher as outspoken advocates for a merciful treatment of
the "discomfited Rebels." The article presented three reasons for mercy.
First, the posture proved that abolitionists had been in earnest; that they
were not hypocrites but people who identified with those who suffered,
and had given up their own popularity to help the downtrodden. Ironically, the downtrodden now included the defeated rebels. Second, the abolitionists had won more than the war; they had achieved their primary
goal of destroying slavery. The writer added that "we hear of no scheme
that looks to a reconstruction of Slavery. That veteran culprit, it is univer-
sally agreed, has constructed a tall gallows named Secession, and hung
himself by the neck thereon until very dead indeed." It was better to work
toward having southern whites consent to this reality than to execute defeated traitors. Finally, third, the abolitionists desired the freedmen of the
South to have the rights of self-protection via the suffrage. Hanging some
of the insurgents would hardly dispose the survivors toward granting the
elective franchise to the freedmen. Kindly feelings between abolitionists
and their former antagonists "may do much toward a removal of these
real, formidable obstacles barring the path of the Nation toward genuine
Peace and durable Prosperity."[61]

Phillips lent his support to the rebel leaders escaping punishment.
In a speech at Boston's Tremont Temple in late April 1865, with the air
thick with cries for vengeance because of the Lincoln assassination, he
reminded his listeners that no cause "was ever crushed by punishing its

advocates and abettors." He said that the blood of martyrs provided the seeds for a new church. This was a common concern among many in the North: executions could create martyrs who inspired further uprisings. With regard to hanging a dozen chief rebels, Phillips repeated a refrain sung around the North that executions presented a practical problem of where to draw the line. After paroling "the bloodiest and guiltiest of all, Robert Lee [loud applause], there would be little fitness in hanging any lesser wretch." Plus, the government had conducted the rebellion as a war, not an insurrection. And the Union could not hang all of the participants. "We cannot hang men in regiments." Covering the continent with gibbets would sicken Americans and sink "our civilization to the level of Southern barbarism." But he did try to capitalize on the mood for punishing rebels in a particular way. Instead of killing them, he advocated taking their property in order to establish a new political arrangement in the South that supported the equality of black people. Banish the worst of the traitors, but do not let a single southern state back into the Union unless every loyal man enjoys the ballot. Give a black man the ballot and arms "and, while he holds them, the Union is safe."[62]

The desire for clemency found part of its impetus in the mentality of antebellum social reformers trying to create a more benevolent and civilized nation, which included a stance against capital punishment. Scholars often classify people by one particular social movement: as abolitionists, as prison reformers, as temperance supporters, and so on, when in fact reformers could be involved in all of these things at once. Beecher and abolitionists like Greeley fit the profile of reformers interested in a broad range of societal problems beyond abolition. Like many of his colleagues, Beecher argued that there was a difference between criminal and political crimes—that to punish people for the latter, or treason, sent a bad message to the world about the kind of nation the United States represented. Republics should behave better. Beecher said the death penalty existed for only two reasons: reform the prisoner and deter the crime. About the first, he said, "Well, hanging never reforms anybody." As to deterrence of the crime, he claimed, like many, that the rebels had suffered enough and would think twice before rebelling again. "I say," he concluded, "take a step of moderation in the direction of humanity, because it will be understood to the advantage of free governments all the world over."[63] Expressing similar ideas, abolitionist Lydia Maria Child said she opposed capital punishment "because I think it has a brutalizing influence on the public mind, and does not tend to diminish crime, as is generally supposed. I consider it a remnant of barbarism, with which the world will dispense, as it advances in civilization." But as long as anybody hanged, she could not see why Jeff Davis would be exempted or why Robert E. Lee should remain "a gentleman at large."[64]

Beecher and Child featured the ethos of people who had been involved in the campaign against capital punishment in the antebellum North. Their efforts had helped to eliminate the death penalty in three states (Rhode Island, Michigan, and Wisconsin) and restrict the sentence to the crimes of murder and treason in the rest of the states—that is, in the free states of the North. It was another of the many reforms that bypassed the southern slave states. The stalwarts in this effort were many of the usual leaders from the antislavery movement and penal reform. Famed poet and abolitionist John Greenleaf Whittier argued against the utterances of punishing and hanging leading traitors without pointing out the cause—slavery, which had brought God's vengeance on a sinful people. He wrote: "Human life is still a very sacred thing; Christian forbearance and patience are still virtues. For my own part I should be satisfied to see the chiefs of the great treason go out from among us homeless, exiled forever, with the brand of Cain on their foreheads, carrying with them wherever they go the avenging Nemesis of conscience." Letting them live, in fact, might be the worst penalty. He reminded his audience that the peculiar institution had transformed men into fiends. "Deprived of slavery," he said, "they are wasps who have lost their stings."[65]

But the most extreme, albeit disturbing, logic concerning clemency came from Lysander Spooner, Unitarian abolitionist, political philosopher, and anarchist. In the 1840s he had tried to break the monopoly of the U.S. Post Office by founding his own company, which created a competitive situation until the government wore him down through lawsuits. Spooner also contributed a controversial book that declared the U.S. Constitution was a proslavery document. After the war, he published tracts titled *No Treason*, which announced his position against punishing the rebels. As the title suggests, he did not think the Confederate South had betrayed its country. He considered the late war a travesty in showing that the nation rested not upon consent of the governed but upon force. The North expended money and blood to "maintain her power over an unwilling people" and did so in the name of liberty. If consent determined the formation of new nations in the modern world, then it also negated the charge of treason if a people decided to break their compact and form a separate nation. This was not betrayal any more than someone committed treason when leaving a church or a voluntary association. As long as a group announced a change in allegiance, as the Confederate South had done through its ordinances of secession passed at conventions, then there was no such thing as committing a crime against a country to which they no longer professed loyalty. He argued that a government that can accuse, shoot, and hang men as traitors for refusing to surrender themselves to an arbitrary will can put into practice any oppression that it pleases. Obviously, Spooner believed that no former Confederate should hang.[66]

No better justification for southern secession presented itself, especially because it came from a northerner and one who had served as a leading opponent of slavery. One could almost hear former Confederates applauding. *De Bow's Review*, a southern agricultural and economic journal that also had promoted slavery and a state rights political philosophy, seized upon Spooner's thought as vindication for the war. In June 1867, this journal which circulated widely in the South published a review of the tracts that took great glee in mentioning that the rationale for the Confederate rebellion had come from one of the "distinguished" members of the antislavery camp. There was no novelty in this affirmation of state rights, the writer alleged, except that it came from someone who lived in Boston and who had belonged to a party (read that as Republican) that had tried to make such views obsolete. Later, the editor of the journal had to apologize for this statement—not because it misrepresented Spooner's position but because the abolitionist chastised the journal for calling him a Republican. He was against slavery, but not a member of that party. Like many abolitionists he detested institutions for the way they made people forsake their individual principles for the group. He did not hold any grudges, however. The editor of *De Bow's Review* not only printed a correction of this political fact but also reprinted, with the permission of Spooner, the entire text of *No Treason*.[67]

Although an extremist within an extreme group, Spooner's popular interpretation of the Constitution voiced themes that echoed not only with Radicals but also with Americans who advocated mercy for the rebels. Here the news was not good for those wishing that the government adopted a consistent posture of protecting black American life, liberty, and property from oppression and violence. If consent of the governed mattered, then the doctrine presented a challenge for the government to regulate life in the postwar South. It was a political philosophy that not only encouraged individualism but also handcuffed the national state by reinforcing the need for respecting local rule. The people of the United States enjoyed touting consent and popular rule as attributes that distinguished the nation from the rest of the world. Did forcing down the throat of white southerners a law that allowed for black suffrage contradict American

principles? Did doing so mean that the United States followed the example of dictatorial governments, instead of democratic ones? Did such
a plan for reunion diminish a democratic republic in the eyes of the rest
of the world? As Spooner had asked, could a government founded on the
belief in consent of the governed *force* democratic rule on a people?

Sadly, these questions gave continuing traction to state sovereignty.
Even among abolitionists who favored a stronger central government that
protected human rights, the old philosophy of state rights kept rearing its
head. So did the structure of the Constitution and laws that protected the
right of states to establish the requirements for suffrage, not the federal
government. On May 2, 1865, Greeley's *Tribune* pondered such questions,
as General Halleck in Richmond ordered oaths of allegiance for pursuing professions and even getting married. In an article titled "What's the
Use?" Greeley decried the use of meaningless oaths by following a logic
that former Confederates developed to defend themselves. The secession
theory had allowed for states to withdraw. Using Lee as an example, the
item noted that the general had been bound by his federal oath until Virginia seceded, which released him from his pledge and carried him into
the rebel camp. With Virginia out of the Union, Lee felt he had to follow. Sounding a bit like Spooner, the author concluded that Lee did not
regard himself as a traitor but as a patriot because he had renounced his
federal loyalty. If he swore an oath of allegiance to the Union and Virginia
again seceded, he would likely go with his state once again. If state sovereignty represented a sound principle, "then swearing fealty to the Union
is a mockery at best—a grimace—a Mormon marriage—a boundary line
run from a crow flying over a forest to a will-o'-wisp flickering through a
swamp." The country did not need more oaths until it figured out what
allegiance meant.[68]

Gerrit Smith entered more treacherous waters in a letter to Salmon P.
Chase. In this correspondence he doubted whether the war had settled
the issue of secession. "I have admitted the plainness of the Constitution
at one point [concerning treason]," he observed, adding, "Its lack of plainness at another and most vital point is of itself a sufficient reason why
the South should not be held for treason. It was not slavery alone, but
slavery combined with the doctrine of State sovereignty, that brought on
the War." He said that no small number of statesmen in the North and
South, dating back to Thomas Jefferson and James Madison, believed that
they found the doctrine of state rights in the Constitution. "Perhaps, the
streams of blood shed in this horrid War have not washed away, entirely
and forever, this pernicious doctrine. Then, let it be provided for, if not

in a Constitutional Amendment, at least in the terms of 'Reconstruction,' that it shall no more return to curse us." Smith claimed that no one should be punished until the doctrine of state rights, especially state sovereignty, was indisputably determined to be wrong, according to the laws of the land.[69]

Despite their differences, one area of agreement among Radicals concerned winning the right of suffrage for black people. The would-be executioners could stand on this principle shoulder-to-shoulder with the forgivers of the Confederate traitors and find themselves in the company of African American activists. But "people," when it came to suffrage, meant men only, no matter the race.

The Militarization of Black Loyalty

Although the occasional cry "Hang Jeff. Davis" found its way into their discourse, African Americans did not give vengeance much of a priority. It simply did not take them where they needed to go. This does not mean they felt no anger against the slaveocracy. During a July 4th celebration in Pennsylvania in 1865, a black soldier shouted his desire to see the ex-president dangle at the end of a rope, but "the other colored troops instantly knocked the orator down." It is doubtful that this episode signaled that the black people wished Davis Godspeed and a long life. Not too long before, an African American newspaper cheered that President Lincoln had occupied the mansion of Davis, and that "Jeff. Davis himself" was "running for his life."[70] The discomfort of the rebels undoubtedly gave African Americans good cheer. However, they were aware of the problematic nature of black violence. Suffrage and an end to discriminatory laws in the North and the South mattered far more than gaining retribution for suffering. Politics demanded that attitudes about hanging rebels remained private in deference to the greater quest for equality. Hatred by black people toward former rebels was counterproductive, although they occasionally shared the observation of Philip A. Bell: "Instead of pursuing a system of 'liberal, but judicious hanging,' as recommended by General Scott, the Government appears to have adopted a system of liberal but injudicious pardoning."[71]

African Americans adapted the rhetoric of treason to make their case for deserving the rights of citizenship signified by male suffrage. Much of the rationale based itself on the performance of black men in the military. It was logical to remind the northern public that the black race had been loyal during the war: that it had compiled a better record of support of the Union cause than had white Copperheads. It certainly struck leaders of the black suffrage movement as hypocritical to grant the vote quickly to rebel traitors while denying it to the men and women who had had labored to build the nation and had fought to keep that same nation together. African Americans did not always appreciate the paternalistic attitude of white abolitionists who viewed suffrage as a gift or as a necessary ingredient for protection from a rebel counterrevolution; they considered it a right that had been earned and that they could protect themselves if only they had due process. They found themselves in perhaps less than a true partnership with white emancipationists than as fellow travelers who, for a while, found themselves heading in the same direction.

To press the cause, 145 African Americans had gathered in Syracuse, New York, roughly a month before the presidential election of 1864 to launch the National Equal Rights League. This was the first nationwide organization devoted to equality by black Americans. Its members worried that Lincoln might not win or, even if he did, that peace might come without a general emancipation. White support among Republicans appeared mixed at best when it came to pushing for an end to discriminatory laws. The convention to form the National Equal Rights League drew the top black leadership from around the country, including portions of the occupied Confederacy. Douglass attended, as well as John Mercer Langston (who became president), George B. Vashon, George Downing, and Henry Highland Garnet. So were about 2,000 spectators, many of them white people. Key themes involved suffrage and elevation of the race, and much of the rationale for equality resided on the performance of black soldiers who had come forward when white Democrats had forsaken the government. The organization established itself throughout the North, then spread to the former Confederacy as the fighting stopped.[72]

Black service to the nation—as contrasted with treasonous rebels— became a justification for good schools, access to public accommodations, participatory justice, and especially suffrage. Also hard to miss was the justification for giving black men the right to vote ahead of white women. Black men had shouldered a musket and fought in the Civil War. They had shed their blood on the altar of the nation. They were not the traitorous enemies whom the nation now seemed hell-bent on restoring to full political rights. African Americans had proved their loyalty when Confederates and northern Democrats had not. Frederick Douglass's observation has often been quoted: "Once let the black man get upon his person the brass letters U.S.; let him get an eagle on his button, and a musket on his shoulder, and bullets in his pocket, and there is no power on the earth or under the earth which can deny that he has earned the right of citizenship in the United States." But that was during the recruitment drives of summer 1863. Two years later he saw that more revolutionary change was required than recognition of black people as citizens. "Slavery," he told a meeting of the American Anti-Slavery Society in 1865, "is not abolished until the black man has the ballot." He and other black abolitionists stressed that males had earned that right through validating their martial prowess in service of the nation.[73]

Until recently, historians have accepted Douglass's interpretation uncritically; now, they have noted the problems of building voting and citizenship rights on a foundation of martial manhood. First of all, it left women out of the picture entirely, reinforcing a gendered citizenship and rights that suggested that black women's swiftest way to achieve civic standing came through marriage. But the prevailing ideology also left black men more vulnerable than one might think. The militaristic road to freedom and citizenship did not automatically define the rights that white people conceded to African Americans and the approach charted an uneven road toward political advancement. Basic citizenship did not necessarily equate to voting. And reinforcing violent civic rituals through such things as paramilitary groups, rifle clubs, and even voting on Election Day placed a premium on an aggressive defense of manhood. Whenever African American men showed themselves unable to defend themselves or their dependents—the product of restrictions on gun ownership, discrimination, or injustice in general—then it raised questions among white supporters about their ability to exercise the rights of males in a democracy. Plus, guns in the hands of black men created nervousness among conservative and moderate white northerners. Even after they were mustered out of service in the U.S. military, armed African Americans remained a striking, and problematic, presence in the South in black militia groups, Emancipation Day parades, and other public events. Even white people sympathetic to emancipation might see this display of martial prowess as a problem—a problem requiring discipline to control the supposed violent tendencies within black people, giving impetus to further restraints on freedom.[74]

Although a central theme, the military rationale for suffrage provided only one part of a larger rhetorical and organizational strategy. Black Americans also argued that they were entitled to the vote because they deserved the natural rights guaranteed to all men. They invoked the Declaration of Independence as their chief authority. And they used male gender as an element to span the racial divide. As one historian has explained, "In their opinion slavery had imposed the unnatural condition of inequality on them; now that the shackles had been removed, they had been restored to their original condition of free men." Langston, who became president of the Equal Rights League, declared that because government rested upon the consent of the governed, it was tyranny to force the obligations of citizenship upon black people—such as taxes—without also granting the right to elect their representatives.[75]

However, when employing the language of treason and loyalty, as well as arguing for suffrage, black military service invariably became an essential trope. Speakers at mass rallies drew upon examples from the past to underscore the loyalty of black male service to the nation. William C. Nell, an African American journalist who in 1863 presided as president of the first Emancipation Day celebration in Boston, provides a good example. In his remarks to commemorate the president's action, Nell cited the sacrifice of Crispus Attucks as one of the first martyrs of the American Revolution. This was partially true. Attucks, a black man killed in the Boston Massacre of 1770, did lose his life in a protest against the British. However, the actual revolution waited another six years to begin. No matter. He provided an invaluable reference point for abolitionists both black and white in making their claims for the continuity of black loyalty to the cause of liberty. Like his colleagues, Nell stressed the fighting ability of black males through the War of 1812, when free blacks in New Orleans helped Andrew Jackson fend off the British. Nell carried his analysis to current times with mention of Robert Smalls, a slave who took a Confederate ship from Charleston harbor to beyond the federal blockade and to freedom.[76]

These expressions found their way into the rituals and rhetoric of the Equal Rights League and shaped the culture of the organization. In February 1866 an observer of the league's meeting in Columbus, Ohio, proudly described how members made their appearance led by a man bearing aloft the "flag of our country." During the meeting, the Reverend Grofton Graham led the group in the singing of one of his songs: "Let the Banner Proudly Wave." The third stanza was particularly noteworthy to the observer: "We've stood and fought like demons Upon the battle-field; Both slaves and Northern freemen Have faced the glowing steel. Our blood beneath this banner Has mingled with the whites, And 'neath its folds we now demand Our just and *equal rights*." The reporter avowed that every man, woman, and child in the audience raised their voices for the chorus: "Let it wave, let it wave, Let the banner proudly wave. Let it wave, let it wave! But never o'er a slave."[77]

Before convincing white Americans that suffrage was a right earned through violent service to the nation, black leaders had to make the case that they and their followers were, in fact, citizens. The *Dred Scott* decision by the Supreme Court in 1857 left a powerful statement to the contrary. Late in the war and into Reconstruction, African American activists increasingly referred to an opinion rendered in 1862 by Attorney General Edward Bates. A revenue cutter—on routine duty to make sure that no contraband goods made it from U.S. ports—had inspected the schooner *Elizabeth & Margaret* off the coast of New Jersey. The U.S. sailors who boarded the ship discovered that a black person named David M. Selsey served as the master. The law at the time required masters of ships to be citizens of the United States. The matter landed in the lap of Treasury Secretary Salmon P. Chase, who asked Bates to answer the question "Are colored men Citizens of the United States?" Emerging from this exchange was one of the authorities not only for U.S. practice at the time but also for African American claims on citizenship until the passage of the Fourteenth Amendment.[78]

The exercise by Bates required a surprisingly high amount of interpretation. The attorney general noted how difficult the question was to answer before finally seizing upon the rationale that became part of the Fourteenth Amendment. He could not find a consensus on a definition. At the time, the Constitution was silent about either what made a citizen or especially the rights that followed. "I find no such definition," he wrote, "no authoritative establishment of the meaning of the phrase, neither by a course of judicial decision in our courts, nor by the continued and consentaneous action of the different branches of our political government." In fact, he added: "Eighty years of practical enjoyment of citizenship, under the constitution, have not sufficed to teach us, either the exact meaning of the word, or the constituent elements of the thing we prize so highly." Eventually, he seized upon "'the accident of birth'—the fact that we happened to be born in the United States." In his reading of the Constitution—as unclear as it was about such an important question—if a person was born on U.S. soil, or the offspring of American parents, that person was a citizen, regardless of color, gender, or any other qualification.[79]

Black people seized upon the opinion, with Langston proclaiming it as "the finest legal document ever written by an American." At the Emancipation Day celebration in Boston in January 1863, William Nell told his audience, "President Lincoln's Emancipation Proclamation, and the Opinion of Attorney General Bates, recognizing the citizenship of color[ed] Americans, inaugurate a national era of fair play for the black man." In

May, Robert Purvis told a mass rally of abolitionists in New York that the "atrocious doctrine of the detestable Taney was no longer the law of the land. The black man was now a citizen and could take his passport and travel over the world under the protecting aegis of the nation."[80] Frederick Douglass also tipped his hat to Bates in the famous speech in which he urged black men to enlist in the army as the way to achieve rights. Under the interpretation of Attorney General Bates, Douglass said that "we are American citizens. We can import goods, own and sail ships, and travel in foreign countries with American passports in our pockets; and now, so far from there being an opposition, so far from excluding as soldiers, the President at Washington, the Cabinet and the Congress, the generals commanding, and the whole army of the nation unite in giving us one thunderous welcome to share with them the honor and glory of suppressing treason and upholding the star-spangled banner."[81]

In Pennsylvania, the state branch of the Equal Rights League used Bates's opinion to push for recognition of African Americans as citizens of the Keystone State. As the Civil War came to a close, black males reminded state representatives that they had held the ability to vote until 1838, when a new state constitution restricted the right to "white freemen." In February 1865, members of the state league sent a petition to the General Assembly insisting that the right be restored. They were citizens of Pennsylvania. And, as citizens, they should be allowed to vote. They claimed that the U.S. Constitution supported their claims. As part of the proof they referred to the opinion by Bates. "Is that opinion regarded as unsound? Let it be judged of in the light of History." The petitioners also reminded the lawmakers "of the proofs of determined manhood and loyalty manifested by Colored men of Pennsylvania, during the course of the existing unholy rebellion, in defence both of the State and of the Union. Your State Captial [sic] was endangered. Straightway a band of Colored men rushed to its rescue. A call for additional troops is issued; and soon twelve thousand black Pennsylvanians respond, and aid in filling up your quota."[82]

This tactic highlighted the need to secure suffrage by also making a claim on state citizenship. The American system of federalism complicated the fight for equality and required a state-by-state strategy alongside national efforts. There were two citizenships in the country: national and state. There still are today, although we do not think of it in the sense of state rights. But states differ in the rights granted to individuals. Their legislatures and legal codes establish regulations regarding marriage, elections, driving, partner benefits, inheritance, and many other components of the day-by-day freedoms that Americans might attribute to national citizenship. Certainly, states cannot establish regulations that conflict with the federal code; that has been determined by the Civil War and by law. However, African American leaders in the middle of the struggle to define freedom understood that the expansion of rights required multiple approaches at varying levels of sovereignty. For historians, this realization now demands—as the next chapter will affirm—a review of the impact of the war and Reconstruction on state constitutions in the North, not just the defeated South. All states, even the northern ones resistant to black suffrage such as Pennsylvania, eventually needed to bring their constitutions into line with the Fifteenth Amendment and work out new ways of understanding the attendant restructuring of freedom and equality.

Obviously, the efforts of black people in the Equal Rights League enjoyed mixed success. The road to black voting rights—as well as desegregation of public accommodations—contained more obstacles to overcome. It was a journey requiring stamina to prevail against the inevitable reverses. It could not be accomplished by simply asserting the muscular manhood of military service, or constantly reminding white people that their suffrage, particularly in the South, could limit the power of former rebels. Fortunately for the cause of African Americans like Douglass, and white men like Chase, there was agreement about the importance of not letting the ex-rebels return to their old ways as they came back into political power. As the Reverend J. M. Manning noted at an Independence Day celebration in Boston, "Let us not be so kind to the disloyal as to be unkind to the loyal."[83] And former Confederates certainly demonstrated enough resistance to warrant their punishment by means other than hanging.

9

SUFFRAGE, DEBT, AND
THE LIMITS OF
PUNISHING THE REBELS

Abolitionist and women's rights activist Lydia Maria Child feared that Reconstruction, done incorrectly, ensured the perpetuation of the former slave-owning oligarchy in a system of free labor infected by undemocratic rule. She was very insightful. Freedom for the enslaved ironically increased the power of white people in the former Confederacy: the three-fifths clause became moot, augmenting representation in the Congress for the South by two-fifths for every black person, while allowing southern whites to create policies and harsh treatment for African Americans who did not enjoy the franchise. Unlike northern moderates, Child favored confiscating the land of the rebellion's leaders as an equalizer. If left with their property, she said, they "will trample on the blacks and poor whites, as of old." But as Grant's army cornered the Confederates at Appomattox in 1865, she sounded a theme about traitors that resonated with Republicans more broadly. Child told George W. Julian, Radical congressman from Indiana, that she did not agree with his pleas to hang some of the rebels. "I trust our record will not be blotted by anything like revenge," she said. The leaders should be contained from doing further mischief, "but I wish there might be no clamoring for blood." Then she hit upon a common solution among those who feared that former Confederates would trade their failed military fight for a successful political one. "I would deprive them of power," she wrote, "but not of life."[1] With confiscation of rebel property highly improbable, the most viable solution to winning the peace became controlling who could vote—not only black people, but also white people; not only southerners, but also the northerners, or the stay-at-home traitors who had demonstrated their disloyalty during the Civil War.

Limiting the power of traitors went hand in glove with concerns for the safety of black people as the forces behind the formation of the Fourteenth Amendment. Punishing ex-rebels through either denying them the franchise or democratizing apportionment through black suffrage first arose as a strategy among Radicals but found increasing support among moderate Republicans as the United States watched new southern governments form with too many of the old faces in place and with the violent repression of African Americans. As the desire for executing the leaders of the rebellion languished, the desire to punish the traitors through other means grew, especially as the rebels fought a rearguard action against the most basic requirements for readmission to political rights—ending slavery, accepting national sovereignty, and repudiating Confederate debts. States' Black Codes in the South seemed to reinstitute slavery by other means. "Magnanimity is very well," army officer C. E. Lippincott told Senator Lyman Trumbull, "but to surrender the Government bodily to the keeping of those who have not learned to be ashamed or sorry that they attempted its destruction seems something else than magnanimity to me."[2] The solutions became the Civil Rights Act of 1866 and the Fourteenth Amendment, with the Fifteenth Amendment providing the capstone on these efforts.

Child's prescription for protecting the gains of the war by denying power to rebels worked just as well for the other disloyal people who had offended Republicans and War Democrats during the conflict—the men and women they called the stay-at-home traitors. And here the Republicans, especially in the borders states, had a slight advantage that they pressed as hard as they could before the inevitable conservative counterrevolution. Northern laws and practices concerning disloyalty left a residue that did not wash away with the mustering out of U.S. soldiers but had to be challenged in courts and through other political action. Proscriptions against disloyal people remained in place, especially in the border states, determining who voted, who held public office, and who practiced professions such as ministers, teachers, and lawyers. In various parts of the North, the federal law that had disfranchised deserters from the Union army became a part of postwar state elections, with Republicans experimenting with this "legal" means to deny certain Democrats the right to vote. Suffrage, apportionment, and national debt were overlapping issues in the continuing debates over treason in early Reconstruction that informed the structure of the Fourteenth Amendment.

It took a Catholic priest to begin unraveling the measures in Missouri against former rebels and their suspected sympathizers. Father John A. Cummings had been convicted in a circuit court that he had taught and preached as a minister of the Catholic faith without having taken the test oath required by the State of Missouri. He clearly had not taken the oath, so he lost the early round. The court sentenced him to pay a fine of $500 and to serve jail time until that amount was paid. Legally sound, the decision nonetheless represented strong measures against a man of the cloth who intended to practice his calling in a country that espoused freedom of religion. He was among the untold numbers of Missourians prevented from engaging in their professions because of a state constitution enacted in 1865. Ministers, teachers, lawyers, doctors, and corporate officers had to satisfy more than eighty-six tests in order to earn the living for which they had trained. These loyalty tests were demanding in that the swearers had to account for past behavior, not only present and future loyalty. The procedure was not designed for people to pass easily. It intended to restrict from power the returning Confederate veterans, guerrilla fighters, and brigands, as well as the citizens who had stayed home and remained peaceful, but who had given supplies to the enemies of the state, cheered for the Confederacy, or discouraged people from enlisting. The U.S. Supreme Court was sympathetic to Father Cummings, as it should have been. It considered the case during its December 1866 term, rendering a ruling in early 1867 that overturned the test oath as unconstitutional. The provisions, according to the court, contradicted the U.S. Constitution's proscription against enacting *ex post facto* laws — making something illegal after the fact, which inflicted punishment upon people without providing a legal hearing.[3]

Using religious freedom as an argument provided a better way to challenge the law rather than, say, betting on the public's sympathies for lawyers. A case involving an attorney did come about, but the U.S. Supreme Court refused the petition of Alexander J. P. Garesché to push aside the test oaths for practicing law in the state of Missouri, recognizing a state's right to regulate such things.[4] But what about a governmental assault on freedom of worship? That kind of case created a sensation. Almost immediately one could see in the public presses that political opponents of the Republicans recognized a delicious chance to embarrass their rivals by capitalizing on unrest among the clergy. One newspaper reported that Democratic newspapers in Missouri urged clergymen to resist the constitutional provision requiring an oath of loyalty to conduct services, pray for their charges, marry their congregants, minister to the sick, and bury their dead. These restrictions struck at the most fundamental phases of life's needs, not to mention the afterlife. The Catholic Church in the region needed little nudging to mount a campaign in the name of religious freedom. Strengthened by the Germans among them, church leaders had poured money into the unsuccessful effort to defeat the new constitution. After the constitution passed, the Reverend Peter Richard, archbishop of St. Louis, openly signaled his opposition to the test oath and indicated that, should the procedure come, he would provide counsel and assistance to his clergy.[5]

What he advised is not known, but he probably did not advocate going quietly. Shortly afterward, two priests—one in Hannibal, Missouri, and another in Jefferson County—were arrested for refusing to take the test oath. Cummings awaited his arrest for another time, but the circumstances suggested an organized attempt to challenge the law. By September the *Baltimore Sun* noted that there was "considerable agitation in Missouri amongst the clergy of different denominations." This writer noted that Presbyterians had resolved not to take the oath and Baptists and Episcopalians had filed their public objections.[6] Key religious denominations had mobilized for a fight. And this fight had the twofold blessing of the fundamental law of the nation and, perhaps more important politically, religious righteousness.

There was only one problem. Although the Supreme Court decided in favor of Father Cummings, allowing professionals to conduct their business without having to swear an oath of loyalty, the ruling did not eliminate a more important restriction. The ballot box clearly remained out of reach to many. In order to vote, Missourians needed to swear their past loyalty to the Union and that they had not helped the Confederate cause in any way. This simple qualification for voting ended up being, in the words of one historian, "one of the most severe and comprehensive disfranchising measures in the nation." This provision disfranchised between 35,000 and 50,000 white Missourians, or roughly one-quarter to one-third of the electorate. It remained in effect until about 1870, given the usual ups and downs of energetic enforcement at the polls. Through these means, Republicans in Missouri seized control of their state, hell-bent on making it more northern than Confederate.[7]

Although Missouri often exhibited extremes in the story of the Civil War, the postwar battles over disloyalty in that state were hardly exceptional. Concerns over test oaths and disqualifying treasonous people from voting had much wider interest—and application. Joining the Show-me State in its proscriptions against disloyal voting was West Virginia, where Republicans held on to control longer than in the other states along the border.[8] The struggles of both states occurred as part of a general reconstruction of liberties in new constitutions throughout the United States. In the decade or so beginning with 1864, most states—both former Confederates and Unionist—had to adopt new constitutions or amend their existing bans on black suffrage. In the border region, this had begun with antislavery constitutions in West Virginia, Maryland, and Missouri. But throughout this region, Republicans were concerned about containing the damage that might come from a speedy restoration of political rights to disloyal people.

The border states featured the most apparent struggles over the electoral rights of white people for a simple reason—former Confederates came home to states that had stayed in the Union. Deciding how to treat these returning enemies presented an issue, especially whether to restore voting rights. Maryland gave perhaps 20,000 of its citizens to the Confederate army and Kentucky between 25,000 and 40,000.[9] Their arrival home ignited controversies over regaining property, exercising the franchise, and holding elective office. Should a former Confederate general officer like Bradley Johnson of Maryland vote for the next congressmen or president of the United States, while under a federal indictment for treason? Former rebels—by that meaning the men who had served in the Confederate army from Kentucky, Missouri, and Maryland—interpreted that the pardons from President Johnson had restored their civic rights. To be sure, they were no longer traitors subject to criminal prosecution, according to the national government. But they were not yet the equal of white Unionists. The nature of the federalist system dictated that the United States could forgive the rebels of treason, but it also meant that the individual states had to figure out what to do with them.

Republicans in the border region attacked this problem by trying to curtail the franchise from the known rebels and the stay-at-home traitors. Maryland and Kentucky joined Missouri in prohibiting former Confederates from casting ballots, as did the new state of West Virginia. We have already seen how Missouri handled this issue by disqualifying problematic voters for five years. Maryland attempted a similar course, although with more limited results, through a change in its constitution that used test oaths and a new voter registration system. West Virginia also instituted a voter registration system as a means to aid disfranchisement of traitors. Kentucky leaned on its expatriate act passed in 1862, which stripped state citizenship from anyone who had fought for the Confederacy or aided the rebellion. "Aided" included in this case, as it had during the war, exclamations of free speech: discouraging enlistments or promoting the success of the rebellion. But Kentucky featured the quickest transition toward re-enfranchising former Confederates. All of these states used similar means in that they established test oaths administered at polling places by either judges of elections or special registrars who had wide latitude in determining the loyalty of the voters who stood before them.[10]

In Maryland, Unionists tried to ensure loyalty at the polls through a voter registration law that established some 600 registrars of elections throughout the state—three for each precinct. Before Election Day, voters were to register themselves with these officials, but the agents of the state also sat at precincts to screen the people casting ballots. In the case of Maryland, the initial appointments for these public servants came under the administration of Governor Augustus Bradford, who was more in line with the Lincoln administration than his successor, Thomas Swann. But Bradford also admitted the daunting responsibility of appointing so many men whose character he could not know. To fill these positions, he had to rely on local people hired largely because of their political affiliation. This procedure reinforced partisanship and allowed local functionaries to decide individual cases without needing evidence.[11]

On Election Day, the first duty of the registrars was to enforce an oath of loyalty to the Constitution of the United States. The best guess is that the law was applied here—as with similar methods in other states—unevenly. Although the law required an oath of all persons coming to the polls, it is unlikely that Republican registrars questioned Republican voters rigorously, especially in an age when no secret ballot existed and most people from communities understood how their neighbors voted. Various elements came into play in disqualifying voters: serving in the Confederate army, leaving the state to set up residency in the Confederate States, giving countenance and support to the rebels, sending money to them, transmitting communications through the line, or declaring the desire for the triumph of the rebels. The work of the registrars was not necessarily finished with the oath, which, according to the governor, was not a "conclusive" test for loyalty. Even if persons took this pledge, a registrar could disqualify someone on the basis of personal knowledge or intuition. Public reputation of the prospective voter mattered, even if that reputation rested upon unsubstantiated rumors. In 1865, Bradford admitted that there was "no longer probably the same necessity for the strict exclusion from the rights of Citizenship of those who a short time since were reckoned a dangerous element in our midst—that the War is practically over, and that Secession orators are no longer dangerous, but will be overruled or neutralized by their more loyal neighbors."[12] But he and his political cronies viewed the law as a very necessary means of preventing rebels from taking over the government.

Hints appeared in newspapers that thousands were affected by the law, which must be taken seriously because of the partisanship surrounding this controversy. The *Sun* reported the opposition to the law by Montgomery Blair, Lincoln's former postmaster general, who tossed out the figure that one-half of the population was prevented from taking part in the affairs of government. A Virginia newspaper estimated that in 1865 a voting population in Baltimore that once was 35,000 would be around 12,000, a proportion supported by one historian.[13] But there were also signs of resistance, and poor enforcement, enabling people to circumvent the law. In the Twelfth Judicial Circuit, voters elected a Conservative to serve as circuit judge. The losing candidate on the Union ticket contested the election, claiming that many voted who were not registered. Another report estimated that illegal votes were cast in Somerset alone. In some districts the judges of elections had no list of certified voters to help them enforce the law. And the November election featured reports of fighting at several election polls in Cecil County; at other polls, judges and registrars were beaten.[14]

If the impact of the law on voting remains difficult to capture, its importance for postwar politics does not. The voter registration law became one of the ways in which the parties fought, and defined, their differences over Reconstruction. Unconditional Unionists urged the necessity of maintaining the Registry Law and indicated that they supported the Congress in its plans for Reconstruction that included proposed amendments to the Constitution. They were not, however, in favor of black suffrage and in one account flatly stated: "The subject of *Rebel suffrage* is one of vastly more importance than *negro suffrage*."[15] (This meant that neither political wing went on record for black suffrage.) They condemned the actions by the people who battled the measure and especially the actions of Governor Thomas Swann, who opposed the law and worked hard to limit its application. The governor appointed the registrars who administered the oaths, and Swann angered Radical Republicans by replacing Bradford's choices with officials who ignored the act. Unconditional Unionists looked upon this assault on voter registration as attempts to place in power the rebels who had tried to destroy the nation.[16] So-called Conservatives had tried to fight the law beginning in September 1865 but lost all the way through to the state Court of Appeals. By 1866, Governor Swann and numbers of others left the Union Party to join the Democrats. Democrats considered the voter registration act an odious attempt to disfranchise thousands of people with the ulterior motive of forcing through black suffrage. The middle ground, if one had truly existed, was rapidly disappearing from Maryland politics.[17]

Matters came to a head in late 1866. Swann attempted to increase his power over political appointees by removing two of Baltimore's police commissioners for alleged corruption and overt partisanship during elections. In the state's largest city, police commissioners had the job of selecting the judges of elections, and these men obviously leaned more to the Republican side. There was a standoff in which the commissioners hoped to overturn their removal by the governor, but they had to go before Swann for the hearing—a losing proposition. The autumn featured political violence again, with a riot at Hagerstown in late October resulting in the death of at least one man, maybe two, and the wounding of perhaps twenty. The accounts are notoriously sketchy and contradictory; however, the riot appears to have been the culmination of agitation since the public elected a "Rebel" mayor the prior spring. Once installed, Mayor William Biershing proposed to add additional police, a plan blocked by the town council composed of Unionists. Undaunted, the mayor raised funds from his constituency to hire a special police force that served his interests and that factored into the confrontation on October 22. A brawl broke out, escalating as the parties—"Johnsonites" and "Union men"—eventually traded fire. Republicans met in groups that appeared to foreshadow a nascent military organization, causing Swann to beg for federal soldiers to intercede. In a complicated series of events that included President Johnson trying to shuttle Grant off to Mexico in order to have a freer hand in Maryland, Grant saw behind the maneuvering, sent a military officer into the state to bring back information, and blocked the dispatching of soldiers. He also tried to personally negotiate a compromise by having Republican and Democratic election officers stationed at polls in Baltimore. Even that effort broke down; however, the balloting passed peacefully. In an understatement, northern newspapers characterized Maryland as a state in turmoil.[18]

Conservatives seized control with the 1866 elections, making it only a matter of time before they removed the portions of the Registry Law they had found repugnant. The balloting resulted in their winning fifty-three of eighty seats in the House of Delegates, a depressing setback for the champions of black equality. The result, one historian has observed, was considerable and, by our contemporary values, tragic: "For the first time since 1861, the friends of black progress, the supporters of emancipation, the Freedmen's Bureau Bill, and the Civil Rights Act, were out of office."[19] Over the next year, the state moved toward adopting a new constitution. That document stated that slavery would not be reestablished, and although black suffrage was not part of the provisions, African Americans were able to serve as witnesses in court, as jurors, and as public officials. Surprisingly, voter registration remained a part of the electoral process. Not surprisingly, the 1867 constitution purged the test oath as a requirement for casting a ballot. Suffrage was now open to virtually any white person, even former Confederates, but not for the African Americans who constituted the most loyal part of the potential electorate for the Republican cause. And they were being counted as full citizens for the purposes of representation, increasing the apportionment for white public officials who did not have to deliver as much as an ounce of pork to this portion of their constituency.[20]

In Kentucky, Republicans enjoyed less success in denying suffrage to traitors because of the state's political alignments. Republicans were on the defensive in the Bluegrass State. Partly because of government oppression of civil liberties and especially because of policies concerning black people, the state had gone overwhelmingly for McClellan in 1864. Conservative public officials were in place who opposed federal interference and congressional Reconstruction. As the war ended, the state contained three factions: Unconditional Unionists, Conservatives, and Democrats. The Unconditional Unionists contained the most Radical element, which had trouble earning wider support because of their willingness to work with federal authorities and more progressive stance on black rights. Democrats, meanwhile, openly welcomed former Confederates not only as voters but also as public officials. Conservatives for a brief time remained in between. They were old-line Whigs who increasingly hated the Radicals and their initiatives but were fearful of turning state power over to the men who had only recently quit killing its citizens in Union uniform. The Republicans repeatedly criticized the opposition as consisting of a party that bowed to ex-rebels, but the attempt to brand the opposition party as harboring a nest of traitors proved to be less effective than during the conflict.[21]

Not that they did not try. Radicals attempted to control the vote in the summer of 1865. In July, Major General John M. Palmer reminded the citizenry that Kentucky remained under martial law. Falling under close scrutiny were ex-rebel soldiers, whether or not paroled; guerrillas; persons who gave aid and comfort to the enemy, including supplies, money, information, or encouragement; and deserters who had not returned to the army. Palmer promised that civil authorities—not the military—would enforce the measures, but in subsequent speeches he made it clear that the army intended to help. And it did. In support, Governor Bramlette issued his own proclamation on July 19 that raised the old justification by Senator Jacob Howard of Michigan for interference by the military at precincts—to maintain the "purity" of the elective franchise. By no means a Radical, Bramlette was a Conservative moderate who actually supported the Thirteenth Amendment but was nervous about giving the reins of government to rebels. The governor reminded his constituents that voting required meeting the tests of the Expatriate Act, which stripped citizenship from anyone who had entered the military or civil service of the Confederate States, held a position with the Provisional Government (the rebel shadow government), or assisted the Rebels in any way. Voters had to swear an oath that they had not done these things since April 10, 1862.[22]

When Election Day came on August 7, 1865, the military stood guard at precincts, irritating Democrats and raising the eyebrows of some Republicans. After all, the federal law of the land at that moment was the February 5, 1865, act that prohibited the army from interfering in elections and that required troops to remain a mile away from precincts. Despite its contentious politics that put it at odds with the national congress, Kentucky could hardly be considered a rebel state under occupation. There was no justification for disobeying the law and placing troops at the polls—beyond, of course, dictating political power. According to reports, soldiers at various places held lists of names of people who should not vote. Persons on these lists who tried to make their way to the precinct sometimes faced interdiction by neighbors, who pointed them out to the soldiers. At Winchester, Kentucky, the lieutenant in command allegedly held a list of 124 names of people who should not vote. The interference by soldiers under General Palmer was so egregious that it elicited commentary even from a newspaper that did not support the Conservative cause. The *Cincinnati Commercial* denounced General Palmer who "has greatly exceeded his authority." The paper chastised the general for making stump speeches to single out favorable candidates and castigated him for "the obtrusive, illegal and unscrupulous use of the military power," which "has disgusted thousands of the friends of the constitutional amendment." It added: "If the integrity of the ballot-box in Kentucky under the laws of the State cannot be maintained without wholesale military operations, it would be better not to have any elections, and to put an end at once to civil government from the Kanawha to the Mississippi." The *New York Herald* joined the list of newspapers condemning Palmer. In October, Johnson declared an end to federal martial law in the state.[23]

The outrage from Conservatives and Democrats seems at first excessive. Yes, the military had tried to dictate the outcome, which should not be dismissed. But despite the manipulation of an election by a federal military officer, the non-Radicals had won. The results had been close, to be sure. Although Conservatives won the congressional vote—sending five of nine congressmen to Washington—the total majority for congress fell out as 57,502 Conservative to 54,008 Republican. Other races were tighter.[24] And Republican accounts claimed that people ignored the law by allowing former Confederates to vote. But this means that without Palmer's illegal interference, the non-Radicals carried the day even more handily, which should have cheered the Conservatives. Historians point to this time in the state's history as when the Radical impulse lost its hold and Conservatives took over, with repeal of the expatriation act quickly following. Yet, despite these successes, protests continued over the election. U.S. senator Garrett Davis of Kentucky led a contingent of prominent citizens to Washington to lay before the president "facts in connection with the military usurpations and outrages perpetuated by sanction of military commanders, on the day of the recent so-called election in Kentucky, setting at defiance, as it is alleged, all law and order, and boldly substituting the bayonet for the ballot."[25]

But there were reasons for concern. Despite winning the election, the Conservatives and Democrats had not quite come together, leaving the political situation somewhat unclear. Then there was the affront that came when soldiers refused to allow a citizen to cast a ballot. Robert H. Ball told such a story to the *Cincinnati Enquirer*. As he approached a precinct in Covington, Kentucky, two soldiers bracketed him on the left and right as an officer stood behind him. He was told to leave. Ball refused and wanted to submit his vote to the judges. The soldiers accused him of rejoicing at the death of President Lincoln, which he denied and asked to swear an oath on the subject. After some more words were exchanged, he backed down.[26] What felt, and functioned, like military occupation by a hostile force certainly undercut Radicals and their scant chances to move forward on black suffrage. On the other side of the political aisle, Conservatives understood that to protect their agenda, the federal military had to go.

Republicans refused to give up the fight over suffrage, although they had to switch from a state to a federal strategy. In May 1867, Conservatives in Kentucky increased their hold on the state victories during the congressional elections in which nine Democrats won. Republicans decided to contest the elections by attacking the loyalty of the men who had won. Remaining in place was the law from July 2, 1862, that required attorneys, federal employees, and elected officials to swear an oath of loyalty that they had never borne arms against the United States or provided aid or encouragement to the rebels. When the Congress met in July, Republicans led by John A. Logan and Ebon C. Ingersoll of Illinois moved to ban the Kentucky delegation from admission. Logan said he desired to protect the House from "contamination." He claimed that rebels returned to the state after the war to find that the law disfranchising them had been repealed in late 1865. "Then they undertook," Logan said, "to transfer their representation from the halls of Richmond, contaminated by treason, to the halls of Congress, which ought to be sanctified by loyalty."[27] The House refused admission of the representatives from Kentucky and sent the matter to the Committee on Elections for adjudication, although it quickly admitted one member from the Eighth District who had been a major in the Union army.[28]

For more than five months the Kentucky representatives lived in political limbo, as a congressional committee deliberated their ability to serve by assessing their loyalty to the United States. Witnesses lined up against them, swearing affidavits that attested to traitorous activities during the war of the six representatives under question. The case of L. S. Trimble provides an example. An incumbent, he had been reelected to another term in Congress in the spring of 1867. At a hearing on June 25, a J. T. Bollinger swore that during the war large quantities of groceries had made their way from northern territory to rebels at Camp Boon, which housed 10,000 Confederate soldiers. The opposition accused Trimble of making disloyal speeches that denounced the policies of the president, the Congress, and the people trying to suppress the rebellion. "His speeches," said Bollinger, "had such a poisonous effect on the people that recruiting for the federal army was almost entirely suspended, while enlistments for the confederate army were going on all the time." This was exactly the behavior that Lincoln in 1863 had targeted in his Corning Letter as requiring arrests. Bollinger also alleged that the May elections were not held in accordance with the law, claiming he had examined the poll books of ten precincts, which revealed persons who had been in the rebel army, or had aided the rebellion, served as election officers. As might be expected, Trimble vehemently denied the allegations.[29]

Ultimately, the political maneuvering only delayed the admittance of most of the delegation. There was no way to prevent duly elected officials from assuming their public office without evidence of corruption of the ballot, which never was advanced as an argument. In early December, Congress cleared three of the Democrats, who then expended energy in aiding their colleagues. By January, three more won their seats. Only one Radical was put into place and one other seat was left empty. The Kentucky legislature, meanwhile, followed up the controversy by passing resolutions decrying the interference by the Congress to decide qualifications for serving on factors that were not provided for in the Constitution.[30]

With the exception of Missouri and West Virginia, by 1867 most former Confederates in the border enjoyed the right to vote before their former slaves did; yet, for a brief moment after the war, thousands of white males had lost the franchise. If we use the most limited figures—35,000 in Missouri, 20,000 in West Virginia, 15,000 in Maryland—at least 70,000 former Confederates and disloyal residents were prevented from casting ballots.[31] This does not even count Kentucky, which presents a problem in calculating a figure because it featured the shortest duration of proscriptions against former Confederates and widespread resistance to the expatriate act. So for practical purposes, the round number of 100,000 might serve as a rough figure for disfranchisements. The numbers are estimates, undoubtedly flawed, but also possibly understated. They appear here to give a sense of proportion rather than an accurate measurement. All told, the policies worked in maintaining Republican regimes in only two of the states; however, white suffrage became a highly divisive issue that also contributed, along with black suffrage, to the erosion of a political middle ground.

If we raise our geographic sights just a little north of the border states, we find a bold experiment that—had court cases dictated otherwise—contained the theoretical potential to disfranchise roughly 200,000 white men from across the Union. Republicans in at least seven states capitalized on the federal law enacted March 3, 1865, that stripped rights of citizenship from deserters from the Union army and navy if they did not report for duty sixty days after President Lincoln's proclamation—a deadline that came on May 9. After that date, the men who had not turned themselves in to provost marshals, according to Lincoln's proclamation, "shall be deemed and taken to have voluntarily relinquished and forfeited their rights of citizenship and their rights to become citizens, and such deserters will be forever incapable of holding any office of trust or profit under the United States or of exercising any rights of citizen thereof."[32]

One study notes that five states moved to disfranchise deserters: Kansas, Pennsylvania, Wisconsin, New York, and Vermont. But this does not tell the whole story. An offhand reference in a newspaper indicated that Indiana and Ohio applied the policy at least haphazardly at election precincts. To an extent difficult to determine, additional states or perhaps localities may have taken advantage of the federal act without passing laws. Clearly, though, the returning deserters concerned many Unionists. In a report to the War Department in September 1865, Provost Marshal General Fry estimated that only 1,755 deserters earned a pardon under the president's proclamation, meaning more than 100,000 deserters from the army remained at large. This, however, did not include the thousands of draft resisters who failed to report—well over another 100,000—many of whom trickled back from sanctuary across the Canadian border into their former communities in the upper Midwest and Northeast. A couple of provost marshals remaining in communities asked to maintain the $30 reward for rounding up these men. They did not have enough administrative staff to regulate the situation even if they had resolved the question about the military's right to intervene when war no longer existed.[33]

Although part of the motivation behind such measures can be attributed to a cynical attempt to ensure a Republican edge in elections, deserters also provoked honest outrage. Just as returning Confederates in uniform jarred the eyes of Unionists in the border states, men who fled from military service, or left the country, seemed out of place at election precincts standing next to the veterans who had sacrificed themselves for the cause. In fact, it is hard to decide who was the more hated figure—Confederates or their sympathizers. Fry's letter to Stanton noted reports of friction between deserters and loyalists from numerous places, including New York, New Jersey, New Hampshire, Indiana, Pennsylvania, Ohio, Minnesota, and Wisconsin. The acting assistant provost marshal general for Maine reported that "complaints of deserters returning and taunting soldiers who have lost limbs in service are made from all parts of the State, but are more numerous from the Fourth and Fifth Districts."[34] With its strong Democratic base and a border that touched Canada, the *New York Tribune* was especially sensitive to this issue. "Do soldiers who did their duty want to be placed on a par with these traitors?" its columnist asked. "Why *should* they vote in a country that they chose to desert rather than defend?" In another column a month later, a writer urged that the states should deny suffrage to the bounty jumpers, skedaddlers, and runaways who hid in Canada. "The purity of the elective franchise" depended on it. The writer exhorted his readers to disfranchise "the Canadian branch of the Democratic party."[35]

Pennsylvania has left one of the clearer paper trails over disfranchising deserters that includes two cases in its Supreme Court, an act by its General Assembly, and a federally generated document used by the state's judges of elections to disqualify voters. Pennsylvania Republicans seized upon the federal law and Lincoln's proclamation to overturn an election for the state senate in the fall of 1865. In the Nineteenth Senatorial District embracing Franklin and Adams counties, incumbent Democrat Calvin M. Duncan squared off against Republican challenger David McConaughy. The first tallies declared that Duncan won reelection, but by a narrow margin of twenty-five votes. Inventive minds set about finding a way to challenge the outcome. At first, McConaughy and his supporters tried to claim the absentee ballots of thirty-one soldiers stationed in Texas but had to abandon that strategy when it was learned they had returned. What else could be done? No fraud or corruption of the ballot had occurred; at least nothing beyond the ordinary. The obvious remedy was the federal act banning deserters from voting. Not all deserters were Democrats, but everyone believed that most of the men who avoided the draft or fled from the military belonged to the party of Jackson. One can almost hear the fingers snap at the epiphany. When all was said and done, the Senate committee that adjudicated the matter threw out ninety-three of the votes for Duncan, claiming they were cast by deserters. A twenty-five-vote loss had become a sixty-eight-vote victory.[36]

Democrats greeted the decision with predictable outrage. The Senate committee had consisted of six Republicans and one Democrat, highlighting the partisan nature of the investigation. The losers cried foul, understandably, but they attacked the judgment with truly meaty constitutional arguments. The U.S. Constitution, they reminded, specifically forbids Congress from passing *ex post facto* laws, or legislation that makes an act illegal after it had been committed. The bulk of Union soldiers had deserted from the military before the law was passed in March 1865. Additionally, Democrats pointed out that the law punished people for crimes without due process. Criminals do suffer disfranchisement, but not until they have their day in court. To strip men of citizenship required their conviction before a military court at the very least, instead of through judges of elections determining guilt on the spot. Finally, Democrats accused the committee of setting aside Pennsylvania's election laws in favor of a federal act, which in their view overturned the state's exclusive authority to qualify voters and establish election procedures. The danger was clear for those who wanted to restrict the franchise to white freemen. The minority report of the lone Democrat on the senate committee said, "Is there any one so bold as to assert that Congress has the constitutional power to declare that none but negroes shall be allowed to vote in Pennsylvania, or that no white man shall be allowed to vote here until he has attained the age of thirty years?" If the national Congress could determine who could not vote, it also might say who could, putting black suffrage on the table for the North as well as the South.[37]

Democrats pushed forward a test case to stop disfranchising deserters. On October 10, 1865, Henry Reily handed his ballot to one of the judges of elections in Franklin County, ironically one of the counties represented by McConaughy. An election judge named Benjamin Huber refused to allow the vote because of the federal law disfranchising deserters. Reily sued, even though it was admitted that he had failed to report when drafted in July 1864. What about Lincoln's proclamation? Did Reily contact a provost marshal after that inducement? No. Had he furnished a substitute or paid a commutation fee to remain home legally? No again. So there was no dispute that he fit the description of the men targeted by the act of the U.S. Congress. According to the federal law, he deserved to lose the franchise.

The court ruled in favor of the deserter Reily, but employed a convoluted logic to get there. The 3-2 opinion recognized the right of the Congress to impose a draft on the country and to craft a law that punished deserters appropriately. Here is where it becomes tricky to follow. The majority dismissed the claim that the law was unconstitutional by interfering with the exclusive right of states to regulate elections. Justice William Strong said the act left in place the organic law of Pennsylvania, allowing officials to confer the right of suffrage as they pleased. Strong also declared that the law did *not* violate the U.S. Constitution's proscription against *ex post facto* laws. The people under question were not being punished for their act of desertion *before* March 3, 1865, but for their failure to report *after* the deadline specified in Lincoln's proclamation. It was their *continued* resistance that came under question.[38] However, the crucial interpretation coming from *Huber v. Reily*—the one that Democrats in Pennsylvania applauded—was that suspected deserters had to face a hearing in order to be disqualified.[39] For the moment, it appeared that Democrats had won a victory. They hoped that the decision would cause McConaughy to step down. As one newspaper crowed: "The pretext upon which he was admitted by a partisan committee is declared untenable, and all 'the props are knocked from under it.' Having, then no right to the seat, will he continue to hold on to it?"[40]

They guessed incorrectly. Pennsylvania Republicans—like their Democratic rivals—were incredibly resourceful when it came to partisan struggles. In fact, the Republicans considered this kind of maneuvering as out-Democrating the Democrats. McConaughy was a Republican attorney from Gettysburg. He had read for the law under Radical Thaddeus Stevens and earned fame for his efforts to establish the Gettysburg Battlefield Memorial Association, the first agency to supervise preservation and commemoration at the site, and for soliciting the artist Peter Rothermel to undertake a famous series of paintings on the Battle of Gettysburg. But he does not come down to history as a politician who won a postwar election by employing the definitions of wartime disloyalty.[41]

As he hit the senate floor at Harrisburg, McConaughy apparently provided some of the force behind amending the state's election laws to disfranchise deserters from the Union military during the Civil War. Democrats gave him the credit for the bill that eventually emerged. Whether he deserved this credit is uncertain, but the Pennsylvania legislature on June 4, 1866, pushed through a state law to disfranchise deserters. The statute referenced the federal act of March 3, 1865, and proclaimed that inspectors of elections risked misdemeanor charges if they allowed deserters to vote. The state of Pennsylvania also requested from the federal government a list of deserters that its judges of elections could use as prima facie evidence of guilt. The War Department complied with a "Descriptive List of Deserters," printed and distributed to courthouses in time for the fall 1866 balloting.[42]

From the newspaper record, the law appeared to influence some elections, although perhaps it is more accurate to say it cemented Republican victories in areas in which they had the political muscle to select judges of elections. As voters approached the precincts, the judges had the power to reject anyone who appeared on the list of deserters compiled by the provost marshal general's office. The document consisted of sheets of broadsides containing 274 pages of information on the roughly 30,000 men who deserted from Pennsylvania's infantry, artillery, and cavalry regiments.[43] Even if all of the deserters were disqualified, the impact might not have swayed many statewide elections: the 1866 gubernatorial race featured nearly 600,000 voters, although the victory margin was a close 17,000. Nonetheless, the measure was used most effectively in local races, such as for district attorney, where the quality of enforcement depended upon the partisan background of the evaluators. As one Philadelphia newspaper observed, "In Republican districts, where the election laws can be enforced, few, if any, of these disfranchised Democrats are allowed to vote. They are known, registered and challenged, and the law is thus vindicated. But in many Democratic districts little or no opposition is made to their votes, and there were probably several thousand votes of deserters cast for Judge Sharswood, last week, which were as illegal as if the voters had been subjects of Great Britain or China."[44]

It took another court challenge to end the practice. Edward McCafferty had made his way to an election precinct in Huntingdon County on October 9, 1866, or after the Pennsylvania Supreme Court's ruling. The three election judges—George Guyer, John C. Dickson, and Alexander Ale—denied him the ballot on the basis of his desertion from the federal army. McCafferty sued and lost in a lower court. But the higher court proved more hospitable. In *McCafferty v. Guyer et al.*, the majority opinion of a divided Pennsylvania Supreme Court unambiguously declared the state law that stripped deserters of citizenship as unconstitutional. McCafferty had met every qualification for voting. He had not been convicted by a court-martial for treason. That the legislature declared him guilty, according to the majority opinion, placed that governing body above the organic law of the state. For all practical purposes, the time of the deserter law had passed.[45]

Again, Pennsylvania was not the only state to search for such solutions to the problem of dealing with wartime disloyalty in the Reconstruction era. New York Republicans eyed the policy approvingly. Ohio attempted to strike the word "white" from its voting requirements, while prohibiting "such persons as have borne arms in support of any insurrection or rebellion against the Government of the United States, or have fled from their places of residence to avoid being drafted into the military service thereof, or have deserted the military or naval service of said Government in the time of war, and had not subsequently been honorably discharged from the service." But the measure failed to become part of the state's constitution.[46] By the time that Pennsylvania's Supreme Court cases resolved the issue in the Keystone State, the strategy withered on the vines of northern Republican intentions.

The point remained that the suffrage rights of the wartime disloyal remained an issue after Appomattox—not only for former rebels but also for the stay-at-home traitors. How to control the ballot box was a concern by Republicans at state and national levels, during a time when political power and individual liberties were being redefined. Republicans worried about the endurance of their party, which was a little more than a decade old and had lost the central ingredient keeping together its various factions—to prevent slavery's expansion. The concerns over voting by former Confederates, and the lack of voting by former slaves, found their way into the Fourteenth Amendment. But before arriving there, we need to add a couple of ingredients to the postwar struggles for power and the desire to punish alleged traitors.

Debt and Treason

On his fourteen-week tour of the South in 1865, northern journalist Sidney Andrews encountered hard feelings among the former rebels at the constitutional convention in Milledgeville, Georgia. It was early November. Other southern state conventions had handled their business already—not heartfelt enough to suit Radical Republicans, but satisfactorily enough for conservative leaders in the North. The conventions had been mandated by the president for readmission of the rebellious states to the Union. The former Confederate states had to elect delegates who created new constitutions that repealed ordinances of secession, outlawed slavery, and repudiated the debt amassed during the war. In Georgia, Andrews ran into an angry group of politicians who hated to surrender their investments in the Confederacy or their state. When he first arrived, Andrews estimated that the delegates favored assumption of debts by a 3-1 margin, which meant ignoring the federal mandate. A Judge Simmons of Gwinette County told his colleagues that they had submitted "to a disgrace deep enough and dark enough already." He wanted the convention to ask the federal government for directions so that a decision to abandon the loans could be blamed on external force. He thundered: "*Let us repudiate only at the express command of military power; and then, when we are again in the enjoyment of our rights in the Federal Union, and are once more a free and independent sovereignty, let us call another Convention and assume the whole debt.*"[47]

Eventually, Georgia repudiated the war debt, but it took a strong telegram from President Johnson and twelve days of further wrangling at the convention to do so. Even then, there were a significant number of holdouts in a vote that came in at 135-117. Georgia was not alone in grudgingly accepting this stipulation for reunion. The debts of the Confederate states collectively totaled $54 million. The Mississippi convention had met in August and refused to repudiate the debt. South Carolina met in September and adjourned without complying; the governor never mentioned the issue in his instructions. In October, North Carolina triggered Johnson's intervention because of its sluggishness in this area. He explicitly told provisional governor William Woods Holden, "Every dollar of the State debt created to aid the rebellion against the United States *should be repudiated, finally and forever.* The great mass of the people should not be taxed to pay a debt to aid in carrying on a rebellion which they, in fact, if left to themselves, were opposed to." Those who had opposed the United States "must meet their fate." Georgia's convention received the directive from Johnson on October 29, which helped tip the scales toward repudiation. By the following summer, a congressional inquiry revealed that most of the former Confederate states had complied; however, South Carolina was stalling, and Mississippi indicated it had instructed its comptroller not to pay out money unless specifically ordered by the legislature. There was no clear sign of repudiation there.[48]

Whitelaw Reid was not convinced that the legislation represented the true sentiments of the people in Georgia and the Gulf states. An editorial correspondent of Greeley's *New York Tribune*, Reid was one of the many northerners touring the defeated South to check the pulse of their former enemies. In Atlanta, he encountered indignation over the law. One man reportedly said, "'If the Confederate debt isn't honestly due, no debt in the world ever was. If we've got to repudiate that, we may as well help the Democrats [in the North] repudiate the debt on the other side too. What's fair for one is fair for the other.'" In Louisiana, Reid found more of the same. "Politicians, whose status depended on the admission of the Louisiana members to Congress, professed great readiness to pay the National debt; but I did not hear one private citizen make a similar expression," he observed. "They did their best in the rural districts to discredit the National currency; till the military interfered, they did the same in some of the city banks."[49]

By the fall of 1865, positions on the war debt served as a barometer for more than finances: it had become part of the definition of treason and loyalty. Republicans in the North made it a part of their political positions. They watched closely for how ex-Confederates responded to the presidential edict that reunion depended in part on their repudiating the debts amassed in the war. Greeley's *New York Tribune* preached forgiveness of the traitors in general, but rejected clemency in this area. "The Rebel debt," the columnist maintained, "is one of the important issues that 'remain of this contest.' To us, this debt is an abomination; to the Southern leaders, a question of honor. They mean to make us pay it if possible."[50] Another New York newspaper reported that former Confederates who vacationed in Saratoga Springs accepted the end of slavery and reunion, but they talked openly about "the federal government assuming and paying the rebel debt, with the alternative of a repudiation of the national debt." In response, a local Union League passed a resolution proclaiming as a traitor anyone who adopted such a position. And in Ohio, former governor David Tod declared that the Democratic Party could not be trusted—that he believed it would repudiate the national debt, imperiling the livelihoods of soldiers' wives and widows. He called it the duty of every patriot to stand by the Union party.[51]

This resistance must be placed into perspective. There is little doubt that the situation stuck in the craw of the men tied to the Confederate debt. Judging by the reactions of some of the white South, repudiation served as a punishment for treason. Their finances melted away overnight, intensifying the problems of a capital-starved South that then had to fall back on a compromise labor arrangement of farming by shares. But some of this recalcitrance undoubtedly represented exaggeration by Republicans, like Reid, who were inclined to cry wolf to break the political power of the former slaveocracy. Not every southern white opposed repudiation. Unionists in the South pressed President Johnson to keep up the pressure. Additionally, for those who had not purchased state or Confederate bonds, repudiating the debt provided relief. They would not face additional taxes to pay off the loans held, as one of the Georgia delegates said, "in the hands of men, fat and sleek, who never saw the forefront of battle, and were careful to keep out of harm's way in the hour of conflict."[52] The disagreement over renunciation of rebel war debts launched the first salvos in the continuing ruptures within southern politics concerning stay laws to protect impoverished people against foreclosures in new constitutions during Radical Reconstruction.

What concerned Republicans was what Whitelaw Reid had confronted—the possibility that newly empowered southern Democrats would join with their northern colleagues to repudiate the national debt. The Civil War had caused an expansion in the country's debt load from $65 million in 1860 to about $2.7 billion in 1865. To fund the war, Congress had taken the nation off the gold standard, created greenbacks, instituted the Internal Revenue Bureau, and passed excise taxes of all kinds. Jay Cook had engineered a bond effort that successfully raised money for the government, embracing even small investors. Changing course at this moment threatened real harm to the American economy, and to the loans held by nations outside of the United States. Republicans heard murmurings from Democrats to eliminate the debt as a solution to the problem rather than increasing the burden on poor people to help pay it off through taxes. In the South, ex-Confederates were not very happy that they had to repudiate their expenses while absorbing their share of the northern debt load.

When Republican Carl Schurz made his now famous report on the conditions in the South, he spent a portion of his time highlighting this problem. President Johnson had chosen the German native and major general in the Union army to tour the South beginning in July, especially the Gulf states, to report on the sentiments of the former Confederates for reconciliation. It was a curious choice, to say the least. Schurz was an anti-slavery Republican who believed in black suffrage. Johnson was a conservative War Democrat who believed in freedom for black people to break the hold of the slaveocracy but not in black equality. Johnson was looking for ammunition to welcome white southerners back into the Democratic Party. Schurz was bound to craft a document that Johnson hated, which is exactly what happened.[53] However, the document became important for Republicans in Congress who used it as part of the argument to end the lenient policy of Johnson with the rebel traitors. Schurz said he had encountered little national feeling on the part of former rebels and noted: "Treason does, under existing circumstances, not appear odious in the south. The people are not impressed with any sense of its criminality."[54]

Although most of the material dealt with the nature of race relations and the status of black people in the former Confederacy, Schurz shared attitudes about the national debt and how the rebels restored to power figured to vote on the subject. The national debt, according to Schurz, "is, and will continue to be, very unpopular in the south." What he wrote next sounds preposterous, although he did hear such opinions expressed. His conversations with ex-Confederates, both politicians and ordinary people, led him to the conclusion that they were more inclined to ask the government for compensation for their slaves and for damage done by the Union armies "than, as the current expression is, to 'help paying the expenses of the whipping they have received.'" Schurz claimed that newspapers, public speeches, and election documents promised that readmission of the rebels to Congress would result in an attempt to lobby for compensation for emancipated slaves. He was not alone in this assumption. In February 1866, Senator Henry Wilson, a Radical from Massachusetts, argued for an amendment to the Constitution that prohibited the compensation to masters for emancipated slaves. He claimed, without substantiation or citing an authority, that former masters in Georgia and Louisiana maneuvered for such an outcome. Did they wish such a thing had come about? Undoubtedly. Did they expect it to happen? This was probably dubious. Politicians may have blustered in this fashion, but the movement had very little chance of gaining traction. But Schurz was on target when he said: "It may be assumed with certainty that those who want to have the southern people, poor as they are, taxed for the payment of rebel debts, do not mean to have them taxed for the purpose of meeting our national obligations."[55]

For Radicals the solution for this problem was apparent: suffrage for black men. In September 1865, Senator Charles Sumner addressed the Republican State Convention meeting in Worcester, Massachusetts. Titled "National Security and the National Faith," the speech urged participants to remember that the work of emancipation would not be completed until the Black Codes disappeared from the South. Varying by states, these codes allowed ex-Confederates to coerce blacks' labor, control their travel, and prevent meetings among African Americans, among other repression. To many Republicans, the regulations replicated the control of black people under slavery. But there was much more to this particular talk. The subtitle best captures the thrust of Sumner's speech: "Guaranties for the National Freedman and the National Creditor." National Security involved twin goals. To protect the national debt from collusion of rebels with northern Democrats—the kind of alliance prophesied by Whitelaw Reid—required suffrage for black males who had proved their support of the nation.[56]

At one point in the speech, the senator created a sensation as he dramatically connected the two goals. He led into the demonstration with, "Repudiation of our bonds, whether to the national creditors or to the national freedmen, would be a shame and a crime; and the national faith is irrevocably plighted to the two alike." Then he held up in each hand an important national document that he flourished for the crowd. "Here is the Proclamation," he said, displaying Lincoln's Emancipation Proclamation, "and here is a Treasury Note." It was a powerful presentation: emancipation in one hand and the nation's financial security in another; a two-fisted declaration to continue the fight for black equality. Sumner privileged emancipation as the more substantive document, but he considered the treasury note as one of the means for moving forward as a strong nation. Later in the talk, he also indicated that one of the means of achieving this came through black suffrage in order to give greater support to the national cause. But he also advocated limiting certain rebels from voting. "They must not be voted for, and they must not vote. On this principle I take my stand."[57] Along these lines, Benjamin Butler, the War Democrat turned Republican, employed a clever argument for the adoption of black suffrage in order to protect white investors. "It is for the interest of bondholders in the United States that the negro should vote," he said. "Your seven-thirties are worth a premium of ten per cent if the negro has the ballot. There will be neither fear of assumption of the rebel credit, or the repudiation of our own, from his vote."[58]

Clearly, the Radicals mustered every argument they could find not only for enfranchising black men but also for blocking the admission of rebel representatives to Congress. Once the conventions in the South did their business, and Johnson recognized them as reconstructed states, it meant a flood of Democrats into the legislature of the United States. But even more meaningful were the public offices at home filled by former Confederates: constables, sheriffs, magistrates, county judges, district attorneys, councilmen, election judges, state legislators, or the men who daily determined for the freedpeople where to walk, how to get paid for work, how to gain justice for the killing of family members. As is well known, the Congress blocked the seating of representatives from the South as the session opened in December 1865. Republicans were trying to wrest control of Reconstruction from the president. In their efforts, treason provided a useful device. As one newspaper stated, "The members from the Southern States who will come to Washington asking for seats in Congress next winter, will be in sympathy with all there is left of treason at the South. And it is plain now to the dullest apprehension, that on all questions of finance, tariff, revenue they will act,—if they are admitted—as the representatives of people who have been whipped and are called upon to pay the cost of their own subjugation."[59] This was smart. The argument introduced a way to conceive of the benefits of black suffrage for white people, especially the small investors in the Union cause.

Yet it is doubtful that the rhetoric convinced Democrats—the dock workers who thumped shoulders with opponents at election precincts and who did worse with African Americans most times, the politicians who harped on the prospects of racial amalgamation in the new era, the amateur constitutionalists who contested the legality of emancipation and the currency, the businessmen who felt the same, and the political philosophers—all of whom made drawing the racial line either with violence or with words a high art form. They would not be swayed by a leading, detested Radical holding up two pieces of paper that they considered to be both unconstitutional and damaging to their interests. This reasoning by the likes of Sumner represented preaching to the Republicans: a way to reinforce solidarity of party when antislavery had disappeared as a cohesive force and when the extremes of the party needed the moderates to hold off an alliance of Democrats across the sectional divide.

Debt and the ability of rebels to recover wartime losses continued as an issue for several years after the war. In fact, some of the boldest legal statements about the criminal behavior of the rebels and secession came in the U.S. courts over questions of recovering wartime financial losses. Here, Salmon P. Chase reentered the story. In the literature of Reconstruction, he holds due credit for denying the legality of secession in *Texas v. White*, a case in which the federal government tried to recover bonds issued in the 1850s that had been sold by agents in Texas during the war to fund supplies for the Confederacy. In this 1869 ruling, the chief justice upheld the supremacy of the Union and, in no uncertain terms, declared secession illegal.[60]

It was not the first time he had grappled with such matters, however. In 1867 he had undercut the legitimacy of the Confederate government in *Shortridge v. Macon*, a circuit court decision that received coverage across the country. Pennsylvanians sued a North Carolina man who tried to get out of paying money borrowed before the war because the note had been seized as part of the Confederate government's sequestration act. T. B. Macon declared that because the Confederate government compelled him to turn over his debt to it, that he had fulfilled the payment to the Pennsylvanians. Chase, however, declared that Macon owed payment. The reason: the war against the United States had been treason. It did not matter that a rebellion had grown to a size considered to be a civil war; war levied against the United States constituted treason no matter the scale. Mercy, or the lack of prosecutions, came down to political discretion as the government worked for restoration and conciliation. According to the law, as Chase defined it, the rebels had committed treason against the United States.[61]

Northern newspapers invariably trumpeted the opinion by Chase as important because it told people who had lived within the rebellious states that they had committed treason against the United States. Chase's opinion did not rely upon Lincoln's notion of preventative arrests or the president's belief in attacking speech that may or may not have discouraged enlistments. The chief justice appropriately cited the sections of the Constitution that declared treason as levying war against the United States, not conspiring or plotting against the nation. By the standards set in the Constitution, it was clear to him that the highest crime against the nation-state had been committed by the rebels. It was not a bad ruling to have on the table as northern Republicans moved to institute a congressional solution to Reconstruction that included renewed military occupation of the South, setting aside the recognized governments, and calling for new constitutions that allowed for black suffrage and the ratification of the Fourteenth Amendment.

A letter that Chase wrote to Horace Greeley—who had publicly chastised the chief justice for this ruling—was even more pointed. The newspaperman had claimed that the opinion denounced opposition to the government similar to the American Revolution. Chase responded: "How could you! / Don't the Constitution say, what shall constitute 'treason.'

Isn't it 'Levying war'? Didn't the rebels 'levy war'? Didn't they, then 'commit treason?'" He saw no middle ground between a de facto government and a "treasonable combination of rebels in arms." Again, Chase believed in the merits of noting the difference between the law and the political process of reconciliation. The rebels could be considered traitors, but that did not mean the government had to take action. Clemency was a political decision—not a legal one—and represented how modern, civilized nations dealt with such matters. In this regard, Chase thought that Congress and the president had been liberal.[62]

What bears remembering is not that repudiation of the rebel debt constituted the principal issue compelling support for hard measures against the former rebels. It remained in the background of larger concerns over liberty and how to maintain the gains of a war against treason and disunion. But it provided a deeper context to the issues of loss and loyalty than has been represented by scholars. It also continued the wartime practice of considering the rebels guilty of treason without trials. Although losing their money and paying for the Union war debt irked the rebels, judging by the reactions of former Confederates during the ratification of the Fourteenth Amendment, more important struggles captured their attention, especially the power play evident in the sections that dealt with representation in Congress and who could hold public office. In sections 2 and 3 resided methods to limit the power of the former slaveocracy—interference in southern voting qualifications and restrictions on state officeholders that may have won approval from people such as Lydia Maria Child, who believed in withholding executions in favor of depriving traitors of their power.

Apportionment and Public Office

Early in 1866 Representative Thaddeus Stevens of Pennsylvania asked his Republican colleagues to solve a math problem. Stevens was a Radical—at home with the concept of black equality. But in this speech, he played to the anti-Confederate sentiments within his listeners. As many northerners realized, freedom for the enslaved had increased the political influence of the old Slave Power, the traitorous slaveocracy that had launched the war against the United States. Emancipation rendered the three-fifths clause for determining representation moot, adding to the potential power of the rebels. By his reckoning, Stevens estimated that the former slave states gained thirteen seats in Congress by adding two-fifths of a person for each of the freedmen and -women who previously had been counted as three-fifths while enslaved. This increased the number of slave-state congressmen from seventy to eighty-three. Stevens then raised the prospect of these former rebels aligning themselves with the traitorous Democratic Copperheads of the North. Republicans expected this to happen: it replicated the alliance from the antebellum era and provided northern Democrats with their only scenario for overcoming the national Republican majority. If they managed to clasp partisan hands across the bloody chasm, the results would cause harm. "Their eighty-three votes," Stevens warned, combined "with the Representatives of the Five Points [Democrats from New York] and other dark corners, would be sufficient to overrule the friends of progress here, and this nation would be in the hands of secessionists at the very next congressional election and at the very next presidential election." Within a few years, he prophesied, the Republicans could lose their majority.[63]

Math problems generally contain a solution, and Stevens offered one. Despite his belief in full political equality for everyone, at this particular moment his solution could not involve black suffrage. Not yet. In early 1866 the white votes did not exist nationally to push through an amendment to the Constitution to franchise black men, not with the border states and plenty of northern states resisting the proposition. Between 1865 and 1868, Wisconsin, Minnesota, Connecticut, Michigan, Ohio, and Nebraska all defeated proposals for franchising black males.[64] Support for what became the Fifteenth Amendment—which would prohibit disqualifying voters on the basis of race—congealed later, a response to continued rebel resistance to the president's lenient Reconstruction, to violence against the freedpeople and white Republicans, to the South's rejection of the Fourteenth Amendment, and to the open combat between the Congress and the president. But if black suffrage proved too difficult to accomplish in early 1866, undercutting the power of the former slaveocracy did not. To solve his math problem, Stevens argued for an equation that became popular in Republican quarters. If the former Confederacy failed to grant suffrage to all of its qualified male residents, then the United States should reduce their representation in Congress by a similar proportion. Such a result meant their eighty-three seats in the House dwindled to between forty-five and forty-eight. Implement this approach, and Stevens believed: "If a State abuses the elective franchise and takes it from those who are the only loyal people there, the Constitution says to such a State, you shall lose power in the halls of the nation, and you shall remain where you are, a shriveled and dried-up nonentity instead of being the lords of creation, as you have been, so far as America is concerned, for years past."[65]

Apportionment was not the only subject put forward. The Fourteenth Amendment took shape from myriad agendas, many of them conflicting. Historian Eric Foner has noted that by January 1866 no fewer than seventy constitutional amendments had been introduced. However, the problem presented by the three-fifths clause captured immediate attention and became a central issue connected to protection of black people in the former Confederacy and to limiting the power of insurrectionists. As Representative Roscoe Conkling of New York put it, "Shall the death of slavery add two fifths to the entire power which slavery had when it was living? Shall one white man have as much share in the Government as three other white men merely because he lives where blacks outnumber whites two to one?"[66] Even business showed concern over how rebels in Congress could menace the retiring of the national debt. *The Nation* considered them to be "determined repudiationists." It added, "It would hardly be a safe thing for the national credit to have such a body of men in Congress, reinforced as they would probably be, by a considered number of Northern men ready to go for at least qualified repudiation."[67]

When Senator William Pitt Fessenden issued the report of the Joint Committee on Reconstruction in June 1866, the subject of treason and representation provided a significant part of the rationale for why the Constitution needed amending. The committee had formed in December 1865 to gather testimony about the conditions within the South, the loyalty of the rebels, and the treatment of the freedpeople. Consisting of fifteen members, only three of them Democrats, the members heard testimony from more than a hundred witnesses including politicians, generals, and citizens from both North and South. Robert E. Lee was called before the committee to testify. Questions invariably dealt with the loyalty of the former rebels—whether they would accept the national government wholeheartedly, whether they would work peacefully with former slaves. The answers were not encouraging, causing the committee to recommend five measures in what became consolidated into the Fourteenth Amendment. Fessenden, a senator from Maine who authored the report, was not a Radical but a centrist Republican. Yet the language he composed laid out in no uncertain terms that the Confederate South had brought any and all government sanctions against itself because the rebels had committed treason. They had seceded from the government, seized federal property, killed large numbers of loyal people, and yielded not because they believed in restoration of the Union but because they could resist no longer. Consequently, the government had every right to exclude the insurrectionists from Congress. Although the rebellion failed, the report asserted "the battle may be still fought out in the legislative halls of the country. Treason, defeated in the field, has only to take possession of Congress and the cabinet." Such a possibility needed to be prevented.[68] Implied treason remained alive as a rationale for punishing the rebels.

The report explained why the committee considered section 2 of the proposed amendment necessary. Section 1 had established birthright citizenship and equal protection for everyone before the law. Section 2 implemented what Stevens and others had presented as a solution to the problem of apportionment: a reduction in southern representation if adult males were wrongfully prevented from voting. Fessenden noted that defeat had increased the political power of the insurrectionary states. "The increase of representation necessarily resulting from the abolition of slavery," the report indicated, "was considered the most important element in the questions arising out of the changed condition of affairs, and the necessity for some fundamental action in this regard seemed imperative." It continued: "It did not seem just or proper that all the political advantages derived from their becoming free should be confined to their former masters, who had fought against the Union, and withheld from themselves, who had always been loyal." Slavery had created a white oligarchy adverse to the spirit of republican institutions. The continuing dominance of that class was anticipated. In response, the committee adopted what it termed a persuasive measure to induce states to adopt full suffrage. That was the ultimate goal.[69]

Along similar lines, Republicans intended to halt the practice of the white South electing former rebels to federal office. In December 1865 traitors entered the national legislative halls. Moderates and Radicals alike were outraged to find former Confederates—especially Vice President Alexander Stephens—laying their credentials on the table for admission to the House and Senate even though they could not honestly have taken the loyalty oath required of public officials since July 1862. "Professing no repentance, glorying apparently in the crime they had committed," and clinging to the belief in secession, these men should not have a voice in national affairs. To prevent this, the committee recommended a third section of the amendment which banned from public office the people who had been elected before the war, or who had served in the judiciary, and then engaged in insurrection.[70]

Politicians were not the only ones expressing sentiments to punish treason by limiting the political power of rebels and protecting loyal citizens through suffrage. A petition to the Committee on the Judiciary in March 1866 from 151 citizens from Bucksport, Maine, expressed alarm that the conditions in the South rendered insecure the lives of loyal people, whether white or black. "They therefore pray your honorable bodies to impose such conditions upon the Rebel States, as shall punish treason—at least with ineligibility to office and loss of power, and reward loyalty with confidence and honor; and which shall demand as an evidence of sincere loyalty and good faith, on the part of those States, the abolition of all distinctions in their constitutions and laws, on account of color or race." Similar statements came from 119 people in Chester, Pennsylvania, and 37 petitioners from Bridgewater, Massachusetts.[71] Undoubtedly, these represented Republican wishes.

It took some doing to hammer out an approach to limit the political power of former Confederates. The apportionment resolution emerged as one of two proposals for amendments to the Constitution from the Joint Committee on January 15, 1866. The initial paragraph contained the germ of the ideas to provide equal protection for all citizens, which became part of section 1 in a revised form. But the second paragraph failed to move forward. It had explicitly stated: "Whenever, in any State, the elective franchise shall be denied or abridged on account of race or color, all persons of such race or color shall be excluded from the basis of representation."[72] The Senate had rejected the wording, with members from both sides of the aisle finding fault, although for different reasons.

Senator Edgar Cowan, a conservative Republican from Pennsylvania, characterized the solution as an unconstitutional application of treason. "Rebellion is treason; treason is a crime, and ought to be punished," he said. "But can Congress inflict that punishment?" No, he answered. The Constitution prohibited bills of attainder, meaning legislative declarations of guilt for treason without conducting a trial. The senator claimed that the apportionment clause, if passed, represented "a bill which of itself inflicts this deprivation of right upon the people of eleven states as a punishment for their alleged treason, which is a species of attainder." He then offered a novel, if totally impractical, idea about how to handle the traitors who showed up in Congress. Try them individually for treason. Hanging a few might discourage others from following. Needless to say, he had few supporters.[73]

Congressman Andrew J. Rogers of New Jersey became one of the first Democrats to speak out against the amendment. He was the lone member of the Joint Committee to vote against the proposal before it went to Congress. He claimed the amendment infringed upon the reserved rights of a state to qualify voters. Rogers reminded his readers that it was a state right to determine the requirements for suffrage, factors such as age, length of residence, race, and so on. He also claimed that the clause hurt states that contained a significant population of African Americans, causing those with a black majority to lose half of their representation. But then he turned his sights on the North and reminded representatives that the proposal affected more than the former Confederacy. New York, because it did not allow black suffrage, would lose seats in Congress under the provision. This was a reality for more than the Empire State. Only a handful of northern states franchised African Americans. Later he added, "Unnaturalized persons, women, and persons under twenty-one years old, cannot vote, yet they are all to be counted in the basis of representation. Why not exclude such persons from the basis of representation, unless they are allowed to vote?"[74]

It was a cogent question, one that Republicans had considered but then abandoned. Basing representation on voters, rather than total population, had been proposed by representatives, including Thaddeus Stevens. But this was dropped fairly quickly when it became clear that northern states stood to lose seats in Congress. New England had a higher proportion of females to males because of western migration. So it would suffer a decline of representation if only voters factored into apportionment. Plus, the North wanted to count its nonvoting immigrant residents for representation. The final amendment stated, "Representatives shall be apportioned among the several states according to their respective numbers, counting the whole number of persons in each state"—not voters, not citizens, but *persons*. That meant the North could use all immigrants who came to the country's shores even if they did not have U.S. citizenship or the franchise. More than 80 percent of the foreigners coming into the country had established themselves in the non-slave-owning states. Stevens knew this. In his speech on January 31, 1866, he estimated—if he had been rightly informed about the numbers—that the North benefited from fifteen to twenty representatives owing to the foreign population. He thought that there were three or four from New York alone. The precise number was not the point: northern Republicans used every means to enhance their advantage over the southern insurrectionists.[75]

One other punishment was attempted that mirrored what had taken place in the state of Missouri, whose constitution had denied the franchise to rebels for five years. When the consolidated Fourteenth Amendment emerged in late April, one of five sections handed down a stiff penalty against former Confederates. Instead of restricting insurrectionists from holding public office, section 3 in the consolidated amendment disfranchised all persons who had participated in the late rebellion against the

United States, whether soldiers or citizens. Former Confederates would be prevented from voting for congressmen or presidential electors until July 4, 1870. This was a bold policy designed to break the power of the former slaveocracy and guarantee Republican dominance in national affairs. Despite this punitive action, as he opened debate on the measure on May 8, Stevens called it "too lenient," preferring to see the time period extended to 1876. "Here is the mildest of all punishments ever inflicted on traitors."[76]

As he anticipated, this portion of the amendment received heated discussion as the House considered it on May 10. Even fellow Republicans, who were generally supportive, wondered if this policy interfered with the president's pardon power. At the least, it created confusion. Future president James A. Garfield predicted that many would question whether the act nullified the pardons or if the penalty did not apply to those who had taken advantage of clemency. If the latter held true, then it was hardly worth the effort to frame the section because of the extent of Johnson's leniency. As other objections came, Stevens mounted a defense, proclaiming, "Give us the third section or give us nothing. Do not balk us with the pretense of an amendment which throws the Union into the hands of the enemy before it becomes consolidated." He repeated that he considered the ban on rebel voting too lenient. "Not only to 1870, but to 18070, every rebel who shed the blood of loyal men should be prevented from exercising any power in the Government. That, even, would be too mild a punishment for them." Evoking a vivid image, he declared that he did not wish to sit next to a congressman whose garments smelled of the blood of slain Unionists. The measure passed the House quite handily—128 to 37.[77]

Disfranchising the rebels found little support in the Senate. The proposal was recognized as containing the potential to scuttle the amendment during ratification. Instead, the upper chamber put into place the proscription against former Confederates holding elective positions, which required a two-thirds vote of the entire Congress to remove the disability. Moderate politicians like James G. Blaine, Republican congressman from Maine, comforted themselves with the rationale that this provision, which did not have an end date, might prove more punitive than stripping rebels of the franchise only until 1870. It was, after all, already 1866. The disfranchisement provision had a shelf life of only four more years at best, and it was highly probable that it would take a year at least to move through ratification and implementation. Practically speaking, that meant excluding rebels from voting for no more than three years. But holding the rebels accountable for an undetermined length of time offered a more enduring punishment. This reasoning, though creative, likely represented a man trying to oversell the merits of a less punitive course.[78] The third section did, however, skirt the constitutional edges by announcing that Congress, and not the president, held the power to lift such sanctions. It was one more attempt by congressional Republicans to constrict the reach of President Johnson. Ironically, this part of the Fourteenth Amendment did have a long life. In the 1970s, Congress finally employed its power to restore citizenship rights to Jefferson Davis and Robert E. Lee.

The Senate had read public attitudes correctly. The portions of the Fourteenth Amendment that restrained the political power of traitors, rather than disfranchising them, created the most discussion and controversy at the time. An outright ban on voting by Confederates had little political support. Legal scholars and historians justifiably spend most of their energy on dissecting section 1, which established birthright citizenship and created the national guarantee of equality before the law. That part of the amendment has generated the most court opinions involving personal liberties, and it provided an extremely important foundation for the country's legal interpretations for federal intervention in areas of discrimination and human rights. However, at the time, section 1 raised little furor; nor did section 4, which reinforced that states could not assume or pay any of the debt incurred by the Confederacy during the rebellion. In 1868, southern whites entertained little hope that they could win reimbursement for Confederate investments or for slaves. More southern white people were interested in the damage caused by sections 2 and 3 of the consolidated amendment—those dealing with limiting representation in the rebel states without recognizing black suffrage and the exclusion of rebels from public office.

Nowhere was this truer than in the former Confederacy. One study of the ratification debates over the Fourteenth Amendment in the southern states has found that sections 2 and 3 garnered the most invective commentary from southern whites. White southerners shrugged at section 1—which clarified birthright citizenship and protection for all before the law—as simply legitimating the "bastard" civil rights bill of 1866. Its acceptance was a foregone conclusion. Section 2, which dealt with representation, struck the white South as "Hobson's choice," meaning no choice at all. According to legend, Thomas Hobson was a livery stable owner in England who told clients to take the horse in the first stall or none at all. In the case of postwar Confederates, black suffrage was Hobson's choice in the Fourteenth Amendment. It was a take-it-or-leave-it proposition. Take it and the South, by Thaddeus Stevens's count, gained eighty-three seats in Congress. Leave it, and southern representation fell to around forty-six. Either way, northern Republicans won, especially as they factored whatever increases they received from immigrants into the equation for political power. It was Hobson's choice: take it or leave it. And the power structure of the South chose—to leave it. None of the former Confederate states consented to the amendment during the first voting. Five of the eleven eventually endorsed the provision by 1868, but only after they had been forced to rewrite constitutions to allow for black suffrage and accept the amendment as part of the bargain for restoration of their state governments.[79]

The third section, which prohibited traitors from holding public office, may have been the most objectionable clause to southern whites. It not only removed incumbents from office but also paved the way for opponents of the Confederates to move into positions of power.[80] This was tantamount to northerners watching deserters from the Union army fill the majority of civic posts. In Louisiana, a conservative newspaper said, "The Southern States would have to submit for an indefinite period to a representation in Congress derived from the scum of her people, in place of a former representation by men of transcendent ability, and the State offices would be filled by those whose only recommendation is their hostility to the States in the time of trial and danger." But a Virginia commentary put this issue into stark relief that related to the recent war and the proscription against Confederate heroes serving as political representatives. The *Richmond Dispatch* strongly objected to the exclusions by section 3 of an entire class of southern men from civic life. "We should not like to be the man to go before the people and ask LEE's, or LONGSTREET's or JOHNSTON's, or HOOD's old soldiers to vote to disqualify their old commanders, or to ask the civilians to vote to disqualify our old judges and justices."[81]

By the time the amendment was ratified, much of it seemed out of date. The committee that produced the amendment wrestled with crafting the language in 1866, in the midst of battles with the president over who controlled Reconstruction. When the necessary states had ratified the amendment in 1868, or two years after its initiation, the nation's political situation had changed. In 1867, Congress seized control of Reconstruction, stripped the Confederate states of their governments, established five military districts in the South, and created conventions that admitted black delegates to create new constitutions. African American suffrage became a fait accompli, imposed by federal lawmakers and enforced by the army on the former insurrectionists. Consequently, there was no need to invoke the provision against the southern states to reduce representation for failing to include all eligible voters. Ex-Confederates had been forced through other means to choose the horse in Hobson's stall; they had to take black suffrage, not leave it. As for section 4, assumption of the Confederate debt was an issue that had been removed from the table. Presidential fiat and federal court cases had rendered this moot. Only section 1 survived out of the five to influence future legal decisions in a significant way.

Oddly enough, section 3—which restricted specific former Confederates from holding elective office—had a somewhat strange application, very much unintended by lawmakers. As the court case against Jefferson Davis dragged on interminably, Chief Justice Chase in 1868 came up with an innovative reading of the newly ratified amendment to make the president's treason trial go away. Reinforcing the interpretation that he did not wish this case to go to trial, he sent hints to Davis's defense counsel that he believed that section 3 of the newly ratified amendment provided a way to argue for a dismissal. The section denied the right to hold public office to former Confederates who had sworn an oath to protect the Constitution of the United States. In essence, Chase concluded that this provision of the amendment already had punished the former Confederate president. It had disqualified him from serving as a public official. Further prosecution, according to this thinking, violated the double jeopardy clause of the Fifth Amendment. The defense adopted this theory, and who knows if it would have won. Chase and Underwood, who also would preside at this hearing, disagreed on this point, sending the matter to the Supreme Court. But President Johnson's blanket pardon on Christmas Day 1868 halted further prosecution. The government, in 1869, let the charges go away by indicating it would no longer prosecute the case.[82]

Although the middle three sections of the amendment were nearly obsolete by the time the country adopted the amendment, such an assessment also misses the point.[83] The so-called obsolete provisions of the Fourteenth Amendment served as invaluable commentary on what mattered most to power brokers in the North, Republicans in particular. The sections revealed perhaps less about the constitutional intentions than about the pulse of the country during 1866, as that pulse was measured by politicians calculating how far they could go in punishing the rebels to secure the achievements of the Union's Civil War. The national debt would be upheld and the rebel debt repudiated. Executions of the traitors, confiscation of property, or even adoption of black suffrage could not be won then. But in the meantime, former Confederates would suffer a loss of power no matter which of Hobson's choices that they made. As one scholar has written about the amendment when it went to the states for ratification, "This, then, in June 1866, seemed to be the declared limit to the exactions of the United States Senate for vengeance. Gone was most of the talk of execution of traitors, confiscation of property and reparations."[84]

But not gone were attempts to limit the power of the former slave-holding oligarchy. There had been some punishment of traitors after all, although not in the civil courts. At least for a time, ex-Confederates in some states had been prevented from voting and from holding public office. They also had lost property through the Second Confiscation Act. They could not recover their debts incurred while supporting the Confederacy, despite trying. Not only did they lose their control over the enslaved, but they also had to accept the participation of the freedmen as citizens exercising the suffrage in elections. Treason may not have been made as odious as some northerners wanted. No former Confederate died because of his or her treason. But the supporters of the failed Confederacy had suffered economic and political consequences, albeit not the hangman's noose. And the punishment had left its footprints on one of the cornerstone amendments of the Constitution of the United States.

CONCLUSION

The "Traitor Coin" Comes Up Heads

Sometime in the 1920s, Lucy Shelton Stewart became angry enough to write a book that defended Union soldiers and restored slavery as a cause of southern secession. A daughter of a Union veteran who had served in Sherman's army, she had earned a degree at Northwestern University and had composed tributes to other war heroes, such as Annie Wittenmyer, a fellow Iowan who served as a nurse, as an agent of the U.S. Sanitary Commission, and after the war as the first president of the Woman's Christian Temperance Union. Stewart, who served as her father's personal aide after graduation, devoted herself to protecting the memory of Union veterans. She had tired of hearing Sherman and his men depicted as vandals who pillaged everything in their path, of seeing Lee mentioned on par with Lincoln as an exemplar of Americanism, and of reading propaganda that elevated the southern cause to a righteous war of constitutional principle without slavery included as a central right to protect. One of the last straws came in a congressional bill in 1924 that authorized the striking of 5 million fifty-cent pieces as an inducement for the carving of Confederate heroes onto the face of Stone Mountain in Georgia. The organization in charge of constructing the memorial could purchase the coins at face value and then sell them as commemoratives at what the market would bear, with the proceeds going toward construction of the monument. The coin featured Lee and Stonewall Jackson on one face, with praise for the valor of the soldier of the South on the other. Stewart referred to the piece as "The Traitor Coin" and pointed out the contradiction in a "scheme to have the United States Government finance a memorial to those who repudiated it and sought to destroy it."[1]

When Stewart's *The Reward of Patriotism* appeared in 1930, the country had come far from the battles of the Civil War and Reconstruction, but to some of the people who treasured the Union cause perhaps it had gone too far down the road of reconciliation. The Confederates had flipped a coin, fought a war to sever themselves from Union, committed treason in the minds of northerners, and lost. Yet the traitor's coin eventually came up heads in their favor. Even this long after the war—after the country had fought two more wars, in fact—there were still a few old veterans around who found this discomforting. Stewart's father, Samuel Franklin Stewart, had been one of them. He had written a letter of protest to Calvin Coolidge asking the president to veto the bill. A veteran of the 31st Ohio in the war, Stewart believed the congressional act opened the door to federal commemoration of Confederate victories. Then he put his finger on motivations that likely did nothing to advance his cause with the president. "If Republican congressmen believe that the policy of conciliating the south, which this bill seems to indicate, will ultimately secure electoral votes or congressmen from this part of the country [Tallahassee, Florida], they are doomed to disappointment and have much to learn." The Stewarts believed that Republicans should pay attention to a constituency in the South that always had been loyal and that deserved a place on the coin "which now bears the likeness of traitors."African Americans needed to be remembered as the antithesis of traitors and as deserving the protection of the Fourteenth Amendment.[2]

A Union veteran and his daughter were not the only ones voicing their concern. The Grand Army of the Republic's Department of Illinois adopted resolutions against the measure that allowed an organization to use federal dollars to carve into the side of a mountain the figures of three traitors: Lee, Jackson, and Jefferson Davis. In 1865, the statement went, the rebels had laid down arms and were forgiven, "but we did not forgive their rebellion nor their treason, which time has not changed any more than it has changed the treason of Benedict Arnold or Judas Iscariot."[3] These were strong words, but they were not strong enough to overcome the wider movement to embrace the memory of Confederates as Americans, of celebrating the common valor of soldiers on both sides, and of relegating African Americans to a footnote in the story of the Civil War and American freedom. The Civil War generation was slowly passing away. With its diminishing ranks came the inexorable numbing of the reflex that reacted against such actions as the federal government endorsing a project that lionized Confederate heroes: the one-time traitors who had killed comrades.

Coming roughly sixty years after Appomattox, these events would have puzzled Unionists who had lived through the Civil War and presidential Reconstruction. With the possible exception of Peace Democrats, and even here the verdict is not clear, a majority of the people loyal to the Union had considered their enemies as traitors. There was little popular doubt over this. The public had divided primarily over the consequences that should fall to those who mounted insurrection against the nation and generally came to accept that only the leaders should face punishment, if anyone. It had divided even more over how to define treason on the part of the Unionists who remained in the loyal states, but who spoke out against the policies of the Republican administration. In this effort, the federal government certainly played a part, but it more often fell to the day-by-day interactions of soldiers with civilians, and civilians with each other, to set the terms and tempo of loyalty and arrests. Although the U.S. Supreme Court supplied valuable interpretations of the enemy as a belligerent traitor, the broader parameters for what constituted treason were set outside of the judiciary.

In this battle over loyalty on the northern home front, the federal government has left a problem over assessing the extent and nature of its reach. On the one hand, it seemingly expanded exponentially, with the creation of the Provost Marshal General's Bureau in 1863 that installed agents of the central government in congressional districts to catch deserters and enforce conscription. On the other hand, even that structure, pieced together as it was, required cooperation from local and state officials to have any chance of being effective. Resistance in communities could be incredibly effective depending on where it occurred and the nature of the political composition within neighborhoods. By 1868, the centralized state remained a work in progress without a strong commitment for state building on the part of its administrators beyond employing the tools to defeat an enemy while securing for the nation the Republican vision of free labor.

Similarly, Lincoln has presented a problem in trying to fit him into a particular niche when considering the tactics he proposed or accepted in the fight against treason on the battlefield and on the home front. Was he a dictator? No. Did he ignore the Constitution? No again. But did he allow policies and procedures of questionable constitutionalism—and even questionable need? Yes. The interference at election precincts by the military throughout the border states should give one pause, although hindsight provides clarity that was missing from the moment. The nineteenth-century political culture had its own peculiarities, very different from today. Elections featured violent political rituals, with occasional riots and intimidation as part of the elective process, especially in the urban areas studied by scholars such as Mary P. Ryan. Even without violence, elections could be swayed by party agents employing bribery to win over voters. And everyone knew that election commissioners could allow their partisan instincts to influence the direction of judgment calls at precincts. This kind of activity typified the prewar, *peaceful* state—not one at war. Add to these habitual election practices an extraordinary civil strife, with known divided loyalties among the electorate, and it perhaps becomes more understandable why excesses occurred, even if they remain questionable.[4]

Lincoln also prevented the ship of state from sailing too far into unconstitutional waters. Even though he suspended habeas corpus, supported the military arrests of civilians who tried to disrupt recruitment, and condoned a frightful policy of preventative arrests before individuals had created treason, he also stopped the government's seizure of churches. He freed prisoners of state. And he looked for the reestablishment of civil courts and less restrictive measures by the military, as soon as the outcome of the war seemed more secure. When the 1864 election came, he did not advocate for postponing it, even if he used executive powers to maximize the voting by soldiers favorable to the administration. The same dynamic that took place concerning emancipation occurred in the realm of treason and loyalty. Military officers and arresting agents on the ground often caused superiors to accept or overturn their decisions. The national government, occupied with trying to win the war on the battlefield, often reacted to the challenges of loyalty that confronted it. General Burnside dropped Vallandigham into Lincoln's lap as a problem; the Ohio politician was not arrested through national orders. Soldiers at the point of contact with civilians, in fact, have contributed more than most scholars have noticed to the practical constitutionalism of the United States.

Nor should the story of treason, loyalty, and civil liberties belong only to Lincoln. Different agents from varying authorities policed treason on the home front. And after his death, the fight continued. Republicans in the border states instituted or continued laws that prevented ex-Confederates from voting and from practicing professions. Deserters in various places found their right to the franchise challenged, especially if they were Democrats. Much of this activity took place at the state level, where the meaning of freedom also was in flux. National punishment of traitors came through forcing ex-Confederates to accept black suffrage and new constitutions, as well as to endorse the U.S. amendments that had been shaped by the battle against treason.

By 1868, the country had seemingly crossed one divide. At the end of the year it became clear that the government would prosecute no former Confederate for treason. National matters appeared to be more comfortable for northern Republicans. One of their own, Ulysses S. Grant, had been elected president. The United States military oversaw the installation of new governments based on congressional principles for Reconstruction. Black suffrage was a foregone conclusion, even though the Fifteenth Amendment waited until the following year to emerge. The Fourteenth Amendment—the most punishment that could be achieved against traitors at the time—was forced on the South through military power. Democratic principles of self-determination were achieved through overpowering a regional majority. It was a situation shrugged off by the conquerors as a necessary evil to combat continued treason. So be it; the rebels deserved it. During the year, the Congress had impeached President Johnson. With his conviction falling short by one vote, Johnson tucked in his horns for the last months of his presidency, but announced his final pardons of the rebels on Christmas Day.

Just a few weeks ahead of the Christmas pardons, Joseph Medill looked around the country and liked what he saw. Owner of the *Chicago Tribune*, Medill was an antislavery Republican who had served the cause of Lincoln during the war. It had been a hard war, and he had been a hard proponent for emancipation. In December 1868 he gave a speech in Washington that showed he was thinking about the next steps for the nation. Expansionism occupied his mind—what we now call imperialism. He was looking for additional territory for the United States. This was a desire that had led the country into war, but it had been held in check pending the pacification of the Confederacy. "The desire for territorial expansion is one of the most natural and certain incidents of collective patriotism," he said. "It is an instinct inseparable from a healthy nationality."As it did during the antebellum era, the health of the American empire depended on expansionism. Medill used patriotism as a key noun, rather than its negative cousin of treason. The speech looked forward, rather than backward. In this new world, a world that deployed antebellum, expansionist impulses under a new name, the treason of Confederates would play less of a role, although enduring in the political campaigns that waived the "bloody shirt" to gain Republican votes against the former rebels and stay-at-home traitors— Democrats all. As he stood before his audience in Washington in 1868, Medill boldly proclaimed, "The reconstruction was settled by his [Grant's] election. Very little remains to be done. The Democracy are going to abandon the issues they have fought us on for four years. He has an opportunity to immortalize his administration and place his fame high above all Presidents who have preceded him."[5]

He was not quite correct. Like many northern progressives, Medill cast his eyes to a wider world once the southern traitors seemed to be pacified. The wider world did not include references to African Americans in the United States, although this does not mean that he, a leading radical Republican, had no interest in them. Perhaps he was swept up in the post-election euphoria around Grant and became too comfortable with what he perceived to be the white South's defeat. Perhaps he only uttered what had been on his mind for some time until a stable Union gave him a platform from which to make such an announcement. But perhaps Medill and his colleagues had miscalculated. Most of them put their faith in the ballot— that if black males gained the suffrage, it provided the best means for their protection. The problem was solved. With their coalition solidified and the ballot for black males in place, Republicans could move on to other things, such as charting their way toward becoming a more powerful nation. The traitors from the Civil War had been handled. For the moment, it was possible to see it that way.

Another man, however, saw things differently. Assigned to command a military division that oversaw Kentucky, Tennessee, Georgia, Alabama, Mississippi, and Florida, Major General George Thomas was less sanguine about affairs in the South. It had been a particularly tense time in Tennessee, with the rise of insurgency that would come to be known as the Ku Klux Klan, causing a delegation from the state to meet with the president to ask for aid. They apparently won a concession that resulted in the War Department asking Thomas to specify his needs for additional military forces to ensure the preservation of peace and law.[6] In September 1868, his report detailed that the rebels since the close of war had been trying to suggest that the cause of liberty, justice, humanity, and equality had suffered with the failed attempt to win independence. He wrote:

> This is, of course, intended as a species of political cant, whereby the crime of treason might be covered with a counterfeit varnish of patriotism, so that the precipitators of the rebellion might go down in history hand-in-hand with the defenders of the Government, thus wiping out with their own hands their own stains; a species of self-forgiveness amazing in its effrontery, when it is considered that life and property,— justly forfeited by the laws of the country, of war, and of nations, through the magnanimity of the Government and people,—were not exacted from them.[7]

Thomas witnessed the beginning of a process that historians in recent decades have traced. Over the intervening years—decades that involved political strife, bloodshed at the polls, night riders who targeted white Republicans and black people, legislative battles, and northern white acquiescence—came the rehabilitation of the Confederate traitors into good Americans, to an extent that troubled people like Lucy Shelton Stewart in the 1930s. As the Great Depression loomed, "traitors" may have remained a label for the people who had supported the Confederate republic, but it was by no means the dominant descriptor. But in 1868, when the country flipped the reconciliation coin into the air, it was not yet clear that it would come down in favor of the former traitors.

APPENDIX A.
COURTS-MARTIAL FOR TREASON

Date	Name	Rank	Place	Specifications	Finding
Feb. 1861	Smith, Thomas M.	citizen	Mo.	burned 2 bridges	guilty
Sept. 1861	Aubuchon, Joseph	citizen	Mo.	took up arms against U.S.	guilty
Sept. 1861	Baker, Joseph	citizen	Mo.	took up arms against U.S.	guilty
Sept. 1861	Beck, Enoch	citizen	Mo.	took up arms against U.S.	guilty
Sept. 1861	Caldwell, John	citizen	Mo.	took up arms against U.S.	guilty
Sept. 1861	Childers, Thomas G.	citizen	Mo.	took up arms against U.S.	guilty
Sept. 1861	Hutton, William D.	citizen	Mo.	took up arms against U.S.	guilty
Sept. 1861	Jackson, Philip	citizen	Mo.	picket for C.S.A.	guilty
Sept. 1861	Phillips, Harley J.	citizen	Mo.	took arms against U.S.; joining Hardee	guilty
Sept. 1861	Thurman, James C.	citizen	Mo.	took up arms against U.S.	guilty
Sept. 1861	Wilcox, Isaac	citizen	Mo.	enlisted in C.S.A.; induced others to join	guilty
Sept. 1861	William, David E.	citizen	Mo.	took up arms against U.S.	guilty
Nov. 1861	Aldereti, Pablo	citizen	N.Mex.	sent information to C.S.A.	guilty
Dec. 1861	Batterdon, Ransom	citizen	Mo.	took up arms against U.S.	guilty
Dec. 1861	Benedict, James H.	citizen	Mo.	took up arms against U.S.	guilty
Dec. 1861	Benedict, Thomas	citizen	Mo.	took up arms against U.S.	guilty
Dec. 1861	Crowder, Richard B.	citizen	Mo.	burned bridges	guilty
Dec. 1861	Cunningham, George	citizen	Mo.	burned 2 bridges	guilty
Dec. 1861	Grismall, Austin	citizen	Mo.	took up arms against U.S.	guilty
Dec. 1861	Jones, George H.	citizen	Mo.	helped bridge burners	guilty
Dec. 1861	Jones, James R.	citizen	Mo.	took up arms against U.S.	guilty
Dec. 1861	Mitchell, John	citizen	Mo.	soldier in C.S.A.	guilty
Dec. 1861	Powell, Barzillia	citizen	Mo.	took up arms against U.S.	not guilty
Dec. 1861	Powell, John	citizen	Mo.	took up arms against U.S.	guilty
Dec. 1861	Rumano, James W.	citizen	Mo.	took up arms against U.S.	guilty
Dec. 1861	Stott, Stephen	citizen	Mo.	aided bridge burners	guilty

Date	Name	Rank	Place	Specifications	Finding
Dec. 1861	Tuggle, James	citizen	Mo.	took up arms against U.S.	guilty
Jan. 1862	Bollinger, Joseph W.	citizen	Mo.	robbery; plunder	guilty
Jan. 1862	Childes, Alfred	citizen	Mo.	took up arms against U.S.	not guilty
Jan. 1862	Wayne, William	citizen	Mo.	took up arms against U.S.	guilty
Feb. 1862	Ellis, Edmund I.	citizen	Mo.	wrote treasonable articles	guilty
July 1862	Higgins, Patrick	1st Lt.	Ill.	helped POWs escape	guilty
July 1862	Hoy, Jeremiah	citizen	Kans.	murdered citizen, soldier; burned bridge	guilty
Aug. 1862	Copewood, W. S.	citizen	?	said he would join C.S.A.	guilty
Aug. 1862	Harding, J.	citizen	Tenn.	hid from capture at Memphis	guilty
Aug. 1862	Hukill, David	citizen	?	sank boat in Mississippi R.	guilty
Aug. 1862	Johns, Samuel	citizen	Ky.	in group of armed men going south	guilty
Aug. 1862	Morris, William	citizen	Ky.	with group of armed men going south	guilty
Oct. 1862	Simms (no 1st name)	teamster	?	Jackson had whipped U.S. every battle	not guilty
Nov. 1862	Ford, George W.	citizen	Ariz.	aided Ben McCullough's army	guilty
Jan. 1863	Atkinson, John M.	citizen	Tenn.	guerrilla	guilty
Feb. 1863	Fortune, J. C.	2nd Lt.	Mo.	language about president, emancipation	guilty
Mar. 1863	Betts, Samuel C.	citizen	Md.	C.S.A. soldier	guilty
Mar. 1863	Dugan, Pierre C.	citizen	Md.	had letters from the South	guilty
Mar. 1863	Kemp, Simon J.	citizen	Md.	had letters from the South	guilty
Mar. 1863	Montgomery, Samuel	Lt.	Pa.	would rather shoot Lincoln than Davis	guilty
Mar. 1863	Oliver, James R.	citizen	Md.	C.S.A. soldier	guilty
Mar. 1863	Rider, James	citizen	Md.	C.S.A. soldier	guilty
Mar. 1863	Scott, John W.	citizen	Md.	spy	guilty
Apr. 1863	Mcelroy, Michael	Pvt.	N.Mex.	language	guilty
May 1863	Cazauran, A. Ringold	citizen	?	language about General Sherman	guilty
July 1863	Etherly, Alfred	citizen	Tenn.	guided Rebels who stole, kidnapped	guilty

Date	Name	Rank	Place	Specifications	Finding
July 1863	Funk, David	citizen	Mo.	raised secession flag	guilty
July 1863	Luckett, Henry	citizen	Tenn.	smuggled percussion caps	guilty
Aug. 1863	Smith, Walter N.	Capt.	Mass.	language on march to Warrenton	guilty
Dec. 1863	Clayton, Elijah	C.S.A.	C.S.A.	spy	guilty
Jan. 1864	Smith, Thomas M.	citizen	Tenn.	smuggling gunpowder, caps	guilty
Feb. 1864	Bringle, Alfred	citizen	?	gave information to C.S.A.	not guilty
Feb. 1864	Stone, William D.	Capt.	Ohio	president and cabinet are corrupt scoundrels	guilty
Mar. 1864	Cargill, John	Pvt.	Md.	said he would shoot sergeant	guilty
Mar. 1864	Scally, John	citizen	Md.	recruiting for C.S.A.	guilty
Apr. 1864	Hill, Frederick	Pvt.	Ill.	desertion; bushwhacking	guilty
May 1864	De Bold, Frank	citizen	Mo.	treasonable language: GD Uncle Sam	not guilty
May 1864	Horton, W. H.	citizen	Tenn.	gave information to C.S.A.	guilty
June 1864	Childress, Robert A.	citizen	Ariz.	went to Rebel camp in Arizona	guilty
June 1864	Hogg, James J.	citizen	Mo.	language: I am a Rebel	guilty
June 1864	Zunts, James E.	citizen	La.	wishes C.S.A. killed colored soldiers	not guilty
July 1864	Tinsley, B. W.	citizen	Tenn.	now a niggers' war, I join Confederacy	guilty
Aug. 1864	Foster, Gabe	citizen	Mo.	Lincoln bigger traitor than Davis	guilty
Aug. 1864	Hughes, Thomas	Pvt.	Nev.	disobedience; language	guilty
Aug. 1864	Reading, Frank R.	citizen	D.C.	language: I am a Rebel	guilty
Aug. 1864	Veitch, James H.	citizen	D.C.	damn capitol should be burned to ground	guilty
Sept. 1864	Bickers, John	citizen	Ind.	?	not guilty
Sept. 1864	Caldwell, Lafayette	citizen	La.	raised company of jayhawkers	guilty
Sept. 1864	Hart, I. B.	citizen	Tenn.	Smuggled 50,000 percussion caps	guilty
Sept. 1864	Johnson, Thomas	Pvt.	Calif.	subversive conduct	guilty

Date	Name	Rank	Place	Specifications	Finding
Oct. 1864	Rutherford, Daniel	Pvt.	Ind.	language sympathetic to Rebels	guilty
Nov. 1864	Etheridge, Samuel	citizen	Va.	harbored guerrillas	not guilty
Nov. 1864	Hutchins, Sarah	citizen	Md.	wrote C.S.A. officer	guilty
Nov. 1864	Ives, William	citizen	Md.	sent sword to Harry Gilmore	not guilty
Nov. 1864	Reynolds, Mary V.	citizen	Tenn.	sent information to C.S.A.; bought supplies	not guilty
Dec. 1864	Gray, S. A.	citizen	La.	delivered $120 to enemy	guilty
Jan. 1865	Spence, John	Pvt.	?	praised assassination of Lincoln	not guilty
Feb. 1865	Anderson, Andy	"colored"	La.	took horses to Confederates	not guilty
Feb. 1865	Green, William	"colored"	La.	took horses to Confederates	guilty
Feb. 1865	Hicks, Rufus A.	Pvt.	Ill.	carried revolvers through U.S. lines	guilty
Feb. 1865	Huff, Peter	"colored"	La.	smuggled pistols	guilty
Mar. 1865	Brainard, Henry	Sgt.	N.Y.	language about president	guilty
Mar. 1865	Julian, Marsena R.	citizen	Tenn.	allowed C.S.A. to tear up railroad track	guilty
Mar. 1865	Rivers, William	citizen	Ala.	treasonous language	not guilty
Mar. 1865	Tierney, Phillip	employee	La.	Language about murder of Lincoln	guilty
Apr. 1865	Bickers, John	citizen	Tenn.	?	not guilty
Apr. 1865	Bickers, John	citizen	Tenn.	gave information to Rebels	not guilty
Apr. 1865	Walker, James	Pvt.	Calif.	language about Lincoln's death	guilty
May 1865	Adams, Henry	citizen	La.	intends to die a Rebel	guilty
May 1865	Allen, Frank	Pvt.	Mich.	glad Lincoln was murdered	guilty
May 1865	Campbell, Jacob	Pvt.	Mich.	wished Lincoln was shot 12 years ago	guilty
May 1865	Collins, John	citizen	La.	glad Lincoln was murdered	guilty

Date	Name	Rank	Place	Specifications	Finding
May 1865	Douglas, Henry Kyd	C.S.A.	C.S.A.	appeared in Confederate uniform	guilty
May 1865	Fletcher, J. E.	C.S.A.	C.S.A.	language: bet Johnson would be killed	not guilty
May 1865	Orrez, C.	citizen	La.	glad Lincoln was murdered	guilty
May 1865	Ryman, John	Pvt.	Mich.	glad Lincoln was murdered	guilty
May 1865	Shields, Patrick	citizen	La.	glad Lincoln was murdered	not guilty
July 1865	James, J. W.	citizen	La.	paroled POW; language	not guilty
Sept. 1865	Latimer, Emma	citizen	Tenn.	tore down, trampled U.S. flag	guilty
1865	Wirz, Henry	Comdr.	C.S.A.	13 total, Andersonville-relayed	guilty

Source: Thomas P. and Beverly A. Lowry, indexing project for courts-martial records held at the National Archives, Washington, D.C.

APPENDIX B.
COURTS-MARTIAL FOR DISLOYALTY

Date	Name	Rank	Place	Specifications	Finding
Feb. 1862	Miller, Charles A.	Pvt.	Calif.	language: said he was secessionist	not guilty
Mar. 1862	Kellogg, John W.	Pvt.	Calif.	language: would vote for Jeff Davis	guilty
Mar. 1862	Morrison, Angus	Pvt.	Calif.	language: government played out	guilty
June 1862	Emerson, Daniel	citizen	Mo.	take down U.S. flag	guilty
July 1862	Divine, Patrick	Pvt.	D.C.	language: threatened to join Rebs	guilty
Aug. 1862	Mansfield, John	?	Wisc.	remove flag; correspondence with C.S.A.	not guilty
Oct. 1862	Ormes, John P.	citizen	Ky.	knew guerrillas; language	guilty
Oct. 1862	Rankin, Elbert	citizen	Mo.	language	guilty
Nov. 1862	McClune, Hugh H.	1st Lt.	Pa.	language: abolition warfare	guilty
Nov. 1862	Smith, Benjamin B.	Pvt.	Ky.	denounced U.S.; stole horses	guilty
Dec. 1862	Ross, J. A.	Sgt. Maj.	?	language: would fight for Rebels	guilty
Jan. 1863	Langley, Sanford	citizen	Mo.	secesh sympathizer	guilty
Jan. 1863	Nichols, Joseph	1st Lt.	Maine	language: opposed emancipation	guilty
Feb. 1863	Coleman, Nicholas	citizen	Va.	helping deserters	guilty
Feb. 1863	Leach, Stephen	Pvt.	Ind.	language: hoped Rebs whipped U.S.	guilty
Feb. 1863	Williamson, Frank	Sgt.	Pa.	language: would join British against U.S.	not guilty
Mar. 1863	Dearth, John	citizen	Tenn.	language: South will whip North	not guilty

Date	Name	Rank	Place	Specifications	Finding
Mar. 1863	Fitzsimmons, Homer	Sgt.	Mo.	language: anti-emancipation; would desert	guilty
Mar. 1863	Hogencamp, Abraham	citizen	Ky.	aided desertion	guilty
Mar. 1863	Jones, Garrett	citizen	Ky.	language: pro-Confederate	not guilty
Mar. 1863	Kirby, L. W.	citizen	Tenn.	hid C.S.A. soldiers and guerrillas	not guilty
Mar. 1863	Kirk, James M.	citizen	Ky.	refused to take oath; sympathy for Rebels	guilty
Mar. 1863	Markel, Solomon	citizen	Ky.	advised desertion; helped desertion	guilty
Mar. 1863	Montgomery, Samuel	Lt.	Pa.	language: wished all would desert	guilty
Mar. 1863	Rutter, Richard	citizen	Ky.	language: took oath to travel	guilty
Mar. 1863	Trowell, James M.	citizen	Ky.	Helped man get to Rebel army	guilty
Mar. 1863	Wilkinson, James	citizen	Ky.	language: all Union men should be killed	not guilty
Mar. 1863	Wilson, William	citizen	Ky.	advised desertion; said he was secessionist	not guilty
Mar. 1864	Coyle, Andrew	citizen	Pa.	language	not guilty
Mar. 1864	Dougherty, Michael	citizen	Pa.	language	not guilty
Mar. 1864	Duffy, Michael	citizen	Pa.	language	not guilty
Mar. 1864	Maley, Charles	citizen	Pa.	language	not guilty
Mar. 1864	Maloy, Mannas	citizen	Pa.	language	not guilty
Mar. 1864	McElhaney, Patrick	citizen	Pa.	language	not guilty
Mar. 1864	McGeady, John	citizen	Pa.	language	not guilty
Mar. 1864	McGill, Frank	citizen	Pa.	language	not guilty
Mar. 1864	Mulligan, John	citizen	Pa.	language	not guilty
Mar. 1864	O'Donnel, Michael	citizen	Pa.	language: resisted draft	not guilty
May 1864	Armstrong, Daniel H.	citizen	Mo.	language: hostility toward U.S.	guilty
May 1864	Arnot, William L.	citizen	Mo.	wrote letter to military prisoners	guilty

Date	Name	Rank	Place	Specifications	Finding
May 1864	Bartlett, James	citizen	Mo.	language: a southern sympathizer	guilty
May 1864	Hamilton, Joseph M.	citizen	Mo.	language: a southern sympathizer	guilty
May 1864	Heberland, August	citizen	Mo.	sold shotgun to Rebels	guilty
May 1864	Judge, James	citizen	Mo.	language in a saloon	guilty
May 1864	Poindexter, Joseph J.	citizen	Ark.	language: GD governor, election Lincoln	guilty
May 1864	Sieber, Robert	citizen	Mo.	sold guns to Rebels	guilty
Feb. 1865	Curley, Patrick	citizen	Pa.	language about the draft	guilty
Feb. 1865	Garner, William H.	citizen	Mo.	language: Rebels are my friends	guilty
Feb. 1865	Huntsucker, James	citizen	Mo.	language: would shoot recruiters	guilty
Feb. 1865	Kemp, Nancy P.	citizen	Mo.	furnished provisions to C.S.A.	guilty
Feb. 1865	Lowe, Joseph	citizen	Mo.	language: Quantrill had good men	not guilty
Feb. 1865	Lownsberry, Samuel	citizen	Pa.	language: advised draft resistance	guilty
Feb. 1865	Mathey, Edward G.	Capt.	Ind.	language: would not fight to free Negroes	not guilty
Feb. 1865	Willhelm, Jacob	citizen	Pa.	language: advised draft resistance	guilty
Mar. 1865	Beatty, A. J.	citizen	?	no entry	guilty
Mar. 1865	Beatty, William S.	citizen	Tenn.	In C.S.A. Army	guilty
Mar. 1865	Bloom, Gainer P.	citizen	Pa.	language about the draft; rescued deserters	guilty
Mar. 1865	Boyer, Benjamin	citizen	Pa.	language about the draft; rescued deserters	guilty
Mar. 1865	Cook, Christian	Pvt.	Kans.	language: wished Rebels would whip U.S.	guilty
Mar. 1865	Dean, John	citizen	Mo.	Gave information to enemy	not guilty
Mar. 1865	Huntsucker, James	citizen	Mo.	language	guilty
Mar. 1865	Johnston, George J.	citizen	Mo.	hurrah Jeff Davis; Quantrill man	guilty

Date	Name	Rank	Place	Specifications	Finding
Mar. 1865	Keller, Charles	citizen	Pa.	language about the draft; rescued deserters	guilty
Mar. 1865	Rousher, George	citizen	Pa.	language about the draft; rescued deserters	guilty
Mar. 1865	Yoas, Henry	citizen	Pa.	language about the draft	guilty

Source: Thomas P. and Beverly A. Lowry, indexing project for courts-martial records held at the National Archives, Washington, D.C.

APPENDIX C.
POLITICAL ARRESTS REPORTED IN
NEWSPAPERS, BY CHARGE/CAUSE

The sampling was compiled from the database America's Historical Newspapers (Readex: A Division of NewsBank, Inc.), with reference secondarily to 19th Century U.S. Newspapers (Gale Press). Search terms used were "arrests," "treason," and "disloyalty." With the assistance of then graduate student Anne Brinton, I recorded a little more than 400 incidents in 11 newspapers. By far, most of the cases came from the *Philadelphia Inquirer* and the *Baltimore Sun*. Not surprisingly, most of the arrests were of people from Maryland or in the Washington-Maryland corridor. A geographical analysis is skewed by the newspapers in the database and cannot be considered as an accurate depiction of trouble spots.

Nor should this compilation be considered comprehensive; it is meant to be suggestive of the kind of arrests made, by which authorities, and of what kind of people. The compilation demonstrates, for instance, that prominent people were targeted, as Attorney General Edward Bates suggested. Journalists, ministers, merchants, and others holding important community positions can be found here. Suspect language— supposedly protected speech—was responsible for numerous arrests, as were the less precise charges of "disloyalty" or "treasonous sentiments." Again, these do not represent all arrests made in communities. Mayor's courts and other municipal units could have numerous people flowing in and out of the judicial system on charges of disloyalty. Newspapers as a source are likely biased toward dealing with more influential people in communities rather than with members of the more anonymous masses.

Person Arrested	Occupation	Jurisdiction	Location	Source	Date	Result
Aiding and abetting rebellion						
Mrs. Emerich	unstated	military	Md.	*The Sun*	6/18/1864	paroled from house arrest
Aiding Confederacy						
William T. Smithson	banker	unstated	D.C.	*Daily National Intelligencer*	1/11/1862	unstated
Aiding desertion						
Daniel Roderick	unstated	unstated	Harpers Ferry	*The Sun*	8/14/1862	Fort McHenry
Wm. S. Stronzinberger	unstated	unstated	Harpers Ferry	*The Sun*	8/14/1862	Fort McHenry
M. E. Winchester	unstated	Marshal Van Nostrand	Md.	*The Sun*	8/25/1862	took oath; discharged
N. B. Pryor	unstated	Marshal Van Nostrand	Md.	*The Sun*	8/25/1862	took oath; discharged
James McSherry	unstated	Marshal Van Nostrand	Md.	*The Sun*	8/25/1862	took oath; discharged
A. Featheake	unstated	Marshal Van Nostrand	Md.	*The Sun*	8/25/1862	took oath; discharged
Henry F. Super	unstated	unstated	Md.	*The Sun*	4/27/1863	sent beyond lines
Thomas McDonald	unstated	provost marshal	Md.	*The Sun*	3/3/1864	released
Thomas Cox	unstated	military	Md.	*The Sun*	6/18/1864	took oath; released
Aiding draft dodgers						
Dr. J. Cartwright	unstated	unstated	Potomac River	*The Sun*	9/4/1862	Fort McHenry
J. J. Briscoe	unstated	unstated	Potomac River	*The Sun*	9/4/1862	Fort McHenry
B. B. Crone	unstated	unstated	Potomac River	*The Sun*	9/4/1862	Fort McHenry
unnamed "colored man"	unstated	unstated	Potomac River	*The Sun*	9/4/1862	Fort McHenry
Mr. Ascour	unstated	unstated	Potomac River	*The Sun*	9/4/1862	Fort McHenry

Person Arrested	Occupation	Jurisdiction	Location	Source	Date	Result
Assisted parties going south						
Miss Sarah Flanigan	unstated	military: Col. Fish	Md.	*The Sun*	3/30/1863	sent south
Attempted release of C.S.A. prisoners						
Walsh	unstated	military commission	Chicago, Ill.	*Plain Dealer*	1/11/1865	unstated
Morris	unstated	military commission	Chicago, Ill.	*Plain Dealer*	1/11/1865	unstated
Marmaduke	unstated	military commission	Chicago, Ill.	*Plain Dealer*	1/11/1865	unstated
Cantril	unstated	military commission	Chicago, Ill.	*Plain Dealer*	1/11/1865	unstated
Daniel (alias Travis)	unstated	military commission	Chicago, Ill.	*Plain Dealer*	1/11/1865	unstated
Semmes	unstated	military commission	Chicago, Ill.	*Plain Dealer*	1/11/1865	unstated
St. Leger Grenfel	unstated	military commission	Chicago, Ill.	*Plain Dealer*	1/11/1865	unstated
Anderson	unstated	military commission	Chicago, Ill.	*Plain Dealer*	1/11/1865	
Attempting to convey information to enemy						
John Lewis	unstated	unstated	Va.	*The Sun*	9/4/1862	took oath; released
Burning railroad bridges						
George M. E. Shearer	unstated	unstated	unstated	*The Sun*	1/6/1864	Fort Delaware
Buying weapons						
R. R. Walter	unstated	military	N.Y.	*San Francisco Bulletin*	10/21/1861	Fort Lafayette

Carrying Rebel mail

Name	Description	Arresting authority	State	Source	Date	Outcome
Dr. Hammitt	doctor	Deputy Marshal Lyon	Md.	*The Sun*	7/31/1862	released
August Anton	unstated	deputy marshal	Md.	*The Sun*	7/31/1862	paroled
James Meghee	unstated	deputy marshal	Md.	*The Sun*	7/31/1862	held
William Acton	unstated	deputy marshal	Md.	*The Sun*	7/31/1862	held
Wm. Woodward	unstated	Deputy Marshal Lyon	Md.	*The Sun*	7/31/1862	paroled
George Putnam	unstated	unstated	Md.	*The Sun*	1/6/1864	Fort Delaware
W. H. Resin	unstated	unstated	Md.	*The Sun*	1/6/1864	Fort Delaware
John Tyler	unstated	unstated	Md.	*The Sun*	1/6/1864	Old Capitol Prison

Cheered for Jefferson Davis

Name	Description	Arresting authority	State	Source	Date	Outcome
Charles Cochrane	unstated	military	Md.	*The Sun*	5/4/1863	took oath; released
Thomas Jordan	unstated	military; Col. Fish	Md.	*The Sun*	5/12/1863	took oath; released
John Jackson	unstated	military; Capt. French	Md.	*The Sun*	5/16/1863	took oath; released
Richard Humphrey	unstated	military; Capt. French	Md.	*The Sun*	5/16/1863	took oath; released

Communication with South

Name	Description	Arresting authority	State	Source	Date	Outcome
William H. Winder	brother of Brig. Gen. John H. Winder	military	Pa.	*San Francisco Bulletin*	10/2/1861	Fort Lafayette
John W. Anderson	merchant	military	R.I	*San Francisco Bulletin*	10/2/1861	Fort Lafayette
Magraw	unstated	military	Va.	*Philadelphia Inquirer*	10/3/1861	unstated
John W. Long	unstated	military	Md.	*The Sun*	3/30/1863	held subject to provost marshal

Person Arrested	Occupation	Jurisdiction	Location	Source	Date	Result
Wm. Penn Goldsborough	unstated	military	Md.	The Sun	3/30/1863	held subject to provost marshal
William O. Wheatley	unstated	military	Md.	The Sun	3/30/1863	held subject to provost marshal
Eugene Williamson	unstated	unstated	Md.	The Sun	1/6/1864	Fort McHenry
Matthew Nolan	unstated	military: Col. Woolley	Md.	The Sun	7/4/1864	released
Confederate soldier						
Jennie De Hart	soldier	military: Col. Fish	?	The Sun	5/8/1863	held on Gen. Schenck's order
Contact with Rebel spy						
William Wilkins Glenn	lawyer	military	Md.	The Sun	7/1/1864	exiled for duration of war
Discouraging enlistment						
Marcus Julius Cicero Stanley	unstated	military	N.Y.	San Francisco Bulletin	10/2/1861	Fort Lafayette
Dr. Thomas M. Hope	doctor	unstated	Ill.	San Francisco Bulletin	9/10/1862	perhaps still in custody
C. L. Weller	postmaster	military	Calif.	Daily Evening Bulletin	7/26/1864	unstated
Disloyal language/sentiments						
Judge Birch	gubernatorial candidate	Col. Boyd	Mo.	Philadelphia Inquirer	6/2/1862	unstated
Wm. Clayton	unstated	military	Ill.	Milwaukee Sentinel	7/29/1862	unstated
Christopher Heiselger	unstated	military	Mo.	Milwaukee Sentinel	7/29/1862	unstated
Christopher Burgess	unstated	military	Mo.	Milwaukee Sentinel	7/29/1862	unstated
Benedict Simpson	unstated	military	Mo.	Milwaukee Sentinel	7/29/1862	unstated

Name	Occupation	Arresting authority	State	Newspaper	Date	Disposition
Rev. Chas. A. Hay	pastor	military	Pa.	Philadelphia Inquirer	10/29/1862	arrested
O. Ferrandini	unstated	Col. Fish	Md.	The Sun	5/4/1863	took oath; released
Wm. Cochran, alias Brown	unstated	Col. Fish	Md.	The Sun	5/8/1863	held for hearing
Wm. Richardson	unstated	Col. Fish	Md.	The Sun	5/8/1863	held for hearing; sent south
James Quinn	unstated	Col. Fish	Md.	The Sun	5/8/1863	held for hearing
James League	unstated	unstated	Md.	The Sun	1/7/1864	taken to D.C.
B. G. Harris	merchant	military	Md.	The Sun	1/16/1864	unstated
Dennis Murphy	unstated	military	Md.	The Sun	1/16/1864	took oath; released
Disloyalty						
David Welford	unstated	unstated	Ky.	Philadelphia Inquirer	10/5/1861	unstated
Pharis Welford	unstated	unstated	Ky.	Philadelphia Inquirer	10/5/1861	unstated
Henry Jenkins	unstated	unstated	D.C.	Philadelphia Inquirer	2/8/1862	unstated
Dr. Ives	correspondent	unstated	D.C.	Philadelphia Inquirer	2/11/1862	Fort McHenry
Brig. Gen. Charles P. Stone	brigadier general	military	N.Y.	Philadelphia Inquirer	2/12/1862	Fort Lafayette
Judge Petts	judge	unstated	D.C.	Wisconsin Daily Patriot	4/29/1862	congressional hearing
Ulyseus[?] Hobbs	lawyer	military	Md.	The Sun	7/31/1862	Fort McHenry
Alexander Armstrong Sr.	prominent citizen	provost marshal	Md.	Philadelphia Inquirer	8/8/1862	took oath; released
Nathaniel Schner	prominent citizen	provost marshal	Md.	Philadelphia Inquirer	8/8/1862	took oath; released

Person Arrested	Occupation	Jurisdiction	Location	Source	Date	Result
Michael Freise	prominent citizen	provost marshal	Md.	*Philadelphia Inquirer*	8/8/1862	took oath; released
Joseph McDowell	prominent citizen	provost marshal	Md.	*Philadelphia Inquirer*	8/8/1862	took oath; released
Martin McDowell	prominent citizen	provost marshal	Md.	*Philadelphia Inquirer*	8/8/1862	took oath; released
Henry Garvin	prominent citizen	provost marshal	Md.	*Philadelphia Inquirer*	8/8/1862	took oath; released
Dr. Smith	prominent citizen	provost marshal	Md.	*Philadelphia Inquirer*	8/8/1862	took oath; released
B. Y. Fechtig	prominent citizen	provost marshal	Md.	*Philadelphia Inquirer*	8/8/1862	took oath; released
Henry Yingling	prominent citizen	provost marshal	Md.	*Philadelphia Inquirer*	8/8/1862	took oath; released
J. H. Powles	prominent citizen	provost marshal	Md.	*Philadelphia Inquirer*	8/8/1862	took oath; released
T. P. Crist	prominent citizen	provost marshal	Md.	*Philadelphia Inquirer*	8/8/1862	took oath; released
William Ragan	prominent citizen	provost marshal	Md.	*Philadelphia Inquirer*	8/8/1862	took oath; released
James Kridler	prominent citizen	provost marshal	Md.	*Philadelphia Inquirer*	8/8/1862	took oath; released
Blackstone Lynch	prominent citizen	provost marshal	Md.	*Philadelphia Inquirer*	8/8/1862	took oath; released
Joseph Ground	prominent citizen	provost marshal	Md.	*Philadelphia Inquirer*	8/8/1862	took oath; released
Henry Freaner	prominent citizen	provost marshal	Md.	*Philadelphia Inquirer*	8/8/1862	took oath; released

Name	Description	Authority	Location	Source	Date	Disposition
Williams	prominent citizen	provost marshal	Md.	*Philadelphia Inquirer*	8/8/1862	declined to take oath; held
Keller	prominent citizen	provost marshal	Md.	*Philadelphia Inquirer*	8/8/1862	declined to take oath; held
Wm. McAtee	wealthy and influential citizen	provost marshal	Md.	*Philadelphia Inquirer*	8/8/1862	took oath; released
Erastus Thompson	unstated	provost marshal	Md.	*The Sun*	8/20/1862	took oath; discharged
Lewis Page	unstated	provost marshal	Md.	*The Sun*	8/20/1862	took oath; discharged by marshal
Allen M. Price	unstated	unstated	Md	*The Sun*	8/25/1862	took oath, released
Mr. Daniel Crummer	unstated	military	Md	*The Sun*	8/25/1862	released on parole
Nathan Dawson	unstated	military	Md	*The Sun*	9/4/1862	awaiting questioning
Richard Dawson	unstated	military	Md	*The Sun*	9/4/1862	awaiting questioning
Stewart Harrington	unstated	military	Md	*The Sun*	11/7/1862	unstated
Wm. T. Craig	unstated	military	Md	*The Sun*	11/7/1862	unstated
Josiah Keene	unstated	military	Md	*The Sun*	11/7/1862	unstated
D. A. Mahoney	unstated	judge advocate	D.C.	*Philadelphia Inquirer*	1/6/1863	refused to take oath
John H. Mulkey	unstated	judge advocate	D.C.	*Philadelphia Inquirer*	1/6/1863	refused to take oath
D. Shewald	unstated	judge advocate	D.C.	*Philadelphia Inquirer*	1/6/1863	refused to take oath
Andrew D. Duff	unstated	judge advocate	D.C.	*Philadelphia Inquirer*	1/6/1863	refused to take oath
Henry Alsquith	unstated	provost marshal	Md.	*The Sun*	4/14/1863	confined awaiting Col. Fish
Edwin T. Fuller	unstated	provost marshal	Md.	*The Sun*	4/14/1863	confined awaiting Col. Fish
Michael Gatty	unstated	provost marshal	Md.	*The Sun*	4/14/1863	confined awaiting Col. Fish

Person Arrested	Occupation	Jurisdiction	Location	Source	Date	Result
Frank Earle	unstated	provost marshal	Md.	The Sun	4/14/1863	confined awaiting Col. Fish
Henry Long	unstated	provost marshal	Md.	The Sun	4/24/1863	confined awaiting Col. Fish
Henry Supper	unstated	provost marshal	Md.	The Sun	4/24/1863	confined awaiting Col. Fish
Solomon Helser	unstated	military	Md.	The Sun	4/24/1863	sent south under guard
John Helser	unstated	military	Md.	The Sun	4/24/1863	sent south under guard
S. D. Fletcher	unstated	military	Md.	The Sun	4/24/1863	sent south under guard
Louis Vines	unstated	unstated	Md.	The Sun	4/27/1863	sent beyond lines
G. Koontz	unstated	Col. Fish	Md.	The Sun	5/4/1863	paroled awaiting hearing
Richard Courtney	unstated	Col. Fish	Md.	The Sun	5/4/1863	paroled awaiting hearing
L. M. Low	unstated	Col. Fish	Md.	The Sun	5/12/1863	took oath; released
Adam Selbert/Seibert	unstated	Col. Fish	Md.	The Sun	5/13/1863	Fort McHenry
H. L. Porter	unstated	Col. Fish	Md.	The Sun	5/13/1863	Fort McHenry
Edwin O'Donnell	unstated	Col. Fish	Md.	The Sun	5/13/1863	Fort McHenry
James Dillon	unstated	Col. Fish	Md.	The Sun	5/13/1863	Fort McHenry
John Leavelle	unstated	Col. Fish	Md.	The Sun	5/13/1863	Fort McHenry
James Snyder	unstated	military	Md.	The Sun	5/13/1863	sent from Fort McHenry to Louisville, Ky.
William Leach	unstated	military	Md.	The Sun	5/13/1863	sent from Fort McHenry to Louisville, Ky.
Daniel Sheckbert	unstated	military	Md.	The Sun	5/13/1863	sent from Fort McHenry to Louisville, Ky.
Frederick Sigmond	unstated	military	Md.	The Sun	5/13/1863	took oath; released
Adam Reed	unstated	military	Md.	The Sun	5/26/1863	took oath; released
C. F. Jones	editor	chief of police	Tenn.	Milwaukee Sentinel	6/4/1863	sent south
Septimus Brown	unstated	unstated	Va.	The Sun	1/6/1864	Old Capitol Prison; released
C. W. Vallant	unstated	military	Md.	The Sun	1/7/1864	released

Name	Occupation	Arresting authority	State	Source	Date	Disposition
J. W. Hyde	unstated	military	Md.	The Sun	1/7/1864	released on parole
T. Bromwell	unstated	military	Md.	The Sun	1/7/1864	released on parole
W. Ring	unstated	provost marshal	Md.	The Sun	3/3/1864	30 days hard labor
Patrick Brannan	unstated	provost marshal	Md.	The Sun	3/3/1864	30 days hard labor
John Brokman	unstated	military	Md.	The Sun	3/10/1864	released after trial with Maj. Hayner
Slater O. Blackiston	farmer	county sheriff	Md.	The Sun	4/1/1864	held military prison
Edw. Cockran	farmer	county sheriff	Md.	The Sun	4/1/1864	held military prison
J. Bratton	unstated	county sheriff	Md.	The Sun	4/1/1864	held military prison
Robt. Bratton	unstated	county sheriff	Md.	The Sun	4/1/1864	held military prison
Irvin Walters	unstated	county sheriff	Md.	The Sun	4/1/1864	held military prison
Henry Kennerly	unstated	county sheriff	Md.	The Sun	4/1/1864	held military prison
Samuel S. Acworth	unstated	county sheriff	Md.	The Sun	4/1/1864	held military prison
W. Wainwright	unstated	county sheriff	Md.	The Sun	4/1/1864	held military prison
Dr. Henry L. Todd	doctor	county sheriff	Md.	The Sun	4/1/1864	held military prison
Jesse Walters	unstated	county sheriff	Md.	The Sun	4/1/1864	held military prison
William H. Hunt	unstated	unstated	Md.	The Sun	5/21/1864	locked up to await trial
John P. Rhodes	unstated	unstated	Md.	The Sun	5/21/1864	locked up to await trial
James H. Washington	unstated	unstated	Md.	The Sun	5/30/1864	took oath; released
George Roth	unstated	military	Md.	The Sun	6/18/1864	released on oath after 5 weeks
John Thompson	unstated	military	Md.	The Sun	6/18/1864	released on $1,000 bond
Geo. Rensel	unstated	military	Md.	The Sun	6/18/1864	released on $1,000 bond
George W. Johnson	unstated	unstated	Md.	The Sun	7/1/1864	released on oath after several days
Daniel Haley	unstated	military: Col. Woolley	Md.	The Sun	7/4/1864	took oath; released

Person Arrested	Occupation	Jurisdiction	Location	Source	Date	Result
Francis Key	journalist	military	Md.	*The Sun*	7/4/1864	held awaiting trial
Victoria V. Trook	unstated	unstated	D.C.	*Philadelphia Inquirer*	7/20/1864	took oath; released
Joshua Ritchie	unstated	unstated	D.C.	*Philadelphia Inquirer*	7/20/1864	took oath; released
Michael Brown	unstated	unstated	Md.	*Philadelphia Inquirer*	7/20/1864	took oath; released
Thomas Donnelly	unstated	military: Col. Woolley	Md.	*The Sun*	8/6/1864	released on oath after 6 weeks
John Betts	African American	military: Col. Woolley	Md.	*The Sun*	8/6/1864	took oath; released
James H. F. McCormack	hack driver	military: Col. Woolley	Md.	*The Sun*	8/6/1864	tried; imprisoned 30 days
Thomas Len	unstated	military	Md.	*The Sun*	8/6/1864	held for trial
Bernard McKeever	unstated	military	Md.	*The Sun*	8/8/1864	held; disposition unstated
Disloyalty: cheering Jeff Davis						
Rufus Belt	unstated	unstated	Md.	*The Sun*	7/31/1862	unstated
Disloyalty: disloyal publisher						
Thomas K. Robson	editor	military	Md.	*The Sun*	5/12/1863	sent south
Disloyalty: "lip-loyalty"						
George D. Armstrong	minister	military: Gen. Butler	Va.	*New Hampshire Sentinel*	4/14/1864	questioned; results unstated
Disloyalty: refusing oath						
David G. Ridgeley	aged	unstated	Md.	*The Sun*	7/29/1862	unstated
Hon. J. Thomson Mason	judge	unstated	Md.	*The Sun*	8/20/1862	Fort McHenry; paroled
Solomon Keller	unstated	unstated	Md.	*The Sun*	8/20/1862	Fort McHenry

	occupation		location	source	date	disposition
Joseph Stonebraker	unstated		Md.	*The Sun*	8/20/1862	Fort McHenry
Joseph Williams	unstated		Md.	*The Sun*	8/20/1862	Fort McHenry
Dennis Prestman	unstated		Md.	*The Sun*	8/20/1862	Fort McHenry
Samuel Price	unstated		Md.	*The Sun*	8/20/1862	Fort McHenry
Timothy O'Connor	unstated		D.C.	*The Sun*	1/6/1864	charged with treason; held for provost marshal
Disloyalty: treasonable language						
Senator Baker	senator, Visalia, Calif.	military	Calif.	*Deseret News*	10/29/1862	released; investigation continues
Disloyalty: treasonable practices						
A. G. Gallett	editor	marshal and military	Md.	*The Sun*	8/20/1862	Fort McHenry
Dr. Charles E. Tarr	doctor	marshal and military	Md.	*The Sun*	8/20/1862	Fort McHenry
Dr. George W. Goldsborough	doctor	marshal and military	Md.	*The Sun*	8/20/1862	Fort McHenry
Dr. John H. Holt	doctor	marshal and military	Md.	*The Sun*	8/20/1862	Fort McHenry
Thos. P. Quigley	unstated	marshal and military	Md.	*The Sun*	8/20/1862	Fort McHenry
Francis A. Lisk	unstated	marshal and military	Md.	*The Sun*	8/20/1862	Fort McHenry
John W. Bryant	unstated	marshal and military	Md.	*The Sun*	8/20/1862	Fort McHenry
Edward Pritchett	unstated	marshal and military	Md.	*The Sun*	8/20/1862	Fort McHenry
Collison Pritchett	unstated	marshal and military	Md.	*The Sun*	8/20/1862	Fort McHenry

Person Arrested	Occupation	Jurisdiction	Location	Source	Date	Result
Wm. T. Elliott	unstated	marshal and military	Md.	The Sun	8/20/1862	Fort McHenry
Francis Gadd	unstated	marshal and military	Md.	The Sun	8/20/1862	Fort McHenry
Dr. P. O. Cherbonier[?]	doctor	marshal and military	Md.	The Sun	8/20/1862	Fort McHenry
Employing men to go south						
Joshua Barley	unstated	unstated	Md.	The Sun	8/25/1862	took oath; released
Enlisting men for Rebel army						
Mr. Atwood Blunt	unstated	military	Md.	The Sun	8/25/1862	released; no proof of wrongdoing
Enticing soldiers to desert						
Fred Debring	unstated	military: Col. Woolley	Md.	The Sun	8/6/1864	took oath; released
Evading military duty						
Hardy Longcope	unstated	military	Pa.	The Sun	8/14/1862	Fort McHenry; released on bond
Joseph F. Passano	unstated	military	Pa.	The Sun	8/14/1862	Fort McHenry; released on bond
L. Durbin Passano	unstated	military	Pa.	The Sun	8/14/1862	Fort McHenry; released on bond
Louis Rosenberg	unstated	military	Pa.	The Sun	8/14/1862	Fort McHenry; released on bond
Leon Sellger	unstated	military	Pa.	The Sun	8/14/1862	Fort McHenry; released on bond
Joshua Passano	unstated	military	Pa.	The Sun	8/14/1862	Fort McHenry; released on bond

Failed to report after visiting South						
C. F. Weldmeyer	unstated	unstated	Md.	The Sun	5/17/1864	locked up for a hearing
Flew Rebel flag						
Caroline Lamden	unstated	criminal court	Md.	The Sun	5/30/1862	indicted
Matthew Hale	17 year old	military	Md.	The Sun	6/28/1862	Fort McHenry
Furnishing horses, mules to Rebels						
R. W. Peay	unstated	civil	Cincinnati, Ohio	Cleveland Herald	2/21/1862	bail of $6,000; committed to jail
Gave liquor to Rebel prisoners						
Charles Cope	unstated	military	Md.	The Sun	5/16/1863	took oath; released
Guerrilla						
D. O. Whitman	unstated	unstated	Md.	The Sun	8/20/1862	Fort McHenry
Guiding Rebel raiders						
John G. Day	unstated	military: Col. Woolley	Hartford, Conn.	The Sun	8/6/1864	held for trial
Had been in South						
David Magee	unstated	unstated	Md.	The Sun	4/14/1863	sent south via Harpers Ferry
Jos. L. Toy	unstated	unstated	Md.	The Sun	4/14/1863	sent south via Harpers Ferry
G. H. Hartman	unstated	unstated	Md.	The Sun	4/14/1863	sent south via Harpers Ferry
Harboring deserters						
James T. Taylor	unstated	military	Md.	The Sun	5/16/1863	questioned; results unstated
Hostages (presumably Rebels)						
Belney Purcell	unstated	unstated	Va.	The Sun	1/6/1864	Old Capitol Prison
Stephen R. Mount	unstated	unstated	Va.	The Sun	1/6/1864	Old Capitol Prison
Impeached for treason						
Judge James H. Hardy	judge	unstated	unstated	Daily Evening Bulletin	4/7/1862	unstated

Person Arrested	Occupation	Jurisdiction	Location	Source	Date	Result
Impersonating government detective						
Thomas Dutcher	unstated	military; Col. Woolley	Md.	The Sun	8/6/1864	held for trial
Interfering with enlistment						
Jonathan P. Cuddington	unstated	U.S. marshal	Newark, N.J.	Atlantic Democrat	12/20/1862	jailed, then released
Knights of the Golden Circle						
Levi Birsch	unstated	military	Md.	The Sun	5/13/1863	took oath; released
William Birsch	unstated	military	Md.	The Sun	5/13/1863	took oath; released
John Duce	unstated	military	Md.	The Sun	5/13/1863	took oath; released
Adam Leese	unstated	military	Md.	The Sun	5/13/1863	took oath; released
Ephraim Feser	unstated	military	Md.	The Sun	5/13/1863	took oath; released
Jacob Hess	unstated	military	Md.	The Sun	5/13/1863	took oath; released
Adam Wantz	unstated	military	Md.	The Sun	5/13/1863	took oath; released
Henry Resel	unstated	military	Md.	The Sun	5/13/1863	took oath; released
John Walker	unstated	military	Md.	The Sun	5/13/1863	took oath; released
M. H. Crouse	unstated	military	Md.	The Sun	5/13/1863	took oath; released
William Feser	unstated	military	Md.	The Sun	5/13/1863	took oath; released
David Utz	unstated	military	Md.	The Sun	5/13/1863	took oath; released
Knights of the Golden Circle/"Wooden Horse"						
Christopher Wistner	unstated	military	Md.	The Sun	5/4/1863	took oath; released
Jacob Wistner	unstated	military	Md.	The Sun	5/4/1863	took oath; released
Peter Bisch	unstated	military	Md.	The Sun	5/4/1863	took oath; released
Nicholas Bisch	unstated	military	Md.	The Sun	5/4/1863	took oath; released
John Gobiel[?]	unstated	military	Md.	The Sun	5/4/1863	took oath; released

Ladies' organization supporting Rebel army						
Miss Alice Pairo	daughter of Mrs. Pairo	military: Col. Fish	Md.	The Sun	3/30/1863	sent south with mother
Machinery for weapons provided to Rebels						
John K. Millner	unstated	military	N.Y.	San Francisco Bulletin	10/5/1864	determined to be citizen
Meeting "inimical to government"						
James H. Buchanan	unstated	military	Md.	The Sun	9/4/1862	no evidence; released
Samuel W. Worthington	unstated	military	Md.	The Sun	9/4/1862	no evidence; released
Dr. E. R. Tidings	doctor	military	Md.	The Sun	9/4/1862	no evidence; released
Dr. J. Davis Thompson	doctor	military	Md.	The Sun	9/4/1862	no evidence; released
Duncan B. Cannon	unstated	military	Md.	The Sun	9/4/1862	no evidence; released
H. P. Hayward	unstated	military	Md.	The Sun	9/4/1862	no evidence; released
Richard Grason	unstated	military	Md.	The Sun	9/4/1862	no evidence; released
J. T. Albert	unstated	military	Md.	The Sun	9/4/1862	no evidence; released
H. Scott	unstated	military	Md.	The Sun	9/4/1862	no evidence; released
Chas. McLane	unstated	military	Md.	The Sun	9/4/1862	no evidence; released
Charles M. McLane	unstated	military	Md.	The Sun	9/4/1862	no evidence; released
W. R. Penniman	unstated	military	Md.	The Sun	9/4/1862	no evidence; released
John J. White	unstated	military	Md.	The Sun	9/4/1862	no evidence; released
Edward Hyatt	unstated	military	Md.	The Sun	9/4/1862	no evidence; released
T. L. Worthington	unstated	military	Md.	The Sun	9/4/1862	no evidence; released
T. T. Tunstall	native of Alabama	military	Md.	The Sun	9/4/1862	no evidence; released
Jnd.[?] Merryman	unstated	military	Md.	The Sun	9/4/1862	no evidence; released
Alfred Matthews	unstated	military	Md.	The Sun	9/4/1862	no evidence; released

Person Arrested	Occupation	Jurisdiction	Location	Source	Date	Result
Objected to newspaper suppression						
Col. James W. Wall	col., senator's son	military	N.Y.	San Francisco Bulletin	10/2/1861	Fort Lafayette
Piloting Rebel raiders						
Charles H. Cockey	unstated	military: Col. Woolley	Md.	The Sun	8/6/1864	Gratiot Street Prison
Preaching armed resistance						
Gen. Tench Tilghman	unstated	military	Md.	Easton Gazette	10/12/1861	released
Preaching treason and rebellion						
Lorenzo Dow Houston	minister, Methodist Church South	state judge	Ky.	Cleveland Herald	10/3/1865	unstated
Preferred southern government						
John R. Lambson	unstated	military: Capt. French	Md.	The Sun	5/16/1863	confined during war
Printing money for C.S.A.						
Conrad Fatzer	lithographer	military	N.Y.	San Francisco Bulletin	10/2/1861	Fort Lafayette
Benjamin F. Corlies	printer	military	N.Y.	San Francisco Bulletin	10/2/1861	unstated
Rebel						
George Hoyle	unstated	unstated	Md.	The Sun	1/6/1864	took oath; released
James W. Holton	unstated	unstated	Md.	The Sun	1/6/1864	Old Capitol Prison
J. H. Barnes	unstated	unstated	Va.	The Sun	1/6/1864	Old Capitol Prison
Francis Fox	unstated	unstated	Va.	The Sun	1/6/1864	Old Capitol Prison
John H. Mills	unstated	unstated	Va.	The Sun	1/6/1864	Old Capitol Prison
N. W. Mills	unstated	unstated	Va.	The Sun	1/6/1864	Old Capitol Prison

Refugee						
John Regan	unstated	unstated	unstated	*The Sun*	1/6/1864	Old Capitol Prison
W. Bentke	unstated	unstated	unstated	*The Sun*	1/6/1864	Old Capitol Prison
Requested arrest to be with wife						
Edward William Johnston	old gentleman	provost marshal	Mo.	*San Francisco Bulletin*	9/10/1862	Gratiot Street Prison
Riot						
Patrick O'Donnell	unstated	military	Md.	*The Sun*	4/19/1863	held for examination
Running/violating blockade						
Henry A. Wood	unstated	military	Md.	*The Sun*	4/24/1863	sent south under guard
Geo. Williams	unstated	military	Md.	*The Sun*	4/24/1863	sent south under guard
William Goddard	blockade-runner	military	Md.	*The Sun*	5/16/1863	took oath; released
Julius G. White	unstated	unstated	unstated	*The Sun*	1/6/1864	Old Capitol Prison
Thomas Fitchell	lighthouse keeper	military arrest	Md.	*The Sun*	1/6/1864	Old Capitol Prison
John A. Taber	unstated	unstated	Md.	*The Sun*	1/6/1864	Fort Delaware
John Goldsmith	unstated	unstated	Md.	*The Sun*	1/6/1864	Old Capitol Prison
Thomas W. Jones	unstated	unstated	Md.	*The Sun*	1/6/1864	Old Capitol Prison
Charles H. Posey	unstated	unstated	Md.	*The Sun*	1/6/1864	Old Capitol Prison
John J. Wilson	unstated	unstated	Md.	*The Sun*	1/6/1864	Old Capitol Prison
John W. Taylor	unstated	unstated	Va.	*The Sun*	1/6/1864	Old Capitol Prison
George Taylor	unstated	unstated	Va.	*The Sun*	1/6/1864	Old Capitol Prison
Samuel G. Taylor	unstated	unstated	Va.	*The Sun*	1/6/1864	Old Capitol Prison
Dearban Johnson	unstated	unstated	Va.	*The Sun*	1/6/1864	Old Capitol Prison
Samuel Johnson	unstated	unstated	Va.	*The Sun*	1/6/1864	Old Capitol Prison
Isaiah Johnson	unstated	unstated	Va.	*The Sun*	1/6/1864	Old Capitol Prison
John A. Scott	unstated	unstated	Va.	*The Sun*	1/6/1864	Old Capitol Prison

Person Arrested	Occupation	Jurisdiction	Location	Source	Date	Result
S. D. Spence	unstated	military commission	Md.	The Sun	3/19/1864	1 year at Fort McHenry
George Hall	unstated	military	Md.	The Sun	7/1/1864	held awaiting trial
Samuel Lewis	unstated	military	Md.	The Sun	7/1/1864	held awaiting trial
Nicholas McKee	unstated	military	Md.	The Sun	7/1/1864	held awaiting trial
Secessionist						
Colonel Kerven	elected to Calif. legislature	military	Calif.	Deseret News	10/29/1862	Fort Alcatraz
George H. Cook	unstated	unstated	Va.	The Sun	3/16/1863	Fort Lafayette
Richard Johnson	unstated	unstated	Va.	The Sun	1/6/1864	Old Capitol Prison
Richard Richardson	unstated	unstated	Va.	The Sun	1/6/1864	Old Capitol Prison
Albert Wren	unstated	unstated	Va.	The Sun	1/6/1864	Old Capitol Prison
Secretary for Hon. Mr. Mason						
E. F. F. Williamson	secretary	military: Col. Fish	Md.	The Sun	5/12/1863	paroled
Sold liquor to soldiers						
Wm. Dunning	proprietor of drinking house	military	Md.	The Sun	5/26/1863	paroled to report 1 week
Spy						
G. A. Satterfield	unstated	unstated	Fort Marshall	The Sun	7/31/1862	10 days confinement
Spy: telegraph wire cutting						
Maria Murphy	unstated	military: Col. Fish	unstated	The Sun	5/8/1863	held subject to Gen Schenck's order
Mary Jane Green	unstated	military: Col. Fish	W.Va.	Alexandria Gazette	5/8/1863	unstated
Spy: violation of laws of war						
William Stokes	citizen	military commission	Md.	The Sun	4/23/1864	held subject to Gen Schenck's order

Substitute deserted

Samuel Sharp	unstated	military	Md.	*The Sun*	5/26/1863	confined awaiting general's decision

Suspected Rebel soldier

John Collins	soldier?	military	W.Va.	*The Sun*	5/16/1863	Fort McHenry
John Dixon	unstated	military: Col. Woolley	Md.	*Alexandria Gazette*	10/23/1863	Fort McHenry
John Clarke	unstated	military: Col. Woolley	Md.	*The Sun*	8/6/1864	determined to be citizen
Charles Britton	unstated	military: Col. Woolley	Md.	*The Sun*	8/6/1864	determined to be citizen
John Sutton	unstated	military: Col. Woolley	Md.	*The Sun*	8/6/1864	determined to be citizen
Robert Anderson	unstated	military: Col. Woolley	Md.	*The Sun*	8/6/1864	determined to be citizen

Treason

Lt. A. Morton	unstated	unstated	St. Louis, Mo.	*Plain Dealer*	10/5/1861	Fort Lafayette
Messrs. Brennan	iron founders	provost marshal	Nashville, Tenn.	*Philadelphia Inquirer*	4/5/1862	
R. B. Cheatham	mayor of city	provost marshal	Nashville, Tenn.	*Daily National Intelligencer*	4/7/1862	unstated—presumed to go to civil court
Mr. Sharp	plough manufacturer	provost marshal	Nashville, Tenn.	*Daily National Intelligencer*	4/7/1862	unstated—presumed to go to civil court
Mr. Hamilton	plough manufacturer	provost marshal	Nashville, Tenn.	*Daily National Intelligencer*	4/7/1862	unstated—presumed to go to civil court
Judge Richard Carmichael	judge	military: Gen. Dix	Md.	*Public Ledger*	5/29/1862	unstated

Person Arrested	Occupation	Jurisdiction	Location	Source	Date	Result
Mr. Doyle	editor	U.S. marshal	Detroit, Mich.	New Hampshire Patriot and State Gazette	6/18/1862	unstated — presumed to go to civil court
John S. Riddison	farmer	deputy marshal	Md.	The Sun	8/14/1862	Fort McHenry
John Hermann	blacksmith	deputy marshal	Md.	The Sun	8/14/1862	Fort McHenry
Joshua Burgan	gardener	deputy marshal	Md.	The Sun	8/14/1862	Fort McHenry
George P. Buckey	unstated	police	Md.	The Sun	8/14/1862	questioned; results unstated
Wm. Lambert	unstated	police	Md.	The Sun	8/14/1862	questioned; results unstated
Robert Saylor	unstated	police	Md.	The Sun	8/14/1862	questioned; results unstated
Wm. Zimmerman	unstated	police	Md.	The Sun	8/14/1862	questioned; results unstated
Charles B. Simpson	unstated	police	Md.	The Sun	8/14/1862	questioned; results unstated
Thomas Lyons[?]	unstated	military: Sgt. Pryor	Md.	The Sun	8/14/1862	questioned; results unstated
Aaron Dailey	aged	military guard	Va.	The Sun	8/14/1862	Fort McHenry
Joseph Mead	aged	military guard	Va.	The Sun	8/14/1862	Fort McHenry
George L. Moore	unstated	unstated	Va.	The Sun	8/14/1862	Fort McHenry
Benjamin Hornett	ex-Rebel soldier	military: Sgt. Pryor	Md.	The Sun	8/14/1862	awaited criminal trial
John Unart	unstated	unstated	Md.	The Sun	8/20/1862	took oath; released
Levi Pettiman	unstated	unstated	Md.	The Sun	8/20/1862	Fort McHenry
William H. Tatspaw	unstated	unstated	Md.	The Sun	8/20/1862	Fort McHenry
John Worley	unstated	unstated	Md.	The Sun	8/20/1862	Fort McHenry
Hugh O'Brien	unstated	provost marshal?	Md.	The Sun	8/25/1862	Fort McHenry
Dennis Whalen	unstated	provost marshal?	Md.	The Sun	8/25/1862	held for examination by marshal
Christian Emerich	unstated	military commission	Md.	The Sun	4/14/1863	unstated

Name	Occupation	Tribunal	Location	Source	Date	Outcome
Fanny James	unstated	civil: Md. City	Md	North American & U.S. Gazette	5/12/1863	unstated
Miss Fanny James	unstated	military	Md	The Sun	5/12/1863	convicted to 2 years hard labor
John Scally	unstated	military commission	unstated	The Sun	4/14/1864	held for hearing
George Emerich	unstated	military commission	Md	The Sun	4/14/1864	held for hearing
William Hall	editor	military	Calif.	Daily Evening Bulletin	7/27/1864	questioned; results unstated
Treason: aiding Sibley						
Diego Armijo	unstated	U.S. District Court	N.Mex.	Philadelphia Inquirer	11/18/1862	held for marshal
Treason: carrying Rebel mail						
Mrs. S. E. Eldridge	unstated	police	Md.	The Sun	9/4/1862	no arrest; sermon turned over
Treason: cheering Jefferson Davis						
William Roundtree	unstated	provost marshal	Md.	The Sun	8/20/1862	awaiting orders of Marshal Van Nostrand
Treasonable language						
Joseph Rogers	unstated	civil?	Md.	The Sun	9/4/1862	took oath; released
Frank Thompson	unstated	unstated	Md.	The Sun	4/14/1863	judge ordered held for Marshal Van Nostrand
Charles Weaver	unstated	military: Col. Fish	Md.	The Sun	5/4/1863	took oath; released
J. A. Barrett	physician	military	Mo.	The Sun	6/7/1864	unstated
Francis Key	unstated	military	Md.	The Sun	8/12/1864	took oath; released
John McElwee	editor	U.S. District Court	Cincinnati, Ohio	Daily Ohio Statesman	11/16/1864	took oath; released

Person Arrested	Occupation	Jurisdiction	Location	Source	Date	Result
Treasonable language and/or practice						
John Hagan[?]	lawyer	military	Md.	*The Sun*	7/31/1862	Camp Chase
Joseph Marshal	unstated	unstated	Md.	*The Sun*	8/27/1862	from police station to McHenry
Kate McCoy	unstated	military	Md.	*The Sun*	1/7/1864	held at marshal's office
Treasonable school activities						
Miss Hull	teacher-principal	provost marshal	New Orleans, La.	*Boston Recorder*	6/5/1863	fined $100
Madame Loquet	principal	provost marshal	New Orleans, La.	*Boston Recorder*	6/5/1863	fined $250
Miss Picot	principal	provost marshal	New Orleans, La.	*Boston Recorder*	6/5/1863	fined $150
Treason and piracy						
John Murphy	unstated	U.S. district attorney	Md.	*The Sun*	6/25/1861	held for examination by marshal
Treason from the pulpit						
Rev. Mr. Stearns	minister	U.S. district attorney	N.Y.	*Philadelphia Inquirer*	10/4/1861	held for hearing
Trying to go south						
Clarence Peters	unstated	military	Md.	*The Sun*	1/7/1864	Old Capitol Prison
Unstated						
Austin E. Smith	former navy agent	unstated	N.Y.	*San Francisco Bulletin*	8/22/1861	Camp Mansfield
Wm. M. Gwin	former U.S. senator	military: Gen. Sumner	Panama	*New York Herald*	11/16/1861	held at Fort Lafayette
Calhoun Benham	travel companion	military: Gen. Sumner	D.C.	*San Francisco Bulletin*	1/9/1862	unstated

Name	ex-minister	military		source	date	disposition
Faulkner	ex-minister	military	N.Y	San Francisco Bulletin	1/9/1862	unstated
Jacob Dalweiner	unstated	deputy marshal	Harpers Ferry	The Sun	8/14/1862	Fort McHenry; took oath; released
John Dalweiner	unstated	deputy marshal	Harpers Ferry	The Sun	8/14/1862	Fort McHenry; took oath; released
Joseph Keyne	unstated	deputy marshal	Harpers Ferry	The Sun	8/14/1862	Fort McHenry; took oath; released
William George	unstated	deputy marshal	Harpers Ferry	The Sun	8/14/1862	Fort McHenry; took oath; released
William Burke	unstated	deputy marshal	Harpers Ferry	The Sun	8/14/1862	Fort McHenry; took oath; released
Henry Weaver	unstated	deputy marshal	Harpers Ferry	The Sun	8/14/1862	Fort McHenry; took oath; released
Henry Dougherty	unstated	deputy marshal	Harpers Ferry	The Sun	8/14/1862	Fort McHenry; took oath; released
J. G. Diffenderfer	unstated	unstated	Md.	The Sun	8/14/1862	Fort McHenry; took oath; released
F. A. Zimmerman	unstated	unstated	Md.	The Sun	8/14/1862	took oath; released
Robert Godfrey	unstated	unstated	Md.	The Sun	8/14/1862	took oath; released
Milton A. Lausre[?]	unstated	unstated	Md.	The Sun	8/14/1862	took oath; released
Jacob F. Pope	unstated	deputy marshal	Harpers Ferry	The Sun	8/14/1862	imprisoned
William H. Carter	unstated	unstated	Va.	The Sun	8/20/1862	took oath; released
Thomas H. Crow	unstated	unstated	Va.	The Sun	8/20/1862	Fort McHenry
Richard Wagner	unstated	unstated	Va.	The Sun	8/25/1862	Fort McHenry
Dr. John Laws	doctor?	Md. Home Guards	Del.	The Sun	10/11/1862	unstated
Judge Hall	unstated	unstated	Ohio	Cleveland Herald	10/17/1862	Camp Mansfield

Person Arrested	Occupation	Jurisdiction	Location	Source	Date	Result
Whitely Meredith	unstated	Md. Home Guards	Del.	The Sun	12/9/1862	imprisoned
Dr. Bachelor	doctor?	U.S. marshal	N.H.	Daily National Intelligencer	12/10/1862	imprisoned
David R. Risley	prominent citizen	military	Mo.	The Sun	5/27/1863	imprisoned
L. M. Shreve	prominent citizen	military	Mo.	The Sun	5/27/1863	imprisoned
J. M. Loughborough	prominent citizen	military	Mo.	The Sun	5/27/1863	imprisoned
W. H. McKnight	prominent citizen	military	Mo.	The Sun	5/27/1863	took oath, released
John Kelchea	unstated, British subject	unstated	unstated	The Sun	1/6/1864	Old Capitol Prison
Samuel Rich	unstated	unstated	unstated	The Sun	1/6/1864	Old Capitol Prison
Jacob Lewis	unstated	unstated	unstated	The Sun	1/6/1864	Old Capitol Prison
Daniel Lambert	unstated	unstated	Md.	The Sun	1/6/1864	Old Capitol Prison
George R. Magglisson	unstated	unstated	Mo.	The Sun	1/6/1864	Old Capitol Prison
Joseph Savage	hardware dealer	by order of government	D.C.	The Sun	3/15/1864	imprisoned
Michael Bosley	unstated	Gen. Butler	Md.	The Sun	4/26/1864	unstated
Southey F. Miles	unstated	Gen. Lockwood	Md.	The Sun	4/26/1864	unstated
Mrs. William Key Howard	unstated	provost marshal	Md.	Alexandria Gazette	4/29/1864	Old Capitol Prison
Eugene McDonald	government hay contractor	by order of secretary of war	Md.	The Sun	6/18/1864	store closed
Urged murder of black troops						
Mr. J. F. Bilderbeck	unstated	native Calif. Cavalry	San Francisco, Calif.	San Francisco Bulletin	5/28/1864	held at Drum Barracks

Urging draft resistance

Dr. J. M. Allen	doctor?	military: U.S. marshal	Ohio	*Cleveland Herald*	10/17/1862	sent south via Harpers Ferry

Violating laws of war

William F. Quinlan	citizen	military commission	Md.	*The Sun*	4/14/1864	Fort Delaware

NOTES

Abbreviations

ALP	Abraham Lincoln Papers, Library of Congress
CG	*Congressional Globe*
CW	Basler, *Collected Works of Abraham Lincoln*
GBMP	George B. McClellan Papers, Library of Congress
HL	Huntington Library, San Marino, California
HSP	Historical Society of Pennsylvania, Philadelphia
LC	Library of Congress, Washington, D.C.
LGM	Letterbooks, Governor of Maryland, Maryland State Archives, Annapolis
MMP	Manton Marble Papers, Library of Congress
NARA	National Archives and Records Administration
O.R.	U.S. War Department, *The War of the Rebellion: A Compilation of the Official Records of the Union and Confederate Armies*
PMG	Records of the Provost Marshal General's Bureau (RG 110), National Archives and Records Administration, Washington, D.C.
PSA	Pennsylvania State Archives, Harrisburg
RG	Record Group
WHMC	Western Historical Manuscript Collection, State Historical Society of Missouri, Columbia

Introduction

1. White, "'To Aid Their Rebel Friend,'" 1–4.

2. On plausibility, see Neely, *Lincoln and the Triumph of the Nation*, 5; Belz, *Abraham Lincoln, Constitutionalism, and Equal Rights in the Civil War Era*, 73–74.

3. Vattel, *The Law of Nations*; Wheaton, *Elements of International Law*.

4. For the work recognized as stating that the Constitution was adequate to handle the crisis, see Hyman, *A More Perfect Union*.

5. On the practical approach to the Constitution, see Belz, *Abraham Lincoln, Constitutionalism, and Equal Rights in the Civil War Era*, 74–75.

6. For a sophisticated discussion of how people, crowds, and public officials felt they had the right to interpret the Constitution, see Kramer, *The People Themselves*.

7. See, for instance, Foner, *The Fiery Trial: Abraham Lincoln and American Slavery*, 176–81; Manning, *What This Cruel War Was Over*; Ayers and Nesbit, "Seeing Emancipation: Scale and Freedom in the American South," 3–24; Berlin et al., *Freedom: A Documentary History of Emancipation, 1861–1867, Series II, The Black Military Experience*, 1–34.

8. For this assessment, see McPherson, *Tried by War*.

9. Neely, *Lincoln and the Triumph of the Nation*, 19–20. White makes a similar point that we need to look beyond court cases, constitutions, and statutes. See his "'To Aid Their Rebel Friend,'" v.

10. Quoted in McPherson, *Battle Cry of Freedom*, 600.

11. Sandow, *Deserter Country*, 7–8, 20–21, 100–103; Weber, *Copperheads*, 103–6; Anbinder, "Which Poor Man's Fight?," 353.

12. *O.R.*, ser. 1, 38:5.

13. See, for instance, Coulter, *The Civil War and Readjustment in Kentucky*. Works on Maryland have taken note of the military interference with elections in that state. A somewhat critical assessment of the actions can be found in Wagandt, *The Mighty Revolution*, 157–84, while Baker dismisses the influence as sour grapes by partisan opponents who lost the elections in her *Politics of Continuity*, 88–89. One of the rare recent works to touch on the subject can be found in Frank, *With Ballot and Bayonet*, 180–81.

14. See, for instance, Hooker, "Soldiers of the State," 1–18.

15. Weber, *Copperheads*, 121.

16. On the importance of Union, see Gallagher, *The Union War*.

17. For the view that these arrests were more targeted than arbitrary, see Neely, *Fate of Liberty*.

18. For a good overview, see Fehrenbacher, "The Anti-Lincoln Tradition."

19. In general, historians have argued over whether the Copperheads served as a loyal opposition whose harm against the state was overexaggerated by Republicans or were truly problematic and threatening. Taking the former view were Klement, *Copperheads in the Middle West*; Silbey, *A Respectable Minority*. More recently, Jennifer Weber has argued for the Copperheads as being not traitors necessarily but a threat to the nation. Weber, *Copperheads*. The seminal study of Democratic racism belongs to Baker, *Affairs of Party*. For a good overview on the Copperhead debate in general, see Sandow, *Deserter Country*, 4–7.

20. Sternhell, "Antiwar Civil War." A representative sampling of works includes Royster, *The Destructive War*; Goldfield, *America Aflame*; Faust, *This Republic of Suffering* and her "'We Should Grow Too Fond of It': Why We Love the Civil War," 368–83; Nelson, *Ruin Nation*; and books on guerrilla warfare typified by Sutherland, *A Savage Conflict*.

21. Bensel, *The American Ballot Box in the Mid-Nineteenth Century*, 251.

Chapter 1

1. Hurst, *The Law of Treason in the United States*, 144; Leek, "Treason and the Constitution," 607–8; Carso, "'Whom Can We Trust Now?,'" 101–5.

2. Tarrant, "Congress and the Law of Seditious Conspiracy, 1859–1861," 107–23.

3. Hurst, *The Law of Treason in the United States*, 150–51.

4. For summaries of treason and the Constitution, see ibid., 75, 139, 141; Chapin, *The American Law of Treason*, 81–84; White, "The Trial of Jefferson Davis and the Americanization of Treason Law," 114–16; Slaughter, "'The King of Crimes,'" 62–74; Hobson, *The Aaron Burr Treason Trial*, 1.

5. Hobson, *The Aaron Burr Treason Trial*, 1.

6. Slaughter, "'The King of Crimes,'" 85.

7. Chapin, *The American Law of Treason*, 80–85; Slaughter, "'The King of Crimes,'" 89–95. Also see his *The Whiskey Rebellion*.

8. *U.S. v. Mitchell*, 2 U.S., 348 (1795), p. 7.

9. Slaughter, "'The King of Crimes,'" 93.

10. Carso, "'Whom Can We Trust Now?,'" 125–26; Chapin, *The American Law of Treason*, 90–97; Slaughter, "'The King of Crimes,'" 96–108.

11. Carso, "'Whom Can We Trust Now?,'" 129–30; Newmyer, *John Marshall and the Heroic Age of the Supreme Court*, 180; Smith, *John Marshall*, 352; Hobson, *The Aaron Burr Treason Trial*, 1–2.

12. Hobson, *The Aaron Burr Treason Trial*, 2–4.

13. *Ex Parte Bollman and Ex Parte Swartwout*, 8 U.S., 75 (1807), p. 125.

14. Haskins and Johnson, *History of the Supreme Court*, 2:259.

15. Ibid., 2:260, 266.

16. Swisher, *History of the Supreme Court of the United States*, 5:247.

17. For the definitive work on the riot, see Slaughter, *Bloody Dawn*, 50–71.

18. Ibid., 64–65, 72.

19. Finkelman, "The Treason Trial of Castner Hanway," 84–85.

20. Slaughter, *Bloody Dawn*, 93.

21. Robbins, *Report on the Trial of Castner Hanway for Treason*, 242.

22. Ibid., 242, 243, 244.

23. Ibid., 245.

24. Ibid., 246.

25. Slaughter, *Bloody Dawn*, 133–35.

26. David Reynolds in his study of John Brown does not make the explicit argument about the role of treason in escalating violence; however, he does reveal a series of events that make Brown's crimes explainable, if not legally or morally defensible. See his *John Brown*, 139. Also see Oates, *To Purge This Land with Blood*, 114–15.

27. Sanborn, *The Life and Letters of John Brown*, 236.

28. Etcheson, *Bleeding Kansas*, 53–59.

29. *National Era*, September 25, 1856.

30. "Message of the President of the United States, Relative to Affairs in the Territory of Kansas," H. Ex. Doc. No. 28, 34th Cong., 1st sess. (January 24, 1856), 4.

31. Ibid., 3, 7. See also the *New York Times*, January 26, 1856.

32. *CG*, 34th Cong., 1st sess. (February 18, 1856), 440.

33. Sanborn, *Life and Letters of John Brown*, 219 (first quotation), 223 (second).

34. Robinson, *Kansas*, 207.

35. For placing the blame on Jones rather than Judge Lecompte, see Malin, "Judge Lecompte and the 'Sack of Lawrence,'" 465–94. For other accounts of the incident, see Etcheson, *Bleeding Kansas*, 102–5; Gienapp, *The Origins of the Republican Party*, 297; Potter, *The Impending Crisis*, 208–9.

36. The most recent estimates place the number of deaths between December 1855 and the end of 1856 at thirty-eight; far and away most of those came after the executions conducted by John Brown's men. Etcheson, *Bleeding Kansas*, 135.

37. Reynolds, *John Brown Abolitionist*, 156, 180–81; Horwitz, *Midnight Rising*, 56.

38. *CG*, 34th Cong., 1st sess. (August 4, 1856), 1900.

39. *Report of the Select Committee of the Senate on the Invasion and Seizure of Public Property at Harper's Ferry, June 15, 1860*, 36th Cong., 1st sess., S. Rep. No. 278, "Testimony," p. 88.

40. *Notes of Debates in the Federal Convention of 1787*, 489–91; Carso, "'Whom Can We Trust Now?,'" 104.

41. Schlesinger, *The Age of Jackson*, 410–13.

42. *New York Herald*, October 26, 1859.

43. Horwitz comes to a similar conclusion about the lack of interest by the Buchanan administration. See his *Midnight Rising*, 194–95; *The Code of Virginia* (1849), 722. I am indebted for this insight to Jonathan W. White.

44. For a comprehensive account of the proceedings, see McGinty, *John Brown's Trial*.

45. Brown and DeWitt, *Life, Trial and Execution of Captain John Brown*, 86.

46. Ibid., 87. Also see the *New York Times*, November 1, 1859.

47. Brown and DeWitt, *Life, Trial and Execution of Captain John Brown*, 72 (Hunter), 51–54 (provisional constitution); for a reprint of the provisional constitution, see Trodd and Stauffer, *Meteor of War*, 110–20. For coverage of the final day and summation, also see the *New York Times*, November 1, 1859.

48. Brown and DeWitt, *Life, Trial and Execution of Captain John Brown*, 92. See also *Report of the Select Committee of the Senate*, S. Rep. No. 278, pp. 48–59.

49. Brown and DeWitt, *Life, Trial and Execution of Captain John Brown*, 93–95.

50. *CW*, 3:502.

51. *National Era*, October 27, 1859.

52. 1860 Grand Jury Presentment Regarding John Brown's Raid, Criminal Case Files, 1791–1970, box 10, Records of the Eastern District of Pennsylvania, RG 21, United States District Court, NARA, Philadelphia (emphasis in original). I am grateful to Jonathan W. White for supplying this source.

Chapter 2

1. For the use of constructive treason by northerners, see White, "'To Aid Their Rebel Friend'"; for treason under the laws of war, see White, "All for a Sword," 163–65.

2. For the observation on little social unrest greeting these arrests, see Neely, "The Lincoln Administration and Arbitrary Arrests: A Reconsideration," 8–9, and for "constitutional plausibility," see his *Lincoln and the Triumph of the Nation*, 5.

3. Edward Bates, December 30, 1861, vol. 7, Attorney General's Office, Letters Received, entry 10, RG 60, Department of Justice, NARA; Neely, *Fate of Liberty*, 120.

4. Randall, *Constitutional Problems under Lincoln*, 75–76; Neely, *Lincoln and the Triumph of the Nation*, 5; White, "'To Aid their Rebel Friend.'"

5. *CW*, 4:428.

6. Robert Dale Owen was still using the term after the war. He hoped for restoration of political rights only for the rebels who purged themselves of treason "actual or implied." See his letter of June 21, 1865, in *The Liberator*, July 7, 1865. For

the Burnside order that prohibited "treason, expressed or implied," see *O.R.*, ser. 1, 23(pt. 2):237.

7. *New York Herald*, August 7, 1862; *O.R.*, ser. 1, 23(pt. 2):108.

8. Binney, *The Privilege of the Writ of Habeas Corpus*. On Binney, see Neely, *Lincoln and the Triumph of the Nation*, 71–80.

9. Binney, *The Privilege of the Writ of Habeas Corpus*, 47–48.

10. Neely, *Lincoln and the Triumph of the Nation*, 86.

11. Beall, *Memoir of John Yates Beall*, 254.

12. *Harper's Weekly*, February 2, 1861.

13. Randall, *Constitutional Problems under Lincoln*, 149–50.

14. William H. Seward to George Ashmun, April 12, 1861, vol. 1, Secret Letters, 1861–1863, entry 955, RG 59, Department of State, NARA.

15. William H. Seward to William H. Barse, September 2, 1861, vol. 1, p. 52, Secret Letters, entry 955, RG 59, Department of State, NARA

16. *O.R.*, ser. 2, 2:32–33.

17. *O.R.*, ser. 2, 1:186.

18. *Daily Cleveland Herald*, June 17, 18, 1861; *Cincinnati Enquirer*, June 16, 1861; Blake, "Ten Firkins of Butter and Other 'Traitorous' Aid," 289.

19. *O.R.*, ser. 2, 2:6–8.

20. *New York Herald*, August 26, 1861; *New York Times*, September 23, 1861.

21. *Philadelphia Sunday Transcript*, May 12, 1861.

22. See, for example, the case of Edward B. Wilder in *O.R.*, ser. 2, 2:693–703.

23. William H. Seward to Seth C. Hawley, November 26, 1861, vol. 2, Secret Letters, entry 955, RG 59, Department of State, NARA.

24. *O.R.*, ser. 2, 2:84.

25. Nevins, *George Templeton Strong Diary*, 176.

26. Bates to J. O. Broadhead, April 16, 1862, Attorney General's Office, Letterbook B, no. 5, vol. 8, pp. 70–71, Letters Received, RG 60, Department of Justice, NARA.

27. Bates to N. P. Banks, June 16, 1861, box 4, Attorney General's Office, entry 14, RG 60, Department of Justice, NARA.

28. Paludan, *People's Contest*, 239–40; Towne, "Killing the Serpent Speedily," 53.

29. *Philadelphia Inquirer*, August 20, 1861.

30. White, *A Philadelphia Perspective*, 108–10, 116. Also see Charles H. Fisher to Abraham Lincoln, September 13, 1861, ALP.

31. Bates to George A. Coffey (U.S. District Attorney at Philadelphia), May 5, 1862, Letterbook B, no. 5, vol. 8, p. 83, Attorney General's Office, RG 60, Department of Justice, NARA.

32. "An Act Relating to Habeas Corpus, and regulating Judicial Proceedings in Certain Cases," March 3, 1863, *U.S. Statutes at Large*, 37th Cong., 3rd sess., 12:755–78. For Butler, see *O.R.*, ser. 2, 2:505–9.

33. Bernstein, *The New York City Draft Riots*, 23–24.

34. See, for instance, the *New York Herald*, May 2, 1861; *Philadelphia Inquirer*, May 1, 1861; and *Daily Cleveland Herald*, January 22, 1862.

35. *New York Herald*, August 26, 1861.

36. *Loyalty of Clerks and Other Persons Employed by Government*, 37th Cong., 2nd sess., H. Rep. No. 16; Hyman, *Era of the Oath*, 1–9.

37. Cole and McDonough, *Witness to the Young Republic*, 376; B. B. French to Abraham Lincoln, October 15, 1861, ALP.

38. Hyman, *Era of the Oath*, 6–11; *Loyalty of Clerks and Other Persons Employed by Government*, 65–66; *New York Times*, January 20, 1862.

39. Neely, *Fate of Liberty*, 23. For his conclusions on the period, see pp. 29–31.

40. *Philadelphia Inquirer*, May 1, 2, 3, 1861; *New York Herald*, May 2, 4, 1861.

41. *United States v. Greiner*, 26 F. Cas. 36 (1861).

42. *Daily National Intelligencer*, May 13, 1862; *New York Times*, May 16, 1862.

43. On Houston, see the *Philadelphia Inquirer*, November 27, 1862, and the *Baltimore Sun*, December 1, 1862; on Schachlett, see the *Milwaukee Daily Sentinel*, April 3, 1863.

44. District Court of Maryland, Docket, 1860–1867, 24-M-1-1.6, RG 21, District Courts of the United States, NARA, Philadelphia; McGinty, *Lincoln and the Court*, 197–99; Neff, *Justice in Blue and Gray*, 152; White, *Abraham Lincoln and Treason in the Civil War*, 59–60.

45. *U.S. v. William Perry et al.*, Records of the U.S. Circuit Court for the Eastern District of Pennsylvania, Criminal Case Files, 1791–1883, box 13; Records of the Circuit Court, Minutes, from August 1, 1860, to April 1, 1862, 42-E-11-1.1, and Minutes, April 5, 1865, to November 30, 1866, RG 21, District Courts of the United States, NARA, Philadelphia.

46. Blake, "Aiding and Abetting," 95–108.

47. *O.R.*, ser. 2, 5:190–91.

48. Lichterman, "John Adams Dix: 1798–1879," 478–80; Trogdon, "The Uninspiring Story of the Dix-Pierrepont Commission."

49. *New York Herald*, February 16, 1862.

50. *Springfield Republican*, February 1, 1862.

51. Smith, *The Borderlands in the Civil War*, 350, 367; Gerteis, *Civil War St. Louis*, 173.

52. Neely, *Fate of Liberty*, 168; for military commissions in general, see Prescott and Eldridge, "Military Commissions, Past and Future," 42–51; for Halleck's instructions in General Orders No. 1, see *O.R.*, ser. 1, 8:477.

53. Records of Courts-Martial for the Union and Confederate Armies and the Union Navy, RG 153, Judge Advocate General, NARA; *O.R.*, ser. 2., 1:282–389; also see appendix A.

54. Neely, *Fate of Liberty*, 162–65.

55. File no. 00540, Courts-Martial Records, RG 153, Judge Advocate General, NARA.

56. See the cases of Solomon Markel, John Dearth, and James Wilkinson, file no. ii777, ibid.

57. For the sampling and an explanation of how it was compiled, see appendix C.

58. For the arrests and newspapers, see appendix C.

59. See, for example, David G. Ridgeley, *Baltimore Sun*, August 20, 1862 (refusing to take oath); Rev. William Davies, *Daily South Carolinian*, July 20, 1861 (prayed for

the Confederate States); Thomas K. Robson, *Baltimore Sun*, May 12, 1863 (disloyal publisher); William Clayton, *Milwaukee Sentinel*, July 29, 1862 (disloyal language).

60. See the *Baltimore Sun* for the following arrests: Charles Cochrane, May 4, 1863; Thomas Jordan, May 12, 1863; John Jackson and Richard Humphrey, May 16, 1863, in appendix C.

61. *O.R.*, ser. 1, 9:380.

62. *O.R.*, ser. 1, 50(pt. 2):55.

63. *Daily Cleveland Herald*, February 23, 1863.

64. Sandow, *Deserter Country*, 80–81. For Philadelphia activity, see White, *A Philadelphia Perspective*, 109; Risley, *Civil War Journalism*, 94. For a fuller discussion, see Randall, *Constitutional Problems under Lincoln*, chap. 19.

65. White, "The First Amendment Comes of Age," 300; Neely, *Lincoln and the Triumph of the Nation*, 18; White, "'To Aid Their Rebel Friend,'" v.

66. Curtis, *Free Speech*, 1–13, 6 (quotation).

67. Ibid., 10–11. For the Ohio newspaperman, see White, "'To Aid Their Rebel Friend,'" 97. The case stood until dismissed in 1869.

68. *Frank Leslie's Illustrated Newspaper*, August 24, 1861.

69. Wesley, *The Politics of Faith*.

70. Francis Lieber to Edward Bates, July 8, 1862, box 23, Francis Lieber Papers, HL; *New York Times*, September 8, 1861.

71. Neely, *The Union Divided*, 90 (quotation), 95.

72. Risley, *Civil War Journalism*, 98–99; Tenney, "To Suppress or Not to Suppress," 248–59, 252 (quotation).

73. Chicago Union League to Abraham Lincoln, June 6, 1863, ALP, ser. 1.

74. Carwardine, "Abraham Lincoln and the Fourth Estate," 11–12; Randall, *Constitutional Problems under Lincoln*, 505–6.

75. Wesley, *The Politics of Faith*, 64–69.

76. Andreasen, "Civil War Church Trials," 235, 240 (quotation).

77. Wesley, *The Politics of Faith*, 76–77.

78. *Weekly Harrisburg Patriot and Union*, April 30, 1863.

79. Sandow, *Deserter Country*, 96–97.

80. Stanton, *The Church and the Rebellion*, 208.

81. White, "'To Aid Their Rebel Friend,'" 66–70, 268–69.

82. Abraham Lincoln to Samuel E. Curtis, January 2, 1863, ALP.

83. Abraham Lincoln to William S. Rosecrans, April 4, 1864, ALP; Boman, *Lincoln and Citizens' Rights in Missouri*, 246–47.

Chapter 3

1. See, for instance, McGinty, *Lincoln and the Court*, 81–82; Hyman, *More Perfect Union*, 127. At least one exception to this is work by legal scholars who have debated the impact of the American Civil War on foreign affairs. See, for instance, Lee, "The Civil War in U.S. Foreign Relations Law," 53–71.

2. For the argument that the judiciary represented a greater threat than scholars have considered, see Neely, "'Seeking a Cause of Difficulty with the Government,'" 48,

53–54. The conflicts between Lincoln and the Radicals are outlined in Tap, *Over Lincoln's Shoulder*. For how the administration used legal technicalities to its advantage, see White, "The Strangely Insignificant Role of the U.S. Supreme Court in the Civil War." For the consensus view that the courts supported Lincoln's prosecution of the war, see Hyman, *A More Perfect Union*, 256.

3. Randall, "Some Legal Aspects of the Confiscation Acts," 90.

4. Randall, *Constitutional Problems under Lincoln*, 70–71; Neff, *Justice in Blue and Gray*, 21.

5. Whiting, *War Powers of the President*, 8th ed., 46; Belz, *Abraham Lincoln, Constitutionalism, and Equal Rights in the Civil War Era*, 35.

6. For a study that has dealt with international dimensions to the law, see Carnahan, *Lincoln on Trial*, chap. 1.

7. Swisher, *History of the Supreme Court of the United States*, 5:841.

8. Lee, "The Civil War in U.S. Foreign Relations Law," 55.

9. Witt, *Lincoln's Code*, 20, 86.

10. Wheaton, *Elements of International Law*, xiv.

11. Vattel, *The Law of Nations*; Neff, *War and the Law of Nations*, 87, and his *Justice in Blue and Gray*, 56; Witt, *Lincoln's Code*, 16–19. Carnahan describes Vattel's book as the "favorite authority" on international law for American lawyers and judges. See his *Lincoln on Trial*, 107.

12. *Brown v. United States*, 12 U.S., 110 (1814). For the link between this case and the Civil War, see Carnahan, *Lincoln on Trial*, 23.

13. *Brown v. United States*, 12 U.S., 125, 133–34.

14. White, "'To Aid Their Rebel Friend,'" 47–56; Neely, "'Seeking a Cause of Difficulty with the Government,'" 54–60 (stump speech).

15. Younger, *The People's Panel*, 106–8; *New York Herald*, April 25, 1861.

16. Charge to the Grand Jury, Judge Peleg Sprague, 1 Sprague 602 (1861).

17. Ibid.

18. On Grier, see McGinty, *Lincoln and the Court*, 99.

19. Swisher, *The Taney Period*, 858–59; *Weekly Harrisburg Patriot and Union*, July 18, 1861; *New York Herald*, July 14, 1861 (sound on slavery).

20. *New York Herald*, July 14, 1861. Also see McGinty, *Lincoln and the Court*, 100.

21. *Boston Daily Advertiser*, July 15, 1861; *Springfield Republican*, July 20, 1861; *Weekly Harrisburg Patriot and Union*, July 18, 1861; *Weekly Wisconsin Patriot*, July 20, 1861.

22. Swisher, *The Taney Period*, 873.

23. McGinty, *Lincoln and the Court*, 133.

24. *Weekly Harrisburg Patriot and Union*, November 7, 1861.

25. Swisher, *The Taney Period*, 870–72. For a good overview of the case, see Weitz, *The Confederacy on Trial*, 132–62.

26. Richardson, *A Compilation of the Messages and Papers of the Confederacy*, 1:115–16.

27. Weitz, *The Confederacy on Trial*, 168–69.

28. Warburton, *Trial of the Officers and Crew of the Privateer Savannah*, 371–72; Neff, *Justice in Blue and Gray*, 24; Weitz, *The Confederacy on Trial*, 188–89.

29. *New York Herald*, November 1, 1861; Weitz, *The Confederacy on Trial*, 157.

30. *New York Tribune*, November 1, 1861.

31. Quoted in Swisher, *The Taney Period*, 873.

32. *United States v. Smith*, 27 F. Cas. (1861), 1135–36.

33. Quoted in Swisher, *The Taney Period*, 875; Randall, *Constitutional Problems under Lincoln*, 93.

34. After the war, the judiciary took up this question once again and, in a case in 1871, mentioned two other possible starting points for the war: the president's proclamations for mobilizing troops and for declaring the blockade. But during the war, the court focused on July 13. See Randall, *Constitutional Problems under Lincoln*, 49–50.

35. *U.S. Statutes at Large*, 37th Cong., 3rd sess., 12:255–58.

36. *The Prize Cases*, 67 U.S., 669 (1863).

37. Ibid., 667.

38. Wheaton, *Elements of International Law*, xix.

39. *Santisima Trinidad*, 7 Wheaton, 283 (1822).

40. *The Prize Cases*, 67 U.S., 692.

41. Wheaton, *Elements of International Law*, 316–17 (n. 153).

42. Swisher, *The Taney Period*, 878.

43. Hyman, *A More Perfect Union*, 95. For similar observations, see McGinty, *Lincoln and the Court*, 85–86; Dunning, "Notes & Suggestions: Disloyalty in Two Wars," 625. On the conspiracy law, see White, "'To Aid Their Rebel Friend,'" 83.

44. *U.S. Statutes at Large*, 12:284.

45. On the general lack of conspiracy trials, see Tarrant, "Congress and the Law of Seditious Conspiracy," 121–22.

46. *CG*, 36th Cong., 2nd sess. (March 14, 1861), 1455; White, "'To Aid Their Rebel Friend,'" chap. 3.

47. *CG*, 37th Cong., 1st sess. (July 10, 1861), 40, and (July 11, 1861), 64.

48. *CG*, 37th Cong., 2nd sess. (December 4, 1861), 9–10.

49. U.S. Senate Historical Office, *Expulsion and Censure Cases*, 106–8.

50. Randall, "Some Legal Aspects of the Confiscation Acts of the Civil War," 79–96. On the Confiscation Act, see Syrett, *The Civil War Confiscation Acts*; Siddali, *From Property to Person*; Hamilton, *The Limits of Sovereignty*; Blair, "Treason and the Second Confiscation Act."

51. For the influence of moderate Republicans, see Siddali, *From Property to Person*, 230; Blair, "Treason and the Second Confiscation Act," 28. Randall was aware that Republicans lacked solidarity on confiscation without specifically identifying the influence of moderates. See his "Some Legal Aspects of the Confiscation Acts of the Civil War," 82.

52. *CG*, 37th Cong., 1st. sess. (August 2, 1861), 414.

53. Ibid.; Vattel, *The Law of Nations*, 12.

54. *CG*, 37th Cong., 2nd sess. (January 24, 1862), 329. For Charles Sumner arguing for emancipation as a war measure, see Stout, *Upon the Altar of the Nation*, 174.

55. Vattel, *The Law of Nations*, 338.

56. Ibid., 339.

57. *CG*, 37th Cong., 2nd sess. (January 24, 1862), 329.

58. *CG*, 37th Cong., 1st. sess. (August 2, 1861), 414.

59. *CG*, 37th Cong., 2nd sess. (February 24, 1862), 933; Johnston, *Studies in American Political History*. Also see Guelzo, *Lincoln's Emancipation Proclamation*, 126.

60. *CG*, 37th Cong., 2nd sess., appendix (May 23, 1862), 178. Trumbull also cited Vattel. See *CG*, 37th Cong., 2nd sess. (February 25, 1862), 943.

61. Ibid., 1875.

62. *CG*, 37th Cong., 2nd sess., appendix (June 3, 1862), 244.

63. Ibid., 261.

64. *CG*, 37th Cong., 2nd sess. (March 3, 1862), 62.

65. *Norris v. Doniphan*, 61 Ky. 385 (1863); on Bullitt, see Klement, *Copperheads in the Middle West*, 188–89.

66. *Norris v. Doniphan*, 61 Ky., 394–95.

67. *Mrs. Alexander's Cotton*, 69 U.S. 404 (1864), 419 (quotation).

68. The issue of jurisdiction and protecting against false arrest is absent from McGinty, *Lincoln and the Court*, 242–43, and Neff, *Justice in Blue and Gray*, 234–35. For the Habeas Corpus Act and false arrest, see White, *Abraham Lincoln and Treason in the Civil War*, 7 and chap. 5.

69. *U.S. Statutes at Large*, 755–58. See especially section 5 for the ability to retry a case in federal court.

70. Hesseltine, *Lincoln and the War Governors*, 329–30. Details of the case are in *The State of Ohio Ex Rel. David Tod v. The Court of Common Pleas of Fairfield County*, 15 Ohio St. 377 (1864).

71. Hesseltine, *Lincoln and the War Governors*, 389, 390. For White's assessment, see *Abraham Lincoln and Treason in the Civil War*, chap. 5.

72. Dyer, "Francis Lieber and the American Civil War," 452–53; Marszalek, *Commander of All Lincoln's Armies*, 167–68; Witt, *Lincoln's Code*, 229–31.

73. Lieber to Halleck, February 20, 1863, in Perry, *The Life and Letters of Francis Lieber*, 330.

74. Witt, *Lincoln's Code*, 237–39.

75. Freidel, *Francis Lieber*, 325; Grimsley, *Hard Hand of War*, 151; Witt, *Lincoln's Code*, 233, 234.

76. *O.R.*, ser. 3, 3:153; Witt, *Lincoln's Code*, 240–44.

77. Carnahan, "Lincoln, Lieber and the Laws of War," 215.

78. See, for instance, Lieber, *Manual of Political Ethics*, 427 (n. i).

79. Freidel, *Francis Lieber*, 320–21; *New York Times*, August 19, 1861.

80. Lieber to Halleck, October 3, 1863, Francis Lieber Papers, HL; Witt, *Lincoln's Code*, 181–82.

81. Freidel, *Francis Lieber*, 339; *New York Herald*, May 20, 1863; *O.R.*, ser. 2, 6:46 (Seddon), ser. 4, vol. 2:1047–48. Also see Witt, *Lincoln's Code*, 245–46.

82. See, for instance, rulings on conscription in the *Baltimore Sun*, June 12, 1863, and *New York Herald*, June 11, 1863.

83. Palmer, *Selected Letters of Charles Sumner*, 1:184 (emphasis in original); Beale, *Diary of Gideon Welles*, 1:381.

84. Whiting, *War Powers of the President*, 7th ed.; Whiteman, *Gentlemen in Crisis*, 307 (n. 22). For another perspective on the distribution of this pamphlet, see Neely, *Lincoln and the Triumph of the Nation*, 81.

85. *Alexandria Gazette*, March 16, 1863; *The Liberator*, April 24, 1863.

86. Neely, *Lincoln and the Triumph of the Nation*, 81.

87. Whiting, *War Powers of the President*, 8th ed., 50.

88. Ibid., 46.

89. Ibid., 54.

90. Ibid., 68–69, 73 (quotation].

91. Neely, *Lincoln and the Triumph of the Nation*, 83.

92. *CW*, 6:408.

Chapter 4

1. Miller, *The Photographic History of the Civil War*, 7:7.

2. Weber, *Copperheads*, 80; Palladino, *Another Civil War*, 11–12. For a brief overview on the treatment of provost marshals in the literature, see Geary, *We Need Men*, 71–73.

3. Phillips, "Netherworld of War," 327–61.

4. Scott, *Military Dictionary*, 475. I am indebted to Carol Reardon for leading me to this source and the following one.

5. Kautz, *Customs of Service for Officers of the Army*, 205–7.

6. On state treason laws, see White, "'To Aid Their Rebel Friend,'" 43. For the importance of national officials remaining cognizant of the needs of state officials, see Earnhart, "The Administrative Organization of the Provost Marshal General's Bureau in Ohio."

7. *O.R.*, ser. 1, 5:30; Sparks, "General Patrick's Progress," 371–73; for shutting down grog shops, see Fairfax County Historical Society, "Letters of Charles Cummings," 64.

8. Moore, "Union Provost Marshals in the Eastern Theater," 121–22.

9. Sparks, "General Patrick's Progress," 379. For more on the feud, see Fishel, *The Secret War for the Union*, 284.

10. Moore, "Union Provost Marshals in the Eastern Theater," 120–22; Gallman, *Mastering Wartime*, 209–11.

11. Sparks, *Inside Lincoln's Army*. For some of Patrick's duties, see pp. 241, 257, 267.

12. Moore, "Union Provost Marshals in the Eastern Theater," 124.

13. See, for instance, the appointment of a "Civil Provost Marshal" by General Wool in the *Baltimore Sun*, September 4, 1862.

14. Eicher and Eicher, *Civil War High Commands*, 819, 825.

15. For the observation that the eastern provost system was more structured than the western, see Moore, "Union Provost Marshals in the Eastern Theater," 122.

16. *O.R.*, ser. 2, 4:34.

17. Ibid.

18. *O.R.*, ser. 2, 5:300.

19. *O.R.*, ser. 2, 4:430. For admonitions early in the war, see the communication of Halleck in *O.R.*, ser. 1, 8:495, and an attempt to demand specification of charges by provost marshals in the Department of the Cumberland (ibid., 738).

20. *O.R.*, ser. 2, 5:245. For a similar situation existing among prisoners in Kentucky, see *O.R.*, ser. 2, 5:93.

21. *O.R.*, ser. 3, 5:750.

22. Copy of order in the *Daily Cleveland Herald*, August 8, 1862.

23. Neely, *Fate of Liberty*, 53.

24. For General Orders No. 140, which established the bureau, see *O.R.*, ser. 3, 2:586. Ella Lonn mentions the bureau in one paragraph. See her *Desertion during the Civil War*, 173. Two scholars who assessed the bureau correctly are Thomas and Hyman, in *Stanton*, 248–49. For the problem of "aliens" showing up to vote, see the *New York Times*, October 31, 1862.

25. *O.R.*, ser. 3, 2:937.

26. Quoted in Carter, *Troubled State*, 104.

27. *New York Times*, June 28, August 26, 1861.

28. *New York Times*, September 28, 1861.

29. *Baltimore Sun*, July 11, 1861.

30. *O.R.*, ser. 1, 20(pt. 2):29–30.

31. *O.R.*, ser. 1, 20(pt. 2):34–35; Sparks, *Inside Lincoln's Army*, 156.

32. Thomas and Hyman, *Stanton*, 248–49.

33. *O.R.*, ser. 3, 3:124.

34. *U.S. Statutes at Large*, 37th Cong., 3rd sess., 12:731–32.

35. Ibid., 755–56.

36. W. B. Lane to Fry, September 6, 1865, microfilm no. 1163, reel 4, Historical Reports of State Acting Assistant Provost Marshals General and District Provost Marshals, 1865, RG 110, PMG, NARA.

37. Thurlow Weed to David Davis, March 30, 1864, ALP.

38. John G. Nicolay to John Hay, June 29, 1864, ALP.

39. *The Crisis*, February 26, 1862; *O.R.*, ser. 2, 2:217–19.

40. *Philadelphia Inquirer*, February 17, 1862.

41. *O.R.*, ser. 2, 2:212.

42. *Philadelphia Inquirer*, February 19, 1862.

43. *North American and United States Gazette*, October 30, 1862; G. D. Stroud to Abraham Lincoln, October 29, 1862, Thomas H. Hicks to Abraham Lincoln, October 31, 1862, and Charles Keener to Abraham Lincoln, October 30, 1862, ALP.

44. *Philadelphia Inquirer*, October 29, 31, 1862; Johns Hopkins to Abraham Lincoln, October 30, 1862, and John E. Wool to Abraham Lincoln, October 29, 1862, ALP.

45. John M. Buck and Others to Governor A. W. Bradford, March 3, 1863, and Governor Bradford to John M. Buck and Others, March 10, 1863, reel 5, pp. 395–403, LGM. Also see White, "'To Aid Their Rebel Friend,'" 271.

46. Bradford to John M. Buck and Others, March 10, 1863, reel 5, p. 401, LGM.

47. John M. Buck and Others to Governor A. W. Bradford, April 2, 1863, reel 5, pp. 415–19, LGM.

48. Scharf, *History of Maryland*, 3:490–91; Fishel, *Secret War for Union*, 335.

49. Lincoln to John W. Crisfield, June 26, 1862, ALP.

50. *New York World*, quoted in *The Compiler* (Gettysburg, Pa.), November 24, 1862.

51. For the proceedings, see the *New York Times*, November 21, 25, 26, 29, and December 2, 1862.

52. *New York Times*, December 2, 1862.

53. E. J. Allen to Brigadier General A. Porter, February 19, 1862, box 1, folder 1, Proceedings, Commission Relating to State Prisoners, entry 962, RG 59, Department of State, NARA.

54. *New York World*, reprinted in the *Wisconsin Daily Patriot*, November 29, 1862.

55. James Fry to Edwin Stanton, November 17, 1863, "Reports and Decisions," microfilm 621, pp. 78–79, RG 110, PMG, NARA; on Pennsylvania, see Sandow, *Deserter Country*, 127–38.

56. James Fry to Edwin Stanton, September 26, 1863, "Reports and Decisions," microfilm 621, pp. 68–69, RG 110, PMG, NARA.

57. R. J. Barry to Fry, July 10, 1865, microfilm 1163, reel 3, RG 110, PMG, NARA.

58. Geo. H. Keith to James Fry, June 12, 1865, microfilm 1163, reel 3, RG 110, PMG, NARA.

59. A. H. Crane to James B. Fry, May 22, 1865, microfilm 1163, reel 3, RG 110, PMG, NARA.

60. A. C. Deuel to James B. Fry, May 23, 1865, microfilm 1163, reel 4, RG 110, PMG, NARA.

61. A. E. Jones to James B. Fry, June 1, 1865, microfilm 1163, reel 4, RG 110, PGM, NARA.

62. File for Dennis Gagan, Department of Missouri, Papers Relating to Persons Charged with Disloyalty and Other Crimes, part I, box 1, entry 2792, RG 393, U.S. Army Continental Commands, NARA.

63. File for Joseph C. Allison, Department of Missouri, Papers Relating to Persons Charged with Disloyalty and Other Crimes, part I, box 1, entry 2792, RG 393, NARA.

64. Darius Caldwell to James B. Fry, May 23, 1865, microfilm 1163, reel 4, RG 110, PGM, NARA.

65. Sandow, *Deserter Country*.

Chapter 5

1. For the interpretation of provost marshals as "islands of order in a sea of violence," see Ash, *When the Yankees Came*, 92. More negative impressions of the provost marshal can be found in the work of Sterling, "Civil War Draft Resistance in the Middle West." For a good discussion of the various positions, see Geary, *We Need Men*, 71–73.

2. Whites, *Gender Matters*, 5.

3. Grimsley, *Hard Hand of War*. For others who place the turn to hard war in the summer of 1862, see Ash, *When the Yankees Came*, 53–54, and Work, *Lincoln's Political Generals*, 165.

4. *O.R.*, ser. 1, 38(pt. 5):778.

5. Colt, *Defend the Valley*, 198; Blair and Wiley, *A Politician Goes to War*, 13.

6. Siddali, *From Property to Person*, 245; Syrett, *The Civil War Confiscation Acts*, 169–89; Randall, *Constitutional Problems under Lincoln*, 288–91.

7. Carnahan, *Lincoln on Trial*, 36.

8. Engs and Brooks, *Their Patriotic Duty*, 83.

9. For the only book to deal with a wide range of issues concerning civil-military relations in the occupied Confederacy, see Ash, *When the Yankees Came*. For increased resistance, see ibid., 46.

10. On Morton's home, see Carnahan, *Lincoln on Trial*, 43–44; for Grant's Jewish order, see McFeely, *Grant*, 123–24.

11. Carnahan, *Lincoln on Trial*, 36; *CW*, 4:531.

12. Harrison, "The Civilians' War," 135.

13. Ibid., 141, 143.

14. West, *When the Yankees Came*, 48.

15. For the Sea Islands, see Rose, *Rehearsal for Reconstruction*.

16. *O.R.*, ser. 1, 16(pt. 2):273–77. Also see Chicoine, *John Basil Turchin*, 65–71; Bradley and Dahlen, *From Conciliation to Conquest*; Grimsley, *Hard Hand of War*, 81–85.

17. Grimsley, *Hard Hand of War*, 85.

18. Chicoine, *John Basil Turchin*, 65–71; Bradley and Dahlen, *From Conciliation to Conquest*, 122.

19. Grimsley, *Hard Hand of War*, 174. Also see Neely, *The Civil War and the Limits of Destruction*.

20. Thomas and Hyman, *Stanton*, 306 (quotation). Also see Bensel, *Yankee Leviathan*, 197.

21. *O.R.*, ser. 1, 15:558.

22. *O.R.*, ser. 1, 17(pt. 2):569.

23. *O.R.*, ser. 1, 15:538.

24. *O.R.*, ser. 1, 15:538–43, 607; 41(pt. 3):574–75.

25. *O.R.*, ser. 2, 1:150–51, 156, 170–71; Gerteis, *Civil War St. Louis*, 174–75.

26. *Daily Morning News* (Savannah), June 2, 1862; Ash, *When the Yankees Came*, 65–66.

27. Chambers, "Notes on Life in Occupied Norfolk," 137.

28. Day, *Rambles with the 25th Massachusetts Volunteer Infantry*, 90.

29. Clay-Clopton, *A Belle of the Fifties*, 222.

30. House, *A Very Violent Rebel*, 82.

31. Rubin, *A Shattered Nation*, 99.

32. *O.R.*, ser. 1, 41(pt. 2):204.

33. *New Hampshire Sentinel*, April 14, 1864 (emphasis in original). Also see Chambers, "Notes on Life in Occupied Norfolk," 139.

34. For a new study that fleshes out the interference by the military in Confederate churches, see Wesley, *The Politics of Faith*.

35. Abraham Lincoln to Samuel E. Curtis, January 2, 1863, ALP; *CW*, 6:34. Also see Gerteis, *Civil War St. Louis*, 182–86.

36. Carter, *Troubled State*, 94–100.

37. *National Intelligencer*, February 25, 1864.

38. Ibid. For the St. Louis orders, see *O.R.*, ser. 1, 34(pt. 2):311.

39. Charles P. McIlvaine to Abraham Lincoln, March 4, 1864, ALP.

40. Abraham Lincoln to Edwin M. Stanton, February 11, 1864, ALP; *O.R.*, ser. 1, 34(pt. 2):452–53.

41. Gerteis, *Civil War St. Louis*, 307; Hyman, *Era of the Oath*, 37; Chambers, "Notes on Life in Occupied Norfolk," 138.

42. Dawson, *A Confederate Girl's Diary*, 316; Rubin, *A Shattered Nation*, 94–100.

43. Ash, *When the Yankees Came*, 60–61.

44. *O.R.*, ser. 3, 3:164. Also see Gerteis, *Civil War St. Louis*, 177–78; Carter, *Troubled State*, 114–15.

45. *O.R.*, ser. 1, 25(pt. 2):496.

46. Engs and Brooks, *Their Patriotic Duty*, 253.

47. *O.R.*, ser. 1, 29(pt. 2):37; Sparks, *Inside Lincoln's Army*, 421.

48. Robertson, *Civil War Letters of General Robert McAllister*, 566–67.

49. Hyman, *Era of the Oath*, 35.

50. Abraham Lincoln to John M. Schofield, October 1, 1863; George R. Dennis to Montgomery Blair, July 21, 1864, both in ALP.

51. Whites, *Gender Matters*; McCurry, *Confederate Reckoning*.

52. Whiting, *War Powers of the President*, 8th ed., v–vi.

53. For this conceptualization of the household, see McCurry, *Masters of Small Worlds*.

54. Whites and Long, *Occupied Women*, 3.

55. On the need for supply, see Grimsley, *Hard Hand of War*, 213–14; House, *A Very Violent Rebel*, 44 (hospital needs).

56. Robertson, *Civil War Letters of General Robert McAllister*, 557.

57. Dawson, *A Confederate Girl's Diary*, 34.

58. Margaret Creighton, "Gettysburg Out of Bounds," in Whites and Long, *Occupied Women*, 68. On helplessness, see Ash, *When the Yankees Came*, 70–72; for symbolic politics, see Faust, *Mothers of Invention*, 211–14; Campbell, *When Sherman Marched North from the Sea*, 11–15.

59. Faust, *Mothers of Invention*, 199–202.

60. Whites and Long, *Occupied Women*, 50–51; Sparks, *Inside Lincoln's Army*, 389. For more examples, also see Lowry, *The Story the Soldiers Wouldn't Tell*, chap. 12, and his *Sexual Misbehavior in the Civil War*.

61. Feimster, "The Threat of Sexual Violence during the American Civil War," 127.

62. Fellman, *Inside War*, 207–8; House, *A Very Violent Rebel*, 21; Blair, "Barbarians at Fredericksburg's Gate," 156. For the North Carolina account, see Schultz, "Southern Women's Diaries," 65.

63. Crystal Feimster, "Rape and Justice in the Civil War," *New York Times*, April 25, 2013; Whites and Long, *Occupied Women*, 49.

64. McKinley, *From the Pen of a She-Rebel*, 15. For a similar example in Winchester, Virginia, see Faust, *Mothers of Invention*, 198.

65. House, *A Very Violent Rebel*, 12. Also see Rable, *Civil Wars*, 163–65.

66. Elvira Scott Diary, folders 4–5, WHMC; McKinley, *From the Pen of a She-Rebel*, 12.

67. Hahn, *A Nation under Our Feet*, 57–60.

68. Cushman, *Bloody Promenade*, 79.

69. Rable, *Civil Wars*, 156 (whipsawed); Phillips, *Diehard Rebels*, 127.

70. McKinley, *From the Pen of a She-Rebel*, 57.

71. Ibid., 31–32.

72. Engs and Brooks, *Their Patriotic Duty*, 235.

73. Ibid., 66–67.

74. Ibid., 130.

75. *O.R.*, ser. 1, 41(pt. 1):220.

76. House, *A Very Violent Rebel*, 27.

77. Ibid., 40.

78. Elvira Scott Diary, July 9, 1862, folders 4–5, p. 119, WHMC (emphasis in original). All subsequent examples of this incident come from this document. I am indebted to Anne Brinton for sharing this document.

79. Ibid., 120.

80. Ibid., 122, 124–25.

81. Ibid., 128–29.

Chapter 6

1. *Official Proceedings of the Democratic National Convention, 1864*, 27.

2. For two of the scholars who have foregrounded concerns over civil liberties and the use of the military to suppress Democrats, see Klement, *Copperheads in the Middle West*, and Silbey, *A Respectable Minority*.

3. Frank Klement first challenged the notion that Copperheadism was a disloyal, pro-Southern movement as he argued for considering the Peace Democrats as conservatives who tried to avert the sociopolitical changes being wrought by war. Klement stressed that the Republicans exaggerated the threat from the Democrats. For the more recent view that Copperheads were a threat, see Weber, *Copperheads*.

4. For the quintessential portrayal of the use of racism by the Democratic Party in elections, see Baker, *Affairs of Party*.

5. Bensel, *The American Ballot Box in the Mid-Nineteenth Century*, 261–62.

6. Stampp, *Indiana Politics*, 254.

7. For the best discussion of these resolutions—and a replication of them—see Sandow, *Deserter Country*, 68–70, 167–69.

8. Ibid., 94; Lawson, *Patriot Fires*, 94; Stampp, *Indiana Politics*, 92–93; Neely, *The Union Divided*, 8–14. Douglas quotation in Paludan, *People's Contest*, 85.

9. *Daily Commercial Register*, July 1, 1861; *Cincinnati Enquirer*, July 7, 1861.

10. White, *A Philadelphia Perspective*, 100–101, 108.

11. Smith, *The Borderlands in the Civil War*, 313–18 (quotation p. 313); *Cincinnati Enquirer*, July 7, 1861.

12. Sandow has made a similar point, indicating that local politics operated with fewer restraints. See *Deserter Country*, 62.

13. Lawson, *Patriot Fires*, 68. See also Sandow, *Deserter Country*, 65–66; Stampp, *Indiana Politics*, 94–95; Neely, *The Union Divided*; Paludan, *People's Contest*, 231.

14. Gray and Ropes, *War Letters*, 19.

15. Tap, *Over Lincoln's Shoulder*, 41–44, 48–54.

16. *The Liberator*, February 14, 1862.

17. Nevins, *George Templeton Strong Diary*, 206.

18. U.S. Congress, *Report of the Joint Committee on the Conduct of the War*, pt. 3, pp. 422–23.

19. Ibid., 430–31.

20. Sparks, *Inside Lincoln's Army*, 106, 110.

21. *O.R.*, ser. 1, 12(pt. 1):41.

22. *Democrat Watchman*, January 9, 1863.

23. Gray and Ropes, *War Letters*, 19. Also see Paludan, *People's Contest*, 93.

24. D. C. A. Clarke, A. H. Fuller to A. G. Curtin, August 2, 1862, folder 1; N. Callendar and S. H. Callendar to A. G. Curtin, July 24, 1862, folder 7, box 15, RG 19, Office of the Adjutant General, PSA.

25. *Hand-Book of the Democracy for 1863 & 1864*, 30.

26. Nevins, *George Templeton Strong Diary*, 268–69; White, *A Philadelphia Perspective*, 193. Also see Wubben, *Civil War Iowa and the Copperhead Movement*, 62, 64, 66–71; Silbey, *A Respectable Minority*, 51.

27. Donald, *Lincoln*, 382–83.

28. Pease and Randall, *Diary of Orville Hickman Browning*, 1:587–89. See also Donald, *Lincoln*, 441; Paludan, *People's Contest*, 100.

29. *New York Times*, November 24, 1862.

30. *New York Herald*, November 26, 1862.

31. *Dubuque Herald*, clipping in *The Crisis*, November 19, 1862; *Chicago Times*, reprinted in *Weekly Wisconsin Patriot*, November 1, 1862.

32. *Philadelphia Inquirer*, January 8, 1863.

33. McPherson, *Battle Cry of Freedom*, 289.

34. George B. McClellan to Nathaniel P. Banks, September 12, 1861, in Sears, *Civil War Papers of George B. McClellan*, 99.

35. McClellan, *McClellan's Own Story*, 147–48 (quotation); for his 1864 account, see Sears, *Civil War Papers of George B. McClellan*, 565.

36. *Philadelphia Press*, September 19, 1861.

37. Hesseltine, *Lincoln and the War Governors*, 270–71.

38. For the celebration of Democrats, see the *Philadelphia Public Ledger*, November 1, 1862.

39. Joshua F. Speed to Abraham Lincoln, September 17, 1862, ALP.

40. William C. Goodloe to Abraham Lincoln, June 30, 1863, ALP.

41. Boman, *Lincoln and Citizens' Rights in Missouri*, 141.

42. *Appleton's Annual Cyclopaedia, 1862*, 590; Siddali, *Missouri's War*, 123; Hyman, *Era of the Oath*, 37; *O.R.*, ser. 1, 22(pt. 2):668–70.

43. *Daily National Intelligencer*, April 21, 1862.

44. For the most thorough analysis of enforcement of the loyalty oaths in Missouri, see Bensel, *The American Ballot Box in the Mid-Nineteenth Century*, 219–40.

45. Boman, *Lincoln and Citizens' Rights in Missouri*, 151; Bensel, *The American Ballot Box in the Mid-Nineteenth Century*, 219–20, 225–27, 233.

46. Boman, *Lincoln and Citizens' Rights in Missouri*, 141–44.

47. White, "Canvassing the Troops," 291–317.

48. *Bangor Daily Whig & Courier*, January 26, 1863.

49. Klement, *Copperheads in the Middle West*, 218.

50. Dana, *Recollections of the Civil War*, 260.

51. Blair, "We Are Coming, Father Abraham," 187–88.

52. Vallandigham, *Speeches, Arguments, Addresses, and Letters*, 467 (quotations), 473.

53. *The Crisis*, April 10, 1863.

54. Anbinder, "Which Poor Man's Fight?," 344–72.

55. Vallandigham, *Speeches, Arguments, Addresses, and Letters*, 465.

56. Curtis, "Lincoln, Vallandigham, and Anti-War Speech," 115–16.

57. Vallandigham, *Life of Clement L. Vallandigham*, 250–53; Curtis, "Lincoln, Vallandigham, and Anti-War Speech," 122; Klement, *Limits of Dissent*, 152–53.

58. *The Trial of Hon. Clement L. Vallandigham*, 11–16; Vallandigham, *Life of Clement L. Vallandigham*, 252–54; Klement, *Limits of Dissent*, 153–54. No extant text of this address exists. The comments have been pieced together by historians from the military commission.

59. *The Trial of Hon. Clement L. Vallandigham*, 7.

60. Vallandigham, *Life of Clement L. Vallandigham*, 255–58; Klement, *Limits of Dissent*, 156–59.

61. *Albany Journal*, May 18, 1863.

62. *CW*, 6:265; Neely, "The Constitution and Civil Liberties under Lincoln," 45–51.

63. Opinion, William Whiting, Solicitor, War Department, June 6, 1863, "Decisions Made," microfilm 621, pp. 6–7, RG 110, PMG, NARA; *O.R.*, ser. 1, 34(pt. 2):231.

64. *O.R.*, ser. 1, 23(pt. 1):728, and ser. 1, 23(pt. 2):572; *Appleton's Annual Cyclopaedia, 1863*, 568.

65. Peter, *A Union Woman in Civil War Kentucky*, 146.

66. Marvel, *Burnside*, 264–65.

67. Coulter, *Civil War and Readjustment in Kentucky*, 178; Richard Smith to Thomas T. Eckert, August 5, 1863, ALP.

68. Coulter, *Civil War and Readjustment in Kentucky*, 176–78; *Appleton's Annual Cyclopaedia, 1863*, 568.

69. *Appleton's Annual Cyclopaedia, 1863*, 563–66, 563 (quotation).

70. Boman, *Lincoln and Citizens' Rights in Missouri*, 226–27.

71. Robert C. Schenck to Edwin M. Stanton, November 1, 1863, ALP; *O.R.*, ser. 3, 3:968. For the Union State Committee chairman, see Bigelow, "Maryland in National Politics," 56.

72. Wagandt, *The Mighty Revolution*, 158–60.

73. A. W. Bradford to Abraham Lincoln, October 31, 1863, ALP.

74. *O.R.*, ser. 3, 3:982.

75. A. Bradford to Abraham Lincoln, November 2, 1862, reel 5, pp. 478–79, LGM.

76. *Report of the Committee on Elections, on Contested Elections in Somerset County*, 14–17; *Daily National Intelligencer*, November 4, 1863.

77. *O.R.*, ser. 3, 3:983.

78. *Report of the Committee on Elections, on Contested Elections in Somerset County*, 10–11.

79. John W. Crisfield to Montgomery Blair, November 14, 1863, ALP.

80. *Report of the Committee on Elections, on Contested Elections in Somerset County*, 9–12, 27–28, 30–31.

81. Francis J. Keffer to Carlos A. Waite, November 6 and 17, 1863; Nicholas Brewer to Abraham Lincoln, November 13, 1863; Donn Piatt to Abraham Lincoln, November 27, 1863, ALP. Also see Thomas G. Pratt and 10 Others to Governor Bradford, November 21, 1863, reel 5, pp. 485–86, LGM.

82. Bigelow, "Maryland in National Politics," 58; House Executive Documents, 39th Cong., 1st sess., No. 14.

83. *Tribune Almanac and Political Register for 1863*, 6.

84. *Daily Constitutional Union*, November 20, 1863; *Daily National Intelligencer*, November 18 and 21, 1863; *New York Times*, November 21, 1863.

85. *New York Tribune*, November 20, 1863; *Daily Age*, November 25, 1863 (quotation). Also see debate over the numbers in *Daily Constitutional Union*, December 5, 1863.

86. Klement, *Dark Lanterns*, 98–99.

87. *New York Times*, November 6, 21, 1863.

88. *CG*, 38th Cong., 1st sess. (February 15, 1864), 660, 2996; 2nd sess., 531. The one person difficult to trace is Webster who appears to have missed voting on February 15.

89. *The Crisis*, October 28, 1863.

90. Bensel, *The American Ballot Box in the Mid-Nineteenth Century*, 261.

Chapter 7

1. De Hauranne, *A Frenchman in Lincoln's America*, 1:331–35.

2. *Hartford Courant*, October 7, 1864, argues that the "Copperheads" tossed stones at soldiers and called them cowards.

3. *Official Proceedings of the Democratic National Convention, 1864*, 27.

4. White, "'To Aid Their Rebel Friend,'" 428–29.

5. *CG*, 38th Cong., 1st sess. (January 6, 1864), 101–8, 103 (quotation).

6. *Daily Constitutional Union* (Washington, D.C.), January 8, 1864.

7. Senate Committee on Military Affairs, *Report to Accompany Bill S. No. 37*, 2, 4–5, 18–19, 32.

8. *CG*, appendix, 38th Cong., 1st sess. (March 3 and 4, 1864), 55–70.

9. Ibid., 62.

10. Ibid., 66.

11. David Sheean to George B. McClellan, June 21, 1864, reel 50, GBMP.

12. *Republican Farmer* (Bridgeport, Conn.), May 27, 1864 (emphasis in original).

13. *Wisconsin Daily Patriot*, January 11, 1864.

14. *CG*, 38th Cong., 1st sess. (May 9, 1864), 2195.

15. W.C. P. to General, October 20, 1864, reel 52, fr. 443, GBMP.

16. Jas. C. Clarke to Genl. Geo. B. McClellan, September 20, 1864, and September 30, 1864, reel 52, frs. 8 and 183, respectively, GBMP.

17. Charles Lanman to Genl. McClellan, October 8, 1864, reel 52, fr. 385, GBMP. For a description of the process of loyalty oaths and voting, see Bensel, *The American Ballot Box in the Mid-Nineteenth Century*, 217–18.

18. Louis C. D'Homergue to Genl. Geo. B. McClellan, October 8, 1864, reel 52, fr. 283, GBMP.

19. R. B. Marcy to McClellan, September 26, 1864, reel 52, fr. 106, GBMP.

20. Benjamin Rush to George B. McClellan, June 16, 1864, reel 5, GBMP; James Harrison to George B. McClellan, August 12, 1864, reel 50, fr. 455, GBMP.

21. (Illegible) to Manton Marble, September 23, 1864, reel 52, fr. 88, GBMP.

22. Address of Colonel Leonidas Metcalf to the Union men of Nicholas County, Kentucky, on April 11, 1864, in the *Scioto Gazette* (Chillicothe, Ohio), May 17, 1864.

23. Balsamo, "Abraham Lincoln and the Election of 1864," 182.

24. Lawson, *Patriot Fires*, 88–90, 99; *Democrat Watchman*, March 6, 1863.

25. Second Annual Report of the Board of Directors of the Union League of Philadelphia, Philadelphia Union League Papers, pp. 5–6, HSP.

26. *Easton Gazette*, February 27, 1864.

27. Lieber, *No Party Now*, HSP.

28. Bellows, *Unconditional Loyalty*, Union League Pamphlets, HSP, 3–5, 6–7.

29. B. H. Hill to Fry, July 28, 1865, Historical Reports of State Acting Assistant Provost Marshals General and District Provost Marshals, microfilm 1163, roll 3, RG 110, PGM, NARA.

30. On Kentucky becoming a rebel state, see Marshall, *Creating a Confederate Kentucky*; Coulter, *Civil War and Readjustment in Kentucky*, 439.

31. Coulter, *Civil War and Readjustment in Kentucky*, 204–6.

32. *Wisconsin Daily Patriot*, March 15, 1864; *Daily National Intelligencer*, March 14, 1864; *Daily Age*, March 14, 1864.

33. Frank Wolford to Abraham Lincoln, July 30, 1864; William C. Goodloe to Green Clay Smith, May 29, 1864, both in ALP.

34. J. H. Hammond to George B. McClellan, May 20, 1864, reel 50, GBMP.

35. *O.R.*, ser. 1, 39(pt. 2):144–45.

36. *Appleton's Annual Cyclopaedia, 1864*, 453; Coulter, *Civil War and Readjustment in Kentucky*, 184–85.

37. *O.R.*, ser. 1, 39(pt. 2):240–41. For the forty-person estimate, see *Appleton's Annual Cyclopaedia, 1864*, 453.

38. *New York Times*, July 23, 1864; Marshall, *Creating a Confederate Kentucky*, 23; Sutherland, *A Savage Conflict*, 220.

39. *O.R.*, ser. 3, 4:689.

40. *Cincinnati Enquirer*, September 26, 1864.

41. "Message of the President of the United States, Communicating, in Compliance with a resolution of the Senate of December 20, 1864, information in relation to the Arrest of Colonel Richard T. Jacobs, lieutenant governor of the State of Kentucky, and Colonel Frank Wolford, one of the presidential electors of that State," 38th Cong., 2nd sess., S. Ex. Doc. No. 16, pp. 12–15.

42. Ibid., 18–21.

43. William C. Goodloe and Charles Eginton to Abraham Lincoln, November 23, 1864, ALP.

44. Richard T. Jacob to Abraham Lincoln, December 26, 1864, ALP.

45. De Hauranne, *A Frenchman in Lincoln's America*, 2:87–88.

46. Klement, "The Indianapolis Treason Trials," 105–7.

47. *Treason in Indiana Exposed!*, 6–7; Pitman, *The Trials for Treason at Indianapolis*; Stampp, *Indiana Politics*, 241–43. For activity with Confederates, see report of Jacob Thompson in *O.R.*, ser. 1, 43(pt. 2):930–36; Klement, *Dark Lanterns*, 154.

48. Klement, *Dark Lanterns*, 163.

49. *O.R.*, ser. 1, 43(pt. 2):931; Pitman, *The Trials for Treason at Indianapolis*, 240.

50. Stampp, *Indiana Politics*, 246–47; Klement, *Dark Lanterns*, 162–63.

51. *Democrat Register* (Lawrenceburg), June 17, 1864, quoted in Klement, *Dark Lanterns*, 112–30.

52. *O.R.*, ser. 2, 7:930–33.

53. McPherson, *Battle Cry of Freedom*, 782–83; *Daily Constitutional Union*, October 17, 1864.

54. Klement, "The Indianapolis Treason Trials," 105–7. He considers Dodd's organization a paper tiger, while, more recently, Jennifer Weber argues for considering the Sons of Liberty as a more considerable threat. Scholar Elizabeth Leonard also takes Holt's concerns as serious. See Weber, *Copperheads*, 148; Leonard, *Lincoln's Forgotten Ally*, 185–86.

55. Burlingame and Etlinger, *Inside Lincoln's White House*, 207; also see McPherson, *Battle Cry of Freedom*, 783.

56. Holt believed the states had the following memberships in secret societies: Indiana, between 75,000 and 125,000 in a state where 130,233 Democrats voted for McClellan; Illinois, from 100,000 to 140,000, where 158,730 voted for McClellan; Ohio, from 80,000 to 108,000, where 205,568 voted for McClellan; Missouri, from 20,000 to 40,000, where 31,678 supported the general. See *O.R.*, ser. 2, 7:934–35; *Tribune Almanac and Political Register for 1865*, 57, 58, 60, 65. Also see Neely, *The Union Divided*, 164–65.

57. Henry Wager Halleck to Francis Lieber, August 19 and September 2, 1864, box 10, Francis Lieber Papers, HL.

58. Henry Wager Halleck to Francis Lieber, October 16, 1864, box 10, Francis Lieber Papers, HL.

59. *Official Proceedings of the Democratic National Convention, 1864*, 7–8, 27 (resolution), 54 (Wickliffe). Also see Silbey, *A Respectable Minority*, 130–31.

60. Klement, *The Limits of Dissent*, 271–77; *Cincinnati Enquirer*, September 26, 1864. For the observation that "mainstream" Democrats erred in ceding control of the convention to the peace wing, see Weber, *Copperheads*, 182.

61. George W. Morgan to George B. McClellan, November 30, 1863, reel 49, fr. 142, and George W. Morgan to George B. McClellan, August 17, 1864, reel 50, fr. 499 (quotation), GBMP; John Bell Robinson to George B. McClellan, n.d., 1864, reel 50, fr. 358, GBMP.

62. S. S. Cox to Manton Marble, August 12, 1864, reel 4, container 8, MMP; Noah Brooks to John G. Nicolay, August 29, 1864, ALP.

63. *Official Proceedings of the Democratic National Convention, 1864*, 30–31, 38.

64. *New York Times*, September 1, 9, 1864. For the factions within the convention, and McClellan's popularity with soldiers, see Noah Brooks to John G. Nicolay, September 2, 1864, ALP.

65. Edgar Conkling to Abraham Lincoln, September 28, October 24, 1864, ALP. For related letters, see Conkling to Lincoln, October 8, 20, 22; Isaac P. Langworthy to Edgar Conkling, October 17, 1864; P. Wellington to Abraham Lincoln, October 16, 1864, all in ALP. Neely, *The Union Divided*, 153–54.

66. *Official Proceedings of the Democratic National Convention, 1864*, 29 (Powell), 50 (Allen).

67. *New York Herald*, September 20, 1864; *Boston Daily Advertiser*, September 21, 1864; *Hartford Courant*, October 7, 1864.

68. *Daily Age*, September 19, 1864; *Daily Constitutional Union*, September 20, 1864.

69. *Cincinnati Enquirer*, September 29, 1864 (testimony on the event); *Daily Age*, September 27, 1864; for Wallace, see the *Daily National Intelligencer*, October 4, 1864; Joshua M. Bosley and James R. Brewer to Abraham Lincoln, October 5, 1864; W. Kimmel and Joshua M. Bosley to Abraham Lincoln, October 8, 1864; Henry Wilson to Abraham Lincoln, October 13, 1864, ALP.

70. *Boston Post*, September 29, 1864.

71. Ibid.; *Philadelphia Public Ledger*, September 26, 1864; *Wisconsin Daily Patriot*, September 19, 1864; *New York Tribune*, September 29, 1864.

72. De Hauranne, *A Frenchman in Lincoln's America*, 2:14–16; *Albany Journal*, September 22, 1864; *Daily Evening Bulletin*, September 22, 1864.

73. *Cincinnati Enquirer*, September 24, 1864.

74. White, "Canvassing the Troops," 309; Thomas and Hyman, *Stanton*, 328.

75. Charles D. Deshler to George B. McClellan, September 13, 1864, reel 51, GBMP.

76. Charles S. Tripler to George B. McClellan, Medical Director's Office, Northern Department, Columbus, Ohio, September 20, 1864, reel 52, fr. 12, GBMP; John H. Ferry to George B. McClellan, Office Chief Quartermaster Depot, Louisville, Ky., October 3, 1864, reel 52, fr. 257, GBMP; Lyman, *Meade's Headquarters*, 247–48.

77. Paludan, *Presidency of Abraham Lincoln*, 286; *CW*, 8:11; Donald, *Lincoln*, 543–44; McKelvy et al., "The David McKelvy Diary," 381–82.

78. *Papers of Ulysses S. Grant*, 12:353.

79. Donald, *Lincoln Reconsidered*, 78–79; Thomas, *Abraham Lincoln*, 451; Randall and Current, *Lincoln the President: Last Full Measure*, 252.

80. Beale, *Diary of Gideon Welles*, 2:97–98 (quotation), 108–9.

81. McKelvy et al., "The David McKelvy Diary," 393.

82. J. G. to George B. McClellan, September 20, 1864, GBMP, reel 52; *Papers of Ulysses S. Grant*, 12:212–15. Grant suggested the orders; the War Department established the procedures. See *O.R.*, ser. 3, 4:751–52.

83. Randall and Current, *Lincoln the President: Last Full Measure*, 256–57.

84. George M. Buck to George B. McClellan, November 10, 1864, reel 52, fr. 546, GBMP.

85. J. G. to George B. McClellan, September 27, 1864, reel 52, fr. 149, GBMP; Unidentified to McClellan, Memphis, October 8, 1864, reel 52, fr. 298, GBMP. For a case study of New York that demonstrates the complexities and problems involving the soldiers' vote, see White, "Canvassing the Troops," 291–317.

86. McKelvy et al., "The David McKelvy Diary," 404.

87. Bensel, *The American Ballot Box in the Mid-Nineteenth Century*, 269–74.

88. Hesseltine, *Lincoln and the War Governors*, 383.

89. *O.R.*, ser. 1, 43(pt. 2):279–80.

90. White, "'To Aid Their Rebel Friend,'" 440; S. S. Cox to George B. McClellan, October 11, 1864, reel 52, fr. 344, GBMP.

91. *O.R.*, ser. 1, 43(pt. 2):486, 498, 519–20, 531–32, 544, 550–51, 576–80; *Papers of Ulysses S. Grant*, 12:339; *New York Times*, November 9, 1864 (quotation).

92. Henry W. Halleck to Francis Lieber, October 26, 1864, box 10, Francis Lieber Papers, HL.

93. *U.S. Statutes at Large*, 37th Cong., 3rd sess., 13:487–91.

94. Engs and Brooks, *Their Patriotic Duty*, 297.

Chapter 8

1. Dykstra, *Clover Adams*, 37.

2. Hacker, "A Census-Based Count of the Civil War Dead," 307–48. For an excellent example of the uglier nature of warfare, see Sutherland, *A Savage Conflict*.

3. Randall, *Constitutional Problems under Lincoln*, 97 (indictments), 103 n. 20 (persons indicted); White, "The Trial of Jefferson Davis," 121. On the Tennessee conviction, see Coulter, *William G. Brownlow: Fighting Parson*, 275–76; *Memphis Daily Avalanche*, May 3, 1866.

4. Winik, *April 1865*, xiv–xvi; Blight, *Race and Reunion*. More recent histories have shown how punishing rebels for treason became waylaid by Reconstruction politics. See Leonard, *Lincoln's Avengers*; Cooper, *Jefferson Davis, American*, 541–42.

5. Benedict, "Abraham Lincoln and Federalism," 1–45.

6. *North American and United States Gazette*, April 26, 1865.

7. Ashton, *Official Opinions of the Attorneys General of the United States*, 11:3–4.

8. Ibid., 206–7.

9. "The Rebel Parole," *The Nation* 1 (August 3, 1865): 133; *Daily Cleveland Herald*, May 23, 1865.

10. Beale, *Diary of Gideon Welles*, 2:404, 407 (quotation).

11. Carroll County resolution in *Boston Daily Advertiser*, April 24, 1865; *Daily Ohio Statesman*, June 9, 1865.

12. For treatment of uniforms, see Blair, *Cities of the Dead*, 52.

13. Court-Martial Case File MM-2040, Court-martial Case Files and Related Records, RG 153, Judge Advocate General, NARA. For Douglas's reminiscence of this situation, see his *I Rode with Stonewall*, 321–24.

14. *United States v. Rucker*, 27 F. Cas. 911 (1866); *Augusta Chronicle*, April 13, 1866 (quotation).

15. *New York Tribune*, June 5, 1865.

16. *Baltimore Sun*, June 20, 1865; *Daily Evening Bulletin*, July 18, 1865.

17. Capt. Lee, *Recollections and Letters of General Robert E. Lee*, 164; *Papers of Ulysses S. Grant*, 15:210–11.

18. MacDonnell, "Reconstruction in the Wake of Vietnam," 121.

19. Simpson, *Let Us Have Peace*, 105–6.

20. *Papers of Ulysses S. Grant*, 15:149. See also Randall, *Constitutional Problems under Lincoln*, 101–2; Simpson, *Let us Have Peace*, 107–8; Thomas, *Lee*, 370–71; James Speed to Lucius H. Chandler, USDA, Norfolk, June 20, 1865, Letterbook E, vol. 11, Attorney General's office, Letters Received, 1818–1870, RG 60, Department of Justice, NARA.

21. Winik, *April 1865*, 88.

22. *Papers of Ulysses S. Grant*, 15:6–8, 10.

23. For Forrest, see Writ of Habeas Corpus for Treason of Confederate General Nathan B. Forrest, 1865, RG 21, United States District Court, NARA, Atlanta, and the *Weekly Union and American*, March 1, 1866; on Semmes, see Beale, *Diary of Gideon Welles*, 2:404–5.

24. Simpson, *Ulysses S. Grant: Triumph over Adversity*, 454; *North American and United States Gazette*, September 2, 1865; *New York Herald*, September 3, 1865; *Papers of Ulysses S. Grant*, 16:143–44; James Speed to William J. Jones, District Attorney, Baltimore, April 2, 1866, Letterbook E, vol. 11, pp. 461–62, Attorney General's Office, Letters Received, RG 60, Department of Justice, NARA.

25. *New York Times*, June 30, August 20, 1865. On Maury and immigration, see Rolle, *The Lost Cause*, 136–40.

26. Levi Alger to Andrew Johnson, June 3, 1865, and Petition to "His Excellency Andrew Johnson," both box 250, Amnesty Papers, RG 94, Adjutant General's Office, 1780s–1917, NARA.

27. F. W. Eshelman and Others to President Andrew Johnson, May 18, 1865, box 250, RG 94, Adjutant General's Office, NARA.

28. For a fuller depiction of the range of opinions on Davis, see Nicoletti, "Did Secession Really Die at Appomattox?," 36–40.

29. Albert Williams to Andrew Johnson, April 21, 1865, quoted in Graf, *The Papers of Andrew Johnson*, 7:609.

30. Spear, *The Punishment of Treason*, 15–16, 18–20, 31–32, HSP.

31. Beale, *Diary of Gideon Welles*, 2:337–39.

32. Ibid., 339. Also see Cooper, *Jefferson Davis, American*, 541–42, Nicoletti, "Did Secession Really Die at Appomattox?," 41–43.

33. White, "The Trial of Jefferson Davis," 120–21.

34. Senate Executive Documents No. 7, 39th Cong., 1st sess., 3–4; Nicoletti, "Did Secession Really Die at Appomattox?," 68–70.

35. Beale, *Diary of Edward Bates*, 481, 483.

36. William S. Groesbeck to Andrew Johnson, November 9, 1865, in Graf, *The Papers of Andrew Johnson*, 9:362.

37. Salmon P. Chase to James S. Pike, July 8, 1865, Chase Papers, LC, reel 35; John C. Ropes to John Grey Jr., May 29, 1865, in Gray and Ropes, *War Letters*, 496–97.

38. John C. Gray to John Codman Ropes, May 24, 1865, in Gray and Ropes, *War Letters*, 493–94.

39. Quoted in Leonard, *Lincoln's Avengers*, 166.

40. Butler, *Butler's Book*, 915–18.

41. Palmer and Ochoa, *The Selected Papers of Thaddeus Stevens*, 15–18, 317–18.

42. On Davis as an impediment, see Cooper, *Jefferson Davis, American,* 542. For an overview of the historical approaches to this issue, see Nicoletti, "Did Secession Really Die at Appomattox?," 107–8.

43. Niven, *Salmon P. Chase Papers,* 5:94 (quotation), 96–97.

44. Niven, *Salmon P. Chase: A Biography,* 395.

45. Niven, *Salmon P. Chase Papers,* 5:64.

46. Beale, *Diary of Gideon Welles,* 2:367–68; Niven, *Salmon P. Chase: A Biography,* 345.

47. Blue, *Salmon P. Chase,* 263–64; Nicoletti, "Did Secession Really Die at Appomattox?," 104–7.

48. Quoted in Nichols, "United States vs. Jefferson Davis, 1865–1869," 281.

49. Foner, *Reconstruction,* 197.

50. Crist et al., eds., *The Papers of Jefferson Davis,* 12:197–98; Davis, *Jefferson Davis: The Man and His Hour,* 656–57; *New York Times,* May 14, 1867 (quotation).

51. *New York Times,* May 12, 17, 1867; *Harper's Weekly,* June 8, 1867.

52. Blight, *Race and Reunion,* 2–3.

53. *The Liberator,* February 5, 1864.

54. Stewart, *Wendell Phillips,* 248–51.

55. *CG,* 39th Cong., 1st sess. (January 29, 1866), 482 (emphasis added). He had first proposed this on January 8. See ibid., p. 138.

56. Donald, *Charles Sumner and the Rights of Man,* 220–21; Palmer, *The Selected Letters of Charles Sumner,* 2:320, 321–22.

57. *CG,* 39th Cong., 1st sess. (February 1, 1866), 569.

58. Fessenden et al., *Report of the Joint Committee on Reconstruction,* part II, p. 7.

59. Ibid., vii–xxi.

60. *Maine Farmer,* November 2, 1865.

61. *New York Tribune,* May 8, 1865.

62. *Boston Daily Advertiser,* April 24, 1865.

63. *Daily Evening Bulletin,* August 30, 1865.

64. Lydia Maria Child to George W. Julian, January 22, 1866, Joshua Giddings and George W. Julian Papers, LC.

65. Banner, *The Death Penalty,* 125; *Lowell Daily Citizen and News,* July 1, 1865.

66. Spooner, *No Treason: No. 1,* 3, 4 (quotation), 6, 9; and *No Treason: No. 2, The Constitution,* 16, 19.

67. *DeBow's Review,* 3 (June 1867): 593–95, and 4 (September 1867): 161–62.

68. *New York Tribune,* May 2, 1865.

69. Letter to Chief Justice Chase, Peterboro, May 28, 1866, reel 36, fr. 491, Chase Papers, LC.

70. *Christian Recorder,* July 29, October 7, 1865.

71. Ripley, *The Black Abolitionist Papers,* 5:357.

72. Davis, *"We Will Be Satisfied with Nothing Less,"* 17–22; Fellmeth, "The First Civil Rights Movement," 5–8; Ripley, *The Black Abolitionist Papers,* 5:324–29.

73. Foner, *Frederick Douglass: Selected Speeches and Writings,* 536, 578.

74. Emberton, "'Only Murder Makes Men,'" 369–93; McCurry, "War, Gender, and Emancipation in the Civil War South," 120–50.

75. Lewis, "The Political Mind of the Negro, 1865–1900," 190–91.

76. *The Liberator*, January 16, 1863. For similar commentary, see Ripley, *Black Abolitionist Papers*, 5:334–49.

77. *Christian Recorder*, February 10, 1866 (emphasis in original).

78. McClure et al., "Circumventing the Dred Scott Decision," 280–82. The article reproduces primary documents surrounding this incident, including Bates's treatise.

79. Ibid., 288–89, 296.

80. *Christian Recorder*, December 10, 1864; *New York Herald*, May 13, 1863.

81. *The Liberator*, July 24, 1863.

82. *Proceedings of the Equal Rights' Convention of the Colored People of Pennsylvania, Held in the City of Harrisburg, February 8th, 9th, and 10th, 1865*, pp. 49–51, box 14, K. Leroy Irvis Papers, University of Pittsburgh.

83. *The Liberator*, July 7, 1865.

Chapter 9

1. Lydia Maria Child to George W. Julian, April 8, 1865, container 4, Joshua Giddings and George W. Julian Papers, LC.

2. C. E. Lippincott to Senator Lyman Trumbull, August 29, 1865, Reel 17, Trumbull Papers, LC.

3. Hyman, *Era of the Oath*, 110–14; Curry, *Radicalism, Racism, and Party Realignment*, 9–10; Kohl, "Enforcing a Vision of Community," 292–307; for the ruling, consult *Cummings v. The State of Missouri*, 71 U.S. 277 (1866).

4. Hyman, *Era of the Oath*, 98–99. Although Garesché lost his petition, another Missourian did successfully fight the test oath for attorneys to practice law. However, Augustus Hill Garland succeeded in overturning the requirement for attorneys to take the ironclad oath in order to conduct business in Federal courts.

5. Ibid., 110–12; Curry, *Radicalism, Racism, and Party Realignment*, 15; *New York Herald*, August 31, 1865.

6. *New York Tribune*, June 16, 1865; *Cincinnati Daily Enquirer*, August 4, 1865; *Baltimore Sun*, September 1, 1865.

7. Kohl, "Enforcing a Vision of Community," 292–93.

8. Webb, *Kentucky in the Reconstruction Era*, 9–10.

9. Harrison, *Civil War in Kentucky*, 95.

10. A good overview of the issues concerning the border states may be found in Curry, *Radicalism, Racism, and Party Realignment*. For a more recent treatment on Kentucky and Missouri, see Astor, *Rebels on the Border*.

11. A. W. Bradford to J. W. Crisfield, May 6, 1865, reel 5, pp. 627–28, LGM.

12. Ibid. For details on the process, see the *Baltimore Sun*, July 25, 1865.

13. *Baltimore Sun*, January 25, 1866; *Alexandria Gazette*, November 7, 1865; Curry, *Radicalism, Racism, and Party Realignment*, 163.

14. *Baltimore Sun*, November 17, 1865; *Philadelphia Inquirer*, November 9, 1865.

15. *Annapolis Gazette*, September 6, 1866 (emphasis in original).

16. *Annapolis Gazette*, May 31, 1866; *New York Herald*, August 16, 1866; Fuke, *Imperfect Equality*, 155–56.

17. *Baltimore Sun*, September 14, 1865; *New York Herald*, November 3, 1865; Fuke, *Imperfect Equality*, 151–53.

18. *New York Tribune*, October 24, November 2, 1866; *Daily National Intelligencer*, November 3, 1866; Curry, *Radicalism, Racism, and Party Realignment*, 168; Simpson, *Let Us Have Peace*, 154–61.

19. Fuke, *Imperfect Equality*, 153.

20. *Daily National Intelligencer*, August 20, 1867; Curry, *Radicalism, Racism, and Party Realignment*, 172.

21. Astor, *Rebels on the Border*, 174–75; Curry, *Radicalism, Racism, and Party Realignment*, 116–17; Coulter, *Civil War and Readjustment in Kentucky*, 273-74; Webb, *Kentucky in the Reconstruction Era*, 12–13.

22. *Appleton's Annual Cyclopaedia, 1865*, 464–65; Curry, *Radicalism, Racism, and Party Realignment*, 117; *New York Tribune*, August 2, 1865.

23. Coulter, *Civil War and Readjustment in Kentucky*, 282–84; Webb, *Kentucky in the Reconstruction Era*, 14–15; *Cincinnati Commercial*, reprinted in *Daily Age*, August 14, 1865; *New York Herald*, August 14, 1865.

24. Coulter, *Civil War and Readjustment in Kentucky*, 282; Marshall, *Creating a Confederate Kentucky*, 38–39.

25. *New York Post*, August 14, 1865; Coulter, *Civil War and Readjustment in Kentucky*, 282–83; *Baltimore Sun*, August 18, 1865; Astor, *Rebels on the Border*, 181–82.

26. *Harrisburg Patriot*, August 17, 1865.

27. *Cincinnati Daily Gazette*, July 4, 1867. Also see address of Ingersoll in *Washington (Pa.) Reporter*, July 24, 1867.

28. Coulter, *Civil War and Readjustment in Kentucky*, 332–33.

29. House Report No. 6, 40th Cong., 1st sess., pp. 7–8, 10–11.

30. Webb, *Kentucky in the Reconstruction Era*, 27–28; Coulter, *Civil War and Readjustment in Kentucky*, 332–39.

31. On West Virginia, see Curry, *Radicalism, Racism, and Party Realignment*, 93.

32. "A Proclamation, Respecting Soldiers Absent without Leave," March 10, 1865, microfilm 621, pp. 261–62, Decisions, RG 110, PMG, NARA.

33. *O.R.*, ser. 3, 5:108–12; Costa and Kahn, "Deserters, Social Norms, and Migration," 327–28. For a reference to Ohio and Indiana, see the *New York Tribune*, November 11, 1865. For reference to the budget, see the *Gettysburg Compiler*, July 16, 1866.

34. *O.R.*, ser. 3, 5:110.

35. *New York Tribune*, October 12, November 1, 1865.

36. *Philadelphia Inquirer*, January 18, 1866; *Gettysburg Compiler*, January 22, 29, 1866; *Harrisburg Patriot*, January 17, 31, 1866.

37. *Harrisburg Patriot*, January 31, 1866.

38. *Huber v. Reily*, 53 Pa., 112 (1866); Brightly, *A Collection of Leading Cases on the Law of Elections in the United States*, 69–81.

39. Brightly, *A Collection of Leading Cases on the Law of Elections in the United States*, 79; *Philadelphia Illustrated New Age*, June 23, 1866.

40. *Harrisburg Patriot*, quoted in the *Gettysburg Compiler*, June 25, 1866.

41. Weeks, *Gettysburg: Memory, Market, and an American Shrine*, 18–24; Spooner, "'Our Country's Common Ground,'" 9–10.

42. Brightly, *Digest of the Laws of Pennsylvania: For the Years 1862 to 1868*, 1425–26; on McConaughy introducing the bill, see *Gettysburg Compiler*, October 6, 1866; for the document generated by the provost marshal general's office, see http://www.libraries.psu.edu/psul/digital/deserters.html (accessed November 13, 2012).

43. Blair, "A Record of Pennsylvania Deserters," 537–38.

44. *Philadelphia Bulletin*, October 17, 1867.

45. *McCafferty v. Guyer et al.*, 59 Pa., 109 (1868); Brightly, *A Collection of Leading Cases on the Law of Elections in the United States*, 44–51.

46. *The Crisis*, July 31, 1867; *Cincinnati Enquirer*, April 9, 1867; *San Antonio Express*, October 29, 1867 (quotation).

47. Andrews, *The South since the War*, 131–32 (emphasis in original).

48. *New York Herald*, October 22, 1865 (North Carolina); McKitrick, *Andrew Johnson and Reconstruction*, 166–68; Andrews, *The South since the War*, 79–82, 130–36; Foner, *Reconstruction*, 194–95; "Laws of the Late Insurgent States," H. Ex. Doc. No. 131, 1–4.

49. Reid, *After the War*, 357–58 (Atlanta), 410 (Louisiana).

50. *New York Tribune*, September 20, 1865.

51. *New York Post*, August 12, 1865; on Tod, see the *Albany Journal*, September 9, 1865.

52. Andrews, *The South since the War*, 133.

53. Mahaffey, "Carl Schurz's Letters from the South," 222–57.

54. Senate Executive Documents, 39th Cong., 1st sess., No. 2, p. 13.

55. Ibid., p. 14; *New York Times*, February 8, 1866.

56. Sumner, *The National Security and the National Faith*, 3–4; also see *The Independent*, September 21, 1865.

57. Sumner, *The National Security and the National Faith*, 6 (proclamation and Treasury note), 12 (voting). I am grateful to Andrew Prymak for providing me with this document.

58. *Cleveland Plain Dealer*, September 29, 1865.

59. *Milwaukee Sentinel*, July 26, 1865.

60. Blue, *Salmon P. Chase: A Life in Politics*, 272–73; Niven, *Salmon P. Chase: A Biography*, 436–38.

61. *The American Law Review, 1867–1868*, 2:95–100; *Shortridge et al. v. Macon*, 22 F. Cas. 20 (1867); *New York Herald*, June 22, 1867.

62. *Boston Commercial Advertiser*, June 24, 1867; Niven, *Salmon P. Chase Papers*, 5:159–60.

63. Palmer and Ochoa, *Selected Papers of Thaddeus Stevens*, 2:72–73.

64. Du Bois, *Black Reconstruction in America*, 293.

65. Palmer and Ochoa, *Selected Papers of Thaddeus Stevens*, 2:72. Also see Blaine, *Twenty Years of Congress*, 2:128–30.

66. Foner, *Reconstruction*, 251–52; Conklin in *CG*, 39th Cong., 1st sess. (January 22, 1866), 357; James, *The Framing of the Fourteenth Amendment*, 60–61.

67. *The Nation*, January 11, 1866, quoted in Du Bois, *Black Reconstruction in America*, 292.

68. Urofsky and Finkelman, *A March of Liberty*, 1:439–40; Fessenden, *Report of the Joint Committee on Reconstruction*, xi. On Fessenden, see Cook, *Civil War Senator*.

69. Cook, *Civil War Senator*, 207; Fessenden, *Report of the Joint Committee on Reconstruction*, xiii.

70. Fessenden, *Report of the Joint Committee on Reconstruction*, xvi.

71. Petition of N. T. Hill and 150 Others, Bucksport, Maine, March 12, 1866, from Chester, Pa., March 5, 1866, and from Lewis Holmes and Others from Bridgewater, Mass., March 2, 1866, HR 39A-H14.2, folder: February 1, 1866 to March 15, 1866, all in RG 233, Committee on the Judiciary, Petitions and Memorials, NARA.

72. "Amendment of the Constitution," 39th Cong., 1st sess., H. Misc. Doc. No. 25 (January 15, 1866); *CG*, 39th Cong., 1st sess. (January 22, 1866), 337.

73. *Appleton's Annual Cyclopaedia, 1866*, 177–79.

74. "Representation," 39th Cong., 1st sess., H. Rep., No. 11, p. 3.

75. Palmer and Ochoa, *Selected Papers of Thaddeus Stevens*, 74. See also Epps, *Democracy Reborn*, 105–6.

76. Palmer and Ochoa, *Selected Papers of Thaddeus Stevens*, 136.

77. Blaine, *Twenty Years of Congress*, 205–7; Palmer and Ochoa, *Selected Papers of Thaddeus Stevens*, 137–38.

78. Trefousse, *Thaddeus Stevens: Nineteenth Century Egalitarian*, 183–84; Blaine, *Twenty Years of Congress*, 211–12.

79. Bond, *No Easy Walk to Freedom*, 8, 105 (legitimated Civil Rights Bill); 123 (Hobson's choice).

80. Perman, "The South and Congress's Reconstruction Policy," 184–85.

81. Bond, *No Easy Walk to Freedom*, 87, 146 (quotation).

82. White, "The Trial of Jefferson Davis," 131; Nicoletti, "Did Secession Really Die at Appomattox?," 632–34.

83. Epps, "The Antebellum Political Background of the Fourteenth Amendment," 177.

84. Brodie, *Thaddeus Stevens: Scourge of the South*, 270.

Conclusion

1. Stewart, *The Reward of Patriotism*, 412–13, 417 (quotation).

2. Ibid., 416, 440.

3. Ibid., 422.

4. Ryan, *Civic Wars*; Bensel, *The American Ballot Box in the Mid-Nineteenth Century*, 75–76.

5. *Daily Cleveland Herald*, December 4, 1868.

6. *New York Herald*, September 13, 1868; *Boston Daily Advertiser*, September 14, 1868; *Daily National Intelligencer*, September 14, 1868.

7. Stewart, *The Reward of Patriotism*, 143; Van Horne, *Life of Major-General George H. Thomas*, 404–5.

WORKS CITED

Manuscripts

Historical Society of Pennsylvania, Philadelphia
   Spear, Samuel T. *The Punishment of Treason: A Discourse Preached April 23d, 1865 in the South Presbyterian Church of Brooklyn*. Brooklyn: Union Steam Presses, 1865.
   Union League Pamphlets
      Bellows, Henry W. *Unconditional Loyalty*. New York: Anson D. F. Randolph, 1863.
      Lieber, Francis. *No Party Now; but All for Our Country*. Philadelphia: Crissy & Markley, 1863.
      Second Annual Report of the Board of Directors of the Union League of Philadelphia, December 12, 1864. Philadelphia: Henry B. Ashmead, 1864.
Huntington Library, San Marino, Calif.
   Francis Lieber Papers
Library of Congress, Washington, D.C.
   Salmon P. Chase Papers, microfilm
   Joshua Giddings and George W. Julian Papers
   Abraham Lincoln Papers, American Memory Project, online
   Manton Marble Papers, microfilm
   George B. McClellan Papers, microfilm
   William Henry Seward Papers, microfilm
   Thaddeus Stevens Papers
   Lyman Trumbull Papers
Maryland State Archives, Annapolis
   Letterbooks, Governor of Maryland
National Archives and Records Administration, Washington, D.C., and College Park, Md.
   General Records of the Department of Justice (RG 60)
      Attorney General Papers: Letters Sent; Letters Received
   General Records of the Department of State (RG 59)
      Commission Relating to State Prisoners
      Secret Letters, 1861–1863
   Records of the Adjutant General's Office, 1780s–1917 (RG 94)
      Amnesty Papers
   Records of the Office of the Judge Advocate General (Army) (RG 153)
      Court-martial Case Files and Related Records
   Records of the Provost Marshal General's Bureau (RG 110)

The Descriptive List of Deserters from Pennsylvania Military Units during the Civil War, http://www.libraries.psu.edu/psul/digital/deserters.html (accessed February 12, 2013)

Historical Reports of State Acting Assistant Provost Marshals General and District Provost Marshals, 1865, microfilm no. 1163

Reports and Decisions Made, microfilm no. 621

Records of the U.S. Army Continental Commands (RG 393)

Department of Missouri: Papers Relating to Persons Charged with Disloyalty and Other Crimes

Records of the United States House of Representatives (RG 233)

Petitions and Memorials

National Archives and Records Administration, Mid-Atlantic Region, Philadelphia

Records of the District Courts of the United States, 1685–1993 (RG 21)

District Court of Maryland, Criminal Case Files

District Court of Maryland, Docket, 1860–1867

Eastern District of Pennsylvania

U.S. Circuit Court for the Eastern District of Pennsylvania, Criminal Case Files, 1791–1883

Minutes, August 1, 1860, to April 1, 1862, and April 5, 1865, to November 30, 1865

National Archives and Records Administration, Southeast Region, Atlanta

Records of the United States District Court (RG 21), 1685–1993

Pennsylvania State Archives, Harrisburg

Adjutant General Papers (RG 19)

University of Pittsburgh, Pittsburgh, Pa.

K. Leroy Irvis Papers

Proceedings of the Equal Rights' Convention of the Colored People of Pennsylvania, Held in the City of Harrisburg, February 8th, 9th, and 10th, 1865. Philadelphia: M. C. Crummill Printer, 1865.

Western Historical Manuscript Collection, State Historical Society of Missouri, Columbia

Elvira Scott Diary

Court Cases

Brown v. United States, 12 U.S., 110 (1814), Lexus Nexis

Charge to the Grand Jury, Judge Peleg Sprague, 1 Sprague 602 (1861), Lexus Nexis

Cummings v. The State of Missouri, 71 U.S. 277 (1866), Lexus Nexis

Ex Parte Bollman and Ex Parte Swartwout, 8 U.S., 75 (1807), Lexus Nexis

Huber v. Reily, 53 Pa., 112 (1866), Lexus Nexis

McCafferty v. Guyer et al., 59 Pa., 109 (1868), Lexus Nexis

Mrs. Alexander's Cotton, 69 U.S. 404 (1864), Lexus Nexis

Norris v. Doniphan, 61 Ky. 385 (1863), Lexus Nexis

The Prize Cases, 67 U.S., 635 (1863), Lexus Nexis

Santisima Trinidad, 7 Wheaton, 238

Shortridge et al. v. Macon, 22 F. Cas. 20 (1867), Lexus Nexis

The State of Ohio Ex Rel. David Tod v. The Court of Common Pleas of Fairfield County, 15 Ohio St. 377 (1864), Lexus Nexis

United States v. Greiner, 26 F. Cas. 36 (1861), Lexus Nexis

U.S. v. Mitchell, 2 U.S., 348 (1795), Lexus Nexis

United States v. Rucker, 27 F. Cas. 911 (1866), Lexus Nexis

United States v. Smith, 27 F. Cas. (1861), Lexus Nexis

Government Documents

"Amendment of the Constitution." 39th Cong., 1st sess, 1866. H. Misc. Doc. No. 25.

Ashton, J. Hubley, ed. *Official Opinions of the Attorneys General of the United States.* Vol. 11. Washington, D.C.: W. H. & O. H. Morrison, 1869. http://www.heinonline. org.ezaccess.libraries.psu.edu/HOL/Page?handle=hein.agopinions/oag0011&id=1 &collection=agopinions&index=agopinions/oag (accessed December 12, 2012).

Brightly, Frederick Charles. *A Collection of Leading Cases on the Law of Elections in the United States.* Philadelphia: Kay & Brother, 1871.

————. *Digest of the Laws of Pennsylvania: For the Years 1862 to 1868.* Philadelphia: Kay & Brother, 1868.

The Code of Virginia: With the Declaration of Independence and Constitution of the United States; and the Declaration of Rights and the Constitution of Virginia. Richmond: William F. Ritchie, 1849.

Congressional Globe. 46 vols. Washington, D.C.: Government Printing Office, 1834–73.

Fessenden, W. P., et al. *Report of the Joint Committee on Reconstruction.* Freeport, N.Y.: Books for Libraries Press, 1971.

House Executive Documents, No. 14, 39th Cong., 1st sess., January 3, 1866.

House Report No. 6, 40th Cong., 1st sess, July 9, 1867.

"Laws of the Late Insurgent States." 39th Cong., 1st sess. H. Ex. Doc. No. 131, June 18, 1866.

"Letter of the Secretary of War," February 18, 1865. 38th Cong., 2nd sess., 1865. S. Ex. Doc. No. 23.

Loyalty of Clerks and Other Persons Employed by Government. 37th Cong., 2nd sess., 1862. H.R. Rep. No. 16 (January 28, 1862).

"Message of the President of the United States, Communicating, in Compliance with a resolution of the Senate of December 20, 1864, information in relation to the Arrest of Colonel Richard T. Jacobs, lieutenant governor of the State of Kentucky, and Colonel Frank Wolford, one of the presidential electors of that State." 38th Cong., 2nd sess. S. Ex. Doc. No. 16, February 1, 1865.

Report of the Committee on Elections, on Contested Elections in Somerset County, Together with the Testimony Taken before That Committee, January Session, 1864. Annapolis: Bull & Tuttle, 1864.

Report of the Select Committee of the Senate on the Invasion and Seizure of Public Property at Harpers Ferry, June 15, 1860, "Testimony." 36th Cong., 1st sess. S. Rep. No. 278.

"Representation." 39th Cong., 1st sess., H. Rep. No. 11, January 22, 1866.

Senate Executive Documents, 39th Cong., 1st sess., No. 2, December 19, 1865.

Senate Executive Documents, 39th Cong., 1st sess., No. 7, January 10, 1866.

Statutes at Large of the United States of America, 1789–1873. 17 vols. Washington, D.C.: 1870–73.

U.S. Congress. *Report of the Joint Committee on the Conduct of the War: In Three Parts.* Washington, D.C.: Government Printing Office, 1863.

U.S. Congress. Senate Committee on Military Affairs. 38th Cong. *Report to Accompany Bill S. No. 37, in the Senate of the United States, February 12, 1864.* Doc. No. 14.

U.S. Senate. "Expulsion and Censure." Washington, D.C.: Senate Historical Office. http://www.senate.gov/artandhistory/history/common/briefing/Expulsion_Censure.htm.

U.S. Senate Historical Office. *United States Senate Election, Expulsion and Censure Cases: 1793–1990.* Washington, D.C.: Government Printing Office, 1994.

U.S. War Department. *The War of the Rebellion: A Compilation of the Official Records of the Union and Confederate Armies.* 128 vols. Washington, D.C.: Government Printing Office, 1880–1901.

Periodicals

Albany Journal

Alexandria (Va.) Gazette

Annapolis Gazette

Augusta Chronicle

Baltimore Sun

Bangor Daily Whig & Courier

Boston Commercial Advertiser

Boston Daily Advertiser

Boston Post

Central Press (Bellefonte, Pa.)

Christian Recorder

Cincinnati Daily Gazette

Cincinnati Enquirer

The Compiler (Gettysburg, Pa.)

The Crisis (Columbus, Ohio)

Daily Age (Philadelphia)

Daily Cleveland Herald

Daily Commercial Register

Daily Constitutional Union (Washington, D.C.)

Daily Evening Bulletin (San Francisco)

Daily Morning News (Savannah)

Daily National Intelligencer

Daily Ohio Statesman

Daily South Carolinian

DeBow's Review: Devoted to the Restoration of the Southern States

Democrat Watchman (Bellefonte, Pa.)

Easton Gazette

Frank Leslie's Illustrated Newspaper

Harper's Weekly

Harrisburg Patriot and Union

Hartford Courant

The Independent

The Liberator

Lowell Daily Citizen and News

Maine Farmer

Memphis Daily Avalanche

Milwaukee Daily Sentinel

The Nation

National Era

National Intelligencer

New Hampshire Sentinel

New York Herald

New York Post

New York Times

New York Tribune

North American and United States Gazette

Philadelphia Bulletin
Philadelphia Illustrated New Age
Philadelphia Inquirer
Philadelphia Press
Philadelphia Public Ledger
Philadelphia Sunday Transcript
Republican Farmer (Bridgeport, Conn.)
San Antonio Express
San Francisco Daily Evening Bulletin

Scioto Gazette (Chillicothe, Ohio)
Springfield Republican
Washington (Pa.) Reporter
Weekly Harrisburg Patriot and Union
Weekly Union and American (Nashville)
Weekly Wisconsin Patriot
Wisconsin Daily Patriot
Zion's Herald and Wesleyan Journal

Printed Primary Sources

American Annual Cyclopaedia and Register of Important Events. Multiple volumes.
    New York: D. Appleton, 1861–66.
The American Law Review, 1867–1868. Vol. 2. Boston: Little, Brown, 1868.
Andrews, Sidney. The South since the War. Baton Rouge: Louisiana State University
    Press, 2004.
Basler, Roy P., ed., Collected Works of Abraham Lincoln. 9 vols. New Brunswick, N.J.:
    Rutgers University Press, 1953–55.
Beale, Howard K., ed. The Diary of Edward Bates. Washington, D.C.: Government
    Printing Office, 1933.
———. Diary of Gideon Welles. 3 vols. New York: W. W. Norton, 1960.
Beall, John Yates. Memoir of John Yates Beall: His Life, Trial Correspondence, Diary,
    and Private Manuscript Found among His Papers, Including His Own Account of
    the Raid on Lake Erie. Montreal: John Lovell, 1865.
Berlin, Ira, ed., Joseph P. Reidy and Leslie S. Rowland, assoc. eds. Freedom. A
    Documentary History of Emancipation, 1861–1867, Series II, The Black Military
    Experience. Cambridge: Cambridge University Press, 1982.
Bethel, Elizabeth. "The Prison Diary of Raphael Semmes." Journal of Southern
    History 22 (November 1956): 498–509.
Binney, Horace. The Privilege of the Writ of Habeas Corpus under the Constitution.
    Philadelphia: C. Sherman & Son, Printers, 1862.
Blaine, James Gillespie. Twenty Years of Congress: From Lincoln to Garfield. Vol. 2.
    Norwich, Conn.: Henry Bill Publishing Co., 1886.
Blair, William Alan, and Bell Irvin Wiley, eds. A Politician Goes to War: The Civil War
    Letters of John White Geary. University Park: Pennsylvania State University Press,
    1995.
Brown, John, and Robert M. DeWitt. The Life, Trial and Execution of Captain John
    Brown, Known as Old Brown of Ossawatomie, with a Full Account of the Attempted
    Insurrection at Harpers Ferry. New York: Robert M. De Witt, 1859.
Burlingame, Michael, and John R. Turner Etlinger, eds. Inside Lincoln's White
    House: The Complete Civil War Diary of John Hay. Carbondale: Southern Illinois
    University Press, 1997.
Butler, Benjamin F. Butler's Book: A Review of His Legal, Political, and Military
    Career. Boston: Thayer, 1892.

Carter, Gari, ed. *Troubled State: Civil War Journals of Franklin Archibald Dick*. Kirksville, Mo.: Truman State University Press, 2008.

Clay-Clopton, Virginia. *A Belle of the Fifties: Memoirs of Mrs. Clay of Alabama*. New York: Doubleday, Page, 1905.

Cole, Donald B., and John J. McDonough, eds. *Witness to the Young Republic: A Yankee's Journal, 1818–1870; Benjamin Brown French*. Hanover: University Press of New England, 1989.

Colt, Margaretta Barton. *Defend the Valley: A Shenandoah Family in the Civil War*. New York: Orion Books, 1994.

Crist, Linda L., Suzanne Scott Gibbs, Brady L. Hutchison, and Elizabeth Henson Smith, eds. *The Papers of Jefferson Davis*. Vol. 12, *June 1865–December 1870*. Baton Rouge: Louisiana State University Press, 2008.

Dana, Charles A. *Recollections of the Civil War*. New York: D. Appleton, 1913.

Dawson, Sarah Morgan. *A Confederate Girl's Diary*. Boston: Houghton Mifflin, 1913.

Day, David L. *My Diary of Rambles with the 25th Massachusetts Volunteer Infantry*. Milford, Mass.: King & Billings Printers, 1884.

de Hauranne, Ernest Duvergier. *A Frenchman in Lincoln's America*. Trans. Ralph H. Bowen. 2 vols. Chicago: R. R. Donnelley & Sons, 1974.

Donald, David, ed. *Inside Lincoln's Cabinet: The Diaries of Salmon P. Chase*. New York: Longmans, Green, 1954.

Douglas, Henry Kyd. *I Rode with Stonewall: Being Chiefly the War Experiences of the Youngest Member of Jackson's Staff from the John Brown Raid to the Hanging of Mrs. Surratt*. Introduction by Philip Van Doren Stern. Greenwich, Conn.: Fawcett, 1961.

Engs, Robert F., and Corey M. Brooks, eds. *Their Patriotic Duty: The Civil War Letters of the Evans Family of Brown County, Ohio*. New York: Fordham University Press, 2007.

Fairfax County Historical Society. "Letters of Charles Cummings, Provost-Marshal of Fairfax Court House, Winter 1861–1862." *Yearbook: The Historical Society of Fairfax County, Virginia* 22 (1989–90): 46–69.

Foner, Philip S., ed. *Frederick Douglass: Selected Speeches and Writings*. 1950. Rev. ed. Chicago: Lawrence Hill Books, 1999.

Graf, Leroy P., ed. *The Papers of Andrew Johnson*. 16 vols. Knoxville: University of Tennessee Press, 1967–2000.

Grant, Ulysses S. *The Papers of Ulysses S. Grant*. Edited by John Y. Simon et al. Ulysses S. Grant Association. 32 vols. Carbondale: Southern Illinois University Press, 1967–2012.

Gray, John Chipman, and John Codman Ropes. *War Letters, 1862–1865*. Cambridge: Massachusetts Historical Society, 1927.

Hand-Book of the Democracy for 1863 & 1864. New York: Society for the Diffusion of Political Knowledge, 1864.

House, Ellen Renshaw. *A Very Violent Rebel: The Civil War Diary of Ellen Renshaw House*. Edited by Daniel E. Sutherland. Knoxville: University of Tennessee Press, 1996.

Kautz, August V. *Customs of Service for Officers of the Army: As Described from Law and Regulations and Practiced in the United States Army*. 1866. Reprint, Mechanicsburg, Pa.: Stackpole Books, 2002.

Lee, Captain Robert E. *Recollections and Letters of General Robert E. Lee*. 1904. New ed. New York: Doubleday, 1924.

Lieber, Francis. *Manual of Political Ethics*. Edited by Theodore D. Woolsey. 2nd ed. Philadelphia: J. B. Lippincott, 1875.

Lyman, Colonel Theodore. *Meade's Headquarters, 1863–1865: Letters of Colonel Theodore Lyman from the Wilderness to Appomattox*. Selected and edited by George R. Agassiz. 1922. Reprint, Salem, N.H.: Ayer Company, 1970.

Mahaffey, Joseph H. "Carl Schurz's Letters from the South." *Georgia Historical Quarterly* 35 (September 1951): 222–57.

McClellan, George B. *McClellan's Own Story: The War for the Union*. New York: Charles L. Webster, 1887.

McCulloch, Hugh. *Men and Measures of Half a Century*. New York: Scribner's, 1888.

McKelvy, David, Margaret McKelvy Bird, and Daniel W. Crofts. "Notes and Documents: Soldier Voting in 1864; The David McKelvy Diary." *Pennsylvania Magazine of History and Biography* 115 (July 1991): 371–413.

McKinley, Emilie Riley. *From the Pen of a She-Rebel: The Civil War Diary of Emilie Riley McKinley*. Edited by Gordon A. Cotton. Columbia: University of South Carolina Press, 2001.

Nevins, Allan, ed. *Diary of the Civil War, 1860–1865: George Templeton Strong*. New York: Macmillan, 1962.

Niven, John, ed. *The Salmon P. Chase Papers, Journals and Correspondence*. 5 vols. Kent, Ohio: Kent State University Press, 1993–98.

Notes of Debates in the Federal Convention of 1787, Reported by James Madison. Introduction by Adrienne Koch. Athens: Ohio University Press, 1966.

Official Proceedings of the Democratic National Convention, Held in 1864. Chicago: Times Steam Book and Job Printing House, 1864.

Palmer, Beverly Wilson, ed. *The Selected Letters of Charles Sumner*. 2 vols. Boston: Northeastern University Press, 1990.

Palmer, Beverly Wilson, and Holly Byers Ochoa, eds. *The Selected Papers of Thaddeus Stevens*. 2 vols. Pittsburgh: University of Pittsburgh Press, 1997–98.

Pease, Calvin Theodore, and James G. Randall, eds. *The Diary of Orville Hickman Browning*. 2 vols. Springfield: Illinois State Historical Library, 1925, 1933.

Perry, Thomas Sergeant, ed. *The Life and Letters of Francis Lieber*. Boston: J. R. Osgood & Co., 1882.

Peter, Frances Dallam. *A Union Woman in Civil War Kentucky*. Edited by John David Smith and William Cooper Jr. Lexington: University Press of Kentucky, 2000.

Pitman, Benn. *The Trials for Treason at Indianapolis: Disclosing the Plans for Establishing a North-Western Confederacy*. Cincinnati: Moore, Wilstach & Baldwin, 1865.

Reid, Whitelaw. *After the War: A Southern Tour, May 1, 1865, to May 1, 1866*. Cincinnati: Moore, Wilstach & Baldwin, 1866.

Richardson, James D., ed. *A Compilation of the Messages and Papers of the Confederacy.* 2 vols. 1905. Reprint, Harrisburg, Pa.: Archive Society, 1996.

Ripley, C. Peter, ed. *The Black Abolitionist Papers.* Vol. 5, *The United States, 1859–1865.* Chapel Hill: University of North Carolina Press, 1992.

Robbins, James J. *Report on the Trial of Castner Hanway for Treason: In Resistance of the Execution of the Fugitive Slave Law of September, 1850.* Philadelphia: King & Baird, 1852.

Robertson, James I., Jr., ed. *The Civil War Letters of General Robert McAllister.* New ed. Baton Rouge: Louisiana State University Press, 1998.

Robinson, Sara T. L. *Kansas: Its Interior and Exterior Life.* 3rd ed. Boston: Crosby, Nichols and Company, 1856.

Sanborn, F. B. *The Life and Letters of John Brown, Liberator of Kansas, and Martyr of Virginia.* 1885. Reprint, New York: Negro Universities Press, 1969.

Scott, Colonel H. L. *Military Dictionary: Comprising Technical Definitions; Information on Raising and Keeping Troops; Actual Service.* New York: D. Van Nostrand, 1861.

Sears, Stephen W., ed. *The Civil War Papers of George B. McClellan: Selected Correspondence, 1860–1865.* New York: Ticknor & Fields, 1989.

Sparks, David S. *Inside Lincoln's Army: The Diary of Marsena Rudolph Patrick, Provost Marshal General, Army of the Potomac.* New York: T. Yoseloff, 1964.

"Speech of the Hon. Benjamin G. Harris, of Md., Delivered in the House of Representatives, May 9, 1864." Washington, D.C.: printed by *Constitutional Union,* n.d. http://wap.archive.org/details/speechofhonbenja00harr (accessed February 8, 2013).

Spooner, Lysander. *No Treason: No. 1.* Boston: published by the author, 14 Bromfield Street, 1867.

———. *No Treason: No. 2, The Constitution.* Boston: published by the author, 1867.

Stanton, R. L., D.D. *The Church and the Rebellion: A Consideration of the Rebellion against the Government of the United States; and the Agency of the Church, North and South, in Relation Thereto.* New York: Derby & Miller, 1864.

Sumner, Charles. *The Equal Rights of All; The Great Guarantee and Present Necessity, for the Sake of Security, and to Maintain a Republican Government.* Washington, D.C.: Government Printing Office, 1866.

———. *The National Security and the National Faith: Guaranties for the National Freedmen and the National Creditor.* Boston: Press of Geo. C. Rand & Avery S. Cornhill, 1865.

Treason in Indiana Exposed! Indianapolis: Union State Central Committee, W. R. Holloway & Co., 1864.

The Trial of Hon. Clement L. Vallandigham by a Military Commission. Cincinnati: Rickey and Carroll, 1863.

Tribune Almanac and Political Register for 1863. New York: Greeley & McElrath, 1864.

The Tribune Almanac and Political Register for 1865. New York: Tribune Association, 1865.

Vallandigham, Clement L. *Speeches, Arguments, Addresses, and Letters of Clement L. Vallandigham.* New York: J. Walter & Co., 1864.

Vallandigham, Rev. James L. *Life of Clement L. Vallandigham, by His Brother.* Baltimore: Turnbull Brothers, 1872.

Vattel, E. de. *The Law of Nations, or the Principles of Natural Law.* Special ed. New York: Legal Classics Library, 1993.

Villard, Oswald Garrison. *John Brown, 1800–1859: A Biography Fifty Years After.* Boston: Houghton Mifflin Company, 1910.

Warburton, A. F. *Trial of the Officers and Crew of the Privateer Savannah on the Charge of Piracy in the United States Circuit Court for the Southern District of New York, Hon. Judges Nelson and Shipman Presiding.* New York: Baker & Godwin Printers, 1862.

West, George Benjamin. *When the Yankees Came.* Edited by Parke Rouse Jr. Richmond: Dietz Press, 1977.

Wheaton, Henry. *Elements of International Law.* Reproduction of 1866 edition by Richard Henry Dana Jr. Oxford: Clarendon Press, 1936.

White, Jonathan W., ed. *A Philadelphia Perspective: The Civil War Diary of Sidney George Fisher.* New York: Fordham University Press, 2007.

Whiting, William. *The War Powers of the President and the Legislative Powers of Congress in Relation to Rebellion, Treason and Slavery.* 7th ed. Boston: John L. Shorey, 1863.

———. *The War Powers of the President, Military Arrests, and Reconstruction of the Union.* 8th ed. Boston: John L. Shorey, 1864.

Secondary Works

BOOKS, DISSERTATIONS, AND THESES

Ash, Stephen V. *When the Yankees Came: Conflict & Chaos in the Occupied South, 1861–1865.* Chapel Hill: University of North Carolina Press, 1995.

Astor, Aaron. *Rebels on the Border: Civil War, Emancipation, and Reconstruction of Kentucky & Missouri.* Baton Rouge: Louisiana State University Press, 2012.

Baker, Jean H. *Affairs of Party: The Political Culture of Northern Democrats in the Mid-Nineteenth Century.* New York: Fordham University Press, 1998.

———. *The Politics of Continuity: Maryland Political Parties from 1858 to 1870.* Baltimore: Johns Hopkins University Press, 1973.

Banner, Stuart. *The Death Penalty: An American History.* Cambridge, Mass.: Harvard University Press, 2002.

Belz, Herman. *Abraham Lincoln, Constitutionalism, and Equal Rights in the Civil War Era.* New York: Fordham University Press, 1998.

Bensel, Richard Franklin. *The American Ballot Box in the Mid-Nineteenth Century.* New York: Cambridge University Press, 2004.

———. *Yankee Leviathan: The Origins of Central State Authority in America, 1859–1877.* New York: Cambridge University Press, 1990.

Bernstein, Iver. *The New York City Draft Riots: Their Significance for American Society and Politics in the Age of the Civil War.* New York: Oxford University Press, 1990.

Bigelow, Marian Elizabeth. "Maryland in National Politics, 1860–1866." M.S. thesis, University of Wisconsin, Madison, 1922.

Blair, William. *Cities of the Dead: Contesting the Memory of the Civil War in the South, 1865–1914*. Chapel Hill: University of North Carolina Press, 2004.

Blight, David. *Race and Reunion: The Civil War in American Memory*. Cambridge, Mass.: Belknap Press of Harvard University Press, 2001.

Blue, Frederick J. *Salmon P. Chase: A Life in Politics*. Kent, Ohio: Kent State University Press, 1987.

Boman, Dennis K. *Lincoln and Citizens' Rights in Civil War Missouri: Balancing Freedom and Security*. Baton Rouge: Louisiana State University Press, 2011.

Bond, James E. *No Easy Walk to Freedom: Reconstruction and the Ratification of the Fourteenth Amendment*. Westport, Conn.: Praeger, 1997.

Bradley, George C., and Richard L. Dahlen. *From Conciliation to Conquest: The Sack of Athens and the Court-Martial of Colonel John B. Turchin*. Tuscaloosa: University of Alabama Press, 2006.

Brodie, Fawn. *Thaddeus Stevens: Scourge of the South*. New York: W. W. Norton, 1959.

Campbell, Jacqueline Glass. *When Sherman Marched North from the Sea: Resistance on the Confederate Home Front*. Chapel Hill: University of North Carolina Press, 2003.

Carnahan, Burrus M. *Lincoln on Trial: Southern Civilians and the Law of War*. Lexington: University Press of Kentucky, 2010.

Carso, Brian Francis, Jr. "'Whom Can We Trust Now?' The Meaning of Treason in the United States, From Revolution through the Civil War." Ph.D. dissertation, Boston University, 2004.

Cashin, Joan, ed. *The War Was You and Me: Civilians in the American Civil War*. Princeton, N.J.: Princeton University Press, 2002.

Chapin, Bradley. *The American Law of Treason: Revolutionary and Early National Origins*. Seattle: University of Washington Press, 1964.

Chicoine, Stephen. *John Basil Turchin and the Fight to Free the Slaves*. Westport, Conn.: Praeger, 2003.

Cook, Robert J. *Civil War Senator: William Pitt Fessenden and the Fight to Save the American Republic*. Baton Rouge: Louisiana State University Press, 2011.

Cooper, William J., Jr. *Jefferson Davis, American*. New York: Alfred A. Knopf, 2000.

Coulter, E. Merton. *The Civil War and Readjustment in Kentucky*. 1926. Reprint, Gloucester, Mass.: Peter Smith, 1966.

———. *William G. Brownlow: Fighting Parson*. 1937. Reprint, Knoxville: University of Tennessee Press, 1999.

Curry, Richard O., ed. *Radicalism, Racism, and Party Realignment: The Border States during Reconstruction*. Baltimore: Johns Hopkins University Press, 1969.

Curtis, Michael Kent. *Free Speech, "The People's Darling Privilege": Struggles for Freedom of Expression in American History*. Durham: Duke University Press, 2000.

Cushman, Stephen. *Bloody Promenade: Reflections on a Civil War Battle*. Charlottesville: University of Virginia Press, 1999.

Davis, Hugh. *"We Will Be Satisfied with Nothing Less": The African American Struggle for Equal Rights in the North during Reconstruction.* Ithaca: Cornell University Press, 2011.

Davis, William C. *Jefferson Davis: The Man and His Hour; A Biography.* New York: Harper Collins, 1991.

Donald, David Herbert. *Charles Sumner and the Rights of Man.* New York: Alfred A. Knopf, 1970.

———. *Lincoln.* New York: Simon & Schuster, 1995.

———. *Lincoln Reconsidered: Essays on the Civil War Era.* 2nd ed. New York: Vintage Books, 1956.

Du Bois, W. E. B. *Black Reconstruction in America, 1860–1880.* 1935. New ed. New York: Free Press, 1992.

Dykstra, Natalie. *Clover Adams: A Gilded and Heartbreaking Life.* Boston: Houghton Mifflin Harcourt, 2012.

Eicher, John H., and David J. Eicher, eds. *Civil War High Commands.* Stanford: Stanford University Press, 2001.

Emberton, Carole. *Beyond Redemption: Race, Violence, and the American South after the Civil War.* Chicago: University of Chicago Press, 2013.

Epps, Garrett. *Democracy Reborn: The Fourteenth Amendment and the Fight for Equal Rights in Post–Civil War America.* New York: Henry Holt, 2006.

Etcheson, Nicole. *Bleeding Kansas: Contested Liberty in the Civil War Era.* Lawrence: University Press of Kansas, 2004.

Faust, Drew. *Mothers of Invention: Women of the Slaveholding South in the American Civil War.* Chapel Hill: University of North Carolina Press, 1996.

———. *This Republic of Suffering: Death and the American Civil War.* New York: Alfred A. Knopf, 2008.

Fellman, Michael. *Inside War: The Guerrilla Conflict in Missouri during the American Civil War.* New York: Oxford, 1989.

Fellmeth, Amanda Marie. "The First Civil Rights Movement: The Pennsylvania State Equal Rights League in Movement Culture." Honor's thesis, Pennsylvania State University, 2011.

Fishel, Edwin C. *The Secret War for the Union: The Untold Story of Military Intelligence in the Civil War.* Boston: Houghton Mifflin, 1996.

Foner, Eric. *The Fiery Trial: Abraham Lincoln and American Slavery.* New York: W. W. Norton, 2010.

———. *Reconstruction: America's Unfinished Revolution, 1863–1877.* New York: Harper and Row, 1988.

Frank, Joseph Allan. *With Ballot and Bayonet: The Political Socialization of American Civil War Soldiers.* Athens: University of Georgia Press, 1998.

Freidel, Frank. *Francis Lieber: Nineteenth-Century Liberal.* Baton Rouge: Louisiana State University Press, 1947.

Fuke, Richard Paul. *Imperfect Equality: African Americans and the Confines of White Racial Attitudes in Post-Emancipation Maryland.* New York: Fordham University Press, 1999.

Gallagher, Gary W. *The Union War.* Cambridge, Mass.: Harvard University Press, 2011.

————, ed. *The Fredericksburg Campaign: Decision on the Rappahannock*. Chapel Hill: University of North Carolina Press, 1995.

Gallman, J. Matthew. *Mastering Wartime: A Social History of Philadelphia during the Civil War*. New York: Cambridge University Press, 1990.

Geary, James W. *We Need Men: The Union Draft in the Civil War*. DeKalb: Northern Illinois University Press, 1991.

Gerteis, Louis S. *Civil War St. Louis*. Lawrence: University Press of Kansas, 2001.

Gienapp, William E. *The Origins of the Republican Party, 1852–1856*. New York: Oxford University Press, 1987.

Giesberg, Judith. *Army at Home: Women and the Civil War on the Northern Home Front*. Chapel Hill: University of North Carolina Press, 2009.

Goldfield, David. *America Aflame: How the Civil War Created a Nation*. New York: Bloomsbury Press, 2011.

Grimsley, Mark. *The Hard Hand of War: Union Military Policy toward Southern Civilians, 1861–1865*. Cambridge: Cambridge University Press, 1995.

Guelzo, Allen C. *Lincoln's Emancipation Proclamation: The End of Slavery in America*. New York: Simon & Schuster, 2004.

Hahn, Steven. *A Nation under our Feet: Black Political Struggles in the Rural South from Slavery to the Great Migration*. Cambridge, Mass.: Belknap Press of Harvard University Press, 2003.

Hamilton, Daniel W. *The Limits of Sovereignty: Property Confiscation in the Union and the Confederacy during the Civil War*. Chicago: University of Chicago Press, 2007.

Harrison, Lowell H. *The Civil War in Kentucky*. Lexington: University Press of Kentucky, 1975.

Haskins, George Lee, and Herbert A. Johnson. *History of the Supreme Court of the United States*. Vol. 2, *Foundations of Power: John Marshall, 1801–1815*. New York: Macmillan, 1981.

Hesseltine, William B. *Lincoln and the War Governors*. New York: Knopf, 1948.

Hobson, Charles F. *The Aaron Burr Treason Trial*. N.p.: Federal Judicial Center, Federal Judicial Historical Office, 2006.

Holt, Michael F. *The Rise and Fall of the American Whig Party: Jacksonian Politics and the Onset of the Civil War*. New York: Oxford University Press, 1999.

Holzer, Harold, Edna Greene Medford, and Frank J. Williams. *The Emancipation Proclamation: Three Views (Social, Political, Iconographic)*. Baton Rouge: Louisiana State University Press, 2006.

Horwitz, Tony. *Midnight Rising: John Brown and the Raid That Sparked the Civil War*. New York: Henry Holt, 2011.

Hurst, James Willard. *The Law of Treason in the United States: Collected Essays*. Westport, Conn.: Greenwood Press, 1945.

Hyman, Harold M. *Era of the Oath: Northern Loyalty Tests during the Civil War and Reconstruction*. New York: Octagon Books, 1978.

————. *A More Perfect Union: The Impact of the Civil War and Reconstruction on the Constitution*. New York: Knopf, 1973.

James, Joseph B. *The Framing of the Fourteenth Amendment*. Urbana: University of Illinois Press, 1965.

Johnston, Alexander, ed. *American Eloquence: Studies in American Political History*. 4 vols. New York: G. P. Putnam's Sons, 1896–1897. Project Gutenberg, http://www.gutenberg.org/files/15392/15392-h/15392-h.htm#2H_4_0008 (accessed June 10, 2011).

Klement, Frank L. *The Copperheads in the Middle West*. Chicago: University of Chicago Press, 1960.

———. *Dark Lanterns: Secret Political Societies, Conspiracies, and Treason Trials in the Civil War*. Baton Rouge: Louisiana State University Press, 1984.

———. *The Limits of Dissent: Clement L. Vallandigham and the Civil War*. Lexington: University Press of Kentucky, 1970.

Kramer, Larry D. *The People Themselves: Popular Constitutionalism and Judicial Review*. New York: Oxford University Press, 2004.

Lawson, Melinda. *Patriot Fires: Forging a New American Nationalism in the Civil War North*. Lawrence: University of Kansas Press, 2002.

Leonard, Elizabeth. *Lincoln's Avengers: Justice, Revenge, and Reunion after the Civil War*. New York: W. W. Norton, 2004.

———. *Lincoln's Forgotten Ally: Judge Advocate General Joseph Holt of Kentucky*. Chapel Hill: University of North Carolina Press, 2011.

Lichterman, Martin. "John Adams Dix: 1798–1879." Ph.D. dissertation, Columbia University, 1952.

Lonn, Ella. *Desertion during the Civil War*. 1928. Reprint, Lincoln: University of Nebraska Press, 1998.

Lowry, Thomas P., M.D. *Sexual Misbehavior in the Civil War: A Compendium*. Bloomington, Ind.: Xlibris Corporation, 2006.

———. *The Story the Soldiers Wouldn't Tell: Sex in the Civil War*. Mechanicsburg, Pa.: Stackpole Books, 1994.

Manning, Chandra. *What This Cruel War Was Over: Soldiers, Slavery, and the Civil War*. New York: Knopf, 2007.

Marshall, Anne E. *Creating a Confederate Kentucky: The Lost Cause and Civil War Memory in a Border State*. Chapel Hill: University of North Carolina Press, 2010.

Marszalek, John F. *Commander of All Lincoln's Armies: A Life of General Henry W. Halleck*. Cambridge, Mass.: Belknap Press, 2004.

Marvel, William. *Burnside*. Chapel Hill: University of North Carolina Press, 1991.

McCurry, Stephanie. *Confederate Reckoning: Power and Politics in the Civil War South*. Cambridge, Mass.: Harvard University Press, 2010.

———. *Masters of Small Worlds: Yeoman Households, Gender Relations, and the Political Culture of the Antebellum South Carolina Low Country*. New York: Oxford University Press, 1995.

McFeely, William S. *Grant: A Biography*. New York: W. W. Norton, 1981.

McGinty, Brian. *John Brown's Trial*. Cambridge, Mass.: Harvard University Press, 2009.

———. *Lincoln and the Court*. Cambridge, Mass.: Harvard University Press, 2008.

McKitrick, Eric L. *Andrew Johnson and Reconstruction*. Chicago: University of Chicago Press, 1960.

McPherson, James M. *Battle Cry of Freedom: The Civil War Era*. New York: Oxford University Press, 1988.

———. *The Negro's Civil War: How American Negroes Felt and Acted during the War for the Union*. 1965. New ed. Urbana: University of Illinois Press, 1982.

———. *Tried by War: Abraham Lincoln as Commander in Chief*. New York: Penguin Press, 2008.

Neely, Mark E., Jr. *The Civil War and the Limits of Destruction*. Cambridge, Mass.: Harvard University Press, 2007.

———. *The Fate of Liberty: Abraham Lincoln and Civil Liberties*. New York: Oxford University Press, 1991.

———. *Lincoln and the Triumph of the Nation: Constitutional Conflict in the American Civil War*. Chapel Hill: University of North Carolina Press, 2011.

———. *The Union Divided: Party Conflict in the Civil War North*. Cambridge, Mass.: Harvard University Press, 2002.

Neff, Stephen C. *Justice in Blue and Gray*. Cambridge, Mass.: Harvard University Press, 2010.

———. *War and the Law of Nations: A General History*. New York: Cambridge University Press, 2005.

Nelson, Megan Kate. *Ruin Nation: Destruction and the American Civil War*. Athens: University of Georgia Press, 2012.

Newmyer, R. Kent. *John Marshall and the Heroic Age of the Supreme Court*. Baton Rouge: Louisiana State University Press, 2001.

Nichols, Roy F. *Franklin Pierce: Young Hickory of the Granite Hills*. 2nd ed. Philadelphia: University of Pennsylvania Press, 1958.

Nicoletti, Cynthia. "The Great Question of the War: The Legal Status of Secession in the Aftermath of the American Civil War, 1865–1869." Ph.D. dissertation, University of Virginia, 2010.

Niven, John. *Salmon P. Chase: A Biography*. New York: Oxford University Press, 1995.

Oates, Stephen B. *To Purge This Land with Blood*. New York: Harper & Row, 1970.

Palladino, Grace. *Another Civil War: Labor, Capital, and the State in the Anthracite Regions of Pennsylvania, 1840–68*. Urbana: University of Illinois Press, 1990.

Paludan, Phillip Shaw. *"A People's Contest": The Union and Civil War, 1861–1865*. New York: Harper & Row, 1988.

———. *The Presidency of Abraham Lincoln*. Lawrence: University Press of Kansas, 1994.

Phillips, Jason. *Diehard Rebels: The Confederate Culture of Invincibility*. Athens: University of Georgia Press, 2007.

Potter, David M. *The Impending Crisis, 1848–1861*. New York: Harper & Row, 1976.

Rable, George C. *Civil Wars: Women and the Crisis of Southern Nationalism*. Urbana: University of Illinois Press, 1989.

Rafuse, Ethan S. *McClellan's War: The Failure of Moderation in the Struggle for the Union*. Bloomington: Indiana University Press, 2005.

Randall, J. G. *Constitutional Problems under Lincoln*. 1929. Rev. ed. Gloucester, Mass.: Peter Smith, 1963.

Randall, J. G., and Richard N. Current. *Lincoln the President: The Last Full Measure*. New York: Dodd, Mead, 1955.

Reynolds, David S. *John Brown Abolitionist: The Man Who Killed Slavery, Spurred the Civil War, and Seeded Civil Rights*. New York: Alfred A. Knopf, 2005.

Risley, Ford. *Civil War Journalism*. Santa Barbara, Calif.: Praeger, 2012.

Richardson, James D., ed. *A Compilation of the Messages and Papers of the Confederacy: Including the Diplomatic Correspondence, 1861–1865*. 2 vols. Nashville: United States Publishing Company, 1905.

Rolle, Andrew F. *The Lost Cause: The Confederate Exodus to Mexico*. Norman: University of Oklahoma Press, 1965.

Rose, Willie Lee. *Rehearsal for Reconstruction: The Port Royal Experiment*. New York: Oxford University Press, 1964.

Royster, Charles. *The Destructive War: William Tecumseh Sherman, Stonewall Jackson, and the Americans*. New York: Knopf, 1991.

Rubin, Anne Sarah. *A Shattered Nation: The Rise and Fall of the Confederacy, 1861–1868*. Chapel Hill: University of North Carolina Press, 2007.

Ryan, Mary P. *Civic Wars: Democracy and Public Life in the American City during the Nineteenth Century*. Berkeley: University of California Press, 1997.

Sandow, Robert M. *Deserter Country: Civil War Opposition in the Pennsylvania Appalachians*. New York: Fordham University Press, 2009.

Scharf, J. Thomas. *History of Maryland: From the Earliest Period to the Present Day*. 3 vols. Baltimore: John B. Piet, 1879.

Schlesinger, Arthur M., Jr. *The Age of Jackson*. Boston: Little, Brown, 1945.

Sears, Stephen W. *George B. McClellan: The Young Napoleon*. New York: Ticknor & Fields, 1998.

Siddali, Silvana R. *From Property to Person: Slavery and the Confiscation Acts, 1861–1862*. Baton Rouge: Louisiana State University Press, 2005.

———. *Missouri's War: The Civil War in Documents*. Athens: Ohio University Press, 2009.

Silbey, Joel. *A Respectable Minority: The Democratic Party in the Civil War Era, 1860–1868*. New York: W. W. Norton, 1977.

Simpson, Brooks. *Let Us Have Peace: Ulysses S. Grant and the Politics of War and Reconstruction, 1861–1868*. Chapel Hill: University of North Carolina Press, 1991.

———. *Ulysses S. Grant: Triumph over Adversity, 1822–1865*. New York: Houghton Mifflin, 2000.

Slaughter, Thomas P. *Bloody Dawn: The Christiana Riot and Racial Violence in the Antebellum North*. New York: Oxford University Press, 1991.

———. *The Whiskey Rebellion: Frontier Epilogue to the American Revolution*. New York: Oxford University Press, 1986.

Smith, Edward Conrad. *The Borderlands in the Civil War*. 1927. Reprint, New York: AMS Press, 1970.

Smith, Jean Edward. *John Marshall: Definer of a Nation*. New York: Henry Holt, 1996.

Spooner, Amelia J. "'Our Country's Common Ground': The Gettysburg Battlefield as Historical Document." Thesis, Columbia University, 2010. http://history.columbia.edu/undergraduate/theses/Spooner_thesis.pdf (accessed November 12, 2012).

Stampp, Kenneth M. *Indiana Politics during the Civil War*. 1949. New ed. Bloomington: Indiana University Press, 1978.

Stauffer, John. *The Black Hearts of Men*. Cambridge, Mass.: Harvard University Press, 2002.

Sterling, Robert E. "Civil War Draft Resistance in the Middle West." Ph.D. dissertation, Northern Illinois University, 1974.

Stewart, James Brewer. *Wendell Phillips: Liberty's Hero*. Baton Rouge: Louisiana State University Press, 1986.

Stewart, Lucy Shelton. *The Reward of Patriotism*. New York: Walter Neale, Publisher, 1930.

Stout, Harry S. *Upon the Altar of the Nation*. New York: Viking, 2006.

Sutherland, Daniel E. *A Savage Conflict: The Decisive Role of Guerrillas in the American Civil War*. Chapel Hill: University of North Carolina Press, 2009.

Swisher, Carl B. *History of the Supreme Court of the United States*. Vol. 5, *The Taney Period, 1836–64*. New York: Macmillan, 1974.

Syrett, John. *The Civil War Confiscation Acts: Failing to Reconstruct the South*. New York: Fordham University Press, 2005.

Tap, Bruce. *Over Lincoln's Shoulder: The Committee on the Conduct of the War*. Lawrence: University Press of Kansas, 1998.

Thomas, Benjamin P. *Abraham Lincoln: A Biography*. New York: Alfred A. Knopf, 1952.

Thomas, Benjamin, and Harold M. Hyman. *Stanton: The Life and Times of Lincoln's Secretary of War*. New York: Alfred A. Knopf, 1962.

Thomas, Emory. *Robert E. Lee: A Biography*. New York: W. W. Norton, 1995.

Trefousse, Hans. *Thaddeus Stevens: Nineteenth-Century Egalitarian*. Chapel Hill: University of North Carolina Press, 1997.

Trevelyan, Francis Miller, ed. *The Photographic History of the Civil War: In Ten Volumes*. Vol. 7, *Prison and Hospitals*. New York: Review of Reviews Company, 1911.

Trodd, Zoe, and John Stauffer, eds. *Meteor of War: The John Brown Story*. Maplecrest, N.Y.: Brandywine Press, 2004.

Trogdon, Matthew. "The Uninspiring Story of the Dix-Pierrepont Commission." M.A. thesis, Pennsylvania State University, 2007.

Van Horne, Thomas B. *The Life of Major-General George H. Thomas*. New York: Charles Scribner's Sons, 1882.

Urofsky, Melvin I., and Paul Finkelman. *A March of Liberty: A Constitutional History of the United States*. Vol. 1. 2nd ed. New York: Oxford University Press, 2002.

Wagandt, Charles Lewis. *The Mighty Revolution: Negro Emancipation in Maryland, 1862–1864*. Baltimore: Johns Hopkins Press, 1964.

Webb, Ross A. *Kentucky in the Reconstruction Era*. Lexington: University Press of Kentucky, 1979.

Weber, Jennifer L. *Copperheads: The Rise and Fall of Lincoln's Opponents in the North*. New York: Oxford University Press, 2006.

Weeks, Jim. *Gettysburg: Memory, Market, and an American Shrine*. Princeton, N.J.: Princeton University Press, 2003.

Weitz, Mark A. *The Confederacy on Trial: The Piracy and Sequestration Cases of 1861*. Lawrence: University Press of Kansas, 2005.

Wesley, Timothy L. *The Politics of Faith during the Civil War*. Baton Rouge: Louisiana State University Press, 2013.

White, Jonathan W. *Abraham Lincoln and Treason in the Civil War: The Trials of John Merryman*. Baton Rouge: Louisiana State University Press, 2011.

———. "'To Aid Their Rebel Friend': Politics and Treason in the Civil War North." Ph.D. dissertation, University of Maryland, College Park, 2008.

Whiteman, Maxwell. *Gentlemen in Crisis: The First Century of the Union League of Philadelphia, 1862–1962*. Philadelphia: Union League, 1975.

Whites, LeeAnn. *Gender Matters: Civil War, Reconstruction, and the Making of the New South*. New York: Palgrave Macmillan, 2005.

Whites, LeeAnn, and Alecia P. Long, eds. *Occupied Women: Gender, Military Occupation, and the American Civil War*. Baton Rouge: Louisiana State University Press, 2009.

Winik, Jay. *April 1865: The Month that Saved America*. New York: Perennial, 2001.

Witt, John Fabian. *Lincoln's Code: The Laws of War in American History*. New York: Free Press, 2012.

Work, David. *Lincoln's Political Generals*. Urbana: University of Illinois Press, 2009.

Wubben, Hubert H. *Civil War Iowa and the Copperhead Movement*. Ames: Iowa State University Press, 1980.

Younger, Richard D. *The People's Panel: The Grand Jury in the United States, 1634–1941*. Providence, R.I.: Brown University Press, 1963.

ARTICLES AND ESSAYS

Anbinder, Tyler. "Which Poor Man's Fight? Immigrants and the Federal Conscription of 1863." *Civil War History* 52 (December 2006): 344–72.

Andreasen, Bryon C. "Civil War Church Trials: Repressing Dissent on the Northern Home Front." In *An Uncommon Time: The Civil War and the Northern Home Front*, edited by Paul A. Cimbala and Randall M. Miller, 214–42. New York: Fordham University Press, 2002.

Ayers, Edward, and Scott Nesbit, "Seeing Emancipation: Scale and Freedom in the American South." *Journal of the Civil War Era* 1 (March 2011): 3–24.

Balsamo, Larry T. "'We Cannot Have Free Government without Elections': Abraham Lincoln and the Election of 1864." *Journal of the Illinois State Historical Society* 94 (Summer 2001): 181–99.

Benedict, Michael Les. "Abraham Lincoln and Federalism." *Journal of the Abraham Lincoln Association* 10 (1988–89): 1–45.

Blair, William. "Barbarians at Fredericksburg's Gate." In *The Fredericksburg Campaign: Decision on the Rappahannock*, edited by Gary W. Gallagher, 142–70. Chapel Hill: University of North Carolina Press, 1995.

———. "Friend or Foe: Treason and the Second Confiscation Act." In *Wars within a War: Controversy and Conflict over the American Civil War*, edited by Joan Waugh and Gary W. Gallagher, 27–51. Chapel Hill: University of North Carolina Press, 2009.

————. "A Record of Pennsylvania Deserters." *Pennsylvania Magazine of History and Biography* 135 (2011): 537–38.

————. "We Are Coming, Father Abraham—Eventually: The Problem of Northern Nationalism in the Pennsylvania Recruiting Drives of 1862." In *The War Was You and Me: Civilians in the American Civil War*, edited by Joan Cashin, 183–208. Princeton, N.J.: Princeton University Press, 2002.

Blake, Kellee Green. "Aiding and Abetting: Disloyalty Prosecutions in the Federal Civil Courts of Southern Illinois, 1861–1866." *Illinois Historical Journal* 87:2 (1994): 95–108.

Blake, Kellee L. "Ten Firkins of Butter and Other 'Traitorous' Aid." *Prologue* (Winter 1998): 289–93.

Carnahan, Burrus M. "Lincoln, Lieber and the Laws of War: The Origins and Limits of the Principle of Military Necessity." *American Journal of International Law* 92 (April 1998): 213–31.

Carwardine, Richard. "Abraham Lincoln and the Fourth Estate." *American Nineteenth Century History* 7 (March 2006): 1–27.

Chambers, Lenoir. "Notes on Life in Occupied Norfolk, 1862–1865." *Virginia Magazine of History and Biography* 73 (April 1965): 131–44.

Chapin, Bradley. "Colonial and Revolutionary Origins of the American Law of Treason." *William and Mary Quarterly*, 3rd ser., 17:1 (January 1960): 3–21.

Costa, Dora, and Matthew E. Kahn. "Deserters, Social Norms, and Migration." *Journal of Law and Economics* 50 (May 2007): 323–53.

Curtis, Michael Kent. "Lincoln, Vallandigham, and Anti-War Speech in the Civil War." *William & Mary Bill of Rights Journal* 7:1 (1998): 105–91.

Dunning, W. A. "Notes & Suggestions: Disloyalty in Two Wars." *American Historical Review* 24 (July 1919): 625–30.

Dyer, Brainerd. "Francis Lieber and the American Civil War." *Huntington Library Quarterly* 2 (July 1939): 449–65.

Earnhart, Hugh G. "The Administrative Organization of the Provost Marshal General's Bureau in Ohio, 1863–64." *Northwest Ohio Quarterly* 37:3 (1965): 87–99 (accessed online, June 18, 2013).

Emberton, Carole. "'Only Murder Makes Men': Reconsidering the Black Military Experience." *Journal of the Civil War Era* 2 (September 2012): 369–93.

Epps, Garrett. "The Antebellum Political Background of the Fourteenth Amendment." *Law and Contemporary Problems* 67 (Summer 2004): 175–211.

Faust, Drew. "'We Should Grow Too Fond of It': Why We Love the Civil War." *Civil War History* 50 (December 2004): 368–83.

Fehrenbacher, Don E. "The Anti-Lincoln Tradition." *Journal of the Abraham Lincoln Association* 4:1 (1982). http://hdl.handle.net/2027/spo.2629860.0004.103 (accessed January 8, 2013).

Feimster, Crystal N. "General Benjamin Butler & the Threat of Sexual Violence during the American Civil War." *Daedalus* (Spring 2009): 126–34.

Finkelman, Paul. "The Treason Trial of Castner Hanway." In *American Political Trials*, edited by Michal R. Belknap, 77–96. Westport, Conn.: Greenwood Press, 1994.

Hacker, J. David. "A Census-Based Count of the Civil War Dead." *Civil War History* 57 (December 2011): 307–48.

Harrison, Noel G. "Atop an Anvil: The Civilians' War in Fairfax and Alexandria Counties, April 1861–April 1862." *Virginia Magazine of History and Biography* 106 (Spring 1998): 133–64.

Hooker, Richard D., Jr. "Soldiers of the State: Reconsidering American Civil-Military Relations." *Parameters: The U.S. Army's Senior Professional Journal* 33 (Winter 2003–4): 1–18.

Klement, Frank L. "The Indianapolis Treason Trials." In *American Political Trials*, edited by Michael Belknap, 101–27. Westport, Conn.: Greenwood Press, 1981.

Kohl, Martha. "Enforcing a Vision of Community: The Role of the Test Oath in Missouri's Reconstruction." *Civil War History* 40 (December 1994): 292–307.

Lee, Thomas H. "The Civil War in U.S. Foreign Relations Law: A Dress Rehearsal for Modern Transformations." *Saint Louis University Law Journal* 53 (February 2009): 53–71.

Leek, J. H. "Treason and the Constitution." *Journal of Politics* 13 (November 1951): 604–22.

Lewis, Elsie M. "The Political Mind of the Negro, 1865–1900." *Journal of Southern History* 21 (May 1955): 189–202.

MacDonnell, Francis. "Reconstruction in the Wake of Vietnam: The Pardoning of Robert E. Lee and Jefferson Davis." *Civil War History* 40 (June 1994): 119–33.

Malin, James C. "Judge Lecompte and the 'Sack of Lawrence.'" *Kansas Historical Quarterly* 20 (August 1953): 465–94.

McClure, James P., Leigh Johnsen, Kathleen Norman, and Michael Vanderlan. "Circumventing the Dred Scott Decision: Edward Bates, Salmon P. Chase, and the Citizenship of African Americans." *Civil War History* 43 (December 1997): 279–309.

McCurry, Stephanie. "War, Gender, and Emancipation in the Civil War South." In *Lincoln's Proclamation: Emancipation Reconsidered*, edited by William A. Blair and Karen Fisher Younger, 120–50. Chapel Hill: University of North Carolina Press, 2009.

Miller, Richard F. "The Trouble with Brahmins: Class and Ethnic Tensions in Massachusetts' 'Harvard Regiment.'" *New England Quarterly* 76 (March 2003): 38–72.

Moore, Wilton P. "Union Provost Marshals in the Eastern Theater." *Military Affairs* 26 (Autumn 1962): 120–26.

Neely, Mark E., Jr. "The Constitution and Civil Liberties under Lincoln." In *Our Lincoln: New Perspectives on Lincoln and His World*, edited by Eric Foner, 37–61. New York: W. W. Norton, 2008.

———. "The Lincoln Administration and Arbitrary Arrests: A Reconsideration." *Papers of the Abraham Lincoln Association* 5 (1982): 6–24.

———. "'Seeking a Cause of Difficulty with the Government': Reconsidering Freedom of Speech and Judicial Conflict under Lincoln." In *Lincoln's Legacy: Ethics and Politics*, edited by Phillip Shaw Paludan, 48–66. Urbana: University of Illinois Press, 2008.

Nichols, Roy F. "United States vs. Jefferson Davis, 1865–1869." *American Historical Review* 31 (January 1926): 266–84.

Nicoletti, Cynthia. "Did Secession Really Die at Appomattox? The Strange Case of U.S. v. Jefferson Davis." *University of Toledo Law Review* 41 (Spring 2010): 587–634.

Paust, Jordan J. "Dr. Francis Lieber and the Lieber Code." *Proceedings of the Annual Meeting of the American Society of International Law* 95 (April 4–7, 2001): 112–15.

Perman, Michael. "The South and Congress's Reconstruction Policy." *Journal of American Studies* 4 (February 1971): 181–200.

Phillips, Christopher. "Netherworld of War: The Dominion System and the Contours of Federal Occupation in Kentucky." *Register of the Kentucky Historical Society* 110 (Summer–Autumn 2012): 327–61.

Prescott, Lt. Col. Jody, and Maj. Joanne Eldridge. "Military Commissions, Past and Future." *Military Review* 83 (March–April 2003): 42–51.

Randall, James G. "Some Legal Aspects of the Confiscation Acts of the Civil War." *American Historical Review* 18 (October 1912): 79–96.

Schultz, Jane E. "Mute Fury: Southern Women's Diaries of Sherman's March to the Sea, 1864–1865." In *Arms and the Woman: War, Gender, and Literary Representation*, edited by Helen M. Cooper, Adrienne Auslander Munich, and Susan Merrill Squier, 59–79. Chapel Hill: University of North Carolina Press, 1989.

Slaughter, Thomas P. "'The King of Crimes': Early American Treason Law." In *Launching the "Extended Republic:" The Federalist Era*, edited by Ronald Hoffman and Peter J. Albert, 54–135. Charlottesville: University of Virginia Press, 1996.

Sparks, David. "General Patrick's Progress: Intelligence and Security in the Army of the Potomac." *Civil War History* 10 (December 1964): 371–84.

Sternhell, Yael. "Antiwar Civil War." *Journal of the Civil War Era* 3 (June 2013): 239–56.

Tarrant, Catherine M. "To 'Insure Domestic Tranquility': Congress and the Law of Seditious Conspiracy, 1859–1861." *American Journal of Legal History* 15:2 (April 1971): 107–23.

Tenney, Craig D. "To Suppress or Not to Suppress: Abraham Lincoln and the *Chicago Times*." *Civil War History* 27 (September 1981): 248–59.

Towne, Stephen E. "Killing the Serpent Speedily: Governor Morton, General Hascall, and the Suppression of the Democratic Press in Indiana, 1863." *Civil War History* 52 (March 2006): 41–65.

Vagts, Detlev F. "Military Commissions: The Forgotten Reconstruction Chapter." *American University International Law Review* 23:2 (2007): 232–74.

Wagandt, Charles L. "Redemption or Reaction?—Maryland in the Post-Civil War Years." In *Radicalism, Racism, and Party Realignment: The Border States during Reconstruction*, edited by Richard O. Curry, 146–87. Baltimore: Johns Hopkins University Press, 1969.

White, G. Edward. "The First Amendment Comes of Age: The Emergence of Free Speech in Twentieth-Century America." *Michigan Law Review* 95:2 (November 1996): 299–392.

White, Jonathan W. "All for a Sword: The Military Treason Trial of Sarah Hutchins." *Maryland Historical Magazine* 107 (Summer 2012): 155–74.

————. "Canvassing the Troops: The Federal Government and the Soldiers' Right to Vote." *Civil War History* 50 (September 2004): 291–317.

————. "The Strangely Insignificant Role of the U.S. Supreme Court in the Civil War." *Journal of the Civil War Era* 3 (June 2013): 211–38.

————. "The Trial of Jefferson Davis and the Americanization of Treason Law." In *Constitutionalism in the Approach and Aftermath of the Civil War*, edited by Paul D. Moreno and Johnathan O'Neill, 113–32. New York: Fordham University Press, 2013.

ACKNOWLEDGMENTS

This project has benefited greatly from the resources and contacts made possible through the George and Ann Richards Civil War Era Center. At Penn State, the Center has helped foster a wonderful intellectual environment of colleagues, graduate students, and undergraduates, many of whom have left their own imprint on this book. During the course of researching and writing this work, the center achieved a significant milestone by completing a *We the People* Challenge Grant with the National Endowment for the Humanities. I am grateful to the leadership of George Richards, Ted and Tracy McCourtney, and Board of Visitor Chairs John Paulus and Hal Rosenberg. Hal went the extra mile by reading a couple of chapters for their legal accuracy. But many other benefactors contributed to our success, as well as a great development team led by Mark Luellen. My thanks to all.

Resources from the center allowed for the hiring of assistants to help with research or check other facets of the work. Some of them, like Barbara Gannon and Timothy J. Wesley, have gone on to produce fine books of their own. But I also owe thanks to Matt Isham, Andrew Prymak, Anne Brinton, William Cossen, Evan Rothera, and Lauren Golder for their assistance. Because of the excellent quality of the students in Penn State's Schreyer Honor's College, I was able to employ a few talented undergraduates. Early in the project, Jim Flook verified the importance of the Amnesty Papers in the National Archives. Later, Amanda Fellmeth and Kristen Campbell augmented the tedious hunt for court cases. They were a joy to work with.

Colleagues also provided invaluable suggestions about the project. At Penn State, Mark E. Neely Jr. and Carol Reardon, both scholars at the center, read various chapters. Beyond Penn State, I received advice from Robert M. Sandow of Lock Haven University, a good historian and friend; Greg Downs of the City University of New York; and Bill Link, University of Florida. Not only did Bill read the entire manuscript; he invited me to participate in the Milbauer Seminar in Southern History at his institution, giving me the chance to gain feedback on key ideas during the early stages of the project. Similarly, James Marten of Marquette University allowed me to test ideas about the nature of clemency after the war in the Frank L. Klement Lectures. The lecture was published as *Why Didn't the North Hang Some Rebels? The Postwar Debate over Punishment for Treason* (ISBN 978-0-87462-337-6, copyright © 2004 Marquette University Press, all rights reserved, http://www.marquette.edu/mupess/). Parts of chapter 8 appeared in *More Than a Contest between Armies: Essays on the Civil War Era*, edited by James Marten and A. Kristen Foster (Kent, Ohio: Kent State University Press, 2008). And I owe a large debt to Jonathan W. White of Christopher Newport University. He went over the manuscript with a close eye and shared additional resources that strengthened the book in numerous ways. His generosity as a scholar remains beyond compare.

I also want to mention David Perry, former editor in chief at the University of North Carolina Press, who was there at the inception of the book and provided encouragement along the way, especially at the annual get-togethers of the Littlefield authors. He did not get to see the finished product on his watch, but I benefited from our discussions and association.

Of course, no work of this kind can happen without good materials. James Mundy, historian of the Union League at Philadelphia, and Gail Farr at the Philadelphia branch of the National Archives were especially helpful in leading me to sources. David Langbart of the College Park, Maryland, branch of the National Archives proved especially helpful in leading me to the records of the Department of State. He served as a model for how archivists can enrich the work of scholars.

Finally, Mary Ann Blair deserves more than I can convey for enduring the highs and lows that inevitably accompany a project that lasts for nearly a decade. Thank you for your love and support.

INDEX

Confederacy and, 209, 210; Confederates after war and, 7, 234, 235, 240–44, 245; conscription and, 167, 176, 180; courts-martial for disloyalty, 57, 316–19; courts-martial for treason, 56–57, 311–15; elections and, 174, 183, 216–17; after end of war, 234, 235, 239–40, 241, 242–43, 245, 255, 270–71; excessive arrests and, 39, 106–7, 114, 168, 169–70, 172, 174, 180, 203–4; government workers and, 49, 50–52, 80; judges and, 119, 207; policy formulation and, 38–39, 42–43, 46–47, 48, 53–54; political arrests for treason and, 38–39, 320–45; presidential power and, 38–39, 49; "preventative" arrests and, 179–80; release from custody and, 45–46, 47–48, 54, 116, 118, 169, 307; social importance and, 46–48, 49, 325–27; suspending the writ of habeas corpus and, 92, 112, 169–70; Union army personnel and, 167, 206; U.S. Department of State and, 42, 44, 51–52, 54; U.S. Department of War and, 48, 54–58, 92, 116, 167; varieties of, during Civil War, 1–2, 40, 57–58, 72–73, 311–19. *See also* Davis, Jefferson; Newspapers; Provost marshals; Union army; Vallandigham, Clement L.; Women; *and particular cities and states*
Articles of War, 69, 93
Ash, Stephen, 132, 139, 145
Ashmead, John, 21
Attucks, Crispus, 264

Baker, Edward, 165
Baker, Lafayette C., 104, 121
Ball, Robert H., 278
Ball's Bluff, 164
Baltimore, Md.: arrests for treason and, 117–19, 170, 242–43; Confederate army veteran voting rights and, 274–76; Confederate sympathizers and,
46, 64; presidential electioneering of 1864 and, 192, 223; provost marshals and, 105, 109–10; Union army and elections and, 170, 185, 230
Baltimore American, 185
Baltimore Evening Post, 223
Baltimore Sun, 271, 274
Banks, Nathaniel P., 46, 91, 109, 110, 170–71, 180
Baptists, 143, 271
Barlow, Samuel L. M., 121
Barry, R. J., 124
Bates, Edward, 91–92, 93, 95, 141, 247, 265–66; policy formulation for arrests for treason and, 38–39, 42–43, 46–47, 48, 53–54
Bax, Adam, 156–58
Bayard, James A., Jr., 82
Beauregard, P. G. T., 164, 221
Beecher, Henry Ward, 253, 256, 257, 258
Bell, Philip A., 261
Bellows, Henry W., 204
Belmont, August, 219
Bensel, Richard F., 189, 229
Bernstein, Iver, 49
Biddle, Charles J., 163
Biershing, William, 275
Binney, Horace, 40, 41
Birch, James H., 173–74
Black Codes, 269, 290
Blaine, James G., 299
Blair, Montgomery, 44, 51, 142, 274
Blennerhassett, Harman, 18
Blockade, 73, 74, 77, 79, 80–81, 99, 337–38, 355 (n. 34)
Boker, George, 47
Bollinger, J. T., 279
Bollman, Eric, 18
Border Ruffians, 24, 25, 28, 30
Border states: arrests for treason and, 10, 114; Confederate army veteran voting rights and, 9, 280; denying vote to disloyal citizens and, 269, 272, 307; guerrilla warfare and, 11, 12, 235; Union army and elections and, 161,

172, 180–81, 189–90, 193, 195–96,
202, 214. *See also* Delaware; Kentucky; Maryland; Missouri
Boston, Mass., 164, 167, 256, 264, 265,
267
Boyle, Jeremiah T., 172, 181
Bradford, Augustus, 118–19, 183, 184,
187, 189, 273–74
Bramlette, Thomas E., 181, 208, 210,
229, 277
Breckinridge, John C., 82
Bright, Jesse D., 83
Brinsmade, Isabel M., 120–22
Brown, Armitz, 70
Brown, Charles, 187, 188
Brown, John: Harpers Ferry and, 13, 30,
33, 252; Kansas and, 24, 25–26, 28,
29, 349 (n. 36); treason against U.S.
and, 13, 14, 16, 30, 31–34, 35, 234,
349 (n. 26)
Brown, John (planter), 140, 144
Brown, John, Jr., 14, 26, 29
Browning, Orville Hickman, 168
Brown v. the United States, 70, 98, 99
Buchanan, James, 90, 35, 42, 73, 212,
350 (n. 43)
Buchanan, J. R., 216–17
Buck, George M., 228
Buckingham, C. P., 111
Buell, Don Carlos, 38, 115, 135
Bullitt, Joshua, 90, 207
Bull Run, first battle of, 73, 163, 164
Burbridge, Stephen G., 206–7, 208, 209
Burnside, Ambrose E., 37, 62, 172, 178,
180–81, 209, 307
Burr, Aaron, 18–19, 20
Bushwhacking, 24, 125, 134, 145, 155. *See
also* Guerrillas
Butler, Benjamin, 4, 120, 248, 290;
Confederate army veterans and,
241; occupation of Confederacy and,
138–39, 140–41, 143, 150; presidential election of 1864 and, 228, 231;
women as traitors and, 129, 158
Butler, Pierce, 47–48

Cadwalader, John, 52, 75
Calhoun, John C., 71
Cameron, Simon, 42, 48, 54
Campbell, John Archibald, 72
Canadian border, 43; draft resisters and,
281; Indianapolis treason trials and,
211, 212; presidential election of 1864
and, 229, 230–31; provost marshals
and, 204–5
Cannon, William, 171–72
Capital punishment, 8, 257–58
Carmichael, Richard B., 119
Carrington, Henry B., 212, 214
Carwardine, Richard, 62
Catholic Church, 270, 271
Catron, John, 72, 73
Chandler, Zachariah, 249, 254
Chase, Salmon P., 51, 260, 265, 267; Civil
War opinions and, 91, 291–93; Jefferson Davis and, 247, 248, 249–50, 302
Chenoweth, James W., 52
Chicago Times, 62, 169
Chicago Tribune, 136, 308
Child, Lydia Maria, 253, 257–58, 268,
369, 293
Christiana Riot of 1851, 14, 20–21, 23
Cicero, 85, 89, 95
Cincinnati, Ohio, 125, 223
Cincinnati Commercial, 277
Cincinnati Enquirer, 223, 224, 278
Civilians, 94; capturing deserters and,
107–8, 124–25, 281; expulsion of from
occupied Confederacy, 138, 145–47,
159, 174; in occupied Confederacy,
115, 116, 117, 128–59. *See also* Ministers and treason; Women
Civil Rights Act of 1866, 269, 300
Clark, John B., 82
Clarke, J. C., 199
Clayton, Milly Ann, 135
Clemency, 52; abolitionists advocating
leniency after war and, 8, 252–53,
256, 258–61; first cases of treason
in United States and, 16, 18; oaths
of loyalty and, 48, 52, 126; paroles

to rebels and, 7–8, 237; punishment after war of rebels and, 235, 255–56, 257, 293; war debt and, 287. *See also* Presidential pardons

Cobb, Howell, 42

Code of war, 3, 68, 93–96, 130, 145, 152, 237

Coffroth, John R., 213

Collamer, Jacob, 27

Colombia, 98

Columbia College, 7, 61, 93, 204, 237

Commerce as treason, 36, 37, 41, 43–44, 140; guns and, 52, 53, 212, 213

Compromise of 1850, 14

Confederacy: abolitionists advocating leniency after war and, 8, 252–53, 254, 256–61, 268–69; arrests for treason after end of war and, 7, 234, 235, 240–44, 245; belligerent enemies vs. rebellious citizens and, 73, 78, 79, 86, 88, 90, 95, 97, 306; conscription and, 111; conspiracy in Indiana and, 211–12; debt after war and, 269, 286–93, 300, 302, 303; general pardon and, 234; limiting power to politicians of, after war, 9, 255, 279–80, 293–303, 307; mobilization and, 149; nation status and, 74, 76, 95; privateers and, 73, 74–75; public opinion of, after war, 305–6; taxes as way to punish rebels and, 129, 138–39; treason and, 19, 58, 67, 138, 234–35; Union army and rumor and gossip and, 153–59; Union army dispensing food during occupation and, 138–41; Union army occupation and, 128–59; Union navy and, 75–76, 237, 242. *See also* Civilians; Clemency; Confiscation; Davis, Jefferson; Oaths of loyalty; Provost marshals; Slavery; U.S. Congress

Confederate army veterans, 57, 236–44, 246; paroles given to, 7–8, 187, 236, 237, 239–40; presidential pardons and, 239, 240–41, 254, 272; travel in loyal states and, 236–37, 238; treason indictments and, 240–44; voting rights and, 8, 9, 12, 268–69, 272–80, 285, 290; wearing military garb and, 237, 238–39

Confiscation: arrests for treason and, 51–52; Civil War beginnings and, 114–15, 130; from Confederate ships, 68–69, 77; Democratic Party and, 90, 91, 98, 198; emancipation and, 84–85, 99; international law and, 67, 68, 78, 84, 85, 87, 89, 90, 95, 98; Lincoln and, 99, 133; military necessity and, 97, 132, 133, 134, 135; Union army and, 98, 114–15, 129, 130–34, 146, 152, 153, 159, 165–66; Union army looting and, 134–37; U.S. Supreme Court and, 70, 78, 91. *See also* First Confiscation Act; Second Confiscation Act; Slavery; U.S. Congress

Conkling, Edgar, 220–21

Conkling, James C., 99

Conkling, Roscoe, 295

Connelly, Margaret, 223

Conscription: arrests for treason and, 167, 176, 180, 321; Confederacy and, 111; Democratic Party and, 175–76; New York City draft riots and, 49, 154, 230; presidential election of 1864 and, 175–76, 215–16; provost marshals and, 5, 11, 100, 101, 102, 107, 112, 123–24, 126, 306; resistance to, 167, 215, 216, 281; U.S. Congress and, 96, 102, 111, 152

Conscription Act of 1863, 96, 102, 152

Conspiracy, 18, 201; Canadian border and, 204–5; crime of, 81; after end of war, 235; Indianapolis treason trials and, 211–12; secret societies and, 214–15

Conspiracies Acts of 1861 and 1862, 53

Constitutional Problems under Lincoln (Randall), 39

Constructive treason, 2, 15, 16, 17, 18, 22, 37, 39, 176–77, 178

Cook, Jay, 288

Desertion, 69, 270, 301, 321; capturing deserters and, 107–8, 123, 124–25, 126, 281, 306; Democratic Party and, 9, 232, 282, 307; provost marshals and, 100, 102, 103, 111, 123, 124–25, 126, 280, 281, 306; voting rights after war and, 9, 12, 232, 280–85, 307

Detroit, Mich., 204, 205

Deuel, A. C., 125

D'Homergue, Louis C., 199–200

Dick, Franklin Archibald, 107, 142

Dickson, John C., 285

Dix, John A., 45–46, 54, 119, 184

Dodd, Harrison Horton, 211, 212, 213, 218

Dodge, George R., 110

Donald, David Herbert, 168, 227

Doniphan, Rebecca, 90

Dorr, Thomas Wilson, 31

Dorr's Rebellion, 31, 177

Doubleday, Abner, 165–66

Double jeopardy, 302

Douglas, Henry Kyd, 238–39

Douglas, Stephen, 27, 162, 168

Douglass, Frederick, 262–63, 266, 267

Downing, George, 262

Draft. *See* Conscription

Draper, Simeon, 108, 110–11, 121

Dred Scott decision, 72, 265

Dubuque Herald, 169

Duncan, Calvin M., 282

Early, Jubal, 240, 242, 243

Eginton, Charles, 210

1865 Customs of Service, The, 102

Elections: army and, after war, 277, 278; Democratic Party boycott and, 6, 187–88, 194; denying vote to disloyal citizens after war and, 273, 275, 307; deserter voting rights and, 282, 284, 307; Kansas and, 25, 26; lack of secret ballot and, 6, 174, 186, 273; midterm, of 1862, 108, 166–67, 168, 169, 174–75, 204; Missouri and, 172–74, 182–83; political culture and, 161–62,

306–7; presidential, of 1856, 27; presidential, of 1868, 307; release of political prisoners and, 169. *See also* Oaths of loyalty; Presidential election of 1864; Union army and elections

Elements of International Law (Wheaton), 3, 78, 84, 88

Elizabeth & Margaret (schooner), 265

Ellsworth, Elmer, 115

Emancipation: elections and, 173–74; international law and, 3, 98, 99; as military necessity, 4, 84–85, 94, 98, 99; presidential election of 1864 and, 10, 160, 198, 254; Ten Percent Plan and, 196, 253–54; Thirty-Eighth Congress and, 189; Union army and, 133, 134, 148–49

Emancipation Day, 263, 264, 265

Emancipation Proclamation, 68, 94, 99, 133, 169, 253; Democratic National Convention of 1864 and, 221; midterm elections of 1862 and, 166, 168; war debt and, 290

Episcopalians, 2, 63, 64, 118, 142, 271

Equal Rights Leagues. *See* National Equal Rights League

Evans, Andrew, 232

Evans, Sam, 132

Evarts, William M., 251

Ex parte Bollman and *Ex parte Swartwout*, 19, 24

Expatriate Act (Kentucky), 272–73, 277, 278

Federal government: branches of, and Civil War prosecution, 66, 353 (n. 1); growth of, during Civil War, 10–11, 100; provost marshals and, 5, 100, 110, 306; workers in, treason and, 49, 50–52, 80

Federalists, 16, 18–19

Federal marshals, 18, 25, 47, 48, 103

Feimster, Crystal, 151

Ferry, John H., 225

Fessenden, William Pitt, 168, 295, 296

for treason and, 48, 54–58, 92, 116, 122, 167; code of warfare and, 67, 93, 94, 96–97; Confederate army veterans and, 241; confiscation and, 165; deserter voting rights and, 281, 284; Ku Klux Klan and, 309; presidential election of 1864 and, 175, 225, 228, 231; provost marshals and, 104, 108, 111, 123, 180; secret societies and, 216

U.S. expansion, postwar, 308

U.S. Sanitary Commission, 46, 168, 204, 304

U.S. Supreme Court, 20, 22, 42, 62, 113, 306; arrests for treason after end of war and, 270, 271; *Brown v. the United States*, 70, 98, 99; confiscation and, 70, 78, 91; Jefferson Davis and, 247, 248–49, 250, 302; *Dred Scott* decision, 72, 265; *Ex parte Bollman* and *Ex parte Swartwout*, 18–19; Indianapolis treason trials and, 212, 213; Lincoln and, 66–67, 79; *Luther v. Borden*, 177; *Mrs. Alexander's Cotton*, 91; oaths of loyalty and, 270, 271; *Prize Cases*, 73, 77–78, 79, 87, 88, 99; *Texas v. White*, 291–92

United States v. Rucker, 239

Utah, 58

Vallandigham, Clement L.: arrest for treason and, 5, 37, 41, 48, 62, 109, 161, 174, 214, 307; banishment of, 154, 178, 183; conscription and military arrests and, 175–76; Democratic National Convention of 1864 and, 217, 218, 219, 220; elections and, 183, 184; government worker loyalty and, 51; Ohio reaction to arrest and banishment of, 178–79; secret societies and, 215; speech in Ohio and, 177–78, 209, 364 (n. 58)

Vance, Zebulon, 242

Vashon, George B., 262

Vattel, Emmerich de: confiscation and, 84, 98, 99; *Law of Nations* and, 3,

69–70, 78, 85, 86, 89, 354 (n. 11); prisoners of war and, 77; warfare and, 85, 86, 88, 89, 95–96, 356 (n. 60)

Veteran Reserve Corps, 123, 126–27

Vicksburg, Miss., 154

Viele, Egbert, 139

Vigol, Philip, 16, 17

Virginia: arrests for treason and, 115–16, 117, 239–40; John Brown and, 13, 31–34; confiscation and, 134, 146; expulsion of civilians in, 146–47; guerrilla warfare and, 145; limiting power of rebels after war and, 301; ministers and treason and, 143; oaths of loyalty and, 144; treason law and, 32–33, 35, 350 (n. 43); Union army occupation and, 133, 134, 141; women and, 150, 151

Voorhees, Daniel W., 212

Voting rights: deserters and, 9, 12, 232, 280–85, 307; oaths of loyalty and, 271–72; property ownership and, 31; state rights and, 260, 266–67, 297–98; voter registration and, 9, 273–76; women and, 262, 263. *See also* African American suffrage; Confederate army veterans

Wallace, Lew, 223, 230

War of 1812, 70, 98, 264

War Powers of the President and the Legislative Powers of Congress in Relation to Rebellion, Treason and Slavery, The (Whiting), 97–98

Washington, George, 14–15, 16

Webster, Daniel, 21

Weed, Thurlow, 113

Welles, Gideon, 97, 227, 237–38, 242, 246, 250

Wells, Robert, 72

Wesley, Timothy L., 62–63

West Virginia, Confederate army veteran voting rights and, 9, 272, 280

Wheaton, Henry, 3, 78, 84, 88, 95, 99

Whiskey Rebellion, 15, 16, 17

White, Jonathan W., 39, 92, 350
(nn. 43, 52)
Whites, LeeAnn, 128
Whiting, William, 96–98, 148, 149, 180
Whittier, John Greenleaf, 258
Wickliffe, Charles A., 88–89, 217
Wigfall, Louis, 82
Wilcox, Cadmus, 243
Wilkinson, James (general), 18, 20
Wilkinson, James (of Kentucky), 57
Wilmot, David, 20, 88
Wilson, Henry, 30, 194, 289
Wilson, James, 31
Wirz, Henry, 234
Wisconsin, 223–24
Witt, John Fabian, 94

Wittenmyer, Annie, 304
Wolford, Frank Lane, 205–6, 208–9, 210, 218, 224
Woman's Christian Temperance Union, 304
Women: apportionment and, 298; in occupied Confederacy and, 129, 149–53, 154, 155–59; rumor and gossip and Union army and, 153–59; as traitors, 6, 11, 38, 120–22, 335; violation of, by Union army, 135, 136, 151–52; voting rights and, 262, 263; white women and Union army and, 147, 148, 149–53, 156–59
Wool, John E., 107, 110, 117–18
Wright, Horatio G., 106, 111